ABEL KIVIAT

NATIONAL CHAMPION

Sports and Entertainment
Steven Riess, *Series Editor*

Abel Kiviat winning the one-mile run, Canadian championships, 1909.
From *Spalding's Annual* (1911).

ABEL KIVIAT

NATIONAL CHAMPION

Twentieth-Century Track & Field and the Melting Pot

ALAN S. KATCHEN

SYRACUSE UNIVERSITY PRESS

First Edition 2009

09   10   11   12   13   14   6   5   4   3   2   1

The paper used in this publication meets the minimum requirements
of American National Standard for Information Sciences—Permanence
of Paper for Printed Library Materials, ANSI Z39.48–1984.∞™

For a listing of books published and distributed by Syracuse University Press,
visit our Web site at SyracuseUniversityPress.syr.edu.

ISBN-13: 978-0-8156-0939-1   ISBN-10: 0-8156-0939-6

Libary of Congress Cataloging-in-Publication Data
Katchen, Alan S.
Abel Kiviat, national champion : twentieth-century track & field and the
melting pot / Alan S. Katchen. — 1st ed.
p. cm. — (Sports and entertainment)
Includes bibliographical references and index.
ISBN 978-0-8156-0939-1 (cloth : alk. paper)
1. Kiviat, Abel.   2. Track and field athletes—United States—Biography.
3. Jewish athletes—United States—Biography.   I. Title.
GV1061.15.K58K37 2009
796.42092—dc22
[B]
2008053592

For Peggy

ALAN S. KATCHEN has taught the history of education at the University of California at Santa Barbara and Howard University. He served for more than twenty years as a regional director of the Anti-Defamation League (ADL). Since retirement from the ADL, he has been an adjunct professor of history at Capital University in Columbus, Ohio, and an announcer at its track meets. Katchen was awarded the J. Kenneth Doherty Memorial Fellowship of USA Track & Field for research on Abel Kiviat and his world.

Contents

LAP FOUR SPRINTING TO THE FINISH

Illustrations

Acknowledgments

THIS BOOK BEGAN as a biography for young readers. Having been fascinated by track and field and its history since childhood, I decided in my fifties that it was now or never to write about it. It occurred to me to tell the story through a great miler, whose long life might reveal the vast social and cultural changes that impacted his sport in the past century. During the years when this idea was germinating, Abel Kiviat was frequently in the news as the oldest living Olympic medalist, a man who began running in 1909 and was still involved with the sport in 1991. I was drawn to him in part because his circumstances paralleled my own. Like Kiviat, I grew up as the son of a rabbi in an outer borough of New York City. How had being Jewish affected him and his career? I wondered. In a larger sense, what might his life reveal about the relationship between amateur athletics, ethnicity, and assimilation in American life?

An early stop in this exploration was at the New Jersey home of Lucy Price, the daughter of Tommy Lennon, Kiviat's lifelong friend. Lucy had cared for Kiviat in his final years and had his papers in her basement. Looking at old photographs, I found one of Kiviat as a meet official at Madison Square Garden. A long-buried memory suddenly came back: this was the man who had derided me for a poor performance in a high school meet forty years earlier and ordered me off the armory track on 168th Street in Manhattan. In the winter of 1955, my coach had assigned me to the seeded heat of the mile run in a big eastern interscholastic meet. I was over my head in this field, and having the flu did not help. When I tottered in near the rear of the pack, a short, stocky, middle-aged official ran after me yelling, "Get off the track; you don't belong!" When I regained my composure, I recall asking two other officials: "Who is that guy?" One said, "Don't pay attention.

He was once, before World War I, one of the world's great runners. But he's crazy now," or words to that effect. I was sixteen and quickly put the incident out of mind. Unbelievably, I was now, four decades later, exploring the possibility of writing this man's biography.

As I proceeded, the phrase "the kindness of strangers" frequently came to mind. Many people have assisted me with this work. At an early stage, I received the J. Kenneth Doherty Memorial Fellowship of USA Track & Field, which enabled me to spend a summer at the organization's Hall of Fame Library, then located at Butler University, doing research in its unique collection and outlining this book. The award was especially meaningful because Ken Doherty had been my college coach, a man who (along with his associate, Boo Morcom) had been exceptionally kind during a difficult adolescence. While I was at Butler, curator Erin Davis answered my inquiries with patience and skill, and I benefited from conversations with Hal Bateman, chair of the Doherty selection committee, and Pete Cava of the USA Track & Field staff, a great friend.

Early on, I decided I wanted to examine in detail what the experience of early modern track and field was like for Kiviat and his contemporaries. I made a list of about two dozen of his teammates and rivals, his coach, and other officials. Based on the sage advice my graduate school adviser, Alfred D. Chandler, Jr., once gave me about doing this kind of social history, I sought out the surviving relatives and friends of these athletes and was surprisingly lucky. I thank the following people for allowing me to study their family archives, for granting me interviews, and for offering encouragement: Stan Saplin, Lucy Price, Glenn Kasper, Bruce Conrad-Reingold, Harold and Adele Kiviat, Esther Kiviat, Erik Kiviat, Dennis Goldner, Litzi Goldner, Frances Kiviette, Dorothy Kiviat, Mary Honey, Lucy Mercer, Mary-Lou Palmer, Marian Robertson, Betty McKeon, Wayne Kohler, John Warner Drebinger, Howard P. Drew, Jean Lightfoot, Grace Thorpe, Phebe Baugher, David Sokosh, Sandy Kalb, Dr. Richard Yeager, Dr. Patricia Halloran, Joe Cloidt, Beatrice Kaufman, Roslyn Attinson, and Sydney Thayer and Bud Greenspan of Cappy Productions.

My work on this book took me to archives and libraries across the United States, Europe, and Israel. For their invaluable assistance, I thank the staffs of the following institutions: American Irish Historical Society (especially William Cobert and Lindsay Wengler); Beaver Co. Research Center; Blackmore Library, Capital University (especially Debbie Flood); Boys and Girls High School Library (New York); Bodleian Library, Oxford; Brasenose College Library, Oxford; Brooklyn Collection, Brooklyn Public Library; Brooklyn Museum Libraries and Archives; Columbia Grammar School; Columbus Metropolitan Library (especially Daisy Hagan-Bolen); Connecticut Valley Historical Museum; Cornell University Library; Curtis High School Library; Georgetown University Library; Harvard University Archives; Historical Society of Pennsylvania; Horrmann Library, Wagner College; Jewish Historical Society of Staten Island (especially Jenny Tango); LA84 Foundation Library (especially Mike Salmon); Library of Congress, Washington, D.C.; Museum of the City of New York; National Archives, Washington, D.C. (especially Mitch Yockelson); New York Athletic Club Library; New York City Municipal Archives; New York Historical Society; New York Public Library (especially Warren Platt); New York Public Library, Staten Island branches at Stapleton and St. George; New York Road Runners Club Library; New York State Archives; New York Stock Exchange Archives; Ohio State University Libraries (especially Joseph Galron); Peddie School Library; Riksarkivet, Stockholm; Roman Catholic Diocese of Brooklyn, Office of the Archivist; Rutherford B. Hayes Presidential Center; St. John's University Archives; State Library of Ohio (especially Paul Immel); *Staten Island Advance* offices (especially Melinda Gottlieb, librarian); Staten Island Historical Society; Staten Island Museum (especially Dottie D'Elletto); University of Illinois, Urbana-Champaign, Library and Archives; University of Notre Dame Library; University of Pennsylvania Archives and Records Center; U.S. Merchant Marine Academy Library; U.S. Olympic Committee Library; Wingate Institute, Netanya, Israel; YIVO.

Others who graciously provided information or shared materials include Lewis H. Carlson and John J. Fogarty, Elliott Denman, Jim Dunaway, Bob Hersh, Fred Jarvis, David Johnson, Eric Seiff, Vincent Seyfried, Ture Widlund (in Stockholm); Richard Mende, Robert Millan, and Richard Packer of Dieges and Clust; Lloyd Albin of Camp Kenmont; Det. Mark D. Warren, New York City Police Department; the staff of the alumni office at Wagner College; the staffs of Public Schools 13 and 14 and Curtis High School, Staten Island; Richard Dickenson, Staten Island/Richmond County

Borough historian; the Civic Center Synagogue; Gisela (Gig) Matheny; coaches Fred Barends, Gene Weil, and Rick Meindl, and historians Tom Maroukis, Harry Jebsen, and David Mayer at Capital University.

Melvin Adelman convinced me to change my original plan and to write instead a study for serious readers of sport history. He introduced me to Steve Riess, as talented an editor as he is an historian. Steve read successive drafts of the manuscript, making numerous marginal notes and suggestions that have improved it greatly. JoDee Dyreson and Pamela Cooper Chenkin also read the manuscript in different stages and made valuable comments. I am grateful to Ellen Goodman, the outstanding former acquisitions editor at Syracuse University Press, for her wise counsel and consistent support of this project. Others at Syracuse who were helpful include Mona Hamlin, Lisa Kuerbis, Lynn Hoppel, and freelance copy editor Annie Barva. Columbus neighbors and seasoned authors Mitchell Snay and Bob Shook took time to advise a rookie about publishing.

Four others helped me the most. I regret deeply that my parents did not live to see the completion of this project. Their profound interest in my becoming an educated person, a lover of literature and Jewish culture, has informed every part of my life. My father also taught me to love sports, although I don't think either he or my mother ever quite understood why their adolescent son was so determined to be a runner.

Frank Sparzo has been the best of friends since Hopkins days. As I worked on this book, he offered insightful suggestions, encouragement, and an unerring critical eye for the written word.

This book is dedicated to my beloved wife, Peggy, who has endured life with me and this project for longer than either of us imagined when I announced a decade ago that I would like to write a short children's book. In spite of the demands of her own profession, she has given me unending intellectual and emotional support, accompanying me on far-flung research trips and contributing indispensable computer and photographic skills.

Prologue

Stockholm 1984

THE LITTLE OLD MAN in the topcoat and hat walked briskly across the stadium infield in Stockholm remembering all those years ago.[1] In the summer of 1912, he had run in an unforgettable race on the same field in the Olympic Games. Although he was barely twenty years old then, he was a star of New York's Irish-American Athletic Club (known as the I-AAC or the Irish Club) and the world record holder for 1,500 meters, having lowered the record three times in thirteen days between May 26 and June 8. Sportswriters made him the favorite to win the Olympic metric mile.

Many people considered his story remarkable. The handsome raven-haired performer for the Irish Club stood at most five feet five inches, was bowlegged, and lived at home with his Yiddish-speaking immigrant parents. Many called him "the Hebrew runner."[2]

Now, seventy-two years later, Abel Kiviat of Lakehurst, New Jersey, had returned to the scene of his glory. At ninety-two, he was the oldest living Olympic medal winner, and the 1984 games would soon be held in Los Angeles. His longtime friend, the filmmaker and historian Bud Greenspan, was producing a two-hour special for the CBS television network entitled *America at the Olympics* that would feature Kiviat talking about his 1912 race.

He was very tired. He had just taken the first plane ride of his life, flying from New York to London the previous night, changing planes, and then going on to Sweden. He had not been out of the United States since he was sent to France as a soldier in 1918, and he had no concept of a plane ride. He said repeatedly to his traveling companion, Sydney Thayer, the associate producer of the film, "This is a lovely boat." Thayer tried to warn him about jet lag, but Kiviat insisted on drinking three glasses of his favorite "two fingers of Scotch Whiskey in a wide-bottom glass," followed by three or four cups of hot black coffee. He refused to sleep.

Although he was still grieving over his wife's death two years earlier, his ebullient personality made it inevitable that he would joke and flirt with the stewardesses. When he and Thayer finally reached the Grand Hotel in Stockholm, he opened the front door again and again for attractive young women, saying: "After you, madam, you are the most beautiful thing I've seen all day," and "Beauty before my old age."[3]

The next day it was on to the stadium to film his memories of the Olympics. The jet lag finally hit him during the interview. He sat in the stands wearing a U.S. Olympic team sweater and talked about those 1912 games. The film crew showed him many pictures of the event that produced vivid recollections. "The Olympics were different in many ways than they are today," he said. He talked about how the 164-member U.S. team traveled to Sweden on a chartered steamship, the S.S. *Finland*. The voyage took fourteen days, with a two-day stopover in Antwerp. Kiviat told the interviewer stories about his famous roommate on the *Finland*, Jim Thorpe. As an athlete, the decathlon winner "was in a class by himself," he said.

There was no Olympic Village in 1912. "We lived on the boat," he recalled about the three weeks' stay in Stockholm. "That included eating and sleeping. . . . There was this small motor boat [that] would tow a half a dozen—to rowboats as we call them in America. And five or six or seven of the boys go on with their little pack or something wrapped up in a couple of towels, running suit or shoes. Maybe a little toilet article or two." The athletes from the other twenty-seven countries that sent teams to the games lived in hotels and homes scattered around Stockholm.[4]

At one point, the interviewer took the old man down to the track, and he relived the memory of what two leading historians of the sport have called "the greatest mile or 1500 meter race ever run from the standpoint of exciting competition between fast runners." Fourteen milers, including seven Americans, lined up for the final at 3:30 P.M. on Wednesday, July 10, 1912. They had qualified by finishing first or second in one of the seven first-round heats the previous afternoon. (There was no limit then to the number of runners from any one country who could qualify for a final.) Track buffs worried, however, that there were too many starters for a fast race.[5]

It was a perfect summer's day. Kiviat looked up at a brand-new stadium, packed with a capacity crowd of more than twenty-two thousand excited spectators. One of the waiting milers remembered: "The stadium had been specially built. . . . We thought it beautiful, as it still is, and technically perfect in plan." The finalists knew this was a great field: at least half were capable of running 4:20 or better for the mile, then the threshold for a world-class performance. Two men, John Paul Jones of Cornell University and Kiviat, had run 4:15 for one mile. Although the Americans were the clear favorites, they expected challenges from the host country's seasoned ace, Ernst Wide, and the two Englishmen, Arnold Jackson and Philip Baker.[6]

It turned out to be a fascinating tactical race until the last lap, when little Kivie moved aggressively ahead of his fellow Yanks, John Paul Jones and Norman Taber, and appeared to have the gold medal in his grasp. Suddenly, from nowhere, in the final meters of the homestretch appeared tall Arnold Jackson of Oxford. "Out of the wide line, running almost as nearly abreast as a military company charging in open order across a field (but almost incredibly faster), shot Jackson, the Englishmen; Kiviat, the Irish-American wonder, and Taber of Brown University," reported Lawson Robertson in the *New York Evening World*. Jackson broke the tape—and Kiviat's heart. As eleven other young men from the United States, Sweden, Great Britain, France, and Germany followed the three medalists, it was as if the stadium were enveloped in a soft glow of confidence and hope that still haunts the imagination. On this "enchanting" afternoon—Cambridge University miler Philip Baker used the word often in nostalgic reminiscence—the amateur athletes of these Western powers had smashed records and inaugurated the modern era of running. An hour earlier, in the 5,000-meter event, Hannes Kolehmainen of Finland and Jean Bouin of France had completed what to observers was "the most interesting, the severest and the finest long-distance race that has probably ever been witnessed." They lowered the world record for the event by twenty-five seconds.[7]

The aura of innocence was illusory. Many of these lads would soon be in real military companies smashed by bullets and cannons in France. Jean Bouin and 5,000-meter bronze medalist George Hutson of England would be killed there in 1914. Arnold Jackson, thrice injured severely, would become a decorated British war hero. Kiviat and many other Olympians would follow them to war.

Moreover, the seemingly indomitable "squad of seven fleet American middle distance runners" in the 1,500-meters can be viewed as a part of America's strategic use of athletics to achieve global power. Organization was the key to their success. The athletes were recruited and supported by colleges, clubs, and vigorous regional and national athletic associations, and they were coached by knowledgeable professionals in the era's best facilities. Some writers, it is true, have dismissed the more casual training standards of 1912 as belonging to the sport's unscientific Victorian past, almost as if the athletes on the track were the subjects of an Eakins painting. Consider, however, that some spectators at Olympic Stadium that July day used their new hand-held cameras for snapshots of the emerging shape of modern track and field. The Stockholm Olympiad was a laboratory of developments that characterized the sport for the next half-century. Kiviat went on to win national championships and then served as the volunteer chief media official of major Amateur Athletic Union (AAU) track meets. By the time a television camera captured Kiviat's return to Stockholm in 1984, its lens had become a potent instrument both in the dissolution of the amateur ethos that had heavily framed his sport and in the rise of professionalism and globalization.[8]

The Olympians of 1912 were also taught to be patriots whose athletic talents would advance America's standing among the nations. For Kiviat, to compete for the United States was "the most wonderful thing in life particularly for a little Jewish boy," whose parents had escaped from czarist anti-Semitism. Nevertheless, despite high-flown rhetoric, the S.S. *Finland* was no melting pot: these milers lived side by side for a month, but ethnic and class consciousness determined their behavior. The Ivy League runners, for example, toured Stockholm and took their meals together; quiet Kivie hung out with Howard Drew, the brilliant young African American sprinter, and with working-class club athletes. This division is, of course, not surprising, given the state of American racial and ethnic relations at the time. Both Kiviat and Drew experienced troubling incidents of anti-Semitism and racism, respectively, during the trip. In future years, Kiviat would face far more destructive forms of bigotry based on his being widely identified as a

Jewish athlete. Yet even while coping with these problems intermittently in his successive careers as an athlete and official, he remained committed to the process of Americanization through sport. The Olympic experience of 1912 and thereafter only intensified the values he had already acquired from the Irish Club before sailing to Sweden.[9]

A story told by Kiviat's Irish Club teammate, the great middle-distance runner Mel Sheppard, is noteworthy. On the morning of the 1,500 final, some of the Americans were fooling around by "wadding up wet towels and heaving them through the portholes" of the ship, Sheppard reported in his memoir. One towel hit an officer of a little launch that took the athletes to shore. The milers thereafter discovered that "transportation [was] temporarily suspended for the remainder of the day. Our race, however, could not wait, so those who were expected ashore were compelled to lower one of the lifeboats and man the oars." The moral (discovered again and again by twentieth-century Americans): they all were in the same boat together.[10]

The life of Abel Kiviat, who learned this simple but enduring truth early in his life, sheds light both on the era of his sport's modernization and on the process of assimilation of immigrant, working-class athletes. In the dynamic interaction between these two sets of developments lies the meaning of his story.

A NOTE TO THE READER. In Kiviat's day, races were often timed in fifths of seconds. For convenience, I have converted those results to the modern tenths of seconds.

LAP ONE

STARTING OUT

1

Staten Island Boy

BY THE JUNE DAY in 1905 that Abel Kiviat became a bar mitzvah and assumed adult responsibilities in Jewish life, a striking personality had begun to emerge. He was already street-smart and high spirited, skilled in relating well to his companions, and respectful of their diverse ethnic and religious traditions. He was also quite ambivalent about his own Judaic heritage. The cultural journey he and his family had taken in thirteen short years goes far to explain this seeming paradox.

His parents came of age in the vital but enclosed world of nineteenth-century Polish Jewry and escaped just before falling victim to the hatred surrounding it. They did their best to inculcate in their New York–born toddler the traditional practices and values with which they had been raised. Much sooner than his mature and distracted parents, Abel began to gain clues to the New World's way of life. After all, as anthropologist Margaret Mead once observed, "[C]hildren of five have already incorporated into their everyday thinking ideas that most elders will never fully assimilate."

Once the family moved from its initial residence in Lower Manhattan's Jewish ghetto to the more open society on Staten Island, a Yiddish-speaking child confronted issues of assimilation that he would have to deal with throughout his life. For Abel Kiviat, the Stapleton neighborhood where he would live from the age of ten became his primary setting for addressing these issues. Even when he was a very old man, removed from the small shorefront village on Upper New York Bay by three-quarters of a century, his idealized memories of the place revealed that it was fundamental to his sense of self. In its public schools, playing fields, and Jewish institutions, the lad began to find his own solutions to the era's competing approaches to the Americanization of immigrants and their children.[1]

IN THE SYNAGOGUE COURTYARD:
BIALYSTOK, WINTER 1890–91

Moishe Kwiat was a most traditional young man. When he was twenty-three, study and prayer filled his fourth and final year in the Bialystoker Yeshiva, a rabbinical seminary. Located in a rundown wooden house near the Great Synagogue, in the courtyard district that was the heart of Jewish Bialystok, the yeshiva demanded much of Moishe. He and his study mate sat bent over a long bench and prepared the text of the day from the Talmud, the sixty-three tractates of commentary on Jewish law that have been the foundation of Judaism for more than two thousand years. The rabbis who lectured to him had themselves studied at well-known academies elsewhere in Poland and Lithuania, and they expected Moishe to explicate difficult problems in the text. In some classes, their methodology was the dialectical process known as *pilpul,* for which intensive student preparation was necessary. At year's end, Moishe would not "graduate": he was expected to pursue lifelong learning of the sacred texts, while "distancing himself as much as possible from the alien technical culture of Western Europe," wrote the leading chronicler of nineteenth-century Bialystok Jewry. "His goal was to be competent in Jewish law."[2]

Moishe had reached this level of education after years of elementary study of the Torah, the Hebrew Bible, as well as of the traditional medieval commentators, notably Rashi, and the Talmud itself. He had received his preadolescent training in his native Piesk, a flour mill town on the Zelbianka River surrounded by forest and streams in what is today Belarus, about seventy miles northeast of Bialystok. Two-thirds of the two thousand residents of this remote shtetl were Jews, most eking out livelihoods as merchants, shopkeepers, and artisans. Evenings presented an entirely different picture, revolving around intensive Hebraic learning and pious observance. Study groups of all kinds met regularly, and it appeared, wrote one memoirist, "that almost everyone in Piesk knew the Psalms by heart." The rabbis and teachers from the Kwiat family stood out, in the words of another townsman, for "Torah, nobility of character, and discernment." Like many other poor but ambitious lads from the small, closely knit towns of northeastern Poland, Moishe, the son of Yoseph and Mary Kwiat, could not resist the lure of the respected yeshiva in the expanding city of Bialystok. An offer of food and lodging for students was decisive.[3]

He matriculated in a surprisingly beautiful city. The great clock tower at the center of Bazarne Street, built of brick and stone more than a century earlier, dominated the landscape. On holidays, people dressed in their finery and gathered there on the square. A surviving early photograph, taken from the balcony of the tower, shows Surazer Street stretched out below, "Main Street" for Bialystok Jewry. Facing left was the courtyard district, from which the Jewish neighborhoods emanated, a maze of narrow streets and small houses. When Moishe had a little time, there was much more to take in, including the commercial hub on Gumjener Street, crowded with people and wagons headed for "stores stocked with all kinds of goods." Gumjener also hummed with "verbal tussle on just about every conceivable topic." The staid boulevard Washlikower Street was the financial center, and on Neistadt Street were the elegant townhouses of the wealthy.

Although Jews had lived in Bialystok since before the arrival of the ruling Polish counts of Branicki in 1703, the town by the Biale (or White) River remained a backwater until the 1880s. The fact that it was a political football, passed back and forth over the centuries between Lithuania, Poland, Germany, and France until Russia's Czar Alexander I captured it in 1815, necessarily impeded its growth. Profound economic and social changes in the concluding decades of the century transformed the city and its Jews, who comprised more than 75 percent of the nearly sixty thousand residents. Silk production in the new factories of Bialystok was the engine of this revolution. The owners, most of whom were Jewish, energetically created markets for their textiles in other countries, while their coreligionists, the weavers, hovered long hours over steam-powered looms. One could sense the new energy everywhere: in the larger modern buildings Jews were beginning to erect, in the new organizations they were creating. Many of the younger generation were enthusiastic modernists, turning Bialystok into a center of early Zionism—the idea of settling in the ancient Jewish homeland in Palestine—and they drew support from the Hebrew Enlightenment's (Haskalah) cultural values. Nevertheless, the traditional Talmudic erudition that Moishe Kwiat pursued devotedly remained the source of "the greatest prestige within the Jewish community" in the 1880s and 1890s.[4]

Not that he could completely escape the grasp of modernity. After all, he needed some means of financial support while he completed his studies. He therefore found employment in one of the great silk factories, most likely as a night watchman, joining other yeshiva students who "would get paid for sleeping."[5]

The job was also a necessity because he was soon to step under the bridal canopy with his fiancée, Zelda Zabludowski. Zelda was an attractive, dignified woman of twenty-five, with an adventurous spirit. She had been born to Abraham (Avram) Zabludowski and his wife, Anna or "Maty," in Kolno, Poland, a small town near the Prussian border. Maty Shapiro Zabludowski had a rich family background: she took pride in being a descendant of Rabbi Yosele Shapiro, and she was also a niece of Rabbi Akibah Rubinstein of nearby Stawiski, himself a scion of rabbinical luminaries. The twenty-two hundred Jews of Kolno, more than 60 percent of the total population, were "influenced by German culture and we considered ourselves superior to and more progressive than our neighbors," a member of that community recalled. Zelda's origins may account, in part, for her early interest in modern literature in Yiddish translation, her studied approach to the Hebrew language, and her profound sympathy for those in trouble.

Economic opportunity had brought the Zabludowskis to Bialystok, where some branches of the family had been established for generations and had achieved great distinction in business and letters. We know from family sources that Zelda's relatives set up textile factories. Industrialization also enabled young women such as Zelda and her four sisters to work outside of the home. She found a place in a silk factory but combined the work with domestic responsibilities after the early death of her parents.[6] As full as the young couple's lives were, the legendary warmth and hospitality of the city engaged them. Because there was yet neither theater nor electrification in the 1880s, their pleasures were simple. Moishe, vigorous and stocky at five feet seven inches, loved the outdoors, especially swimming. Together, they enjoyed the company of friends. As another Bialystoker described the youth of those days, "we walked through lanes and alleys, and effortlessly beyond, along country paths, until abruptly all was still. And from that stillness there arose the humming of more primitive worlds: swamps, lakes and rivers, untamed, forbidding, yet studded with jewels; slim white beryoskes, chestnuts in silver bloom, and warm nights ablaze with stars hovering over a luminous dream we called Bialystok."[7]

Sometimes the dream turned into the nightmare of anti-Semitism. The irrational hatred of Jews was always in the air, ready to explode into a pogrom. Polish peasants had started one in Bialystok in 1882, months after the assassination of Czar Alexander II by Russian revolutionaries. Jewish butchers and wagon drivers, armed with knives, drove off the peasants before anyone was hurt. Years later in America, with tears in her eyes, Zelda would tell her children of her own fears of such a pogrom when she was their age.

Increasing the terror was the possibility of a beloved Jewish boy's being conscripted into the czar's army. Moishe knew well the consequences: twenty-five years of forced military service, farewell to his Zelda, and the end of any Jewish life. In the spring of 1891, the scenario became all too real. His son Abel told the story to an interviewer nearly a century later: "They were doing quite well, when all of a sudden a friend tips off my father and says 'Morris—or he called him by his Jewish name, what is it, Moishe?—get out of here. The army is coming for you next week.' So he grabs his wife to be . . . they escaped through the underground from Russia to Hamburg, Germany. The same friend of my father who warned him took them to the border in a hay wagon with them lying buried in the bottom of the wagon." The wedding of Moishe and Zelda took place in Hamburg. "Then they went to Liverpool and Ellis Island."[8]

Having immersed himself so deeply in "the sea of the Talmud" and the cohesive world that was its safe harbor, would this young man survive the Atlantic passage to the starkly different New World culture that he had been trained from birth to resist? And what would be the fate of his bride?

A CHILD OF THE TENEMENTS:
THE LOWER EAST SIDE, 1891–1896

Moishe and Zelda headed for America, an early part of the great wave from Russian Poland that would crest in the first decade of the twentieth century. Hundreds of Bialystoker had already settled there and had written home of its promise. The ocean crossing from Liverpool on the steamship *Italy* was miserable and traumatic. Although built in 1870 as the second largest of the new vessels for transatlantic trade, the old steamer was small and cramped by the standards of the 1890s—just more than four thousand tons, less than four hundred feet in length, with a single funnel. A thousand or more emigrants and other poor folk were packed into steerage. They lacked any semblance of privacy or comfort, and "filth and stench" were pervasive. There was no provision for the specially prepared kosher foods that Moishe and Zelda required.

"They had a tough life," Abel's younger brother Harold remarked in an interview a century later. "I can't believe it, my mother and father at the bottom of the ship. And they cooked their own food on the deck of the ship below decks. And they brought their own bedding, a big sheet filled with cotton down," which Zelda called *perrene* in Yiddish. "They were the heroes, the pioneers, my mother and father, all the Jews that came over in the 1800s. Geez, I don't know where they had the guts," Harold Kiviat said in wonder. This was Harold's version of family history. Like many similar post–World War II nostalgic memorials to the eastern European Jews transplanted to the Lower East Side, it drew on the hard facts of parental struggles.

On September 18, 1891, the ship reached New York Harbor and the unforgettable first sight of the city's tall buildings. Upon docking, the Kwiats were taken with their baggage to the turreted Barge Office at the Battery, where U.S. Immigration Bureau officials and doctors examined them. (The year 1891 was the midpoint of a two-year interlude between the closing of Castle Garden and the opening of Ellis Island, and the Barge Office served as the temporary immigrant depot.) After they were admitted to the United States, they were probably greeted by waiting Bialystoker, who took them the last few miles to their new home.[9]

The couple "didn't have a dime" and had few options at this stage. According to family legend, some Kwiat relatives had fled from czarist conscription in the 1880s, but "when they came to this country they simply buried their identities. No one knew where they were." Moishe and his bride settled into a tenement house apartment on the corner of Grand and Allen Streets. It was the center of the Lower East Side, a district packed with Yiddish-speaking immigrants from eastern Europe. By 1891, this four-square-mile triangle had more than five hundred people per acre and was the most thickly populated neighborhood in the world. Allen Street was a dark and sleazy "red-light" area, with the largest "disorderly house" (brothel) next door to a school and synagogue. The street's notorious tenements were "great prison-like structures of brick, with narrow doors and windows, cramped passages and steep rickety stairs," the *American Magazine* noted in 1888. These tenements were also "perfect death-traps": "the flimsy fire-escapes" were "so laden with broken furniture, bales and boxes that they [were] worse than useless."

The Lower East Side was of course much more than rows of tenements; it was becoming a lively center of culture and commerce. Synagogues and schools, Yiddish theaters, cafés for intellectual conversation, settlement houses, newspapers and periodicals, labor and Socialist groups, made this period the formative era for what would develop into a kind of adult university without walls long before anyone thought of a name for it. Yet men such as Moishe, whose entire upbringing had been focused on traditional religious study and observance, suffered especially during this early phase of Jewish immigration. Later immigrants would refer to the newcomers of the 1890s as *farloyrene menshn*, "lost souls." The evidence indicates that Moishe never fully recovered from the psychological affects of the profound disruption. However, the fact that the East Side was a familiar all-Jewish world eased, to some extent, the shock of adaptation to the new and alien culture. In this serried mass of humanity, amidst extreme poverty and social pathology, the Kwiats found a center for their lives in a small but vital community of Bialystoker. More than a decade earlier (1878), two Bialystoker societies and prayer groups, the Anshei Chesed and the Adath Jeshurun, had merged to form the Bialystoker Synagogue. The result of this early involvement was that the East Side remained the couple's American Jewish lodestar all their days.[10]

The reality was, however, that Moishe needed to find work quickly. His hope was to find "a pulpit in the Rabbinate, but it did not come his way." He therefore joined dozens of other erstwhile yeshiva students in the basic trade of the peddler. In one sense, it was an opportunity to begin to learn English and American ways while supporting himself and Zelda. He set out "with a pack wrapped up in an old, black oilcloth strapped to his back," walking the streets of New York and undoubtedly crying out the inimitable "suspenders, collah buttons, 'lastic, matches, hankeches—please lady, buy," as he sold his wares. Like other peddlers, Moishe may have been rejected by housewives, chased by bullies, or harassed by the police, but he continued to sell. No matter how much he disliked peddling, he had new responsibilities.[11]

On June 23, 1892, Zelda Kwiat gave birth to their first child, a son. They called him Avraham (Abraham, "Abel" a few years later), after her late father. He was born at home in the tenement, with a midwife to assist Zelda. As an adult, he constructed a revisionist narrative of his origins in which his parents moved to Staten Island when he was six months old. His six younger siblings, he claimed, were all born on the island. In fact, however, his parents lived on Allen Street until at least the second half of 1896. His sister Anna (Anne) was born there in 1894 and brother Iser (Izzy) the following year. The Second Avenue Elevated trains—little steam locomotives that pulled the wooden cars—ran on tracks overhead and were, as one foreign visitor wrote, an "ever active volcano" and "a severe trial to the average nervous system." When Abel described for historian Lewis Carlson his parents' problems with the "Els," he was actually relating his own troubles as a toddler. Little "Avramele" always had to worry about ashes, oil, and cinders falling down on him. The Els also "made a racket all day and night, choo, choo, choo," Abel recalled. "They were little bits of things. My parents took a long time to get used to all that noise. They used to have to go to bed at 5 or 6 o'clock because it would take them so long to get to sleep." Otherwise, he retained only vague memories of his preschool years on the Lower East Side.

Why did Abel deliberately distort his life history? In the oral memoir, he revealed that he was ashamed of the pervasive culture of Yiddishkeit of his earliest years. He did not wish to be thought of, in Jacob Riis's memorable phrase, as one of the East Side's pale "children of the tenements." His was a deliberate effort to reinvent himself as a fully assimilated athlete with all-American roots.

After five years of struggle and with two more children, Moishe decided the tenements were no place to raise a family. "So a couple of his Jewish friends from Russia said, 'Why don't you try Staten Island? You'll be the first Jew down there, and you could open up a general store and you wouldn't have to go peddling,'" Abel recounted a century later. "It worked out."[12]

"A COUNTRY BOY" OF THE GREAT CITY: ROSEBANK, 1896–1902

One day in 1896 the young family boarded the five-cent steamboat ferry at the foot of Manhattan for the six-mile trip across Upper New York Bay to Staten Island. From the enclosed cabin on the main deck of the side-wheeler, they could see the verdant hills of the island, located at the entrance to New York Harbor, and, on the western side, the coast of New Jersey. They had reason to be excited as they passed the Statue of Liberty, for awaiting them was "a wooded land" of promise and opportunity. To the map maker, it resembled an oversized diamond, almost fourteen miles long and more than seven miles wide. To the Kwiats, escaping at last from the East Side's density, it was a different kind of jewel: a place of natural beauty enjoyed by a scattered population.

Approximately sixty-five thousand people lived on the island at the time, many on the three hundred or so farms growing potatoes, corn, oats, wheat, and rye. Dairy farming was also an active occupation. Large wagons carried much of the produce to market in Manhattan or Jersey City. Oystering and shipbuilding remained the important industries they had been since well before the American Revolution. In the mid–nineteenth century, the island's beauty and beaches had drawn the wealthy and famous for vacations. "The people that came to Staten Island," Harold Kiviat exclaimed with pride, "[were] kings and ambassadors and poets. The New England poets—Longfellow and all those poets—they summered on Staten Island." There were hotels and villas, as well as swimming, boating and fishing, clambakes, tennis clubs, and other forms of recreation.[13]

Industrial development began to change the face of the island rapidly after the 1880s. Entrepreneurs and promoters recognized the rich potential offered by its location and natural resources. Adding to its attractiveness, the chamber of commerce pointed out, was the relatively inexpensive cost of living and "an abundant supply of all classes of labor." The latter included new immigrants such as the Kwiats, settling in the villages along the shores and in new manufacturing sites.[14]

When Moishe, Zelda, and their three small children landed at the St. George terminal, they went to the nearby village of Tompkinsville and moved into an apartment at 7 Henry Street. Moishe Americanized his name to "Morris Kiviat" and became a peddler again. He sold "a little of everything: mostly clothes, haberdashery, you would call it, except shoes." He became acquainted with the few Jewish families. They worshipped in their handsome frame synagogue, Congregation B'nai Jeshurun, the first on the island (1891), at Victory Boulevard and Pike Street, a few blocks from their home. They also brought in a kosher butcher from the East Side, who opened a shop in the neighborhood.[15]

On January 1, 1898, Staten Island joined the consolidated City of New York as the Borough of Richmond. With the stroke of the clock, the Kiviats were living in the largest and most populous city in America. By then, they had moved again, this time to Rosebank, or "Little Italy," a village three miles to the south on the eastern shore. In contrast to "the beautiful buildings in Bialystok," Morris and Zelda "were surprised at the shanteys [sic] in Rosebank," according to Anne Kiviat's later account of her conversations with her mother. Jewish friends took Morris "to this big Italian real estate man" who put the Kiviats in a three-story building on Chestnut Avenue, a narrow road that ran perpendicular to the main artery, Bay Street. Morris continued his peddling, but he also opened a general store with Zelda. The family crowded into a small apartment above the store. Many of Morris's customers were immigrants from southern Italy who had arrived in Rosebank in the late 1880s. They displaced the older Yankee residents, as well as the German and Irish immigrants who had come in midcentury. But if the face of Rosebank became more southern European, the dwindling Irish population remained in control. By 1898, the Irish-dominated St. Mary's Roman Catholic Church, "at the front of my street," as Abel put it, and its wooden parochial school building "right around the corner" from the Kiviat home, were the soul of the neighborhood.[16]

Although Zelda, who would retain a thick Yiddish accent, had not yet begun to master English, Morris was learning the language as he dealt with customers. Abel always put a happy face on the family's relations with others: "We got along wonderful. I never got hurt. I never got in a fight, because the other kids took care of me." This comment reflects the beginning of a life-long tendency by the Kiviats' oldest child to avoid interpersonal conflict with his non-Jewish neighbors, some of whom were anti-Semitic. His shrewd strategy was always to secure bigger folk as protectors.[17]

The family kept growing at one- or two-year intervals. David was born in December 1897, followed by Samuel and Irik (Harold). (Charles was born in 1903, after they moved away from Rosebank.) Zelda had the burden of caring for them, coping with the era's terrible childhood diseases, housekeeping, cooking, as well as working in the store. She maintained a traditional home in this strange New World. It was "perfectly kosher," Abel remembered, meaning they strictly observed the dietary laws. Zelda had "two sets of dishes," one for meat and a second for dairy foods. The two were never served together. Morris rose early every day, put on his dark leather tefillin (phylacteries), and recited the morning prayers. "And we would just read the prayer with him, 'till we got old enough and we became bar mitzvah, all the boys," Abel recalled. Morris spent as much time as possible each day studying the Talmud. For him, Jewish learning was both its own reward and a refuge from the profound dislocations in his life.[18]

Shabbos, the Sabbath, was the high point of the week. "Everything was done before sundown Friday," Abel said, as if they were observing the sacred day of rest in Bialystok. Zelda used her gifts as cook and baker to prepare a Sabbath feast: gefilte fish, a variety of noodles, beautifully brown challahs (braided loaves of bread). At dusk, she would light the Shabbos candles; thereafter, there were "no matches, no lights," and all work would cease until sundown Saturday. For little Abraham, games were not allowed. "My parents would send us out to call a non-Jewish boy to light the lights and start the stove once the Sabbath began. . . . We'd give the fellow a little money for lighting the stove." This was the eastern European custom of the Shabbos goy.[19]

There were a few other Jewish families in Rosebank and, given the distance that strict Sabbath observers would have to walk to the B'nai Jeshurun synagogue, they held prayer services in the home of the Payve family. Morris led the worship and was given the honorary title of *gabbai,* or official.

The high holy days and the major Jewish festivals were also dramatic events for a young child. The transformation of the Kiviat home at Passover was especially impressive, however confused the details became with age. "We had the pots and pans taken to Allen Street and had them shired [*sic*]," Abel recalled about the elaborate preparation for the holiday. "That's a Jewish word for 'sandblasted.' They looked new, you know, whitish. . . . And the copper would shine like a mirror." On Passover morning, the family walked the "three miles from where we lived" to services at B'nai Jeshurun in Tompkinsville.[20]

Learning to relate well to peers while exploring the world was also a central component of Abel's early development. "In some ways I was a country boy on Staten Island," he recalled. There was open land all around, where young Abe and his chums "played children's games," including a version of hide-and-seek. A short walk away was Clear Comfort, the Victorian Gothic cottage that was the home of the gifted photographer Alice Austen and her family. Here the magnificent view of the Narrows and the quiet beauty of wide lawns presented a strikingly different and unfamiliar landscape.[21]

This brief childhood Eden was interrupted on September 12, 1898, when Abraham registered at Public School (P.S.) 13. He recalled the event vividly: "So the Italian kids I played with took me to school and this Irish woman who was in charge of the grade school asked them, 'What do you call this boy?' They said, 'We call him Abe.' She said, 'There is no such thing as Abe. His real name from the Bible is Abel.' So that's how I got to be Abel. My real Jewish name I couldn't spell, and I couldn't pronounce, so I never told anybody what it was. I was just Abel." As the head teacher looked down her nose at the six-year-old child and made that arbitrary decision, she initiated the formal process of his "Americanization." At P.S. 13, he took the first of many steps in breaking with his parents' Yiddish-speaking, Orthodox culture and achieving "the American standard." That, after all, was the stated mission of New York's schools in educating the children of the new southern and eastern European immigrants. He attended P.S. 13 through the 1901–1902 school year, when the family moved two miles north to the larger village of Stapleton.[22]

THE AMERICANIZATION OF ABEL: STAPLETON, 1902–1907

Morris and Zelda rented a home at 101 Broad Street in the center of Stapleton. Their dry goods store was on the first floor of the solid two-story brick building, and the family lived in a more spacious apartment above it. At this location, they attracted a more diverse clientele than in Rosebank. The immediate neighborhood was a rich microcosm of the American melting pot: the Irish, Germans, Italians, Poles, a few Rumanians, Swedes and Norwegians, and a number of Yiddish-speaking immigrant families. Across the road on Quinn Street and a block or two away on fashionable Harrison Street lived the comfortable old-stock Americans, including some with southern roots. However, most of the Kiviats' walk-in customers were their working-class neighbors.[23]

Stapleton was a good choice for a home. The Kiviats arrived when the town was entering its most productive period. At the beginning of the nineteenth century, it had been an area of lovely farms facing the Upper Bay, including one that Cornelius Vanderbilt had lived on as a boy during Thomas Jefferson's presidency. In 1832, with land acquired from the Vanderbilts, the developers William J. Staples and Minthorne Tompkins had laid out streets for a new village. It had quickly become one of the most important villages on the island, and its location at a branch of the Upper Bay that "form[ed] a natural anchorage place for vessels of the deepest draught" suggested even brighter prospects as a seaport. At midcentury, German refugees established several major breweries for lager beer, taking advantage of the island's pure spring and well water. They made the place a center of German culture. Following the Civil War, it began to assume its modern form. The state legislature approved taking the vacant marsh in the center of the village and converting it into the "Central Park of Staten Island." Within the park, a striking Village Hall was built in 1889. A line of stores along Bay Street, with residences above them, created a main street and commercial center. Homes for workingmen sprang up near the water, and picturesque houses in the exuberant Queen Anne style, for the new managers and professional men, on the nearby heights. Consolidation of Richmond County into New York City in 1898 promised further rapid development.[24]

1. Morris (Moishe) Kiviat and son Harold in rear of their home, c. 1914. Courtesy of Lucy Price.

Zelda ran the store while Morris continued as a peddler, although he was more creative than before. He bought a second-hand pie wagon and, for twenty-five dollars, a horse "from a friendly Irish neighbor." "The wagon had a lot of shelves inside where you hang all kinds of material, even a suit," Abel remembered. "The wagon had a place for hats, a place for shoes and other things." Morris also carried "general furnishings." His customers were the island's farmers and their immigrant laborers.[25]

Morris enrolled Abel in the fourth grade of P.S. 14, a respected local institution located only about one hundred yards from their front door. At first glance, it seemed more promising than his former school. Built in 1895, the four-story building educated more than twelve hundred children, making it nearly three times the size of P.S. 13. It was well equipped, with a large auditorium, a gymnasium, and special rooms for instruction in science and cooking. Harold Kiviat believed "we got a good schooling, we were intelligent when we left that school," but Abel's younger brother did not remember the lockstep curriculum and the archaic teaching methods. Despite the energetic efforts of New York City's reformist school superintendent William Maxwell to introduce a more progressive course of study, Abel's teachers focused almost exclusively on the basic skills—the so-called three Rs—and required endless recitation, often with the class in unison. There were frequent trips to the blackboard to practice writing. Discipline was severe for laggards and dullards. According to one P.S. 14 alumnus, during Friday morning assembly terrified students recited Tennyson's poem "Charge of the Light Brigade" and other set pieces, accompanied by a teacher playing background music on the piano. An unscholarly and vigorous child such as Abel must have had his patience sorely tested.[26]

One component of the curriculum did have an impact on him. The school used the critical upper grades to solidify the formal process of acculturating the neighborhood's many immigrant children. The "concern for homogenizing American beliefs and behavior" pervaded the lessons and the textbooks, but Abel paid a high price for the instruction. In part, his embarrassment about his mother's Yiddish accent and culture stemmed from this teaching. The irony was that only doors away, his parents were every bit as committed to the life of the mind, in their own idiom, as was Principal A. Hall Burdick's faculty.[27]

A few favorite teachers provided support and diversion that lightened the experience. There was Watson F. Keeley, who encouraged Abel's interest in sport, and his eighth-grade instructor, who recognized his difficulty in memorizing a four-verse poem for the graduation ceremony and mercifully substituted a shorter version. "'May you live as long as you want,'" Abel recited, "'and never want as long as you live.'"[28]

For Abel, the saving grace of elementary school was the new opportunity for interscholastic sports competition. In the fall of 1903, Dr. Luther H. Gulick, the city's director of physical training; General Albert Wingate, a member of the board of education; James E. Sullivan, the head of the nation's Amateur Athletic Union (AAU); Superintendent Maxwell; and others formed the Public Schools Athletic League (PSAL). Its mission was to provide a varied sports program for the young of New York, including afternoon practices in school facilities and matches between elementary schools culminating in borough championships. "The Athletic League was formed to bring back into the lives of our children their birthright of competitive play, and to weld it into the educational procedure of a great city," one of the founders wrote. In the process, city children would become healthier, better students and more disciplined and loyal members of a democratic society. Here was an ambitious attempt at social uplift combined with a Victorian quest to control youth.[29]

Such high-flown rhetoric had little meaning for Abel and his friends, who simply loved to play baseball. He had a good throwing arm, was fast, and ranged widely in the field, even though he was small in stature and slightly bowlegged. The P.S. 14 team, which he played on for three years, won the Staten Island PSAL championship in the spring of 1907, with Abel as captain and shortstop. Although the team then lost in the semifinals of the interborough games to P.S. 10 of Brooklyn, the eventual city champion, Abel was acquiring a reputation as an outstanding ballplayer.

P.S. 14 boys also established their prowess in track and field, mainly because of an excellent coach. Clarence "Chief" Barkley of Stapleton had been a star sprinter in AAU races from 1895 to 1900, and with the formation of the PSAL he found his calling. After organizing a squad, he would wait at the school entrance for classes to end and would gather his boys and take them a few blocks to the Old Lawn, a large field sloping down to Bay Street, which P.S. 14 used as its sports playground. Here, Chief Barkley "trained, lectured, and started the young athletes in the running game." For Abel, it was the beginning of an association that would last for more than twenty years.

The coach's first project was the PSAL's athletic badge tests for elementary schools. Abel won a 60-yard dash for boys under thirteen and took home a "half bronze and silver" button. Not surprisingly, Barkley's track team won the 1904 championship for Staten Island elementary schools. In the team photo, a determined-looking Abel was in the center of the front row. Shortly before graduation in June 1907, while still playing for the city baseball title, he was one of thirteen hundred entries in the PSAL's fourth annual citywide

2. P.S. 14 track team, Staten Island champions of 1904. Kiviat is in the front row center; future sportswriter John Drebinger wears the striped singlet in the front row, fourth from the right. Courtesy of Lucy Price.

elementary schools meet at Celtic Park, near Long Island City, home of the national track champions, the Irish-American Athletic Club (I-AAC, or Irish Club). Entries in the several events were according to an athlete's weight bracket. Abel competed in the "70-Yard Dash, 115 Pound Class." His event had seven heats; he finished second in his round but did not survive the semifinals. However, he was the only boy from Staten Island to advance at all because Manhattan and Brooklyn dominated the meet.[30]

Outside of school, there was plenty of excitement for a child experiencing the startling social and economic changes that impacted uneasily at times on an older way of life. Abel recalled seeing one of his first automobiles: "a couple driving a car with lenses, a cap, a big [linen] duster they called them, sitting way up in the car. . . . And the wife would have blinders on, we called them. You know, sunglasses—driving glasses—the big ones. And she'd wear a big hat with a big veil on it, holding it [on]." A few of these open cars shared island roads with the traditional horse and buggy. Morris bought a "fancy carriage," a surrey with the fringe on top. He would dress up Lady, his mare, and proudly take his young family of nine for a Sunday drive in the country, visiting with his customers, the farmers.[31]

Stapleton, too, retained a countrylike atmosphere. There were woods and open lots everywhere, ideal for sports and games as well as for mischief. Abel made friends quickly and played ball with them whenever he could. Acting like "fresh but ambitious" city kids, the gang played soccer between the trolley tracks on Bay Street. His new gang was as ethnically diverse as the neighborhood itself. It included Tom Walsh of Gordon Street, an Irish American lad and a future county judge, and another boy who was a future chief county clerk. Abel also befriended African American children from Stapleton's ghetto, inviting them as guests for Friday night dinners with the encouragement of Zelda, who detested the pervasive "racial hatred in those days." His sister, Anne, who was "a bit of a tomboy" and "a damned good runner," would play with them.[32]

His parents did not really understand his passion for sports. They retained the eastern European notion that "athletics [was] an arena for gentiles" and that profound scholarship was the essential component of a manly personality. Morris and Zelda must have sympathized with the father who had written about baseball to the *Jewish Daily Forward* in 1903, "I want my son to grow up to be a *mensh,* not a wild American runner."[33]

Opportunity for fun and mischief abounded. The Kiviat kids "stole grapes and peaches from our neighbors, the farmers," Harold Kiviat remembered. "Holy geez, you took a bite into a peach, and you got a bath." They walked two blocks to Dock Street, where a fascinating world awaited them: ocean liners and large tugboats, ship repair and salvage companies such as Merritt & Chapman. Abel swam uneasily off the docks (he was never much of a swimmer) and occasionally rode on motorboats or sailboats, watching the fishermen. "Did you ever smell fresh fish just caught, out of the water?" he asked eighty years later. "What an odor it gives you? And then the saltwater and the sailboat bobbing." The gang also marched in patriotic parades down Bay Street with the military bands "striking the familiar oom-pah-pah beat." At Halloween, they built bonfires and played tricks on unsuspecting islanders. In winter, they enjoyed sledding down hills. Directly across Canal Street was the Rubsam and Horrmann (R & H) Atlantic Brewing Company, the most successful company on the island. "We kids would come in the back way where they were repairing the beer barrels," Abel said. "The foreman was the father of three of my buddies. We learned how to drink beer there. . . . [Afterward] a lot of the kids would come to my place and have a glass of milk on top of the beer and some Jewish cookies that my mother would make. Then the kids would go home, and they couldn't eat their dinner."[34]

The grounds in front of the small frame building of the old Immaculate Conception Church, diagonally across from the Kiviat home, offered another playground for the favorite game of Lost Tracks, a form of Hare and Hounds. One day the gang had the bright idea to sneak Abel into the church as an altar boy. They put a surplice on him, gave him a censer, and had him repeat the words of the Latin liturgy. Who should stroll by but Father William McClure, the strong-minded and dynamic priest? As the boys tried to suppress their laughter, the kindly father demanded that Abel turn over the religious objects but permitted him to remain with his friends.[35]

One of the neighborhood gang was Tommy Lennon, whose family lived in a flat near P.S. 14. Although Tommy was two years younger than Abel, they became fast friends. The boy's father, Thomas Sr., was a native Staten Islander of Irish immigrant parents, a struggling young attorney, and a long-time member of Staten Island's volunteer fire department. After the elder Lennon lost his life heroically while fighting a fire, Abel's friendship helped Tommy to cope.

The bond between the boys was based in part on the fact that they were the two fastest runners in the area. One day Abel had a brainstorm. He would slip Tommy into Sabbath services as "a Jewish altar boy." When Morris and a few neighbors organized a prayer service in the back of Rivkin's kosher butcher shop on Broad Street, Abel's moment of ecumenical reciprocity had arrived. He "got Tommy Lennon to put a Yamulka [skullcap] on his head and wear a tallis [prayer shawl]." Morris found out about the scheme in advance, and "he damned near broke my neck," Abel reminisced. "He gave me the back of the hands, knocked me about ten to fifteen feet away." Long after the sting wore off, the two buddies delighted in regaling listeners with their youthful interfaith adventures.[36]

All of this activity notwithstanding, Abel was a surprisingly shy and introverted child and sought release in reading. His family provided the model: Morris always had a substantive Jewish text at hand, and Zelda was a constant reader, usually of the newest novel in Yiddish translation. His siblings acquired the habit early. Abel chose simple and popular novels about the active life. Tales of cowboys and of his hero Teddy Roosevelt charging up San Juan Hill with the Rough Riders appealed to him at first. When he was an older youth in Stapleton, the dozens of books by Horatio Alger, Jr., about poor boys who succeeded through hard work and thrift reinforced the practical virtues he learned at home and in the neighborhood. Most intriguing, however, were the stories of Frank Merriwell at Yale by Gilbert Patton (who wrote under the pen name "Burt L. Standish"), which intensified his interest in sport and in what President Roosevelt called "the strenuous life." Reading about Merriwell winning a sprint or starring in baseball became another vicarious means of acculturation.[37]

Even while Abel learned competing visions of American life from P.S. 14 and his informal peer network, the one narrow and the other expansive, his family remained rooted in the culture of Yiddish and religious Orthodoxy. The parents spoke Yiddish at home, although increasingly using some English. Despite good relations with a variety of neighbors, their close friendships were with Jewish families. The visits of Zelda's sisters, who had followed her to America, extended the family circle of Yiddishkeit. Abel's married aunt and her husband "would come down Friday night for the prayer and Kosher dinner." She would then join the family for Saturday morning services, sitting with Zelda and Anne in the separate women's section. When another of Zelda's sisters, Aunt Sarah, had a short-lived romance, the Kiviats took in the suitor as a boarder for six months and helped him to secure work at the R & H Brewery across the street.[38]

Of profound importance to Morris and Zelda was to give Abel some kind of formal Jewish instruction, especially as he approached his bar

3. Zelda Kiviat. Courtesy of Esther Kiviat.

mitzvah at age thirteen. Having themselves taught him a basic knowledge of customs and ceremonies, the Hebrew alphabet, and reading simple prayers, these Jewishly literate parents wanted more for their eldest. As it happened, turn-of-the-century America offered an unappealing solution to their dilemma. In Poland, the heder was the privately funded (but publicly controlled) Jewish elementary school that played an historic role in shaping the cultural character of Jewry. The New York version was a despised and pathetic copy of the original. A rabbi or *melamed* (teacher) who lived around the corner from the Kiviat house taught a few neighborhood kids to read from the prayer book and, in preparation for bar mitzvah, some Hebrew blessings and a selection from the biblical prophets. He charged Morris twenty-five cents a session. It was not really a class: Abel and the other boys straggled in at the conclusion of the P.S. 14 day, and the *melamed* tutored each in turn for fifteen minutes while the other lads "were fresh" with mischief, according to Harold Kiviat. Compounding Abel's difficulties with the Hebrew text, the teacher spoke to him partly in Yiddish, which by now he did not understand well. In frustration, the teacher grabbed his ruler with the tin edges and rapped Abel across the knuckles. After minutes that seemed an eternity, the class was released. "Then we'd break our neck, run out to play baseball and football" before darkness fell, Abel recalled.

In June 1905, Abel celebrated his bar mitzvah. (Late in life he told an interviewer: "I don't remember where. Maybe in the home," rather than at B'nai Jeshurun.) Prepared by the heder study and by coaching from Morris and Zelda, he recited the blessings from the prayer book. Afterward, family and friends hugged and kissed him and called him "a mensch." As was the case for the overwhelming majority of his peers, Abel's brief formal Jewish education ended that day. His parents apparently did not push him to pursue further religious study or to continue the family's traditional observances. Although Abel thought they made this decision because "they were fairly broad-minded," a more realistic assessment would be that they coped as best they could with the painful state of contemporary American Jewish education.[39]

As Abel suggested, his parents were inevitably themselves becoming transformed by their experience in a modernizing America. They mingled with neighbors and customers who enjoyed a more relaxed lifestyle. "Everyone knew everyone else," Stapleton residents said. And even the struggle to feed a large family became a part of the Kiviats' assimilation process. Consider the pressing need to provide daily quantities of milk for seven young children. Morris began to indulge a passion for animals by keeping a cow in back of the house, a black-and-white Holstein he named "Dolly." He assigned Abel and his younger siblings to take Dolly to pasture land he rented on property formerly belonging to the Vanderbilts. The children took turns rising before dawn and making the mile or more round trip "along a country road" to bring Dolly home each morning. Zelda milked the cow by hand, which provided as many as fourteen quarts of milk a day. "My mother," Abel

4. The Kiviat children, 1905, about the time of Abel's bar mitzvah: *(from left)* Anne, Abel, Harold, Charlie, Sam, Izzy, and David. Courtesy of Esther Kiviat.

reminisced, "could make anything—God bless her—out of milk. Sour milk, buttermilk, cream cheese." Zelda also sold the milk to neighbors for four cents a quart to supplement the family income. Fortunately, in 1905 Dr. John Halloran built a rowhouse for his Irish Catholic family two doors away, and the Kiviats acquired both an able veterinarian and a kindly social ally in their acculturation.[40]

For kids who demonstrated a passion for athletics, Morris was in one respect a positive role model. He was famous for diving into the icy bay in April and being "the last one out in October." He would use powerful strokes to swim from the Stapleton side to Bay Ridge in Brooklyn and back. However impressed Abel was with his father's physical skills, Morris's frequently hostile behavior and emotional distance interfered with the family's adjustment process. Abel rightly felt that his poppa was "too strict" a disciplinarian. If Morris acted out the traditional role of eastern European patriarch with his brood, there was no love lost. Morris's emotional distance left Abel an angry child. His siblings emerged from childhood with similar resentments, which they would then act out in their relations with each other. "Nobody in that family got along with anybody else," one relative has said.[41]

Zelda therefore had to serve as both the glue of her family and the supporter of her children's efforts to reach out successfully to the larger world. As a girl in a traditional Jewish society, she had learned that the woman's claim was the home, which included handling the family budget and running a business to ensure sustenance. She continued this tradition in Stapleton with skill, efficiency, and warmth. Although she could be a firm disciplinarian, she worried about each of her offspring and, perhaps to overcompensate for her husband's aloofness, was engaged in their lives. Her children adored their momma. Either in a cultivated Yiddish or in halting English speech—and even more by example—she taught them to strive for good relations with others and to be charitable. For example, she found a homeless African American woman in Stapleton's ghetto, a child of slaves, that "everybody shunted aside." According to Harold Kiviat, "Mom adopted her," nicknamed her "Sadie," and had her live with them and help in the kitchen. In the evenings, Sadie would tell the Kiviat children tales of her youth picking cotton in the South. This and similar actions by Zelda set the course for young Abel's life. "My mother told me never to say no," he repeated often. "She said if you want to say no, say maybe. . . . [W]hen she learned American slang, she said 'If you never say no, you'll never get a black eye or a bloody nose.'"[42]

WHAT MADE ABEL RUN? COUNTY FAIR, SUMMER 1907

Abel once recalled for an interviewer a summer day when he took his parents and siblings to the new county fairgrounds in Dongan Hills to watch him race in a special 75-yard dash for schoolboys. He had free tickets from the sheriff who ran the fair ("fifty cents was a lot of money to pay in those days for admission"), and the family drove out in Morris's horse and carriage. Their bleacher seats were near the finish line.

Abel lined up against stiff competition, including the island's PSAL sprint champion. Slow to respond to the starter's pistol, Abel was the last off the mark. He gathered himself quickly and powered ahead of the other boys to win. Sister Anne was screaming, "Abel won! Abel won! Abel won!" Morris and Zelda watched the start but never saw the finish. "He turned around to talk to a neighbor he recognized," Abel remembered. "And my mother put her hand over her eyes. But it was a kick to win with them there."[43]

Although the tale has a kind of Frank Merriwell cast, it was etched in his memory because it represented basic issues in his childhood. Here he was, a schoolboy, taking his immigrant parents to the county fair, an institution synonymous with the traditional American culture in which he aspired to succeed. Like Merriwell, he came from behind and used his gifts to win his first big race against talented competitors from beyond Stapleton. Yet Poppa turned away indulgently at Abel's climactic moment, and Momma—perhaps still traumatized by her Polish youth, perhaps still in the grip of the eastern European Jewish aversion to sport for its own sake—could not bear to watch her firstborn giving his all in a physical contest. His adoring thirteen-year-old sister, already trained to be a nurturer of her brothers and the essential intermediary in family conflicts, exulted in his triumph. Having demonstrated pluck and skill, Abel was now ready to conquer a wider world. On September 9, 1907, he enrolled as a freshman at Curtis High School.

2

All–New York

THE AUTUMN 1907 TERM of the New York public schools began the week after Labor Day. Abel walked approximately two miles from the Kiviat home to the high school, passing the newly erected Borough Hall and ferry terminal of St. George, the island's civic center. The school was located on a hill overlooking the neighborhood, with a commanding view of New York and the Manhattan skyline. "You climb the hill, and there's Curtis High School. A beautiful building," he recalled.[1] Named after George William Curtis, the nineteenth-century editor of *Harper's Weekly* and local communal leader, the four-story brick structure in a campuslike setting opened in 1904 as the island's first public high school.[2] The design by C. B. J. Snyder, the prolific superintendent of buildings for the city's board of education, was a classic example of the English collegiate gothic style in vogue during the rapid spread of the public high school nationwide after 1890. Snyder's characteristic use of medieval forms and ornament—the central turreted tower and gargoyles, for example—created the appearance of a gentleman's academy. Indeed, Curtis's unofficial role, at least for the chamber of commerce and other civic leaders, as well as for the largely middle-class student body and their families, was to serve as the capstone of popular education for the industrialized community that Staten Island had become. The school population was further enlarged by children of the new immigrant masses, such as Abel, who brought with them their own aspirations for professional or managerial careers in the expanding social order. As the borough's Association of Women's Teachers wrote of Curtis that year, "[I]t stands as a pledge to all newcomers that education is held in the highest esteem, and the work of the elementary schools is of a character to make possible such a high school."

Abel's arrival at Curtis also coincided with the booming interest in the PSAL program at the high school level. Athletics teams became central to creating institutional unity and loyalty, and the city's educators developed a year-round schedule of lively interscholastic competition in a variety of sports. Abel wasted little time in availing himself of the opportunity; in a sense, his own growth paralleled that of the PSAL. True to its purpose, the league became his prime agency for cultural and social integration into the life of the city. It enabled him to travel all over the metropolitan area, to mingle easily with a wide variety of youths, and to begin to develop his capacity for a leadership role. During his two years of enrollment at Curtis, he would discover not only his extraordinary athletic skills, but also, less happily, his lack of aptitude for academics. Although this outcome was not quite what his scholarly parents had in mind, his time at Curtis would prove to be a milestone in his life.[3]

CURTIS: A MIDDLE-CLASS EDUCATION

Abel was in unfamiliar territory. Although the Curtis enrollment of 783 students was much smaller than at P.S. 14, he knew only the kids from the old school. He therefore faced a difficult period of transition as a lowly freshman, a fact of life about which the upperclassmen, who took such matters seriously then, were quick to remind Abel and his classmates. ("He who knows not, and knows not that he knows not is a freshman, shun him," ran the seniors' lampoon in the 1908 yearbook.) Still, as the newcomer walked the halls, he encountered a pleasant, but clearly serious, academic atmosphere for which he was not ready.[4]

He signed up for the rigorous first-year classes of the General Course and the standard curriculum in New York, including both the classical subjects and the moderns—English, Latin, algebra, science, drawing, music, elocution, and physical training. His teachers were educated people, with high expectations of their students. In their commitment to intellectual discipline, they followed the lead of their respected principal, Harry F. Towle, a Dartmouth graduate and a scholar of Latin and Greek. Many of the thirty-five faculty members held master's degrees and even Ph.D.s from Yale, Chicago, Columbia, Cornell, Syracuse, and New York Universities. Several had studied in Berlin, Hamburg, and London. Abel's excitement during those first days must have been tempered by the sudden realization of the daunting challenges he faced.[5]

Curtis faculty members used the lecture-recitation methods with which he was all too familiar from P.S. 14, but the content was more complicated and the teachers' demands far greater. Because recitations and tests were regular events, the students memorized the textbooks. Homework was the key to mastery. Abel learned quickly that completion of his assignments required at least two hours nightly. He used a free class period to begin the homework, but he attempted most of it in the apartment after dinner, surrounded by six noisy Kiviat children. The goal of this formalistic pedagogy was preparation for the dreaded state regents' examinations. The teachers' basic function was to ensure that the students passed these tests in order to graduate, and they simply spoon-fed the lessons. Everyone, from Superintendent Maxwell to the freshmen, was critical of this system but was forced to endure it.[6]

In the first two marking periods, Abel failed Latin, science, and algebra, requiring him to repeat these subjects during the spring term. He barely passed English and had modest success with the progressive subjects— drawing, music, and elocution. Not surprisingly, he excelled in the physical training class (with a score of 97) taught by John Blake Hillyer, the able and dapper athletics director. Hillyer, who initiated the tradition of athletic excellence at Curtis, had a genuine interest in his students, and Abel responded positively to him.[7]

Morris Kiviat was not impressed and was even less happy about Abel's misbehavior. At a time when busy parents rarely visited the high school, Morris was called to see Principal Towle. "My father would have to go to see the principal," Kiviat recalled. "I have no idea what happened between them, but it was normally followed by my getting a licking. It was never one's mother who went to the school on times like these."[8]

As a result, Abel buckled down academically during the spring term. He repeated successfully the first term's work in Latin (92), algebra (70), and science (60). He also advanced into the second semester of the subjects he had passed in the fall. His grades in English 1B (65), drawing 1B (83), elocution 1B (75), music 1B (70), and physical training 1B (89) rounded out a productive six months of study.[9]

In sum, Abel's Curtis was a self-consciously conservative institution, mirroring the aspirations of Staten Island's expanding middle-class, business culture. His teachers taught this culture's values, which included study of the traditional liberal arts and the acquisition of social skills. The children of the middle class dominated school life and brought with them their prejudices against the children of "the plain people," including anti-Semitic stereotypes.[10]

Abel built a wall of denial and plunged into extracurricular activity. Yet occasional not so subtle cracks by gentile boys stung. "Once in a public school athletic guide, there were a couple of people named Kiviatsky—Kiviat with a -sky at the end. The guys started kidding me about that," he recalled decades later. Or they said, "Jews aren't athletes." But Curtis compensated by offering its students a rich variety of activities, with sports teams at the top of the list. Morris and Zelda, to their credit, let Abel participate in these activities even though they badly needed the income from his after-school jobs.[11]

"THE JEWISH HONUS WAGNER," 1907–1908

Abel went out for football immediately after enrolling at Curtis. He loved to play it on the open lots with his buddies, and by 1907 football had become a popular high school sport.[12] It offered glory and, Curtis students believed, was an avenue to social status and school leadership roles. This cultural development was in itself striking. During Abel's childhood, the modern game was virtually invented by the Ivy League colleges, its rules and structures formulated, and its contests, especially on Thanksgiving Day, so sensationalized by the competitive New York dailies that youthful imaginations were captured. The nation's secondary schools adopted the game and made their teams cornerstones for creating institutional loyalty.[13]

Abel reported to Curtis Field, one hundred feet behind the high school building, on a sloping plain surrounded by an almost square-shaped, one-fifth-mile running track. A grandstand was being built that fall to seat more than one thousand spectators.[14] He made the Curtis second team as an end, essentially equivalent to a modern wide receiver, rather than being assigned to the freshman eleven, a testament to his athletic skills and reputation. He was only five feet tall and weighed about 115 pounds, "depending on how much milk and beer I drank." The squad's specialty was the newly legalized but still experimental forward pass because the boys were "much smaller and lighter than any that we have had," the *Curtis High School Monthly* reported. With his ability to accelerate and his sure hands, Abel made some good catches and scored two touchdowns. But with his small stature, he paid a high price. When he fractured his collarbone and shoulder blade, Zelda said to a neighbor, a German woman, "For this I send him to high school?" She and Morris made him quit the team.[15]

Following a period of recovery, Abel went out for the track team by convincing his parents it wasn't a "body contact sport." He joined "a little band of some six track athletes" who worked out on Monday, Wednesday, and Friday afternoons by running around the ground floor of the high school. This was how the city's schoolboys ordinarily practiced in winter, without accessible indoor tracks. The team had the good fortune to be tutored by Chief Barkley, Abel's old mentor at P.S. 14, who had also become the first track coach at Curtis. Assisting the Chief was Blanchard "Legs" Preble, the school's former middle-distance ace. Having graduated with the Curtis class of 1907, Preble was waiting to enroll as a college freshman the following September and was acting as a graduate track adviser.

During a meeting on Friday afternoon, January 10, 1908, the team elected sophomore John Drebinger, Abel's pal from P.S. 14, as the manager. The "puckish" Drebby was a sports-loving lad "with an infectious ho-ho-ho laugh" and was also a gifted pianist who had hoped to follow his German-born father—a violinist with the Metropolitan Opera's orchestra—onto the concert stage. A thumb wound sustained while sharpening ice skates ended that dream and sent him to the track, where he was a promising sprinter. Years later, Drebinger would become a Hall of Fame baseball writer for the *New York Times*.

On Saturday afternoon, January 25, the team entered two events in the fourth annual PSAL indoor championships held at the Twenty-third Regiment Armory in Brooklyn. Abel ran the second leg on a "120-lb. relay team," with Drebinger as anchorman. The quartet finished fourth in their heat and failed to qualify for the final. "Although Curtis did not win a point in the meet," the *Curtis Monthly* noted, "we have at least proven that there are men in the school who can run. We are certain that there are many others who would make good runners if they only would come out and try." A six-man squad "is a poor showing for a school of our size, and if we are to make any marks at all in track work we must have more men to run."[16]

The boys returned to Brooklyn three weeks later to compete in the Poly Prep games. With eight thousand spectators crowding the same fortresslike armory building, Abel anchored the novice 880 relay event against eight other schools from New York and New Jersey. The teams "were bunched at the finish," and Kivie didn't place as Cathedral High nipped Newark Academy.[17]

Then it was March, and "the season for hibernating was over," the *Curtis Monthly* announced. "The baseball season is close at hand." Baseball was the country's leading sport in 1908. Millions of men and boys were fanatics, and Curtis High was no exception. Although the school's size meant a smaller pool of candidates for the varsity than other PSAL teams had, the excellent new diamond on Curtis Field might "serve to balance the scale." Therefore, the *Monthly* urged, "when you hear the call for candidates and spectators—come out!"

Kivie's reputation preceded him. He received a Crimson uniform, put "homemade spikes" on leather shoes, and was chosen the shortstop and lead-off batter. With other children of immigrants, his role model was a great Pittsburgh Pirates shortstop. "I read so much about Honus Wagner," Kiviat said later. "Honus and I were both bowlegged and long-armed so I was christened the Jewish Honus Wagner. I walked around with a photo of Honus Wagner, walking like a gorilla with his hands way down."[18]

Opening day was Saturday afternoon, April 11. The talented team that took the field included Abel's classmate, big, handsome Elmer Ripley, an outfielder, who later had a long professional basketball career playing with the "Original Celtics" in the American Basketball League and achieving renown as a collegiate coach. The Crimson beat Brooklyn's Eastern District High ten to four in a wild game plagued by a raw wind. Runners on both sides had a field day, stealing second base sixteen times. "We didn't know how to slide," Kiviat recalled. "We just barreled into the base." No picnic for a shortstop in his first game, but Curtis scored six runs in the bottom of the second inning to put the game out of reach.

The team won three more games at Curtis Field that week, as Abel drew praise for his infield play. He had a strong arm and got rid of the ball quickly on double plays.[19]

He also continued to run track after the indoor season, and therein lies a curious tale. Legend has it that Abel's track career began with a spontaneous act that April. According to the tale Kiviat spun over the years to columnists and historians, he was standing around baseball practice, bat in hand, when he saw the track team working out on Curtis Field. "Impatient for some action," stated a 1952 account of the incident by Hal J. Squier (a longtime Staten Islander and columnist for the *Staten Island Advance*), "Kiviat took off after the runners and whipped them all with plenty to spare." Then, according to Kiviat's own later version, the coach of the track team, "Legs" Preble, challenged all comers to a special 880-yard race, with the runners chipping in "nickels and dimes and even pennies" to buy a bronze medal for the winner. (A few years later, Preble achieved notable success as a collegiate runner for Harvard.) Preble offered everyone a fifty-yard head start. The challenge included the ball team: "Come on, let's see how good you baseball players are," Kiviat remembered Preble saying. Encouraged by teammate Elmer Ripley, Abel went to the starting line wearing either a borrowed pair of "sneakers" (in order to protect his "bow legs") or, in another version, his baseball uniform and spikes. After the starter's gun, Kiviat related in his oral memoir of 1984, "I run like the dickens, passing everybody." His margin of victory also became wider with each passing year. From a few feet in 1952, it became "almost the fifty yards I got as a handicap" by the 1980s. Either way, Coach Preble's "eyes almost popped out of his head," Kiviat recalled. "From that day, I began participating a little in track." The epilogue to this oft-repeated Staten Island legend was written by Hal Squier's successor, Jay Price, after Kiviat's death: "All these years later, maybe it's enough to know the story's too good to have been fabricated."

The reality, insofar as we can reconstruct a high school time trial a century later, still seems impressive, if slightly less melodramatic. On Tuesday afternoon, April 28, "a special half mile was run, in which Preble allowed the other starters 50 yards," the *Curtis Monthly* reported. Abel realized Legs was a formidable half-miler. He had taken off his baseball uniform, he admitted later to a group of Staten Islanders, and we can assume he wore a running suit and spikes for the race. It is also likely he didn't know what to expect at the gun because his longest competition until this point was 220 yards. Preble made up the 50 yards handicap quickly, and "was out in front" by the end of the first lap. For the final one and a half laps, Abel "hung on determinedly." The two lads battled down the final stretch, with Abel using a long sprinter's kick to win a narrow victory. It was, the *Monthly* noted, "an exciting finish." Although there is no record of the race's time, one can imagine Abel's pride in receiving his medal, which remained one of his prized possessions. On that afternoon, a fifteen-year-old youth discovered his gift of sustaining foot speed over a middle distance.

Over time, a simple event took on greater significance for Kiviat, based on his views of the world and of himself. Despite his inattention to schoolwork as a boy, he was an avid reader of the sports pages and Frank Merriwell stories. For the rest of his life, in his account of this incident of early adolescence he resembled a character in a Merriwell saga, jumping naturally and without training from sport to sport, starring at shortstop and then stunning the varsity track star in a half-mile race. In one sense, he never gave up that juvenile attitude. The Preble race was a corking tale that provided a convenient origin for his ongoing narrative of his track career, but it also served to boost his self-esteem at various moments of his adulthood. He was still retelling it enthusiastically at age ninety.[20]

Daily life in 1908 quickly brought Abel down to earth. The following Saturday he failed to place in the 880 in the New York University schoolboy meet. Then, a week later, he began to show real promise as a middle-distance runner, although he had to fight with Coach Preble to get to the starting line. The schedule called for a quadrangular meet with city schools; Preble planned to enter him in the 220-yard junior event. Abel protested the decision "long and loud," telling Preble, "'I can't run a 220 . . . I don't get time to get started. Let me run in the half and the mile and maybe I might win some points.'" The team manager, John Drebinger, said to Preble: "'Let him run his fool head off. He'll get his belly full of the mile.'" Preble gave in, and Abel went out and won the half-mile. He repeated the performance the following Saturday in a dual meet with Bryant High School of Queens. In recording this tale fifteen years afterward, Drebinger remarked that "even as an ambitious schoolboy," Kiviat "seemed to know instinctively, what he could do and what he couldn't" on the track.

The *Curtis Monthly* likened the ten boys of the outdoor track squad "to a comet with a woefully short tail." Of Abel it said: "he filled the gap left by the lanky B. Preble." His participation in the PSAL during that initial year at Curtis filled significant gaps in his young life. It gave him a role and identity in school. It eased his transition from neighborhood life in Stapleton to life in the wider community. It also brought him into close, equal-status contact with his teammates the Ripleys, Drebingers, Maloys, and Bernsteins, thereby accelerating the process of his cultural assimilation, already far along when he arrived at Curtis. In the process, he began to develop the social skill of networking with youthful Staten Islanders who would later be invaluable to him in adult life. It was a skill that would, in fact, prove to be his strong suit in his postathletic career.[21]

OLYMPIAN DREAMS, SUMMER 1908

One late July day, Abel and several of his gang were hanging around the B & O Railroad station near the waterfront, a few blocks from the Kiviat home. Like American boys everywhere, they gravitated to the local rail depot as a place of endless fascination. Their friend, Elias Bernstein, was a telegraph operator there, and he let his pals read the morning papers that were delivered. A story about Johnny Hayes's sensational triumph in the Olympic marathon race over the fallen Italian, Dorando Pietri, inspired Tommy Lennon to take up long-distance running before Chief Barkley at Curtis convinced him to switch to his natural event, sprinting. Another banner headline caught their eye: "Sheppard Wins the 800 meter, 1,500 Meter, World's Champion." Kiviat recalled the moment precisely: "We all looked at it. So they started kidding me. Look, Abel, look, Abel. You can beat all of us running. . . . Why don't you take it up?" From that moment, he was hooked: his dream of glory turned to a faster track. Some years later, Kiviat's Olympic hero, Mel Sheppard, wrote in his memoir that Abel "often told me that the accounts of my victories in the 1908 Olympics served as his inspiration in the running game. This was a strange coincidence, inasmuch as he turned out to be one of my toughest opponents."[22]

5. Tommy Lennon, 1910. Courtesy of Lucy Price.

Although Sheppard stood out at the London Olympic Games, his countrymen also did well. American athletes returning to New York in August had won fifteen of the twenty-six track and field events, three with world records, thus stirring the imaginations of schoolboys such as Abel. To express their appreciation, New Yorkers organized an unprecedented public celebration for a sports team. Thousands of regular army and National Guard troops joined civic and athletic associations in a parade from Forty-sixth Street to city hall. The Olympians "rode in motorcars," the *New York Times* wrote in a laudatory editorial, as "great crowds thronged the streets." Among the one hundred thousand cheering fans jammed into City Hall Park was Abel Kiviat. "'I went into the city to watch the Olympic parade,'" he told President George H. W. Bush during a White House ceremony eight decades later, "and I'm standin' in the crowd when a car comes up. These people asked me if I wanted to go to Sagamore Hill where Teddy Roosevelt lived. I met him briefly, and he just shook my hand. He didn't know me from a hole in the wall. He shook everyone's hand. Meetin' a president doesn't help you run." It can, however, give you a sense of direction.[23]

STORM AND STRESS

During the fall term of his sophomore year at Curtis, Abel seemed to have renewed purpose and made academic progress. Still catching up with his classmates, he was diligent, passing science 1B (80), Latin 1B (70), and even math 1B (67), a subject he felt "was a great weakness." At the same time, he began the second-year sequence by completing satisfactorily English 2A (74), ancient history 2A (75), and the arts appreciation classes.[24]

His home life at 101 Broad Street was a study in contrast. Compounding the normal stresses and adjustments of adolescence, Abel's relations with his parents became increasingly tense and discordant. An obvious source of conflict was the cultural dissonance between his Yiddish-speaking parents and the high school's emphasis on assimilation, but a subtler, more disturbing factor was the family dynamic itself. Although thousands of other New York Jewish adolescents had to cope with similar problems that fall, the long-term impact of dysfunction at home was profound. However, the fact that Abel was not an overly introspective lad, but a doer, all action and reaction, may have made his situation more bearable.[25]

For Morris and Zelda, now in their early forties, the challenges of making a living and raising a family of seven children absorbed them. They worked hard, with the little clothing store below their apartment the focus of their lives. Morris continued to sell merchandise around the island, much of which he bought on frequent trips to the familiar world of the Jewish Lower East Side, sometimes accompanied by Abel. Morris outwardly appeared the same, but cracks began to appear in the persona he had projected since his Polish boyhood. Although seemingly devoted to Orthodox ritual and a fixed schedule of Talmudic study, he would secretly eat the forbidden pork at his customers' island farms. Zelda discovered this and "called him a hypocrite." His sons thought he was "such a phony in that respect." He also began to drink lots of beer. He became absent from home for longer stretches. It is likely his liaisons outside of marriage began at this time, leading ultimately to separate lives for the couple.

His treatment of Abel and his other kids grew harsher, and the teenager's anger toward his father intensified. Morris expected more of his oldest after the passage to high school. Abel helped out in the store in addition to selling afternoon newspapers and running errands for a drugstore, at which jobs he made up to seventy-five cents a day. He still had to wake up at 5:30 many mornings to bring the cow home from pasture before leaving for Curtis. Yet Morris offered no expression of appreciation. Poppa was at best a difficult role model for a teenage boy.[26]

In consequence, the family increasingly became Momma's family, and her burdens were even greater. Beyond the responsibilities of running both the store and the household, she had to be the major emotional resource for a tribe of six vigorous young boys, of whom only Abel (sixteen) and Izzy (thirteen) were adolescents. Granted, Anne (fourteen), who was herself about to begin the physical and social changes of adolescence, aided her immeasurably with child care, and Sadie continued to assist her with household duties, Zelda's job was nevertheless impossible. She worried about each of her kids, but somehow maintained her sense of humor, with the right Yiddish expression or jest as the occasion required. She seemed to take special pains with Harold, age seven, who was already showing signs of the disturbed behaviors that would characterize his long life.

Always she taught them, by word or deed. She emphasized the importance of reading, and she encouraged them to borrow books from the newly opened Stapleton Public Library (1907). She demonstrated civic responsibility more effectively than any formal class on the subject by finding the time to trek down to the Lower East Side for "a lot of charity work." Aided by her boys, Zelda would carry coal or food to the poor Jews on Eldridge or Hester Street, where she had started her American life. She also maintained her interest in two other East Side institutions, the Hebrew Institute, a combination of settlement house and Jewish center, and the Rabbi Jacob Joseph Yeshiva. Her grace and good cheer in fulfilling this communal responsibility had a profound impact on Abel's life.[27]

Try as Zelda might, however, she could not overcome the emotional damage already done to her firstborn. She may have, in fact, unintentionally exacerbated the problem by establishing too protective a relationship with him. That is one explanation for Kiviat's noticeable slips of the tongue in his oral memoir when he called Zelda his "wife." Compounding Abel's problem was the utter lack of privacy so vital in the development of a psychologically healthy modern adolescent. He had to share room space in the apartment with his siblings. While they ate, played, and prayed together in close quarters, the boys were already acting out their feelings of intense rivalry.

It would be a distortion, however, to read only dysfunction into the family situation. Consider a poem Anne composed for her six brothers in 1969, sixty years after these events:

Do you Remember
When we were all together, and
When we were poor, and
When we all sat together, slept together, and
When we were aware of each other, and
When one got the measles, we all got them, and
When birthday gifts were a head of cabbage, or a big Yellow turnip
  wrapped in newspaper, and
When pajamas were all the same size, and
When Harold lost the cow, and
When tomorrows were another hopeful day, and
When we had a weekly bath, and
When arguments ended at the next meal, and
When there were no separate ways, and
When misunderstandings were only words, and
When "THOSE WERE THE DAYS"?

Nevertheless, Abel was caught between an abusive father and troubled brothers, and it was at this time that a pattern of intermittently hostile behavior took root in him. When the track writer Howard Valentine wrote of him a few years later that he "is quite easily upset by little things at times," the cause was deeper and more destructive than his sports colleagues realized.[28]

As Morris's religious fervor diminished, he demanded less strict observance from his children. Although Abel still attended services on the Jewish holidays as well as the family dinners on Friday nights, his Saturday afternoons were now often devoted to sports. His old neighborhood gang, which included three Jewish pals, continued to play football and baseball together. They named themselves the Norwood Athletic Club, short for "the North Woods." Perhaps the fantasy of escape to the remote Alaskan wilderness appealed to them. Each boy "had a little green jersey with white stripes and a swastika on it," Kiviat recalled in his oral memoir, quickly adding, "then swastika wasn't bad." At the time, even the Boy Scouts used this symbol as a decoration. Hanging out with his friends on weekends, he "started eating a little bit outside, having non-kosher foods."[29]

"OUR CRACK HALF-MILER," 1909

Abel's body filled out over the summer, and he soon demonstrated how much physical maturation, combined with talent and an opportunity for competition, can produce. On Saturday night, January 23, 1909, he and eight teammates participated in the major schoolboy event of the winter, the PSAL indoor track championships at the Forty-seventh Regiment Armory in Brooklyn. PSAL officials "spoke glowingly of the good work being done by the league in developing the physical prowess of the American youngsters."[30]

Abel ran the half-mile against a strong schoolboy field and surprised everyone by taking second place. What made this achievement noteworthy was that two other medalists, Brooklynites Cedric Major of Boys High, the winner, and Ollie DeGruchy of Erasmus Hall, in fourth place, were in top shape, having dominated the PSAL cross-country meet in December. To Abel's chums, the sophomore looked like a future champion.[31] A month later, the Curtis track team elected him—"our crack half-miler"—as captain.[32]

In stark contrast, his studies went badly again during the spring term. Although he squeaked by English 2B and history 2B, and even began the elective study of German (61), he failed both Latin 2A (55) and geometry (58). It was becoming clear that Abel might have a problem finishing high school, but he was hardly unique in that the Curtis drop-out rate was the highest in the city, with about 50 percent of freshmen leaving before senior year.[33]

Sports were his saving grace. The Crimson baseball team was promising enough for athletic director Hillyer to enter it in the PSAL's competitive Manhattan division. John Patrick Maloy, the team's manager, and Charles Bailey, the captain, talked to Kiviat, their shortstop, and the track captain, and came up with a novel proposal for Hillyer. They asked the athletic director to schedule baseball games and track meets against the same school on one day, "so that Abel could participate in both." It helped that "several of the other ballplayers were pretty fast" and ran track, too, Kiviat recalled. His buddy Elmer "Rip" Ripley, for example, doubled as a sprinter and center fielder.[34]

On the afternoon of April 13, the boys put gloves and bats aside as Curtis held its sixth annual Closed Meet, the interclass track and field competition. "During the last year, rivalry among the four classes has existed more noticeably than ever before," a student wrote. "So when the time for the meet arrived, the four classes were thoroughly on edge." It turned out to be a close competition between the seniors and juniors for bragging rights, but Abel Kiviat was the boy who shone. Despite the miserable weather, he won the first event, the 440-yard dash, in 55.8. He returned a short time later and sprinted to victory in the half-mile run in 2:10.6, both new school records. At day's end, he anchored the class of 1911's winning relay team.[35]

The next week concluded with the demanding two-sport contests with Bryant High School. After a long trip, the boys from Queens arrived at Curtis Field early on a beautiful Saturday morning, April 24, for the track meet. Bryant dominated the field events and won the meet easily, but Abel gave them a fight on the track. He doubled, taking the first event, the 440, and later the 880. By far the best performance belonged to John Drebinger, whose winning time of 10.4 for the 100-yard dash equaled the PSAL record. Drebby's teammates nicknamed him "Ten Flat."

Because a number of the track athletes on both sides were ballplayers, the afternoon baseball game was sloppy, indicative of how worn out the boys were. Curtis evened the score with the visitors, winning a laugher, 24-2. Kivie went three for five at the plate, with two triples, and scored three runs. A right-handed batter, he was becoming a consistent opposite field hitter. "I stood back a little and swung slow toward the right field, between first and second, over their heads, over second," he recalled. "Very seldom ever hit a ball in left field, even a left field foul."[36]

The following Saturday, May 1, the Curtis track team went by ferry to Hoboken, New Jersey, to compete in a schoolboy meet sponsored by Stevens Institute of Technology. Before the officials could even start the opening event, the heats of the 100-yard dash, heavy rains forced everyone to take cover. Late in the afternoon, Abel went to his mark on a waterlogged cinder track against a good field of half-milers. He "ran a pretty race and won hand-ily" in 2:12.6 for his first victory in a big meet.[37]

Throughout May, as the Curtis baseball team worked their way through the PSAL's tough Manhattan division, Abel's focus was on the diamond. He continued to hit effectively in the leadoff spot, score runs, and field his position beautifully. Three of the games were played at Hilltop Park on Broadway in upper Manhattan, home of the American League's New York Highlanders, later named the Yankees. This experience may have been the basis of reports that the Yankees scouted Abel for a possible big league career, which he himself denied. However, his efforts were recognized at season's end, when he was selected for the *Evening World*'s prestigious "All–New York" team. "The Staten Island boy is a wonder for speed," Ward Kremer wrote in a story about his picks. "He covers more ground around the shortfield than any shortstop seen in the high schools for several years."[38]

Abel kept up some track training during the month. Playing baseball daily, walking to and from Curtis, and hustling on his after-school jobs, he was in shape and mentally ready on the last Saturday in May when the city-wide PSAL outdoor track championships were held at Curtis Field. Beyond an obvious home-field advantage, the good weather that morning—which brought four thousand athletes and fans over to the island—brightened his prospects for fast races. Abel had decided to try what was then a schoolboy glamour event and went to the starting line for the first mile race of his life. His competition included Cedric Major of Boys High, the region's standout middle-distance runner. Kiviat would say later that he "ran without knowing what to do," but the results suggested that his innate toughness, talent, and desire simply took over. He surprised himself and Major, who evidently had taken him too lightly, by running a smart race. "Using both legs and head to better advantage than the Brooklynite," an observer noted, Kivie beat Major to the tape by twenty yards, as excited Staten Islanders cheered from the grandstand. The winning time was 4:43.2.

After only a half-hour's rest, he went back to the starting line with Major and Ollie DeGruchy of Erasmus Hall for his primary event, the half-mile. Here Cedric Major seemed invincible. The tall senior, already recruited to Cornell by its great distance-running coach, Jack Moakley, had defeated Abel indoors at the 880. Yet the cinder track "was well cut up" by midafternoon, which suggested it would be a slow race. Perhaps that would be to Abel's advantage in the homestretch, given his closing speed as a quarter-miler.

With the starter's gun, Major moved in front, and little Kivie tucked in behind him for the next two and a half laps. "Every spurt by the Brooklynite was answered with an equally good one, and the two came down the final stretch neck and neck," the *New York Herald* wrote. "The Curtis runner had a little more in reserve and won by a margin of six inches in record time." Abel's 2:04.8 was a new PSAL meet record by six-tenths of a second. The *Herald* called him "the real hero of the big meet."[39]

He felt like one. He had beaten his conqueror, Cedric Major, the indoor titleholder, and now he was a champion on his home turf. After all the family tension, the pressure of helping out in the struggle to make a living, the failures at school, this acclamation by his neighbors and in the New York dailies was unforgettable. Linked always in his mind with recognition of him as all-city shortstop, the events of that innocent spring of 1909 were for him, in spite of all his later accomplishments, among his most cherished memories.[40]

A LETTER TO THE IRISH CLUB

Among those present at the PSAL track meet was Lawson Robertson, newly named coach of the Irish Club. "Someone pointed, [and said] 'that's a prospective Olympic coach,'" Kiviat later remembered. In this account, Robertson approached Abel on Curtis Field and asked, "How would you like to compete in the Amateur Athletic Union? You're eligible." Abel explained his circumstance to the coach: "'I'm not working, and I come from a poor family, and it's got to be expensive. I can't afford it.' See, I was always honest. No two face."

Once again, this child of Bialystok garment workers took a few facts and wove a silky legend. More likely, when Robertson, himself an Olympic medalist, saw Kivie's raw promise and his fighting spirit, which the Irish Club prized in its recruits, he approached him to offer encouragement. Perhaps the coach said a word about his national championship Winged

Fist team. A boy who loved to compete and avidly read the sports pages let his imagination fill in the rest.

The encounter stayed in Abel's thoughts until the school term concluded in mid-June. Never short of chutzpah, he sat down and wrote a heartfelt letter to David Keane, chairman of the Irish Club's athletic committee. "Please, Mr. Keane, won't you give me a trial on your track team?" he wrote. "I'm 18 years old [*sic*] and very strong for my age. I want to become a fast runner and think I can succeed if you will give me a trial at Celtic Park." Keane talked it over with P. J. Conway, the Irish Club's president, and invited Abel to join Robertson's team. With the invitation came promises of carfare to Celtic Park and a summer job. Morris and Zelda Kiviat gave their approval.[41]

3

The Phenom of Celtic Park

IN LATE JUNE, Kiviat went into Manhattan and took the Thirty-fourth Street ferry to the busy terminal in Long Island City. Almost certainly joining him was John Drebinger, who had also decided to try out for the Irish Club. They transferred to a trolley that brought them quickly to Celtic Park, set in the mosquito-infested fields and farmland of the Laurel Hill area (residents called it "Klondike") near Long Island City, within view of the great Calvary Cemetery. The two boys stepped into a fine athletic complex: surrounding a Gaelic football field there was a 440-yard cinder track, a handsome wooden grandstand, and additional bleacher seating for ten thousand fans. At the edge of the park stood a pavilion with a dance hall, a restaurant featuring "high chef" Patty Kyne, and dormitory rooms off the second-story balcony.[1]

Here was a capstone of the crowded world of urban athletic clubs in 1909. On the one hand, organizations for the privileged classes formed a necklace of restricted societies stretching from midtown Manhattan to the Pacific. Wealthy Bostonians played at their athletic association clubhouse in the Back Bay area, midwesterners at the Chicago Athletic Association on South Michigan Avenue, the West Coast elite at Portland's Multnomah Athletic Club and San Francisco's Olympic Club. On rare occasions such as the national track championships, they competed against each other and lower-class athletes for glory and the vindication of their kind. No club was grander than the New York Athletic Club (NYAC). Descendants of the old Knickerbocker families and their friends socialized, played sports, and arranged business transactions in the comfort of its Fifty-fifth Street clubhouse and its elegant "country home" on Travers Island in Long Island Sound.

On the other hand, the large majority of the athletic clubs served the city's masses, led by the NYAC's powerful rival for national supremacy in track and field, the Irish Club. Providing competition for the two leaders were hundreds of small clubs, perhaps as many as seven hundred. Most had limited funds and relied on the athletic facilities of the city's parks. The more competitive ones that summer included the Pastime Athletic Club, the Xavier Athletic Association, the St. Mary's Total Abstinence Club, and, from Brooklyn, the Acorn Athletic Association and the Loughlin Lyceum. For two decades leading up to the 1904 Olympics, the Pastime, with its ethnically diverse roster of medal winners, had challenged the NYAC on the track. Its runners had included James E. Sullivan, now the powerful administrator of the national AAU, and, in 1890, a Jewish youth named Ehrich Weiss, who would achieve renown a decade later as Harry Houdini. Interclub rivalry was not limited to the fields of play, but involved fierce recruitment battles for potential stars and for loyal supporters. "The clubs of those days displayed an interest in their teams that would be hard to understand at present," Mel Sheppard remarked in his memoir. "They turned out in mass to support their athletes and fought from the grandstands just as hard as we fought on the field."[2]

In the larger sense, these clubs functioned both as agencies for the Americanization *of* the British sport of track and field and for their members' Americanization *through* track and field. Abel Kiviat's experience at Celtic Park illustrated these dual roles of the prewar urban athletic clubs, while revealing the rich complexity of the assimilation process itself.[3]

The early phase of Kiviat's Irish Club career was also a case study in the pressures and expectations placed on a middle-distance prodigy. Kiviat arrived at Celtic Park when the vast majority of his peers were either still attending high school or beginning at the bottom of the job ladder. With his raw talent, he fared better. He literally sprinted overnight from a novice to a world-class performer, the first of a select group of American teenagers—Lou Zamperini, Jim Ryun, and Alan Webb followed him—to excel at the prestigious mile run.

ENCOUNTER WITH ROBBY

Awaiting Kiviat and Drebinger at Celtic Park was the Irish Club's new coach, Lawson Robertson. Although only twenty-five years old, he made a distinct first impression on young athletes. The "tall man with a rather long face" (he was at least six feet one inch), dapper appearance, and gruff Scottish burr in his voice intimidated them. However, after a few minutes, his sudden smile, wit, and puns warmed them up. Although Robertson's dialect stories occasionally had an edge, he was a genuinely tolerant man in an intolerant age. Moreover, his thoughtful comments revealed his kindness "and a profound consideration for his athletes' health," recalled one runner. For a gifted boy escaping from a troubled father, it was a perfect match.[4]

Robertson had already developed the outlines of a philosophy of coaching that he would continue to teach with elaboration but no significant changes for the next four decades. Although his ideas were basically the unremarkable orthodoxy of the age, they seemed fresh because they were rooted in his reflections on his own experiences. He was born in Aberdeen, Scotland, in September 1883 and came with his parents to America when he was nine. The family eventually settled in Brooklyn, where the gawky adolescent attended Boys High but "believed himself unsuited for athletic endeavor and was content to remain a spectator." One day in 1901, just after graduation, a friend persuaded Lawson of the value of exercise, and he joined a Brooklyn Young Men's Christian Association (YMCA). He entered a track meet and, "despite his awkwardness," discovered to his surprise that he was a natural, winning the Y's all-around championship—high jump, pole vault, shot put, 440- and 880-yard runs.[5]

To pursue his new athletic interest more seriously, he joined the Knickerbocker Athletic Club. This longtime track and field power was coached by Ernie Hjertberg, a son of Swedish immigrants who had turned himself into a champion distance runner and then a brilliant coach during the last part of the nineteenth century. When Hjertberg was hired away by the upstart Greater New York Irish American Athletic Association (GNYIAA) in 1903, Robertson went with him. Lawson Robertson's leadership qualities were quickly recognized, and he was elected track captain.

However much Robertson learned from Hjertberg, his own experimentation and intuition were the keys to his approach. "He 'never stops thinking'" was the Irish Club's perception of him. Defying the conventional wisdom that a big man could not be a top sprinter, he became a student of the discipline and was a finalist in the 100 meters at the St. Louis Olympics and again in 1906 at Athens. He also mastered the now-discontinued standing high and long jumps, winning three Olympic medals—one silver and two bronzes. Withal, he maintained his wonderful sense of the playfulness of sport, teaming with his friend Harry Hillman, the NYAC's champion intermediate hurdler, to set world records for three-legged racing. The pair established a new mark of 11 seconds for 100 yards in an indoor meet in Brooklyn.[6]

When the young Scot organized a group of his teammates at the conclusion of the 1908 London Olympics and guided them to a series of victories against Swedish, Scottish, and Irish national teams, his administrative and diplomatic skills impressed Patrick J. Conway, president of the Irish Club. Upon his return home, Robby and two friends organized a steamship business in New York, but it failed within the year. Just as he was considering his future, Conway released Hjertberg as the Winged Fist coach and made the surprising decision to offer the position to Robertson on an interim basis. "I had to do something," Robby later recalled, "so I coached the Irish-American club."[7]

Robby had been on the job for only a few weeks on the day Kiviat came out to Laurel Hill.[8] To begin, the laconic Robertson most likely presented the eager lad with an early version of his straightforward "general rules of health" and training. He would reiterate and amplify them for Kiviat during the coming months.

"Always be sure to warm up before active exercise. This gives the heart and other muscles a chance to gradually accustom themselves to the demands which you are to place on them. After exercise always terminate your activity gradually. Having completed a run, graduate your movement to a jog, then to a walk, never stop short. If you massage your muscles after exercise with a suitable rubbing preparation you will be delighted to find that you will have far less trouble in the way of strains which may pave the way to a dangerous curtailment of your athletic abilities."

Build up gradually in training: "three days a week, one half an hour each day, will be sufficient." "But it is critical not to do too much work."

"Be sure of nine hours of sleep in a well-ventilated room." ("Eight hours of sleep is hardly sufficient sleep for an athlete in training.")

"Eat plainly cooked food, avoiding greasy fried foods and heavy pastries." *"Meat once a day"; "vegetables, more vegetables, and then some vegetables." "A wise plan for a daily diet is a good breakfast, lunch, and a heavier evening meal."[9]*

After Robby said his few introductory words—and with him it was always a few words, even for the younger athletes to whom he devoted so much attention—he directed the boys to the field. What Kiviat and Drebinger saw was unlike anything they may have anticipated. During the brief time Robby had been the coach, it was as if "a regular revolution had hit the place," wrote a veteran track writer. "Imagine the surprise of one who goes to Celtic Park expecting to see runners grinding around the track, burly weight tossers heaving the great missiles with awful grunts, etc., when coming over the brow of Laurel Hill the visitors beholds [*sic*] a game of baseball in progress." Play, after all, was the point of the exercise to Robby. Distance runner Jim Sullivan was hurling the discus 100 feet to strengthen the weak back that had hampered his performance at the London Olympics. Harvey Cohn was "manipulating a couple of dumbbells while prancing up and down the track" in order to alleviate the problem of his arms tying up at the end of his mile races. Only then would Robby's athletes begin the afternoon's serious training.

Robertson was no eccentric. Kiviat observed how respectfully the veteran stars treated their coach and former teammate. They knew whatever his latest radical theory, he could back it up with deed. "Robertson is the only athletic coach in the game to-day who can outrun the men he is training," a visitor to track practice at Celtic Park remarked. The street-smart schoolboy champ took it all in. His new coach, a late convert to amateur athletics and Olympism, had found his first and lasting acolyte.[10]

IRISH CLUB: LORE AND LEGEND

Kiviat had asked for a tryout with the Irish Club because of its impressive and growing reputation as an athletic powerhouse. He had run in PSAL competition at Celtic Park while still in elementary school, and he read the sportswriters' frequent articles about the club's prowess. Its leaders' democratic approach was also appealing and stood in stark contrast to that of its great rival, the NYAC. It was "a poor man's club with very few college men. The Irish-American Athletic Club was made up of guys out of grammar school or from high school or kids who worked. If you could run or jump, you could try out," Kiviat said. Whereas the wealthy and elitist NYAC discriminated against Jews and other white ethnic, working-class athletes, the Irish Club welcomed them. Kiviat was well aware that several Jews had competed successfully for the club, including champion jumper Myer Prinstein and sprinter Harry Hyman. However, he could not have had any real idea of what he was getting himself into.[11]

Along with receiving the club's meet uniform—white singlet with a green winged fist emblem, white shorts with green stripes around the waist and down the sides—the lad began to absorb its lore and legend. "They were a fabulous group," Arthur Daley, the *New York Times* columnist who knew many of them, once remarked, "a roistering, carefree set of hellions who engaged in sports purely for the fun of it." But the Winged Fistites were far more than some Broadway stereotype of wild Irish characters, with their "tremendous, earthy humor," or worse, the incarnation of the Victorians' Celtophobic images of drunken, apelike Paddys. Their athletic accomplishments during the preceding decade had marked them as among the best in the world.[12]

Of about one hundred American athletes in all sports that had sailed from New York on the steamship *Philadelphia* to the 1908 London Olympics, nineteen were Irish Club track athletes. When Britain's Queen Alexandra presented the gold medals in twenty-six track and field events on the final day of the games, Irish Club members received nine. "The Irish-American Athletic Club could have won the world's championship without the assistance of any other organization," declared James E. Sullivan, U.S. commissioner to the Olympic Games. Their names and achievements were nearly as familiar to schoolboys as the names of baseball stars Ty Cobb and Christy Mathewson. Among those in the locker room with Kiviat were his hero Mel Sheppard, the middle-distance star at London; distance-running medalist George Bonhag; and the so-called Irish Whales, John Flanagan and Martin Sheridan, New York policemen who doubled as gold medalists in the hammer and discus throws, respectively. Many other 1908 Olympians were working out all around Celtic Park.[13]

6. The great Irish Club track team, loaded with Olympic and U.S. champions, at Celtic Park, ca. 1909–10. Kiviat is in the front row, fifth from the right. Courtesy of American Irish Historical Society, New York.

Some at Celtic Park still had fresh memories of the club's origins and of the older legends who had helped to establish it. In fact, there was an Irish-American Athletic Club as early as 1879, holding track meets and social events at several sites in Manhattan. Its purpose was in part to provide an outlet for the more talented athletes among the 275,000 natives of Ireland and their children living in Manhattan and Brooklyn and experiencing the shocks of assimilation. Two of its members won distance races at the national outdoor championships, but by 1882 the club disappeared from public view. Irish Americans renewed their enthusiasm for amateur sport in 1888 when Ireland's Gaelic Athletic Association (GAA) sent the so-called Invasion Team of track stars and football players on an American tour. The "Invaders" were well received by the immigrant community, and seventeen chose to remain in New York, including the Irish GAA's new secretary, William F. Prendergast, and the young weight-throwing champion James S. Mitchell.[14]

The New York Irish had no field of their own. Prendergast, who had joined the police department, decided to solve the problem and identified the land in Queens that would become Celtic Park. One Sunday afternoon in the spring of 1897, a small group met with Prendergast in the kitchen of Doria's Restaurant at Sixty-sixth Street and Third Avenue in Manhattan to develop a plan. They formed an organization and decided to build an athletic field for the development of track and field as well as Gaelic sports such as football and hurling. They called themselves the GNYIAA and chose Patrick J. Conway, a thirty-four-year-old native of Limerick and onetime horseshoe champion, as their president. "Pay Jay" or "Chief," as everyone called him, was from that moment the principal force behind the club's accomplishments over the next two decades. After the granting of its charter, the club raised funds quickly to buy nine acres for the bargain price of nine thousand dollars; the organizers then built their sports complex for an additional forty-eight thousand dollars. Conway himself donated one thousand dollars to cover the initial expenses. "The site of Celtic Park was a barren tract with few modern residential buildings in the vicinity and transportation was limited," Conway recalled later. He knew what he was doing. Because he and his friends had close ties to Tammany Hall, the predominantly Irish organization of Democratic Party politicians in New York City, he learned how valuable the empty lands in Queens would become as plans for better transportation took shape. In the meantime, Celtic Park was only ten minutes by trolley from the Long Island City terminal of the Thirty-fourth Street ferry from Manhattan. It was also close to Calvary Cemetery, a place long familiar to Irish mourners as the "City of the Celtic Dead." Celtic Park was soon ready for use, and by the standards of the 1890s, it was an impressive place. "The track and grounds are perfectly adapted for the sport," a reporter wrote. But the GNYIAA was not yet ready to compete at an elite level.[15]

A group of superstars changed that soon enough. The first was the big Irishman Dennis Horgan, who signaled the club's future. In 1900, when he held the world shot put record at 48 feet 2 inches, Horgan joined the GNYIAA during a brief stay in America, won the national shot put title, and single-handedly put the club on the athletic map.[16]

Another early club legend was Myer Prinstein, who immigrated to New York as a child with his Russian Jewish family. As a law student at Syracuse University, he set a world record in the long jump and was the leader after the qualifying round at the 1900 Paris Olympiad. The final was held on a Sunday, but Syracuse, a Methodist-affiliated institution, refused to allow him to compete on that day. Prinstein's great rival, Alvin Kraenzlein of Penn, apparently reneged on their agreement not to compete and took gold. An infuriated Prinstein gathered himself on Monday and won the triple jump. After college, he joined the GNYIAA. The club's breakthrough came in

1904 when Prinstein led its athletes to the national outdoor title and then to glory at the St. Louis Olympics, where he won the long and triple jumps. The team, renamed the "Irish-American Athletic Club" in 1906, began a string of successive victories at the outdoor nationals. Prinstein and his club mates also excelled at that summer's Athens Olympics.[17]

This success was not an accident but the design of a coach who recruited and trained gifted athletes. Coach Ernie Hjertberg and his Irish Club stars were innovators in several disciplines. They had inherited the nineteenth century's more casual and primitive styles of performance and, through study and practice, transformed them into recognizably modern events.

The turn of the century was a moment in history when aspiring Americans were realizing for the first time the value of paid experts in many fields. Hjertberg brought to the team wide-ranging professional expertise. Even though he was a distance runner, he specialized as a coach in the technically demanding throwing and jumping events. To read his masterwork *Athletics in Theory and Practice* (1914) is to realize how analytic he was. (One 1908 British Olympian wrote about "his almost magic analysis of athletic movement.") He outlined detailed and thoughtful training schedules, drawing on the admittedly limited scientific knowledge of the pre–World War I age. Applying physiology, psychology, and other sciences to world-class sport would not occur until later in the twentieth century, so Hjertberg was ahead of his time.

Theory was one thing, but results were another. Hjertberg also produced results. His book was sprinkled with innovative photos of world-record holders and Olympic champions in action. Most were Hjertberg's stars from the Irish Club. These early photos capture the history of the remarkable team that Kiviat joined in the summer of 1909.[18]

Take the case of Martin Sheridan, who emigrated from County Mayo, Ireland, in 1901 and five years later became a member of the New York Police Department. He embodied the Irish heritage of talented athletes. From ancient days, the Celtic clans had competed against each other in throwing heavy objects and in leaping and jumping events. The Tailtin Games, which originated in Teltown, County Meath, had similarities to the Greek Olympics and survived until the twelfth century A.D. Nineteenth-century Irish youth such as Martin Sheridan rediscovered this tradition and brought it with them to America. Standing just under six feet three inches and carrying 195 pounds of solid muscle, Sheridan was then the greatest all-around athlete in the world, winning Olympic medals in the discus throw, the shot put, and the standing high and long jumps. He excelled in the discus, a classic event of the ancient world that had been revived by modern Greek athletes. Track's leading historian has called Sheridan the "prince of the discus pioneers," and Sheridan demonstrated why in winning the event in the successive Olympic Games of 1904, 1906, and 1908, and in breaking his own world record six times. In a perfect world, he would have competed for Ireland in the decathlon, but in the first decade of the twentieth century British-ruled Ireland could not enter an official team, and the decathlon event as such had not yet been created.

As much as Sheridan's teammates admired his athletic talents, he also impressed them with his modesty and leadership. Consider, too, his patriotism: according to knowledgeable track writer Arthur Daley, the night before the opening ceremony at London, Sheridan and other Irish Club men spoke with the American flag-bearer, shot-putter Ralph Rose, and warned him not to dip the flag as he passed in front of King Edward of England. Sheridan's remark—"This flag dips to no earthly king!"—began a tradition that American Olympic teams still follow.

His appetites for whiskey and food were also memorable. Kiviat was still slapping his thigh a quarter-century later (1935) when he told a writer: "'Why, I once saw Martin Sheridan gobble THIRTY-TWO FRIED EGGS WITHOUT BREAKING THE WHITES!'" Surviving accounts by other teammates confirm that this story was no mere tall tale.[19]

Another leader of the Irish Club was the Olympic hero of 1908, Mel Sheppard. Sheppard grew up in a working-class Protestant family in the Philadelphia area, and his running ability earned him a scholarship to Brown Prep School, where at the advanced age of twenty he set national interscholastic records for the 880 and the one- and two-mile runs. Immediately after he won an invitation race in New York in December 1905, Coach Hjertberg recruited him for the Irish Club by assigning one of the club's runners, Harry Hyman, a Jewish alumnus of Penn, to accompany Mel home to Philadelphia by train before other coaches could speak to him. Early the next morning Hjertberg showed up at Sheppard's front door and signed him up.

Sheppard faced a major headache right from the start. An obscure professional athlete named Robert Hallen went to AAU officials with the trumped-up charge that Sheppard had been racing for money at East Coast track meets using an alias. After reviewing the evidence for weeks, the AAU Registration Committee dropped the charge. But because of the sensational headlines and the cloud raised over his name, the American Olympic Committee excluded Sheppard from consideration for the U.S. team going to the 1906 Athens Games.[20]

Sheppard's experience illustrated a problem that would continue to plague track and field for most of the twentieth century—the idea that amateur athletics represents the purest form of sport. Americans borrowed the amateur ethos from the aristocracy and upper middle class of England, whose Oxbridge colleges invented modern track meets. Amateurism essentially meant a Victorian gentleman-athlete played sports only as a hobby, "for personal satisfaction not material gain." A powerful underlying motivation for English gentlemen in the pursuit of this ideology was to avoid physical contact with the lower classes and their professional athletes. America's AAU thus ruled after its founding in 1888 that amateurs could not participate in open competition against professionals, could not accept money for competing, and could not make their living as a coach or trainer. Nevertheless, from the beginning many American meet promoters winked at the idea and gave "money orders, gift certificates and under-the-table cash" as rewards to so-called amateur athletes, and some officials looked the other way. In later years, cynics would call this kind of cheating "shamateurism."[21]

The organizational genius behind the AAU's drive to sharpen the American definition of the term *amateur* and to institutionalize it through a network of regional associations was James E. Sullivan of New York. There were layers of irony here: himself the son of an Irish immigrant, a railway construction foreman, Sullivan was appointed secretary of the new AAU in 1889. For the next twenty-five years, he was "the first sports czar," ruling amateur athletics "with an iron hand" from his office on Park Place in New York. Serving concurrently as the manager of the A. G. Spalding & Brothers' American Sports Publishing Company, he advertised their sporting goods in every volume he brought out for the amateur market. Although Sullivan admired Mel Sheppard as much as he would soon have high regard for Abel

Kiviat—two working-class, non-Celtic stars of the Irish Club—his AAU's rulings about their amateur status would disrupt their careers repeatedly.[22]

In contrast, the "pedestrians," as the professionals were known in nine-teenth-century Britain and America, were mostly working-class Irishmen who competed for cash prizes, often in handicap distance running and walk-ing races enlivened by spectators' heavy betting. Whether in sprints or the longer distances, including the contemporary craze of six-day races, down-stairs bested upstairs—the professionals simply outpaced the amateurs. Two middle-distance runners of the 1880s struggled with the athlete's dilemma in the amateur era: How does one earn a living as an amateur while devot-ing oneself to training and competition? Both Lon Myers of the Manhattan Athletic Club, its Jewish paid secretary and unbeatable from 300 to 1,000 yards, and Englishman Walter George, unsurpassed at one mile, solved their problem by turning pro and racing each other in a series of matches in the United States and Australia in 1886–87. Despite their unsophisticated train-ing by later standards, Myers's 1,000 yards in 2:13 in 1881 (he was techni-cally still an amateur then) and George's 4:12.75 in the mile in 1886 (as a pro) would last for twenty-nine years and would leave lofty goals for Mel Sheppard and his pre–World War I generation.

Early on, young Sheppard liked the glamour of being a miler, but Ernie Hjertberg observed his speed and turned him into an 880 runner. "Peerless Mel's" Hall of Fame career took off immediately. From 1906 to 1908, he ran up a string of successive victories in the 880 at "the big three" outdoor meets of the era: the AAU nationals, the Canadian championships, and New York's Metropolitan AAU games. Indoors, he won national titles at diverse middle distances. Shep peaked at the London Olympics, winning three gold medals for the 800, the 1,500, and the 1,600 relay, which he anchored. Of his upset victory in the metric mile, President Theodore Roosevelt told him when they were introduced, "It was the greatest race I ever read about."[23]

ATHLETIC PRODIGY, SUMMER 1909

If Lawson Robertson hoped to maintain Ernie Hjertberg's legacy and build an even stronger Irish American team, he needed to do whatever he could to encourage raw talent. To recruit Kiviat, for example, Robertson promised that the Irish Club would find him a summer job and pay his carfare to Celtic Park. The club quickly placed him on Wall Street. "Not exactly a runner," Kiviat recalled, "but a little bit higher than a runner. . . . I'd get more than three dollars a week." Whereas runners or pages would carry messages around the floor of the Stock Exchange, he would be delivering important communications back and forth between the trading floor and the members' firms. Wall Street was a lively place that summer. After the Panic of 1907, the stock market had bounced back in 1908, surviving a European war scare, and had one of "the 10 best years of the twentieth century," according to an eminent analyst. The continuing upbeat mood during Kiviat's apprenticeship made his first experience in the financial district memorable. At the close of the workday, he traveled from Lower Manhattan out to Queens for track practice or competition.[24]

Because Kiviat was in good shape after the PSAL season, Robertson told him he would enter him in his first races almost immediately. As he began to prepare for these meets, he was still "a little fellow," measuring about five feet three inches and weighing less than 130 pounds. Robby had him train twice a week, with emphasis on speed work with the sprinters, which meant repeat 100-yard dashes. With his coach's tutelage, he began experimenting for the first time with the crouch start. "I became a good starter," he recalled. "I could shoot off the mark like a sprinter." Robby believed speed work would also enable him "to anticipate a jump on the part of an opponent."[25]

Kiviat made his first start on Saturday, July 10, in the AAU's metropolitan-area junior championships at the Travers Island field of the NYAC. That almost five thousand men and women turned out to watch a junior meet attested to the sport's appeal in 1909. Clustered together on the banks surrounding the track, they did all they could to hold on to their hats and parasols as gales from Long Island Sound blew across the field. John Drebinger competed in the 100-yard dash and, frustrated after failing to advance out of the semifinals, decided to end his brief career with the Winged Fist club. Then Kiviat won the second of three preliminary heats of the half-mile in 2:04.8, by far the fastest time in the rounds, matching his PSAL record of six weeks earlier. Reporters noted his inexperience and that he "was entirely overlooked by the prophets" when he lined up for the final. (He claimed later that "it was the first A.A.U. competition he had ever seen, let alone entered.") Dick Egan of the Pastime Athletic Club led the race by ten yards at the 660 mark when he began to come back to the field. Kiviat wisely bided his time in the wind-buffeted pack, and Egan faltered. As they came through the final bend into the home straight, Kivie "let out with a burst of speed" and drew away easily, winning by five yards in 1:59.4. An observer thought Kiviat finished "the freshest one in the field" and demonstrated "the judgment of a seasoned campaigner." In the face of difficult conditions, he had lowered his personal 880 record by more than five seconds! He took the ferry home to Staten Island knowing he had established himself "as a contender for senior honors," as the *New York Herald* put it.[26]

His commanding win against a veteran field in a 600-yard race the following day in a meet at Celtic Park drew headlines. Having "sprung into prominence on the cinder track about as fast as a mushroom grows," the *New York Herald* remarked, Kiviat must have caused even Robertson to shake his head in surprise.[27]

These races were only previews. Track and field in 1909 gave the "young athletic prodigy" every opportunity to develop his talent. Each weekend, athletic clubs large and small joined religious, ethnic, social, and political organizations in sponsoring well-publicized track meets in cities and towns all over the country. Most were on the East Coast, where modern means of transportation were increasingly widespread, comfortable, and affordable. Railroads and electric trolleys enabled the more gifted and ambitious to compete in two meets every weekend.[28]

On Saturday, July 24, Kiviat ran in his first out-of-town meet, the fourteenth annual St. Augustine Parish Carnival of Sports held in South Boston. Directed by Cornell's Jack Moakley, a native Bostonian on summer vacation from his coaching duties, the meet attracted the season's elite athletes, and there were good performances. The most exciting event was the popular medley relay race (220, 440, 880, and one mile), featuring the Irish Club and the Boston Athletic Association (BAA).

Kiviat and Bill Bingham of Boston started the third leg of 880 yards together. Bingham was a challenge: although nearly twenty and having worked for five years in a Lawrence textile mill, he had just completed his freshman year at the elite Phillips Exeter Academy by setting a national interscholastic 880 record of 1:59 at Harvard Stadium. The two gifted high school recruits battled each other and touched off their anchormen dead even.

The milers, Olympian Joe Bromilow of the Irish Club and Joe Ballard of the BAA, ran together until the gun lap, when Bromilow pulled away and won by twenty-five yards. When the winning time was announced, the Irish Club had set a world record of 7:44.4. Exactly eight weeks had elapsed since an unheralded Kiviat had upset Cedric Major to win the PSAL championship.[29]

Based on these initial races, Lawson Robertson decided "Kivie would do better at the mile than at the half." Indeed, the coach predicted to reporters that his protégé would develop rapidly into the best miler in the world. Many track fans doubted Ernie Hjertberg's young and inexperienced successor. "Poor judgment," some said. "Robbie should keep Kiviat at the distance in which he has shown such grand form." But Robertson now demonstrated he was both a shrewd judge of talent and a pragmatic strategist. The mile better suited Kiviat's size, speed, and stamina. Besides, with Mel Sheppard and Emilio Lunghi, Italy's 1908 Olympic silver medalist at 800 meters, now living in New York and competing for the Irish Club, the coach arguably already had the world's best half-milers on his squad.

Encomiums about Kiviat's "grand form" certainly did not extend to his running style, about which Robby could do little. One writer remarked bluntly that Kiviat "was as bowlegged as a cavalry officer. . . . [He] seemed to run on the rims of his feet, and there was a peculiar twisting from the hips. He was nothing for a poet's rhapsodies, but he was a terrifically hard man to beat."[30]

On Sunday, August 1, Robby entered Kiviat in his first AAU mile race at a Clan-na-Gael athletic meet and picnic at Celtic Park. The Clan was a politically radical, although essentially middle-class organization of Irish Americans committed to the republican cause. Ardently supporting the eviction of the British from Ireland by force, Clan members developed a cult of masculinity that they expressed in part by sponsoring athletic meets. Not coincidentally, here was a sure-fire way to attract new recruits to the cause. Nearly seven thousand enthusiastic spectators, including politicians currying the group's favor, got their money's worth watching hurling, Gaelic football games, and the Irish Club's exceptional triple jumper Dan Ahearn, a recent immigrant from County Limerick. However, "the star event on the schedule was the one-mile handicap," commented the *New York Daily Tribune*. The mainstays of amateur clubs were ordinarily the handicap events, in which less-able contestants were given advantages of yards or meters over the better athletes, who started from "scratch" and thus ran the full distance. Although starting from scratch behind runners with big yardage allowances, Kivie and Joe Bromilow passed most of them during the first three laps. Their sprint duel on the backstretch of the gun lap ended with Bromilow's fading and Kiviat's falling four yards short of catching Dave Noble of the NYAC, who had started with a twenty-five-yard handicap. Kiviat's second-place time was 4:27.2 on a slow track against a strong wind. At a time when "few Americans . . . have beaten 4:23 for one mile," Coach Robertson now believed Kiviat "can go 4:20 this summer." Having participated unwittingly in the revolutionary struggle for a free Irish republic, Kiviat returned to his Yiddish-speaking home.[31]

The following Saturday, Kiviat and some teammates took a Jersey Central train to Asbury Park, the popular boardwalk resort of the northern Jersey shore. Two thousand summer residents watched the athletes compete on a three-laps-to-the-mile bicycle track in the Asbury Park Athletic Association meet. Little Abel stole their hearts. He raced the odd distance of two-thirds of a mile. He was on scratch, with the other runners having handicaps of at least sixty yards. From the crack of starter Johnny McHugh's pistol, he was away flying, and his pressing pace left him without the closing sprint to catch a fast fading YMCA runner. Amazingly, three timers caught him in 2:47.6, fully a half-second ahead of the world record set by the great Englishman Walter George in 1882. Although track conditions precluded recognition of a world record, Kiviat's smashing success and the widespread publicizing of the result stimulated an immediate revival of interest in racing at this distance among the elite runners.[32]

Two weeks later, a reporter for the *New York Tribune* caught up with "the boy wonder" at Celtic Park. Kiviat informed him he was being recruited heavily by the leading colleges, including Yale, Cornell, and Princeton. "I really have two more years yet at high school," Kiviat said somewhat disingenuously, "but by working very hard this year I think I will be ready for college the following fall, and Yale is the one I expect to enter." In a case of life imitating art, he was hoping to become his fictional inspiration, Frank Merriwell of Yale. Zelda and Morris Kiviat may have *qvelled* (Yiddish for "beaming with pride" in offspring) when their kids read them the story, but one cannot imagine Curtis principal Harry Towle's reaction.[33]

The track writers also began to note not only Kiviat's rare talent, but his keen intelligence or "generalship" in competition. Their exaggerated—and repeated—emphasis on his mental capacity throughout his running career drew on both his real tough-mindedness under fire and the hoary stereotype of the innately "crafty and intelligent Jew." Unfortunately, some of the writers' inspiration derived from the not so subtle comments of Coach Robertson about his protégé's cunning. Kiviat's maturity also drew their attention: he was "a most consistent performer" in spite of his youth, one wrote.[34]

Ahead lay Kiviat's two major events of this first outdoor season, mile runs in the Canadian and New York metropolitan senior championships. A summer under Robertson's care, especially the hearty diet of rare roast beef, green vegetables, and milk, filled him out. "In two months' time I actually scaled 135 and found that I had grown TWO INCHES IN HEIGHT!" he recalled years later for a writer.[35]

The beautiful train ride to Montreal was an adventure. Mel Sheppard remembered, "[W]e were always anxious to compete in these games, not only because of the fact we were treated so well by the Canadians while in Montreal, but also because the track there was considered one of the fastest this side of England. The only disadvantage it had was that it was three laps to the mile instead of the customary four." To a rookie like Kiviat, the Montreal Amateur Athletic Association Grounds appeared enormous: "[G]eez, you could put the Yankee Stadium and the Polo Grounds in there," he recalled. Undaunted, he won the mile in 4:23.2, beating Joe Bromilow and Joe Ballard of the BAA. Kiviat and his Irish Club teammates won the meet with sixty-seven points, setting two new world and three Canadian records. After competing, the Irish Club went sightseeing. The club's "favorite trip" was to go up Mount Royal by horse and buggy. From the top, "Montreal looked like a toy city below," Mel Sheppard wrote.[36]

When reports of the meet reached New York, Kiviat's Staten Island friends bragged: "How is this for a soph. of Curtis who was entered in the third mile race he ever ran?" Many others in the sport's growing army of fans eagerly awaited the metropolitan-area championships later that week at Travers Island. Lawson Robertson's team demolished the NYAC by more than fifty points. Kiviat drew a headline, demonstrating to a large crowd his "sterling ability" as a miler. He beat a fast-closing Joe Bromilow to the tape by eight yards in 4:26.4. At seventeen, he was the champion miler of metropolitan New York at a moment when that title really mattered.[37]

There occurred at this juncture a peculiar interruption of the outdoor campaign for the widely anticipated national AAU indoor championships at Madison Square Garden. It was expected to be a truly national meet: for the first time in track history, leading athletes from all of America's regions, plus athletes from Canada and even Europe, would compete against the powerful New York clubs.[38]

Kiviat was proud of his reputation "for not being of the nervous type" before big meets at the Garden. ("Lawson Robertson would take us across the street to the hotel, and I'd be one of the ones could fall asleep, and ringing the phone never woke me up," he recalled.) Nevertheless, his debut there must have been exciting. Located off Madison Square at Madison Avenue and Twenty-sixth Street, the mix of new commercial buildings and the elegant homes remaining from the novelist Edith Wharton's childhood were the backdrops for a constant traffic in humanity, trolleys, horse-drawn carriages, and the new motorcars. Stanford White's blockwide "palace of pleasure" dominated the area known as "the heart of New York." His architectural inspiration of 1890 was the Giralda Tower of Seville; he topped the exterior of buff brick and terra cotta tile with a tower thirty-two stories high, at whose peak he placed St. Gaudens's nude statue of the goddess Diana. Inside, he designed a theater, a concert hall, a roof garden cabaret, a restaurant, and an eight-thousand-seat arena. But when Kiviat and Robertson walked through one of White's marble arches and entered the arena on Monday evening, October 4, 1909, the shine was long gone from the original pale red walls. Only a small crowd of about three thousand was in attendance, a number far below expectations, as the Garden continued to lose money that year. Ticket receipts did not begin to match the deficits incurred from the operating costs, unsteady bookings, and a large mortgage. Yet even with the drabness and the empty seats, the atmosphere was electric:

the knowledgeable fans seemed almost on top of the athletes, and competitors in various events bustled around the Garden floor.[39]

Reporters often wrote facilely that the track was fast, but they did not have to race on it. The athletes wore short spikes to negotiate the flat or unbanked surface of pine board. After competing on the 176-yard track, they had stories for a lifetime. One middle-distance great remembered, "[T]he boards . . . were loose and rattled like a wooden bridge when the field of runners pounded against it. There was always a terrible feeling that the far end of a plank would smack you in the face."[40]

Kiviat's first big indoor race, the 1,000-yard feature, was a lesson in tactics from seasoned masters. He "was badly interfered with on the turn" of the bell lap and finished in third place. Kiviat, whose short physique was perfectly suited to the tight quarters of the Garden, learned he must use his sprinting ability off the mark to position himself in a race. However, he failed to apply this lesson the following night in the final of a fast 600-yard run, finishing a badly beaten fifth behind Mel Sheppard, who was back to his Olympic form. Despite Kiviat's personal disappointment, when the points were tallied, the Irish Club took the national title with sixty-nine to the NYAC's sixty-two, adding one more notch to its reputation.[41]

Kiviat was outdoors again at Celtic Park the next weekend for the Irish Club's fall games. The pleasant weather brought out more than eight thousand fans, with the four-by-one-mile relay advertised as the meet's highlight. Although the Irish Club also advertised its cinder track to the public as state of the art, Kiviat knew differently. "Instead of cinders," a teammate wrote years later, "the surface of the track was composed of sand and loam with plenty of cobble stones." It was therefore slow and even dangerous, with the athletes' spikes occasionally hitting a rock. Injuries were common. That did not deter the Irish Club's leadoff runner Tom Collins, who started at scratch against the NYAC and the Mohawk Athletic Club, with allowances of 170 and 190 yards, respectively. Collins whittled their lead to 25 yards; Olympian Frank Riley ran second and held that position. On the third leg, steady Joe Bromilow made up the deficit and touched off Kiviat 25 yards in the lead. Kivie "set out with remarkable speed in the final mile, and rapidly increased the distance between himself and his opponents." He broke the tape 100 yards ahead of the NYAC anchorman as all five timers caught the

Winged Fist's relay in 18:08.8, breaking the University of Michigan's world outdoor record.[42]

FACING LIFE

Kiviat's initial months with the Irish Club marked the beginning of his transition from an adolescent to a responsible adult. Achieving instant fame as a track star opened up doors of opportunity in other aspects of his life. Although he continued to live with his family in Staten Island, his talent brought him into a much wider circle of activity.

Through the intervention of the Irish Club, the Wanamaker Department Store hired him as a sporting goods salesman. John Wanamaker had built the sixteen-story structure at Eighth Street and Broadway, at the southern end of the so-called Ladies' Mile of shops, as a branch of his Philadelphia store. Wanamaker's fascinated New Yorkers from the moment it opened in 1907. The variety of merchandise displayed, including previously unimaginable luxury items, made shopping there an adventure. Kiviat was fortunate to land this position because Wanamaker's did not usually hire Jews. As one of a small number of children of Jewish immigrants who were able to find work as salesmen in American department stores before 1920, Kiviat was also a pioneer.[43]

It was an exciting introduction to life in the big city, but it required a demanding schedule for a seventeen-year-old. He arose at 5:30 in order to catch a trolley car, ferryboat, and subway to Wanamaker's. He worked there most nights until six o'clock before returning home. He was paid thirty dollars every two weeks—which "meant a lot when there were seven kids to feed." Some evenings he would earn extra change by making deliveries for the Jacob Messing drugstore. One or two afternoons a week in the warm weather he would leave Wanamaker's a little early for track practice at Celtic Park. He would take his workout under Coach Robertson's supervision, eat dinner with teammates in the park's restaurant, and then have to make the long trip back home to Staten Island.[44]

With his belief in being "polite and courteous," his good looks, and his determination, he was a natural as a salesman. His reputation as a young superstar assured his success in selling sporting equipment to schoolboys, who were a staple customer of the department. Other shoppers, too, came in to get Kiviat's autograph. Zelda brought her younger children into Manhattan to see their big brother at work and to enjoy Wanamaker's Christmas concerts by famous choirs. "It was," Harold Kiviat recalled, "a big deal" for the eight-year-old younger brother.[45]

Yet there was more to Kiviat's success. At this time, Rodman Wanamaker, son of the founder, became interested in the health and welfare of his "store family," a term he used for his employees. As a sportsman himself, he decided to create the Wahna Athletic Association ("Wahna" was the Wanamaker trade name), whose purpose was to encourage his employees to participate in physical exercise and athletics "under the rules of the Amateur Athletic Union." He hoped that providing games for his personnel would promote a spirit of loyalty and community at the store. As a businessman, he also realized that sponsoring an elite track team in big meets was an excellent advertising strategy. The store hired four well-known track stars, of whom Kiviat was the youngest by far, to compete as a relay team in a league established by the big department stores, including Macy's. They wore white jerseys with a thick diagonal sash, featuring a red W superimposed on an upside down white W. The Wahna team quickly became the stars of the department store league. Between Wanamaker's and the Irish Club, "I ran for two organizations at the same time," Kiviat said.

Kiviat's employment highlights the hypocrisy of the rules of amateurism in 1909. Coaching athletes in his sport for a salary would make the trackman a professional, automatically disqualifying him from AAU competitions. However, holding a job at a company such as Wanamaker's in order to compete for the store in its league play and of course helping to advertise it was acceptable. Here was another confusing example of "shamateurism." Yet a poor boy like Kiviat had no realistic alternative if he wished to succeed.

Viewed from another perspective, Kiviat's job helped him play a modest but not insignificant role in the growth of the sporting goods industry at the beginning of the twentieth century. The recruitment of star athletes, professional coaches, and administrators into a commercial network with sporting goods manufacturers and retailers resulted in a new and widespread interest in organized games. As sports historian Stephen Hardy has shown, Americans' fascination with athletes who had mastered the new scientific techniques and approaches of modern sports—which the Irish Club under Coaches Hjertberg and Robertson exemplified—positioned the champions as key links in the rise of this new industry.[46]

Although Kiviat was still enrolled at Curtis for the fall term, he was not attending classes, and he withdrew officially from school in November. A Jewish high school dropout may seem unusual to readers today, especially given the myth that all Jewish immigrant children were excellent students who used education as the open door to success. In fact, those Jews who managed to matriculate in high school left early in large numbers at the time, as did other ethnic groups in the population. It was not until the decades following World War I that adolescents were expected to remain in high school until graduation. School superintendents in the early twentieth century knew that large families struggling with poverty needed additional income from their oldest children. The educators also recognized that the idea of a full-time job in an exciting city such as New York was an attraction for a restless teenager. Kiviat was ready to move on with his life, but he never stopped being ashamed of dropping out. In later years, he either lied about it, saying he graduated in the class of 1909, or if someone assumed he was a Curtis graduate, he did not correct the mistaken impression. A touching remark he made during his return trip to the Stockholm Olympic stadium revealed how he felt, at age ninety-two, about what he considered his youthful failure. Speaking on the CBS television network, he likened his winning an Olympic silver medal to receiving a high school diploma. If that seems strange today, when having a diploma is as common as having an Olympic medal is uncommon, it suggests that unconsciously Kiviat still felt deep regret about dropping out.[47]

In October, Robertson invited Kiviat to join his National Guard unit, the Thirteenth Coast Artillery of Brooklyn, also known as the Thirteenth Regiment. The National Guard was a volunteer militia of citizen-soldiers that served as a backup or reserve force to the regular army. The Thirteenth Regiment had a long record of gallantry in battle dating back to the Civil War, but its main role until 1900 was as the "policeman of industry"—a force trained to defend wealthy Brooklynites against imagined mob riots and other civil disturbances by the working poor. By 1909, Americans' fears of social class warfare between business and labor were changing to more realistic worries of a coming war with European countries. To recruit poor youths such as Kiviat in order to create a larger and prepared military reserve, the National Guard's leadership adjusted its program to include sports events and other activities. The Thirteenth, in particular, gained fame as the "Athletic Regiment": Robby coached its track team and recruited many of his Irish Club stars and other AAU athletes. For elite runners, one said, "it was almost necessary to join one of the regiments in order to have an indoor track upon which to train." The Guard also had another powerful appeal for Kiviat. Its emphasis on patriotism provided him with a concrete way to demonstrate he belonged in America and respected the society's middle-class values and lifestyles. What began as a summons to winter track practice developed into a commitment to serious soldiering. He decided to sign up for the five-year term.[48]

The regimental home on Sumner Avenue in Brooklyn was quite a sight when Kiviat first approached it. The four-story armory occupied almost three acres, or a full city block. Its design as a medieval fortress, with two battlemented towers and a turret that served as a signal tower, seemed strangely out of place in Stuyvesant Heights, a lovely middle-class neighborhood of rowhouses and brownstones. The armory's drill shed was "the largest in America, if not in the world," *Harper's Weekly* reported. The basement had rifle and pistol ranges. On the upper floors were officers' quarters, a mess hall, a kitchen, and a lecture room. In short, Kiviat had, as an English visitor wrote that fall, "an exceedingly pleasant club at his disposal during his service." He had drill one night a week, but "they were light on the ones that came a long distance," Kiviat said.[49]

He was there to run, of course, and the Thirteenth provided a preeminent sports arena. The drill shed had a new and fast flat floor track and a 120-yard straightaway for dashes and hurdles. High above the floor on either side of the building, the galleries accommodated at least four thousand spectators. Some fans sat behind a fence on the armory floor, closer to the action.[50]

The Thirteenth's track team competed in the popular and successful Military Athletic League (MAL). Since 1897, the MAL had been sponsoring sports events for the National Guard, the naval militia, and the regular army and navy in the regimental armories then being constructed all around

New York. MAL track meets were intensely competitive affairs between the city's many regiments with longstanding rivalries. In this setting, too, Robby planned to take advantage of Kiviat's versatility by using him in the mile, in the 880, and on several relay teams during the coming winter. In the meantime, Kiviat did his "training between 8 and 10 o'clock at night" before "returning home to Staten Island by moonlight."

In retrospect, the amount of activity young people undertook in those days was remarkable. They spent many hours traveling long distances on public transportation, and they were quite matter-of-fact about it. All Kiviat said was: "I ran for Wanamaker's now and then. I ran in the military athletic league now and then, and I ran regularly for the Irish Club. You don't have to do much training when you compete that often."[51]

"A TYPICAL COUNTRY FAMILY"

A teenager seeking to find his place in the larger world may return often to the safe harbor of family, and Kiviat was no exception. He lived at home, as did most boys in that era, especially the millions from immigrant families. It was an economic necessity. With Abel's new income surely a factor, and with the maturing of their children another, Morris and Zelda Kiviat decided to move from the apartment at 101 Broad Street down the block to "a whole house with the store in front and a garden in the back." Their new home at 156 Broad had a roomy lot, Abel remembered. The yard was the family's delight, providing concrete proof that they were finally making it in America. Near the gate was a well from which they pumped their water and where they cooled big cans of the milk given by their cow, Dolly. At either end of the garden were two sheds for the horse, the cow, some ducks, and chickens. During the week, the Kiviat children were assigned to bring the eggs into the house. Sam, age nine, was so clumsy in picking up the eggs of the baby chicks Morris was breeding that Poppa mocked him cruelly. Before the Sabbath, a *shochet*, or ritual slaughterer, came and prepared some chickens for the traditional Friday dinner.

Morris insisted the sheds be kept clean. He was so proud of his animal husbandry skills, he would think nothing of rushing into the kitchen to show Zelda a newborn colt. She would shoo him out with a broom saying "take your *vilde chai*—wild animal —out of here," Harold Kiviat remembered. The new property also gave Pop the opportunity to exhibit his other talents. "My father was a great one in the yard," Abel recalled. "He'd raise a few vegetables. What we didn't eat right away, he'd put in barrels. He'd pickled [*sic*] things. I remember him trimming the green mold. He made sauerkraut and pickles. He'd pack fruit and vegetables. He was a very handy man."[52]

Zelda used the produce to prepare memorable meals. On the evenings Abel did not have dinner on the training table at Celtic Park or at the Thirteenth Regiment Armory in Brooklyn, he enjoyed eating his mother's food. "I'd have a piece of gefilte fish Fridays and Saturdays." But he kept in mind Coach Robertson's rules of diet: "I wouldn't put horse radish on. I didn't go for condiments."

However deep the strain in their relationship, Morris and Zelda continued to live together and to create the illusion of unity. They were, in Kiviat's fantasy about his early years, a "typical country family." The function of this distorted image was to assure him, even as he ventured boldly into the stressful life of Gotham, both of his normality and of his capacity to adjust to his workaday life in his non-Jewish milieu. After all, were not his circumstances similar to that of the others with whom he mingled?[53]

The mental gymnastics worked. In January 1909, he had been an unknown high school sophomore in a relatively isolated corner of New York City struggling to pass his classes and hoping to succeed in PSAL events. At the end of this magical year, he was in the midst of his apprenticeship with a dynamic organization, quietly preparing himself to play a significant role in his sport at a turning point in its American experience. When the *New York Times* published its annual list of notable achievements in sport for that year, the newspaper listed the Irish Club's four-mile relay, with Kiviat as anchor, a few lines below the Pittsburgh Pirates and Honus Wagner, winners of the World Series. Arguably, no other seventeen-year-old New Yorker has ever made such a remarkable entry into big-time athletics. His future appeared limitless.[54]

LAP TWO

SETTING THE PACE

4

"The Champ" in the Melting Pot

AFTER FLASHING ONTO THE AMERICAN TRACK SCENE as a "phe-
nom," Kiviat began a hectic schedule of year-round, big-time competition
in 1910. It was a time for maturing and gaining experience in competition,
with inevitable inconsistency. The first phase was his introduction to the
exciting rhythm of the indoor season, with its weekly meets in Madison
Square Garden or the armories. Although this season was already an established component of the American sporting scene, Kiviat participated, in an
important sense, in the creation of the modern wintertime tradition, beginning with a brilliant victory in the inaugural Baxter Mile.

In the process, he was also being socialized to the lifestyle of a big-
time amateur athlete, which, in reality, meant being a quasi-professional
performer. Although the Irish Club did not pay him a salary, they covered
all his expenses for training and competing at the elite level, provided him
with a good job, and gave him wide publicity. The elastic rules of amateurism allowed for this level of support, though flagrant violations would result
in swift banishment. The consensus that legitimized the AAU's policy did
not gainsay the fact that he had become an eighteen-year-old jock for hire.
Although by 1910 his career path was well worn, the new transportation and
communications technologies, with their fuller capacities to reach diverse
audiences more quickly, redefined the terms of the athlete's experience. Kiviat arrived at a moment when the outlines of a modern career in track seemed
promising, even for a poor boy. He had been shrewd in evaluating his gift
and exchanging it for the prospect of fame and fortune in America.[1]

To smooth his path, Celtic Park also offered him informal instruction in Americanization. Through immersion in his teammates' world, he
absorbed their attitudes, values, and patterns of behavior. Yet whatever he

adopted from their particular version of the American melting pot culture, he remained different. What Bialystok had wrought, County Limerick—and its American cousin, the Irish athletic center at Laurel Hill in Queens—could only partially alter.

ROBBY'S APPRENTICE, 1910

Kiviat began with a bang on Saturday night, February 5, 1910, in the Irish Club's annual indoor meet at Madison Square Garden by anchoring his team to an indoor world record of 5:06.2 in the popular 2,400-yard relay race (four by 600).[2] However, if one event marked his arrival on the national scene—the point of departure for his career, as it were—it was his participation in the invitation Baxter Mile race of Columbia University's annual indoor meet at Madison Square Garden on Saturday night, March 12. The Baxter would serve de facto as the championship indoor race because at that time the mile was not contested at the AAU nationals. In fact, the Baxter was a new event on the track calendar, replacing the prestigious Martinique Mile at the Columbia meet. Broadway's Hotel Martinique had inaugurated a tradition by donating a cup to the 1909 winner. Harry Trube, a Cornell alumnus and 1908 Olympian, seized the occasion to run the first sub-4:20 indoor mile (4:19.8). When the Martinique decided to discontinue its sponsorship, Hugh Baxter, a banker and dean of the sport, donated $250 for a new cup bearing his name. Baxter had been a pioneering pole vault champion in the 1880s and the organizer of the NYAC team that in 1895 competed against the London Athletic Club in the first significant international track meet. Newspaper hype increased interest to the point that the race was "long looked for as the athletic treat of the season," the *New York Herald* reported.[3]

Both of Coach Robertson's best entries, Kiviat and George Bonhag, were prepared when they went to their marks for the inaugural Baxter race against their teammate Joe Bromilow and four NYAC runners, led by Harry Gissing. The Garden crowd was as quiet and tense as the seven runners awaiting the starter's pistol. Gissing, the reigning indoor champion at 1,000-yards, and Bonhag were the favorites. At twenty-eight, the tallish, striking George Bonhag was king of the boards. A Columbia graduate in civil engineering and a disciple of Ernie Hjertberg, the keenly intelligent and courteous Bonhag ("Gentleman George" was his popular nickname) approached distance running as a scientist and statistician. An Olympic medalist in 1906 and 1908, he had already won six AAU indoor titles at two and five miles, and held indoor records at a variety of distances. Yet with his great confidence and an iron will he was reaching to a different level of performance that winter, while shattering the conventional theory that a runner was at his best only until about age twenty-five. In February, at Buffalo's Seventy-fourth Regiment Armory, he lowered his own two-mile record by more than thirteen seconds to 9:14.2, in a match race with Jack Tait of Canada. He felt "it was the best effort of his life."[4]

Carl Walther of the NYAC, the "rabbit" or assigned pacemaker, sprinted to an early lead of ten yards, with the six other starters bunched tightly. Walther passed the 440 in a very fast 58.6. From laps four through six, Bonhag took over and measurably slowed the pace, with Walther falling back. Bonhag's time at 880 was 2:10. On lap seven, Kiviat made his first move, racing ahead of Gissing of the NYAC into second place behind Bonhag, who passed the three-quarters in 3:17. With the bell for the last 176 yards, first Kivie, then Gissing passed Bonhag on the backstretch; little more than a yard separated the trio as they sped across the finish line in that order. Although Kiviat's winning time of 4:22.2 was slower than the hyped expectations, "the Garden was pandemonium for fully five minutes," the *New York Times* reported, "as every spectator was on his feet cheering the clever and brilliant running of the little Irish-American athlete. It was a popular victory, popularly received."[5]

From the beginning of the invitation board races, such intense competition by top-notch runners in the close quarters of the indoor arenas marked the classic distance of the mile as particularly appealing to the athletes and their fans. Yet for all the hyperbole about Kiviat's tactical brilliance, his race was characteristic of mile running before the advent of Finland's Paavo Nurmi and his strategic innovations in the 1920s. Although the two halves of the race seemed fairly even—a 2:10 followed by a 2:12.2—consider the successive quarter-mile split times: a very fast 58.6, a dawdling 71.4, a bit up-tempo 67.0, and finally a quicker 65.2. Comparison of the 1910 Baxter with several truly outstanding races of the pre–World War I decade indicates the universality of Kiviat's approach. The elite milers "ran hard and fast in the opening and closing stages but indulged in a long 'float' midway in the race," noted one track historian. Above all, competitive conditions dictated performance. Following the success of the great Finn, better advance planning and training by milers during the interwar decades would lead to more evenly distributed lap times—and better overall results.[6]

Nonetheless, Kiviat was remarkably tough-minded and shrewd for an eighteen-year-old competing at that level. As he gained experience on the board circuit, his confidence grew, and he realized his small frame and his savvy were uniquely suited to indoor meets. "Indoor running is as much a brain race as it is speed," he believed. "Because of my size . . . I could usually hold the pole if I got a good jump, or else pass the big guys . . . on the turns."[7]

He did face a major challenge, however. In the closed and smoky air of the arenas, he began to suffer from what his generation euphemistically called "indoor sickness," whose miserable symptoms included nausea, labored breathing, and the like. At this stage, his affliction was known only to a closed circle at the Irish Club; later, as it became more pronounced and had serious repercussions, he talked about it more openly.[8]

After his striking winter successes, great things surely loomed as the trackmen moved outdoors for the summer campaign. His season started slowly with several narrow losses to Sheppard.[9] In late August, at the Ancient Order of Hibernians meet, Kivie made a fast Celtic Park record at one mile (4:20.4) in a duel with the NYAC's Wilton "Billy" Paull, the record holder for the collegiate mile. Given the wet and slow cinders, the experts predicted Kivie and Paull would make a run at Tommy Conneff's world amateur record of 4:15.6, set in 1895, when they would meet again at the faster Travers Island track on September 10.[10]

Kiviat rested for a week and then added an enduring mark to his national reputation by anchoring the Irish Club's two-mile relay team (four by 880) to an impressive world's record. It came in the Tailtin games at Celtic Park on Labor Day before ten thousand spectators. The quartet of Riley, Bromilow, Sheppard, and Kiviat faced tough competition from the Irish Club's second team, which had an allowance of forty yards, and a Mohawk team with a seventy-two yard advantage. After Riley's slow opening leg (2:01.8), Bromilow

(1:56.8) and Shep (1:58.2) made up ground on the handicap teams. Kivie nevertheless started thirty yards behind Dick Egan of the Irish Club's second team. He had almost caught Egan when the veteran eased up near the finish, enabling Kivie (1:56.2) to win by two yards in 7:53. This time lowered by 1.8 seconds the old mark set by an Irish Club team in 1905. No relay team would better it for a decade, and it remains on the books as the first official record for this event recognized by the new International Amateur Athletic Federation (IAAF) in 1913.[11]

The long summer now reached its climax. For the athletes and their fans, all of the furious competition was once again but prologue to the short championship season that really counted—the Senior Metropolitan championships (Senior Mets), the Canadian meet, and the AAU nationals. First on the calendar was the metropolitan district meet at Travers Island on September 10. Although Kiviat reported for the mile as the defending champion, he would have to overcome the formidable obstacle of little Billy Paull to repeat that win. It turned out to be the best race of 1910. The two milers were like scrappy and skilled lightweight boxers, with Paull leading from the start, trying to take away Kiviat's closing sprint. Kiviat stayed right behind him for all five laps. They were dead even as they kicked home. The crowd was in a frenzy of excitement as Kiviat gave it his last ounce of strength, but Paull managed to breast the tape by inches in 4:22.2. That "brought a sudden hush over the I.-A.A.C. contingent who had been loudly blowing their tin horns, believing their favorite was invincible," crowed the *New York Athletic Club Journal*.[12]

Two weekends later Kiviat defended his Canadian mile title at the Montreal Amateur Athletic Association grounds.[13]

Robby turned now to preparing his motley collection of champions for the outdoor nationals, to be held in mid-October in New Orleans. Following the club's "rule to do everything on as big a scale as possible," thirty-six athletes joined coaches and officials on a delightful five-day steamship voyage to the Gulf of Mexico. This was Kiviat's first trip away from the Northeast. He and his teammates exuded confidence. The sportswriters agreed, selecting the Gothamites as the team to beat and Kiviat in the mile. At eighteen, he was now being talked about as one of the world's great runners.[14]

The AAU had awarded the meet to New Orleans to broaden the base of its operations beyond the East Coast and to expose southerners to the excitement of major track competition. The idea resonated, and leading athletic clubs from all sections of the nation sent teams. A local executive committee, recruited mainly from the powerful Democratic Party machine, spent money freely to create a first-class event. New Orleanians poured out the city's legendary hospitality and gaiety. The visitors stayed at the elegant Grunewald Hotel, and, if so inclined, received unlimited gin fizzes and Sazerac cocktails. "New York money" was not acceptable, they were told in jest.[15]

Dissonant notes sounded in all of this jazzy harmony, however. Although the Crescent City was supposedly at its best in the fall, the visitors had a shock. Oppressive heat and humidity, strange water and diet, and "savage and ceaseless attacks of underfed mosquitos" caused some athletes to become ill quickly. They lost weight, sleep, and the competitive edge from their training. When several of the early-arriving athletes went out to inspect the track at the new Tulane Stadium, they discovered it was built with Mississippi River sand and was mushy after the steady rain of the past two weeks. Mayor Martin Behrman, the efficient political boss of the racially segregated city, set about quickly to solve the problem. He "put 200 negroes to work with steam rollers, night and day, and at length they got the track in tolerably good condition; at least, compared with what it was before."[16]

More than ten thousand excited spectators, the largest gathering yet for a national AAU championship meet, packed the stadium on a Saturday afternoon so intensely hot even the usually staid officials removed their jackets. The softness of the track further guaranteed subpar races. Many of the pale-looking athletes were not ready for a track meet. When the milers were called, Billy Paull, the cofavorite with Kiviat, "was as gaunt as a skeleton." Others in the field included the Irish Club's Jack Monument and a promising newcomer, Oscar Hedlund, the New England champion. As they raced through the backstretch on the first lap, they discovered large ridges on parts of the track. An exhausted Paull dropped out at the half-mile post. But this turned out to be a career day for Jack Monument, the short and balding middle-distance veteran of the Irish Club. He finally upset Kiviat in a sprint to the tape, although the time was a very slow 4:31. Kivie beat out Hedlund for second place in their first meeting at the mile. The two young men would shortly become fierce but friendly rivals in memorable competitions.

Favorites in other events also wilted in the heat. The NYAC led narrowly in the team score when the final event, the triple jump, was called. In a touching scene, twilight had enveloped the stadium, and the fans had emptied out of the stands onto the field, forming a kind of large phalanx around the Irish Club's Dan Ahearn and the NYAC's Platt Adams as the two great jumpers took their turns. Ahearn won as expected, with a leap of 48 feet ¼ inch, enabling the Irish Club to defeat its cross-town rival by a single point, forty-nine to forty-eight. The other clubs were left far behind. As quickly as the New Yorkers could, they headed for the Southern Railway station.[17]

All told, Kiviat had scored 76 points in the major championships, placing sixth on the team behind such Olympic stars as Sheppard and Sheridan. At year's end, the *New York Times* included two record-setting relay teams he had anchored—the 2,400-yard indoors in February and the two-mile outdoors in September—in its annual list of leading accomplishments in sports. Yet like all track prodigies starting out, he also lost close races while developing poise in competition against the best middle-distance runners in the world. In consultation with Coach Robertson, he was acquiring a shrewd sense of strategy and tactics that he would put to good use in the near future.[18]

YETTA, OCTOBER 1910

One evening in October 1910, Anne Kiviat was to play the piano at a dance, accompanied on the violin by her gregarious twelve-year-old brother Dave. Abel decided to go along. Perhaps a glimpse of New Orleans had impelled him toward some normal teenage fun. His proud siblings introduced their big brother, the champion, to the other young people. He spotted a girl standing by herself and was instantly smitten. Her petite frame and features and her black hair were striking. He thought she was "awful cute, a little short, about 5 foot tall." She had a good sense of humor and high intelligence.[19]

Her name was Yetta Schimansky. She was about to turn eighteen and was the oldest daughter of a prominent Staten Island Jewish family. The

Schimanskys had been one of the founders of the B'nai Jeshurun synagogue in 1884, and Yetta's father, Joseph, had a successful grocery store in the shorefront New Brighton neighborhood. She lived comfortably with her three sisters, her brother, Al, and their parents in the family home on Bement Avenue. She had "always wanted to be in a creative field," she wrote later, and she had already demonstrated her distinct flair in drawing and painting, and was studying at the pioneering and progressive New York School of Applied Design for Women.[20]

Abel asked if he could take her home, and she agreed. However, the inexperienced lad was not too subtle in his approach. "I walked her home taking a short cut up a hill that we used to go to the synagogue," he remembered. "We got to the top of the hill about eleven o'clock. And I put my arms around her. She says, 'What are you trying to do?' I said, 'I want to kiss you.' 'Why?' she said with her eyes popping. I said, 'I love you.'" His family must have been astonished at the lateness of his return home. Not only had he been too busy for a social life (Zelda, using the common vulgarism of the day, liked to say Abel was the responsible son who "wasn't a chippy chaser"), but he was ever mindful of Coach Robby's insistence on getting to bed early. Until now, the Kiviats could set their clock by his being at home by seven on nontrack nights. Without telling them what was going on, he began to court Yetta.[21]

BREAKTHROUGH, WINTER 1911

Kiviat began to prepare for the major cup races of the coming indoor season at his best distance, the mile. To stir the bubbling interest in the sport, the BAA introduced plans for a new invitation mile race at its annual indoor meet, which would be held on Saturday night, February 11, 1911. A wealthy BAA member named George L. Hunter offered a trophy worth three hundred dollars, which a college or club had to win three times for permanent ownership. Beyond creating a New England version of the Baxter Mile, Hunter's gift established the second jewel in the crown of the nation's emerging indoor track program.[22]

Kiviat looked forward to the trip. He later recalled, "I got along very fine with the Boston gang because we'd go out with them afterwards to drink a couple of beers. Or go over to their clubhouse" in the Back Bay area. The meet was held at the old Mechanics' Hall, an imposing red brick exposition center, now the site of the Prudential Center. The Mechanics' track was a challenge: fourteen laps to the mile, with short, sharply banked turns.[23]

The BAA meet had been sold out for weeks. Fan interest was at fever pitch when Kivie and teammate Jack Monument went to the starting line against a strong field, including the local favorite, twenty-two-year-old Oscar Hedlund of the Brookline Gymnasium. Two weeks earlier, Hedlund had set the track record for the mile in Mechanics' Hall with a 4:27.4. He was the man Kiviat had to watch.

Like Kiviat, Hedlund was small, standing only five feet five inches and weighing 128 pounds. A native of the Boston area, he had the blond-haired good looks of his Swedish ancestors. His immigrant parents worked on a Brookline estate, where they had raised Oscar and his twin sister. He had taken up competitive running for the Brookline Gymnasium Athletic Association in 1908 while attending a business college. He had immediate success at the 880, but by 1910 he had discovered the mile was his natural distance. Largely self-trained, he ran with a "short, snappy stride," high arm carriage, and a perfect sense of pace. His style reminded one track authority of Tommy Conneff, the great Irish American miler of the 1890s.[24]

With the gun, Kiviat sprinted into the early lead for three laps, then dropped back as others set the pace until the half-mile mark. Beginning in the rear, Oscar Hedlund had been moving through the pack and now took command, with Kivie coming back up on his shoulder. The two began to separate themselves from the rest of the field. After twelve and a half laps, Kivie suddenly sprinted past Oscar into the lead. It was a masterful move: he had the pole, forcing Hedlund "to run wide, which was a great disadvantage on the small track. In this manner, Kiviat leading and Hedlund glued to his shoulder, but unable to gain an inch, the men finished." The time was 4:29.6. The sportswriters called that respectable, given the track, but all agreed the first Hunter Mile was a terrific race. More important, the two young immigrants' sons gave promise of creating the first really exciting and sustained modern rivalry in the indoor mile event.[25]

The pair went at it again the following weekend at Madison Square Garden in the second annual Baxter Mile race, now sponsored by the NYAC, with Kivie again outkicking Hedlund to secure a second leg toward the permanent retirement of the Baxter trophy.[26] Indeed, as "Herbert," the *New York Tribune*'s sports columnist commented, by winning the Hunter and Baxter races on successive weekends, Kiviat had "set the seal" on his recognition as a great miler. But such achievement might ultimately exact a high price. "The boy, for he is still in his teens, has taken desperate chances with his future, however, and he would be well-advised at this time to take a long much-needed rest," Herbert wrote. "Constant training and exhaustive efforts are bound to work havoc with a growing youth, and it would be a pity for him to overdo it as Mel Sheppard did in making too many engagements." This advice was so sensible that Lawson Robertson got the message and did not let Kiviat compete again for six weeks. Herbert's warning would become a continuing refrain of thoughtful sportswriters covering the runner over the next five years.[27]

Kiviat returned to competition with a bang in April, winning armory races in world or meet record times on successive weekends. His 880 time at the Thirteenth Regiment's games (1:57.8) broke Mel Sheppard's indoor record for the distance, set in 1907. However, the absence of an established mechanism both for precise measurement of the diverse indoor tracks, especially those located outside of the more knowledgeable eastern cities, and for systematic record keeping made questionable the claims for indoor records in this era. Even as Kiviat's highly successful indoor campaign was ending, track officials were already "predicting great things for the Hunter and Baxter winner on the cinder path" during the outdoor season.[28]

ABEL'S IRISH POSE

The Irish Club was becoming the center of Kivie's life, a second family, providing the emotional attachment he did not always find at home. He inevitably experienced an intensification of the process of Americanization begun during his childhood on Staten Island, but in an unexpected way. He was influenced in forming his attitudes and values not only by his teammates and coach, but also by the club's governing leadership. In reaction, like other American Jews of his generation confronted head-on with seductive gentile cultures, he seemed at times ashamed of his heritage. Yet throughout this period, neither the world nor Zelda Kiviat ever let him forget who he was.

By now, a new generation of world-class athletes, Robby's boys, had succeeded to center stage, although veterans such as Sheppard, Bonhag, and Sheridan, now in his last season, remained to provide leadership. If anything, this talented crew was even more high-spirited than its predecessors.[29] The high jinks were nonstop at Celtic Park, especially by the "Irish Whales," Pat "Babe" McDonald, Matt McGrath, and Patrick Ryan. Like many huge and intimidating figures, these weight throwers were gentle and good-natured fellows who "never bullied smaller men." They developed a protective attitude about Kiviat, the handsome, reserved, and gritty "little Jewish boy" who went out of his way to be helpful to his teammates.[30]

The friendliest was shot-putter Babe McDonald. Standing six feet five inches and weighing more than 250 pounds, Babe had "arms and legs . . . like the boles of oak trees." The twenty-three-year-old son of a poor farmer in County Clare, Ireland, had arrived at Ellis Island in 1901 and within four years was appointed by Tammany Hall as a traffic policeman at the emerging "Crossroads of the World," Times Square. Thrust into the fascinating entertainment district, where elite institutions such as the new Times Tower (1905) and Oscar Hammerstein's lavish Victoria Theater (1899) were neighbors to rows of public brothels, he made his presence felt on the street between 4:00 P.M. and midnight. With his size, his brogue, and his cheerful demeanor, Babe was already a city landmark in 1911, "the favorite of dandies, stage folk and newsboys."[31]

At Celtic Park, Babe was the inheritor of Martin Sheridan's mantle of leadership—and of his gargantuan appetites for food and beer. He had taken up the shot put in 1907, and although he had won significant championships early in his career, only now, after years of hard training, was he coming into his own. He had surprisingly quick movements and fine form for such a big man.[32]

In 1911, Babe had gifted training partners in Paddy Ryan, a recent immigrant from County Limerick, and Matt McGrath, a Tipperary native and a decorated New York patrolman, whom Kiviat admired for his intelligence. McGrath represented the NYAC throughout his long track career;

7. Coach Lawson Robertson and four of his stars about to depart for a meet, ca. 1911–12: *(from left)* sprinter Dan Ferris (the future secretary of the AAU), Abel Kiviat, distance runner Willie Kramer, sprinter Jim Rosenberger, and Robertson. Courtesy of Marian Robertson.

however, he occasionally switched allegiance and competed for the Winged Fist. As competitive with each other as the three throwers were, they formed an inseparable fraternity, training together at Celtic Park and indulging at local pubs. One athlete reportedly "discovered them fortifying themselves behind the stands at the old Celtic Park with an elixir poured from a bottle labeled Irish whiskey."[33]

Other team leaders included the lanky captain and middle-distance man Frank Riley and the "Greyhound," Jimmy Rosenberger. A national sprint champion, Rosenberger was Kiviat's pal, but he was known in the track world as "a very temperamental sort of fellow, with a tendency to rouse to anger and lose his head over trifles."[34]

At age twenty-seven, Lawson Robertson had had two years of successful experience managing this collection of temperamental all-stars. His low-key, at times even sardonic personality masked his diplomatic skills and his managerial genius. "Robby fitted in among the wild Irishmen as gracefully and as naturally as if he'd been born in Dublin instead of Aberdeen," Arthur Daley observed in an obituary column.[35]

The conventional wisdom today among many track historians and officials is that later in Robertson's career, when he served as the head coach of four successive U.S. Olympic teams from 1924 to 1936, his refusal to allow his athletes to extend themselves in training set back the sport for a generation. They argue that he did not adopt modern approaches such as the formidable and more scientific training that would eventually make the Finns superpowers in distance running. Although the impact of Robertson's unprecedented Olympic tenure on the Depression generation is open to discussion, the revisionist critics' harsh judgment of him would have astonished Kiviat and his peers. They viewed Robertson as a keen student of track, who set an example of devotion and hard work for his charges. If anything, his one major fault was to allow his runners, especially Kiviat and the seasoned Mel Sheppard, who knew better, to exhaust themselves by competing too frequently. Yet it was Shep who best summed up Robby's impact in 1911: "All the boys, I know, would work harder under him than for anybody else. What else can you say about him? Look up the results and judge for yourself."[36]

Robertson's philosophy of moderate training and careful attention to diet and sleep was the mainstream philosophy then. In the final analysis, an athletic figure's accomplishments can be evaluated only according to the standards and conditions of his era. Robertson's contemporaries honored his talents in building the Irish Club into a great team through aggressive recruiting, brilliant management, and intelligent preparation of his athletes for championship competition. In some ways, Robby was the first modern track coach and thus belongs in the USA Track & Field Hall of Fame.[37]

Having created an atmosphere for championship training, Robby allowed his established stars maximum freedom to prepare themselves for competition while he attended to the newest recruits. The true measure of the veterans' respect was that they were quick to come to him for advice when they needed it.

This approach worked for Kiviat. In accord with his coach's belief in "conservation of strength," he trained no more than twice a week at this point. His training sessions seem rather quaint today:

> Some days I did sprints. Some days I did distance running. But if I were training for a mile, I'd run a mile and a half once or twice during the week. I went a steady pace, not the 100 percent mile race pace, but I'm figuring around a five minute, ten seconds speed for a workout mile. That's a little faster than a jog. For shorter distances, the half-mile or 600 yards, I'd do more sprints.

He often worked out by himself on Staten Island's Forest Avenue. In 1911, that main island thoroughfare "was all woods, broken down trees, before they built it up. And I used to run there between the trees and the woods, the soft ground. . . . Wasn't road running," Kiviat noted in disapproval of the modern practice. "I didn't jar my stupid brain or my spine or my rear end. Or ruin my feet."[38]

However, there was much more to the Irish Club than track practice and meets. In the process of establishing himself as an outstanding and popular Winged Fist athlete, Kiviat came face to face with a fundamental reality of New York life—Tammany Hall, the Democratic Party machine that ran New York City and dominated the Irish Club. Rooted in the working-class Irish community, the Tammany political organization had sponsored sporting activities for its constituency for decades. Although historian Steven A. Riess and others have emphasized the central role of Tammany politicians in the development of professional sports for a mass audience rather than amateur athletics for WASP elites, the Irish Club experience suggests how the machine also influenced the growth of modern track and field. Just as Tammany shared its clout, patronage, and insiders' knowledge about property values and projected developments in mass transit with early-twentieth-century boxing, horse racing, and baseball promoters, enabling them to flourish, it provided similar assistance in the rise of the Irish Club's track team. Patronage jobs, for example, were powerful tools in the recruitment and retention of talented athletes; hurdlers and weight throwers became policemen, firemen, and sanitation workers.

Irish Club political clout benefitted the athletes in other ways, as illustrated by something that happened to hammer thrower Paddy Ryan. Needing to blow off steam one Saturday night after working in construction, Ryan demonstrated his capacity for throwing six policemen around. Lawson Robertson liked to tell about how he went straight to the magistrate and then saw his protégé in jail. "Now it's all fixed for you," he told Paddy. "Just take it easy."

The compliant magistrate acted as the voice of official rectitude, of course, first lecturing Ryan, then asking him: "And now, young man, are you sorry? What have you got to say for yourself?"

"You can go plumb to hell," Ryan shouted at him. "This case is all fixed."

Paddy spent that night behind bars and next morning muttered at Robby: "And sure it's a helluva club that can't even keep its members out of jail!"[39]

Tammany's support also was a factor in the increasing popularity of track with a wide urban audience before World War I. The presence of machine politicians at Celtic Park or Madison Square Garden meets, for example, was frequently noted in the press.[40]

Many of the Irish Club's officers, members of the board of directors, and standing committees were Tammany sachems and loyalists. One such individual was Daniel F. Cohalan, chief adviser to Democratic boss Charles F. Murphy and the power on the club's Finance Committee. Cohalan was just then vying for the state supreme court; fittingly, when the newly appointed judge took his seat in June, Irish Club president Pat Conway and vice president Michael Cosgrove were there to present him with "a beautiful silver mounted gavel." During his career on the bench, Judge Cohalan would develop a viewpoint about the peopling of the great metropolis that balanced his devotion to Irish nationalism with a cosmopolitan appreciation of "each of the great races, that in turn have poured their blood and brain into our great melting pot." Among them were the Jews, who contributed their "inherited tendency for commerce" and a "broad humanitarianism." He hoped the "new type" of American emerging from the crucible would have a brotherly spirit and a sense of common humanity. Therefore, he urged New Yorkers to reject those Americanizers who "set out to make this land into an Anglo-Saxon country, servile imitator of England and things English."

Judge Cohalan's theory, however derivative and superficial, reflected a hard political reality that Mr. Murphy had understood for years: Tammany needed more than Irish and Roman Catholic voters to stay in power. The genius of the machine was to build a winning coalition with the Jewish community. It was this model of assimilation—a democratic social process in which the Irish were somehow first among equals—that the club offered Kiviat and other non-Irish lads.[41]

The theory was widely shared among other Irish Club leaders from Tammany—men of the stature of state senator James J. Frawley, Judge Victor J. Dowling, and Manhattan borough president John Cloughen, chair of the athletic committee. No track club in American history has had a more colorful governing body. For the most part, they were native New Yorkers, the acculturated children of immigrants who owed their success to the political machine. Like Judge Cohalan, their involvement in the Winged Fist was an expression of their Irish nationalism, their pride in the role of athletic prowess in Irish culture, and their belief in achieving equality of opportunity through sport.[42]

Kiviat was no Israel Zangwill. He may never have heard of the writer or his popular play *The Melting Pot* (1908), and he was not one to speculate about the larger meaning of his Americanization. He loved the Irish Club for its athletic opportunities and its fellowship, and he took it on its own terms. Kiviat's Jewishness seemed to make no difference to his teammates. In one sense, this was surprising: anti-Semitic attitudes and behaviors were common among the New York Irish early in the century, rooted in the historic Christian teaching of contempt for Jews and evoked by competition with them for jobs and turf. "The Russian Hebrew seems too greedy and too clamorous for one who claims to have suffered as much as he says he has," the *Irish-American* editorialized. "Americans thrown into close contact with him often come to the conclusion that he has not suffered more than he deserved. Some go as far as to say that the other fellow had a good deal to put up with." The Kiviat children had heard far worse statements during their own struggles with anti-Semitic youth on Staten Island, but Abel had grown up making friends with Irish kids. Indeed, his best neighborhood buddy was still Tommy Lennon.

The two groups' common experiences eased his way. Both the Irish and the Jews had recent histories of economic struggle, and both had been victims of political oppression in Europe and blatant discrimination in New York. They shared an aversion, for example, to WASP urban reformers' campaign against Sunday sin. The Irish believed it was a war against a poor man's recreation, including outings at Celtic Park. To Jews who were Sabbath observers and worked instead on Sundays, the so-called blue laws were an attack against their meager livelihoods. Kiviat matured with his encounters, becoming comfortable with "goyem," or non-Jews, as adult companions. Celtic Park was his night school—giving him an appreciation for the Irish people's rich use of language and tales, and lessons about how local government really worked. Each March he participated with the Irish Club's delegations in their "National Celebration"—the great St. Patrick Day parades up Fifth Avenue. "They gave us white pants, a white jacket, and a little white cap with a green wing fist," he recalled. "We looked like the street cleaners all dressed in white." The result of all this was a deepening of the assimilation process he had begun in childhood, even while its direction turned slightly. Given the firm social distinctions drawn between the club's dues-paying members and the athletes, his melting pot was a lower-middle-class world of clerks, policemen, and government functionaries, Irish American style.[43]

The club never established the elitist policies of the rival NYAC—in part because it could not. President P. J. Conway was not "supported as he should be," complained the *Irish-American*. "The wealthy Irish of this city. . . . contribute little to the upkeep of this unrivalled institute of physical culture." Yet the Irish Club headquarters at 165 East Sixtieth Street provided Kiviat's introduction to a more middle-class lifestyle, and it therefore left an indelible impression. The three-story brownstone, across the street from today's Bloomingdale's, had a bar on every floor, a dining hall, and a ballroom. Kiviat and his teammates went there only for award ceremonies or other special events. Because the club had virtually doubled its membership in 1910–11 and had outgrown this clubhouse, it opened a new and grander headquarters at 110 East Fifty-ninth Street with a series of boxing exhibitions for more than five hundred members of the sporting fraternity. In one match, the fierce middleweight Stanley Ketchel, the Michigan Assassin, fought one of his last bouts before he was fatally shot by an enraged cuckold. The club also held fancy balls at the Lexington Avenue Opera House.[44]

At eighteen, Kiviat was unsophisticated politically and, by all accounts, would remain that way. The Tammanyites were interested in him as a great athlete who might connect to the Yiddish-speaking masses. The politicos could not then have seen in the quiet and pleasant young man the more engaging and voluble public personality of later years. Indeed, prominent machine officials would encourage him to run for the state legislature in the 1930s. The ties he formed with Tammany early in his life would literally save him during the Great Depression, securing for him a position with the federal courts and a pension.[45]

"THE HEBREW RUNNER," SUMMER 1911

The Kiviats were all too familiar with Jewish-Irish tensions in New York. Zelda, who was active with the Ladies' Auxiliary of the Rabbi Jacob Joseph Yeshiva on the Lower East Side, had only to recall the riotous behavior by Irish workers and subsequent police brutality during the funeral procession for the beloved rabbi in 1902. Nevertheless, she and Morris went along with their son's membership in the Irish Club. His increasing fame eased their fears, Kiviat felt, especially when their Stapleton neighbors came over "all pop-eyed." Making the Irish Club even more acceptable were the stories that began to appear in the Yiddish newspapers. His brother Harold recalled that "Father got a little publicity out of it. Oh, 'he's the father of Abel, that's Mr. Kiviat, Morris Kiviat.'" But "Mom took it in her stride. 'So what, I still gotta cook,'" she said, bemused, in her Yiddish accent.

His success meant more to his younger siblings, who still faced anti-Semitic taunting on the island. As Abel's star rose with the Irish Club, the harassment subsided, Harold stated emphatically. Harold also expressed admiration that Abel, who "lived in tougher times than the younger brothers . . . prepared the way" for them by working in the gentile world and helping to support the family financially. In that sense, Abel opened his brothers' eyes—and those of thousands of other young Jewish boys from eastern European families—to the worldly possibilities resulting from athletic excellence. Consider thirteen-year-old Sam Friedland, who "came from Russia where a Jew was reviled, abused, spat on, beaten and occasionally murdered by the czarist Russians." He wrote years afterward:

> Here in America around 1910 things were better but not much. This was still pre–Bennie Leonard Nat Holman and Bennie Friedman days of Jewish athletic pride.
>
> Baseball was Irish and German the McGraw and Wagner days.
>
> Football was the Yales versus the Harvards.
>
> Boxing was Sullivans Corbett's and Fitzsimmons.
>
> Then out of the complete void of Jewish athletics the name Abel Kiviat started to show up regularly on the sport pages. . . .
>
> We Jewish kids, who could read, started to walk a little straighter, we had a hero, a Jew who could beat Goyim.

Sam Friedland went on to make a fortune in the supermarket business, but he remained grateful to Kiviat for lessons not normally taught by a boy's parents or religious instructors.[46]

The lessons were rich and came at regular intervals during the summer of 1911. After the early spring lull, Kiviat and his teammates began preparing seriously for the full outdoor schedule. Robertson already had the team pointing to the national AAU meet, which would take place much earlier than in past years—on July 1 in Pittsburgh. Meanwhile, the newspapers were full of stories about the collegiate athletes' spectacular efforts. At the Intercollegiate Association of Amateur Athletes of America (IC4A) outdoor championships at Harvard Stadium, John Paul Jones, a Cornell sophomore, took the measure of Billy Paull (who was completing his dental course at Penn as well as his track career), going 4:15.4 to break Tommy Conneff's unofficial amateur record by 0.2 seconds. To the meet referee, James Sullivan, it seemed clear that Walter George's professional record of 1886 (4:12.75) was well within Jones's capacity. The track writers called for a matched race with Kiviat.[47]

First, Kivie faced the challenge of the AAU nationals. He found almost everything to be at a different level for this meet at Forbes Field, home of the Pirates. Donated for the meet by team owner Barney Dreyfuss, the concrete and steel stadium, finished in gray terra cotta, also made a statement about the city's commitment to architecture designed for beauty and comfort. It had a roofed three-tiered grandstand, with a row of luxury boxes on the third deck. There were modern runways and elevators, telephones, and even attendants in the ladies' rooms.[48]

The track was another matter. Coach Mike Murphy of Penn supervised construction of a quarter-mile cinder track on the ball field. When the track makers were done spreading and rolling the cinders, Mel Sheppard wrote, they "prayed for a nice hot sun." Ever the master of hype and spin, the AAU's James Sullivan announced that "the track is perfect." The runners quickly found it otherwise when they dug in their spikes.[49]

More than twenty-five thousand spectators packed the place on Saturday afternoon to watch hundreds of athletes representing thirty-seven athletic clubs from thirty-two cities nationwide. There had never before been a crowd remotely close to this size for the national championships. This high attendance was due in part to cosponsorship by the *Pittsburg Press,* which promoted the meet vigorously. When the gates opened, excited society women and debutantes elbowed businessmen and working-class fans for seats on a "first come, first served" basis. The athletes and officials lined up at the flagpole in deep center field, a band played the "Star Spangled Banner," and then the entire group marched under a broiling sun to the grandstand near home plate. As the band played additional patriotic tunes, Pennsylvania's governor John K. Tener stood, hat in hand, and the crowd followed, leading one observer to note that it felt like the bottom of the ninth of a Pirates-Cubs thriller.[50]

The mile run was a triumph for Kiviat. His principal competitors were Oscar Hedlund and Arthur F. Baker of the Cleveland Athletic Club. Kivie went out fast and stayed in front for the first lap. He let Hedlund pass him and take the field through laps two and three. But he began to move soon after the start of the gun lap, taking over the lead and running away from Oscar "with a wonderful burst of speed at the finish." Kivie beat Oscar to the tape by twenty-five yards in 4:19.6, lowering by 3.2 seconds the old meet record set in 1906. He received a deserved ovation from the grandstands. In the glare of the biggest AAU meet yet, he broke 4:20 and won his first national title on the home field of his boyhood hero Honus Wagner. Even the tough and knowledgeable Boston writers, partisans of Hedlund, conceded that "his wonderful performance," marked by his speed and his "exceptional judgement," propelled him into "a class with the fastest in the world." He had turned nineteen only the week earlier.[51]

Lawson Robertson's men excelled all afternoon on the track and in the field and won the team trophy, fifty-eight points to twenty-eight for the NYAC, which finished second. The dominant New Yorkers scored nearly double the points of all the other big city clubs combined.[52]

From wherever the sport's leaders came to Pittsburgh, they knew that American track and field had entered a new stage of its history. AAU president Everett C. Brown of Chicago told a newspaperman "that he had never witnessed such a meet for good sport, large crowds and enthusiasm." Jim Sullivan was more emphatic, telling a reporter he felt "like the Yankee when he saw the Colorado canyon for the first time. All he could say was 'Gosh!'" For once, the hype was justified, given the attendance figures and the level of performance. Some even savored thoughts about just what Kiviat and John Paul Jones would do to the middle-distance runners of the world at the following summer's Olympic Games in Stockholm.[53]

The Irish community read a more personal meaning into the meet results. "The Irish-American Athletic Club is surely the greatest aggregation of star performers the world has ever seen," began the weekly editorial of *The Irish-American*—greater than the athletes of the classical age, who "have been commemorated in bronze and marble"; greater than the wealthy NYAC, which "has had to lower its colors to the Irish-American on many a well-fought field." Naming the Irish Club's top stars, including Kiviat, the editor underscored that the club was "an organization to be proud of." Abel Kiviat's pose was complete: for his part in strengthening Irish identity and recognition in American life, he gained acceptance as an integral part of the Irish team. Over the long haul, however, this acceptance would prove to be chimerical. He was simply too strongly identified as a Jew.[54]

Kiviat unwisely went directly from Pittsburgh to Boston to race Oscar Hedlund again. The potential cost to his career was not a pressing concern for a vigorous nineteen-year-old athlete. More worrisome, his coach let him go.[55] He became debilitated. In spite of his poor condition, Coach

Robertson entered him in a mile race against the world record holder, John Paul Jones of Cornell, in late July. This competition was Kiviat's most appealing to date, a classic confrontation between two attractive young champions—one representing the wealth and power of the Ivy League establishment, the other the huddled masses of Gotham. The sports pages played up the story, subtly contrasting Jones's graceful style with Kiviat's more plebeian one.[56]

The race was to take place at Washington Park in Brooklyn, home of baseball's Dodgers, as the feature attraction of the St. Agnes Athletic Club meet. Public interest was high. When rumors began to circulate in the press that the meet sponsor was guilty of falsely advertising Kiviat's appearance, the rector of St. Agnes's Church "denounced the attack on the club officials from his pulpit," and there was talk of legal action against the accusers. It was a tempest in a teapot, as Kivie prepared for the race at Celtic Park while Jones kept training at his home in Washington, D.C.[57]

The handsome, dark-haired, twenty-year-old Jones stood five feet nine and a half inches, weighed a slim 141 pounds, and was as natural a talent as American track had yet seen. He had a beautiful and economical running style, a sprinter's speed, and the strength and guts of a distance man. Training with Cornell's outstanding coach of distance runners, Jack Moakley, entailed a severer regimen than Kiviat experienced under Robby. As Jones recalled, "we worked out about three hours a day and usually twice on Sunday." He also did "100 push-ups every night." Jones had set the mile record while only a sophomore. Coach Moakley believed Jones was capable of breaking "every record on the books, from the half-mile up to two miles." But the classic one-mile distance was his best event.[58]

Jones was track's answer to the charisma of baseball's Christy Mathewson. He was an all-American "good fellow," as admired by track stars as he was by his Cornell classmates. People appreciated his modest and pleasant manner, and especially his spunk. While he was preparing for Cornell at the elite Phillips Exeter Academy, his circumstances changed with the early death of his alcoholic father, a prominent Washington real estate lawyer, and he had to work his way through college. Jones still made good grades in the difficult mechanical engineering course and was a leader in campus social life. He was also a dangerous runner, and Kiviat knew he faced his most important challenge.[59]

The setting at Washington Park was in stark Victorian contrast to that of the national championships at Forbes Field. Located in the Red Hook section of Brooklyn, it was a wooden stadium with seating for sixteen thousand, but many fans chose to watch Charles Ebbets's Dodgers or other sporting events free of charge from the rooftops of the surrounding tenements. For the thirty-five hundred paying customers that afternoon, there was no escaping the odors from the nearby Gowanus Canal and the factories or the dark smoke suspended in the air. The "rough" and "uneven" track of 352 yards, or five laps to the mile, was laid out on the ball field grass.[60]

Fearing Jones's closing sprint, Kiviat planned to burn him out with an unexpectedly fast pace. Jones started on the pole, Kiviat lined up next, with Jones's Cornell teammates L. C. Conner and Edward Hunger on Kiviat's right and Jack Monument on the outside. All except Jones, who ran unattached, were representing the Irish Club. Kivie went off flying, and was twenty-five yards ahead of the tightly bunched pack after one lap. He accelerated on lap two, adding ten more yards to his lead. His estimated time for the first quarter, 53 flat, was unheard of for milers then. Jack Monument had moved into second place on this lap, with Jones and the others following. On lap three, Kiviat continued to lead by a full thirty yards. He passed the half-mile under 2:10; Jones's time was 2:14. When the second pack reached the final straight on the fourth circuit, Jones began to lengthen his stride and closed the gap with Kivie. Jones's time at the three-quarters mark was 3:25. Kiviat was clearly tiring. At the crack of the gun for the final lap, Jones drew even with Kivie. "As he flashed past me on his famous finishing spurt I opened my mouth, stopped short and just stared at Jones," Kiviat later recalled. "Never have I seen such superb form—such a rhythmic blend of legs and arms and body— such a free, unhampered stride. Say what you will, Jones is my idea of the greatest of all milers."

Jones won going away in 4:28.8 on the slow grass track. Beaten but unbowed, Kivie finished twenty yards back.[61]

The Ivy Leaguer's performance made quite an impression on blasé New Yorkers, including the Irish American community. Kiviat was more realistic about the experience, and he began "planning with his coach and adviser, Lawson Robertson, how he can get back at the fellow who trimmed him." His chance would come later on the biggest stage of his life. In retrospect, however, what is most revealing about this event—other than Kiviat's courage in competing when he was clearly not at his best—is the disrespectful way he was portrayed by the media in contrast to Jones. One reporter referred to Kivie as a "wild hare" in describing his early pace setting; another, who knew that Kiviat was not at full strength, called him "a selling plater," a derogatory term borrowed from horseracing. Although the reporters did not use blatantly stereotypical language about Jews and WASPs, especially because they liked the affable Kiviat, their constant contrasts between the runners suggest they were responding as much to cultural difference as to Jones's patent talent and achievement.[62]

That difference was then firmly fixed in sports fans' minds by a set of handsomely colored trading cards of 150 champions distributed by the Mecca Cigarette Company of New York. Kiviat's trading card called him "the Hebrew runner." It summarized a few of his achievements until 1911 (although the text had several errors and omitted important accomplishments), and it pictured him, round-faced and boyish, in his Wanamaker track team uniform. Although designed to put Mecca ahead of the competition in the burgeoning market for young Jewish smokers, the card also underscored how the contemporary worlds of media and advertising routinely and casually labeled individuals of so-called non-Aryan "races."[63]

Having a Jewish companion in his locker room was an unexpected source of support for Kiviat. Alvah Meyer joined the Irish Club that spring. The two young men shared a common faith, but their social origins and experiences were markedly different. If not quite up to the wealth of "our crowd," as the close-knit network of elite German Jewish families that led New York's Jewish community called themselves, the Meyer family ran a close second. Twenty-two-year-old Alvah had roots deep in American soil. Both his parents were American born, as were his paternal grandparents, children of immigrants from the Germanic states who landed in New York and Louisiana in the early nineteenth century. Albert A. Meyer was a successful stockbroker, and

KIVIAT, the Hebrew runner, was born on Staten Island, New York, in July, 1892. He attracted attention as a runner when attending high school, and became so fast that he linked his fortunes with the Irish-American Athletic Club in New York and went into training in 1908. The following month, at Travers Island, he won the Junior Championship for one mile for the Metropolitan District, making the fast time of 4:24. In the same year he won the Baxter cup in the Columbia University races at Madison Square Garden, making the fast time of 4:23 2-5. He broke the world's record in the 2,400-yard relay race, his time for his 600 yards being 1:16, and 5:4 for the entire distance. He also won the Canadian mile championship in 1909 and again in 1910.

MECCA CIGARETTES
SERIES OF
CHAMPION ATHLETES
FACTORY N° 649 1ST DIST N.Y.

8. "The Hebrew runner," Mecca Cigarettes sports card, 1911. Courtesy of Esther Kiviat.

Alvah, his oldest child, grew up in a comfortable home on New York's Upper West Side staffed by servants. The Meyer family's culture was a configuration of at least three significant components: the influence of Wall Street, Reform temple, and a circle of wealthy and educated friends. In high school, Alvah first demonstrated his exceptional sprinting ability, but he opted to skip college for a clerkship in his father's brokerage. Six years later, in the spring of 1911, he realized time was running out to find out how good a sprinter he could be. His affluent lifestyle should have made the NYAC the natural place to pursue his quest, but its entrenched anti-Semitic policy obviated that choice. Instead, he sought out Lawson Robertson and, in a scenario strikingly similar to Kiviat's beginnings with the Irish Club, "asked the coach to give him a chance." When he defeated hurdler Jack Eller in a sprint time trial at Celtic Park, a stunned Robby added him to his roster.

Without any prior big-meet experience, the former schoolboy star exploded from his sprinter's crouch into prominence during the summer. Robby entered him in the 100-yard dash at the Junior Nationals in Pittsburgh on July 1, and he took the silver medal, narrowly losing to the brilliant young African American sprinter Howard Drew of Massachusetts. Standing five feet eight inches, Meyer was dark-haired, muscular at 143 pounds, and "dressed like a dude. We always joshed him about being dressed up," Kiviat said. "His clothes were always good quality." The apprentice stockbroker had an aura of success about him that stopped the humor from getting nasty. Kiviat identified with him.[64]

Kiviat kept running his way into better shape, pointing to the series of championship meets in September.[65] He had an easy victory in the mile run of the Senior Mets at Celtic Park, and the mercurial press promptly dubbed him "the champ." A week later in Montreal, he took the Canadian title from Oscar Hedlund, now representing the BAA, and Jack Tait, Toronto's veteran miler.[66] That race concluded Kiviat's successful 1911 season. He had won the grand slam of mile championships—the U.S. nationals, the Senior Mets, and the Canadian nationals—and had set a notable meet record at Pittsburgh in oppressive heat. He had met and defeated the country's leading milers, but had lost badly and erratically to the most gifted, John Paul Jones, when he was not in good condition. Yet when the *Times* published a feature story on track's record-setting superstars of 1911, Jones drew raves, and Kiviat was not mentioned. The son of Exeter and Washington society had earned his recognition, but the son of New York's eastern European "Hebrew race" surely deserved the newspaper's plaudits as well.

Nevertheless, Kiviat had much in which to take pride. Still a teenager at the conclusion of his first two full years with the Irish Club, he had matured as a runner in ways that the timers' stopwatches did not fully reveal. Although he competed more often than was good for him, he was now a far more consistent and confident miler. Inherently savvy and tough-minded, he had grown through experience into a master of the event. In addition, the freewheeling fellowship of the Irish Club deepened his personal development. His participation helped him to begin to fashion an adult identity out of his Staten Island experiences, the inherited culture he brought with him to Celtic Park, and the way of life he confronted there.

Kiviat's advanced course in Americanization was a factor in preparing him for greater challenge and opportunity. As he was putting away his spiked shoes for the season, the attention of the athletic world began to turn in earnest toward Stockholm and the upcoming Olympic Games.[67]

5

Olympic Trials

"WHAT WAS THE MOST IMPORTANT YEAR in the history of track and field?" Hal Bateman, the former information officer of USA Track & Field, the national governing body, once asked me. "1912," was his immediate answer to his own question. Bateman had a point: the year was a watershed in athletics, and during it Abel Kiviat was a lead actor in the transformation of his sport.

There is substantial evidence to support this argument. The Stockholm Olympics placed the games on a firm foundation for the future. At its conclusion, delegates from seventeen participating countries established the IAAF, the sport's international federation. Out of this meeting came a consensus that track and field needed to standardize its program of competitions, technical equipment, and world records. Throughout the year, the world's athletes recorded many marks of exceptionally high quality and consequence.

American athletes and officials were at the heart of this renaissance, with Kiviat's achievements at or near the top of the list. One need look no further than the results of the Eastern Olympic Trials at Harvard Stadium on June 8, 1912, to appreciate that the Americanization of track was nearly complete. Inevitably, the process of battling for places on the Olympic team and then representing the nation in spirited international competition strengthened these athletes' American identity. For members of minorities, such as Kiviat or Pat McDonald, the Olympic experience went far to enhance their own Americanization through track and field. Moreover, their success confirmed their standing as popular role models for their ethnic and religious groups.[1]

THE INVINCIBLES, WINTER 1911–1912

The Olympic year actually began on the night after Christmas 1911 with the national indoor championships at Madison Square Garden. For this first of two sessions, Kiviat demonstrated to the enthusiastic crowd the extent of his maturation in the 1,000-yard competition. Carl Walther of the NYAC led from the gun for 220 yards, but Kivie took over and "made his field look like so many novices." He beat Walther by 35 yards in 2:16.2, breaking Mel Sheppard's five-year-old indoor record by 1.6 seconds.[2]

The following night, Kiviat confirmed that he had become a master of indoor running. He was totally in control as he captured the 600-yard event. Ollie De Grouchy of the NYAC, an old New York high school rival, led another field of solid journeymen around the first two and a half circuits of the Garden floor "on sufferance," the *New York Times* reported. When Kivie "got ready to move he literally ran over his man, and, striding strongly, opened up a big gap on the back stretch of the last lap, finally coming home full of running in 1:14." His time tied the indoor record already shared by the late Dr. John Taylor of Penn, Mel Sheppard, and Harry Gissing.

Kiviat had accomplished more than winning a 600/1,000 "double" at the nationals, done only by Harry Gissing in 1910. Taken together with the 880-yard mark he had made the previous April at the Thirteenth Regiment Armory, the teenage miler now either held alone or shared the world's indoor records for the 600-, the 880-, and the 1,000-yard events. His teammate, Alvah Meyer, swept the 60-, 75-, and 150-yard dashes from an all-star lineup. Meyer was, the *Times* commented, "the best sprinter seen hereabouts" this year. Over the two nights, the Irish Americans' Jewish duo won five national titles by themselves. The final point score for the meet: Irish Club, sixty-six; NYAC, fifty, with other teams left far behind.[3]

During the East's coldest January since the 1860s, thoughts of the upcoming summer Olympics filled the sports pages. In anticipation of Stockholm, Coach Robertson (who believed strongly in sprint and relay work for distance men) had Kiviat use the time to sharpen his speed. Almost all of his early winter races were on short-distance relays. Contrary to Kiviat's later self-effacing remark that he was an occasional fill in on the mile relay, Robby selected him to be a part of his powerhouse quartet, the so-called "Invincibles" or "bullet four": Sheppard, Gissing, Rosenberger, and Kiviat.[4]

The heart of Kiviat's indoor season occurred in mid-February, with his defense of his 1911 victories in the Hunter and Baxter Mile races. In the days leading up to the BAA meet in Boston's Mechanics' Hall on February 10, there was much speculation about the duel between Kiviat and the host's star, Oscar Hedlund, in the Hunter. Hedlund almost did not make it. On Monday, February 5, as he was running a time trial on the little track in MIT's strangely contoured gym in downtown Boston, a sprinter suddenly appeared out of nowhere and collided with him. Oscar picked himself up and finished his mile, but the next day he "was bruised and sore stiff." By Friday, his new coach, the BAA's Jack Ryder, and Hedlund "decided that I had better not run in the Hunter Mile. So I put the race completely out of my mind," he said. At the last moment, he was overcome with temptation. He took a cab to Mechanics' Hall on Saturday evening, arrived thirty minutes before the Hunter race, dressed, and warmed up. "Ryder asked me how I felt," Hedlund recalled, "and I told him pretty good. 'Well,' he said, 'why don't you go ahead and run? If you fail to make a race of it everybody'll understand.'" In retrospect, he realized enforced idleness without worry about the competition had relaxed him—and probably made the difference in his performance. He ended up running "the race of his life."[5]

This was the first time Kiviat encountered two young men who would be significant actors in his career. Dwarfing Abel and Oscar at six feet two inches was Tell Berna of Cornell; also at the line was Norman Taber, a still unsung twenty-year-old junior at Brown University who was returning to competition after a year's absence. Kiviat's strategy was to lie back and let Berna lead the field for the first two and a half of fourteen laps. Then Oscar took command, with Kivie on his shoulder. The strategy was a mistake, but considering his lack of distance work, he had no alternative. When Kivie attempted to pass Hedlund at the three-quarters mark on lap eleven, the BAA runner picked up the pace and fought off Kivie's challenges. Robbed of his kick and thoroughly beaten, Kivie eased up and finished about thirty yards back, with Taber and Berna trailing him.

Given the notoriously poor track, Hedlund's time of 4:23.6—a new Mechanics' Hall record—was excellent. Some judged it at least "as good as 4:18 on a fast outdoor track." When the official result of the race was announced, the sponsor, George Hunter, was delighted. It was a short-lived sensation because Hedlund would never again defeat Kiviat in the Hunter or in any other significant race.[6]

Kiviat was too confident of his ability to accept such a defeat easily. He and Robby wasted little time in planning a response to Hedlund. Their first opportunity would be the following Saturday in the prestigious Baxter Mile. In preparation, Kiviat ran a fast three-quarter mile at the Forty-seventh Regiment Armory and a good two miles two nights later.[7]

The hoopla in the papers all that week, reminding everyone this was an Olympic year, whipped up spectator interest. On Saturday night, an unexpectedly large crowd of ten thousand jammed Broadway and Sixty-eighth Street in front of the Twenty-second Regiment Armory, proving a problem for an inadequate police detail and delaying the start of the meet for an hour. When Hugh Baxter, the middle-aged donor of the Baxter Cup, realized he might not make it through the crush into the building, he followed the example of the Cornell and Dartmouth relay teams and climbed up on the roof and through a skylight.

Once again Hedlund used the same relaxed approach that had worked the previous week. He stayed at the office of his insurance business in Boston until noon and took the one o'clock train to New York, arriving in time to warm up for his race with Kiviat. The atmosphere in the armory was electric, presaging better-known, but no more engaging Cunningham-Venzke-Bonthron, Wilt-Gehrmann, and Coghlan-Scott mile rivalries later in the century. For the second straight week, Kiviat, starting in the outside lane, let Hedlund set the early pace, but the Bostonian, loping along in his beautifully economical style, made the fatal mistake of taking it out too slow. After Hedlund passed the 880 mark in 2:12, Kivie jumped into the lead in accord with his plan. His tactic of speeding and then "'slowing up' continually" worked perfectly. Although the pair began the gun lap neck and neck, Kivie had taken away Hedlund's extra reserve. They sprinted together toward the tape, but "at the final, crucial moment Kiviat threw himself ahead and crossed the tape nearly two feet in the lead." In the excitement, "hundreds of excited spectators rushed to the track, surrounded the course, and for a few moments the result was in doubt." When the announcer proclaimed

Kiviat's victory, a huge roar went up from the crowd. His time of 4:22.2 on an armory floor was impressive. For the third Baxter in a row, Kiviat ruled New York—or nearly ruled it. Incredibly, given the advance billing for the Baxter race, the Sunday *Times* headlined "John Paul Jones Wins for Cornell" on the anchor leg of the collegiate two-mile relay event, thus diminishing Kiviat's achievement.[8]

About this time, Kiviat made another well-planned change. He accepted an offer from the downtown firm of Dieges & Clust, the nation's leading maker of medals. The firm made sure the newspapers noted that their new salesman was the national mile champion. The position turned into a kind of brief apprenticeship for his post-Olympic career in the jewelry business. He would stay with Dieges & Clust for only about eight weeks before taking what amounted to an extended leave of absence for the Olympics.[9]

Meanwhile, with his new firm's encouragement, he finished his indoor season. On the Thursday night following the Baxter, Washington's Birthday, Kiviat was upstate in Troy to run the mile relay with his fellow "Invincibles" in a special match race against the NYAC and the BAA. Never did an athletic team have a less appropriate nickname than did the Irish Club relay team that night. In time, Kiviat and his family would look back on the event with profound regret.

The meet sponsors had disappointments from the outset. They anticipated a much larger attendance at the state armory on this still lively industrial city's riverfront, and Lawson Robertson's Irish Club stars chose to run only in the relay. They should have stayed home. After Jimmy Rosenberger and Kivie led on the first two legs, Bill Prout of the BAA overtook Mel Sheppard on the third, and Donnell Young, Boston's reigning IC4A quarter-mile champion, ran away from Harry Gissing, who faded to third place behind the NYAC's anchorman.[10]

The night belonged to Oscar Hedlund. He came over from Boston and destroyed a big field in a handicap one-mile race. Running on a small armory floor, Oscar tied the world indoor record of 4:19.8 set by Olympian Herbert Trube at Madison Square Garden three years earlier. When Roscoe Campbell, the AAU official in Troy, remeasured the armory track, it turned out to be twelve yards more than a mile. Although Hedlund never received proper credit for his fastest mile ever, his time should have been at least 4:18—more likely closer to 4:17, as some Bostonians claimed.[11]

If, in later years, Hedlund resented Roscoe Campbell's ineptitude, his feelings were not comparable to Kiviat's. In 1915, Campbell would resurface with the charge that the four "Invincibles" were paid $125 under the table to run in the relay race that night. He would claim to have letters verifying his allegation. As we shall see, in spite of Kiviat's denials, this accusation would essentially end his career.[12]

Kiviat ran only one race, a regimental mile relay, in March. In retrospect, the winter's work had been valuable. He had responded well to Robby's training strategy, "running the shorter distances remarkably fast for a miler," Howard Valentine noted in the *New York Globe*. On several occasions he ran his 440 legs in fifty-one seconds. He was ready for the spring of his life.[13]

TRAINING WITH JIM THORPE, SPRING 1912

While Kiviat rested in early April, American Olympic Committee officials, finally acceding to the wishes of many athletes, leaked word to the press that Lawson Robertson was its choice for assistant coach of the U.S. track team. Head Coach Mike Murphy of Penn had been seriously ill during the past year, and Robby's services were badly needed. Within a week, Robby was at Celtic Park making "arrangements for the strenuous campaign which will be necessary to fit the members of the Winged Fist for the tryouts for the Olympic Games" in early June. On Thursday, April 25, Kiviat and twenty-one of his teammates went out to the Queens field to begin their spring workouts with Robby. They included Mel Sheppard, sprinters Alvah Meyer and Jim Rosenberger, and distance runners John J. Daly and Mike Ryan, the latter having won the Boston Marathon only a few days earlier.[14]

Kiviat left his job at Dieges & Clust and moved into the Pavilion at Celtic Park. He lived in a dormitory room off the upstairs balcony. It was one of the few times in his career he was able to put everything else aside and concentrate on sustained training for the mile distance. The results would soon speak for themselves. Although separated for an interval of months from his family and his girlfriend, Yetta Schimansky, he enjoyed his teammates' company. He would "wake them up in the morning, Sunday, to go to church with a big, big pot of black coffee," he recalled later. Particularly welcome were the "big training tables with big hunks of rare roast beef, and each of us got a small pitcher of milk. When you ran out of milk, they'd give you another pitcher. It was real good. All you could drink, three or four quarts of milk. And we got plenty of green vegetables on the table, big platters full of them. And lots of meat. At breakfast you could have as many eggs as you wanted with all the toast you could eat and plenty of buttermilk. Nothing fried and no coffee except in the morning for the older guys."[15]

He took it easy at first, with "plenty of walking and gymnasium work." "Figure it out for yourself," Kiviat told a writer. "A man starting to train early in April, as most of the American athletes have done, will have to hold his form for three full months to be at his best in the Olympic games. I have tried year after year to keep on edge through an entire summer, and every time I lose my edge after I have been in fine condition for seven or eight weeks."[16]

Having emphasized speed work during the indoor season, Coach Robertson had Kiviat gradually build up his stamina through longer runs up to two miles. He also did occasional sprints. After the first week of Robby's training regimen, an invitation by the PSAL to participate in the opening ceremonies for a new athletic field on the Lower East Side offered the team a pleasant break. On a field decorated with American flags, Kiviat returned a hero to the neighborhood of his birth, the Jewish immigrant capital. The afternoon began with the high-flown rhetoric of uplift by well-known reformers: General George Wingate of the PSAL, District Superintendent of Schools Julia Richman, and Rabbi Judah Magnes, a charismatic "uptown Jew" working to build a communal structure for the East Side masses. It was a relief when the P.S. 21 band played and fifty boys from P.S. 62 competed in an interclass relay. The highlight of the occasion was a series of exhibition runs by "America's foremost athletes." Kivie ran an easy mile and a half, and Mel Sheppard did a half-mile around the one-twelfth-mile oval. But it was the late-arriving Martin Sheridan, an idol of East Side boys for his long-standing interest in their welfare, who received the crowd's adulation.[17]

They went back to training at Celtic Park. On Monday afternoon, May 13, Robby held a time trial for Kiviat at two miles.[18] The next afternoon, he had the distinct pleasure of returning to Curtis High as the celebrity performer in the annual interclass track meet. The whole school turned out for the occasion. It felt like old home week, his academic failures a distant memory to everyone but himself.[19]

He now had only two weeks left to prepare for a series of races leading up to the Eastern Olympic Trials on June 8 at Harvard Stadium. If Robby pushed his men, there was good reason. Reports were coming in of fine performances in collegiate championships at home and at Olympic trials being held around the world. On Saturday, May 18, for example, the English held theirs in London; on the same date, the American Olympic Committee, in an innovative effort to create a truly nationwide team, held the first of its three regional trials, at Stanford University, with some formidable results.[20]

There were, however, a few lighter moments that quickly became enduring inspiration when Kiviat had his first look at Jim Thorpe. The Olympic Pentathlon trials were held at Celtic Park that weekend. Avid sports fan that he was, Kiviat knew all about Thorpe, who had been the sensation of college football during the 1911 season, creating his own legend as a superstar. The nearly twenty-four-year-old Carlisle Indian Industrial School student, of mixed Sac and Fox, Irish, and French descent, stood "about five foot, eleven, no neck, built like a wrestler," was Kiviat's description of Thorpe's physique. "He weighed about 178 and walk [sic] with his head sort of back of his body. He always walked on his heels with his toes up in the air." Thorpe arrived at Celtic Park days before his trials, and he watched the Winged Fist men training. When he began to practice the javelin and discus for the five-event pentathlon, Kiviat observed he "was a natural great without good coaching." Glenn "Pop" Warner, the famed Carlisle coach, was a football expert who "didn't know track and field from his nose," according to Kiviat's blunt assessment. First, Thorpe tried to throw the javelin from the discus circle. Then he ran with the discus as if it were a javelin—"fifty, sixty feet and he throws the discus. But with brute strength he threw it pretty good," Kiviat recalled. Sheridan and Robertson "caught him and showed him the right way to do it." He also had "brute strength" as a runner. For his running events, especially the 1,500 meters, he worked out with the middle-distance men. Remarkably, "he stuck with them," Kiviat said. "He wasn't good at the finish, but he stuck till the last 50 or 60 yards and we'd sprint away. Mel

Shepard [*sic*] and myself." So much for the myth of the lazy Native American phenom who succeeded without expending effort![21]

Thorpe dominated the four-man pentathlon field. He won the 200 meters, the broad jump, and the discus. With an even more remarkable demonstration of his ability to learn quickly, he finished second in the javelin throw to Bruno Brod, the Winged Fist's former national champion, and barely lost in the 1,500-meter race. His time was an excellent 4:49.8. Unfortunately, Jack Eller of the Irish Club, who might have given Thorpe more competition, had to scratch because of his duties as a New York Police Department officer. AAU chief James E. Sullivan served as referee for the event. Wearing one of his many other hats as chairman of the Olympic Selection Committee, Sullivan abruptly cancelled the eastern decathlon trials and added Thorpe to the Olympic team for that event.[22]

THIRTEEN DAYS THAT SHOOK THE TRACK WORLD, MAY 26–JUNE 8, 1912

Now it was Kiviat's turn to demonstrate the effect of his training. After track writers and fans' endless speculations about who was the world's best miler, he would finally be able to prove on the cinders that he, not Jones or Hedlund, deserved the title. Jones seemed to guarantee such a direct confrontation when he mailed in his entry blank to the Olympic Committee for the trials on June 8, thus quashing rumors that he intended to be head counselor in a summer camp rather than run in Stockholm. In the meantime, Kiviat had his first rendezvous with several of his rivals—and destiny—in the games of the New York Post Office Clerks' Association on May 26 at Celtic Park.[23]

The meet sponsors had planned a kind of "monster Olympic athletic carnival" for the working classes. Ten thousand spectators crowded into Celtic Park on a beautiful Sunday afternoon. As many as a thousand of them were allowed to roam around the infield of the track. The 1,500 meters was one of the first events called. Hedlund drew the pole position, and his three Irish Club rivals—Riley, Sheppard, and Kiviat—lined up across the track in the next three lanes. Behind them in bright sunlight stood the AAU officials, including Martin Sheridan, as serried rows of fans in straw boater and derby hats pressed against the wooden fence separating them from the runners. In

9. Set to break the world record for 1,500 meters at Celtic Park, May 26, 1912: *(from left)* Abel Kiviat, Mel Sheppard, Frank Riley, and Oscar Hedlund; Martin Sheridan stands directly behind the runners. Courtesy of the Staten Island Museum.

an oft-reprinted photograph, four trim and attractive young men, the cream of America's athletic club milers, leaned forward, legs and arms ready to spring into action, awaiting the starter's gun. Their race was one of the first important skirmishes in America's campaign to capture the world championship that summer. Olympic supremacy would be a sure sign of the nation's emergence as a world power, many believed—and the picture captures the athletes as the embodiment of the innocent but powerful springtime hopes of the pre–world war generation.

The 1,500 meters is about 120 yards short of a mile. Adopted by the French as a standard distance for their 500-meter tracks during the late 1880s, it was, in the elegant words of historian Roberto Quercetani, "a *free* translation of the English mile." Yet it had been run mostly during Olympic years—1912 would put the event on the global athletic map in bold relief.[24]

Oscar Hedlund led for about 700 yards when a cramp in his side forced him to drop out. Riley took over, but with one and a half laps to go Kivie raced into first place and went past the three-quarters mark in 3:16. With the bell, Kivie began to push the pace, and when he approached the final straight, he opened up. Riley cracked, and Shep, the defending Olympic 1,500 champion, passed him again, trying to make a run at Kiviat. Excited, wildly cheering fans spilled onto the track and formed two lanes "the length of the home stretch." "There was no let-up to the pace of Kiviat, who came down the stretch like a sprinter," the *Times* reported, "and finally beat Sheppard home by fifteen yards."

When the announcer called out the results, Kiviat had broken four minutes and set a world record for the metric mile—3:59.2. His time bettered by 0.6 second the standard that Harold "Pony" Wilson set at the English Olympic trials in 1908. Kiviat ran his successive quarter-miles in 59.6, 67.4, and 69.0, and his final 320 yards in 43.2. Behind him, Mel Sheppard and Frank Riley ran by far their best performances for the event. Sheppard's 4:01.2 was more than two seconds faster than his winning time at the London Olympics.

Equally impressive was the new discus throw record of 156 feet 1 inch by Jim Duncan, which soared almost 13 feet beyond the old record. Duncan had joined the Irish Club to train under Martin Sheridan, and his feat, asserted James Sullivan, was "one of the most remarkable in the history of athletics." No one, including Duncan, would come close to it for another twelve years.[25]

Olympic fever rose another few degrees when the press announced that U.S. team manager Matt Halpin had placed more than five hundred athletes' entries in a mailbag shipped to Stockholm on the later ill-fated *Lusitania*. Not surprisingly, the first three middle-distance entrants were Jones, Sheppard, and Kiviat. Following the two remaining Olympic trials on June 8, at Evanston for the Midwest and at Cambridge for the East, the Selection Committee planned to meet in a suite at New York's Waldorf-Astoria Hotel and then cable their final list of team members to the host committee in Sweden.[26]

On Sunday, June 2, the metropolitan-area AAU clubs held a benefit meet for the Olympic team. Ten thousand fans paid their way into Celtic Park to watch a first-class event, the last tune-up before the "official Olympic tryouts" in Boston. Kiviat ran from the scratch mark in a handicap race against a mediocre field with big yard allowances. No record survives of Kiviat's splits en route, but the final result was indisputable. "By long odds the greatest bit of distance running ever accomplished by any amateur in the world," was how the *Times* reported Kivie's victory by fifteen yards over Frank Joyce of the Mohawk Athletic Club—who started with a thirty-eight-yard handicap. His time, 3:56.8, was fully 2.4 seconds faster than the record he had established the previous Sunday. As some track experts watched Kivie finishing comfortably, they regretted the "sterling little champion" had not continued on to the one-mile mark, realizing he could have broken Jones's year-old unofficial world record. Their regret was well founded: as it turned out, that was to be the best chance Kiviat would ever have to own the outdoor mile record. But his wonderful performance at the metric mile was consolation enough. The *Irish-American* pointed out it was "likely to stand for some time, unless the little wonder is driven so hard at Sweden that he will be forced to smash his own figures again."[27]

Now all that remained were the real trials to select the Olympians. Leaving nothing to chance, Robby took the team to Boston by boat a day early in order to get in a light workout on the Harvard Stadium track. A full contingent of seventeen Irish Club athletes went with him. By then, Kiviat knew his anticipated duel with John Paul Jones, long the subject of sportswriters' speculations, would not take place. Cornell notified the Olympic Committee that Jones faced "examinations on Friday and Saturday that detain him in the university" at Ithaca. The great miler had no worries: the less stringent selections process of the era allowed the American Olympic Committee to supplement the winners from the trials with athletes whose exceptional achievements elsewhere promised success at the games. Nor was the committee restricted in 1912 by the international rule, adopted later, limiting each nation to three competitors in an Olympic event.

Nevertheless, because of Cornell's admirable insistence on academic standards, Jones missed something. America had never seen the likes of the track meet on Saturday afternoon, June 8. Although old-timers in the "immense crowd" of twenty thousand may have harked back to the classic United States versus England meet of 1895 and younger fans may have recalled the past year's AAU nationals in Pittsburgh, these trials revealed as never before the quality and depth of America's elite athletes. Here was the clearest signal to the Old World that the Yanks who were coming had transformed the nature of athletic performance.

Of course, holding the meet at Harvard Stadium made a great difference—the track was considered the country's fastest. This was Kiviat's first opportunity to race on a top-notch track. It was at Harvard, after all, on the cinders of America's first steel-reinforced stadium, that John Paul Jones had raced to his mile record exactly one year earlier. Yet there is no clearer indication of the wide gap between the tracks of Kiviat's era and those of our era than his recollection of an encounter he had while warming up for his race on that hot afternoon. Because the track had become so hard from the sun beating down on it, he had, on the advice of a friendly coach, Tom Keane of Syracuse University, filed his spikes down to the size of tiny indoor ones for better traction.[28]

Nine 1,500-meters runners toed the starting line, a mix of club and collegiate veterans with whom Kiviat was quite familiar. They included Oscar Hedlund, Ed Hunger, the Cornell and Irish Club distance runner, and Jake Driscoll of Buffalo and Boston College. However, Kiviat was also well aware of the presence of Norman Taber, a Brown University junior. Although Taber had made little impression on Kiviat when he competed unsuccessfully against him and Hedlund back in February in the Hunter Mile, he had come from nowhere to finish in a dead heat with John Paul Jones at the IC4A championships on June 1. Many observers thought Taber "had beaten the hitherto invincible Jones."[29]

As Taber got set for his first of many memorable encounters with Kiviat, he was approaching his twenty-first birthday. At five feet eight and a half inches and 145 pounds, he was, in Kiviat's words, "a husky chap with a torso like a prizefighter." At a second glance, he resembled a "bulldog" with an "'underslung' jaw," signifying an unusually determined runner who trained constantly. In fact, when Taber's coach at Brown, Eddie O'Connor, told him that riding a bicycle would slow his progress on the track, he began to run everywhere on campus. He worked tirelessly to lengthen his stride, which became in consequence longer than any other contemporary miler. Success did not come easily to Taber. Over the years, other athletes and coaches would say unkindly that he ran like a "plodder," but they overlooked his speed for the half-mile: he could unleash a dangerous kick at the end of a race. This son of Providence's city purchasing agent had been elected recently to Phi Beta Kappa, and he knew how to use his good mind to his advantage in a race. Taber's time for the mile kept getting faster with each meet that spring, capped by his stunning performance of 4:20.6 in tying Jones for the IC4A championship. That impressed Olympic officials enough to guarantee him a spot on the team. Originally thinking he would skip the trials, Taber had not trained much during the past week and did not feel sharp.[30]

Now it was Kiviat's opportunity to demonstrate anew who was the best miler. Oscar Hedlund took the lead early in the race and held it for about five hundred meters, with Ed Hunger and Jake Driscoll just behind him. Then Kivie bolted past them and took over. When he passed the half-mile in a very fast 2:03.6, Oscar was still second but Norman Taber had moved into third place. It had become a three-man race.

Kivie led the trio past the three-quarter-mile mark in 3:09.2, which was close to his best time in races at that distance. The pace was becoming too much for Hedlund, and now Taber went by him, as all three men "began a long sustained dash for the tape 300 yards away." It was a tactical situation made to order for Kivie's style of running. Still, Taber kept inching up on Kivie, and it began to look like a reprise of his IC4A race against Jones. Kiviat felt that Taber "was at my throatlatch every yard" of the way. Indeed, "there was no quit in Taber's makeup," Kiviat once told a writer. "Up to that stretch around the last turn and down the last 120 yards no such race has ever been seen in America," the *Times* reported breathlessly. Kivie was able to hold off Taber, who was only a stride behind, and he broke the tape by a bare yard. Hedlund was another fifty yards back. Kiviat's time at 1,500 meters was 3:55.8, a full second better than the record he had set only six days earlier. It was the last in his series of "annihilation performances"— three world records in thirteen days.

He was not done yet. As he ran through the tape, he recalled later, the officials "yelled, go on for the mile! go on for the mile! They had an extra set of timers and judges." Although he had nothing left after the duel with Taber and Hedlund, both of whom had stopped, he continued on. "Well, by the time I picked myself up sort of, you know—being standing up, you know—tired, with arms down around my ankles, almost—bent over," he managed to complete the additional 120 yards in 19.8 seconds. (One New

Englander noted, "He wobbled badly in the stretch.") Even so, he missed Jones's mile record by only two-tenths of a second. His time for the full mile was 4:15.6, the fastest of his life. As he staggered onto the infield, an Irish Club teammate grabbed him around the shoulders for support.

Ever after, Kiviat was proud of two facts about this shining day in his life. His metric mile time lasted as a world record for five years and as an American record until 1928. Of equal importance to him, he tied the great Irish American miler Tommy Conneff's classic 1895 one-mile record of 4:15.6—never mind that John Paul Jones had broken it by 0.2 second the previous year. Conneff's time was *the* standard of excellence of Kiviat's youth, and now he had equaled it wearing the green Winged Fist on his singlet. In the fuller perspective of history, when the newly formed IAAF created an official list of world's records in 1913, Kiviat's 1,500 went into the books as the first one.[31]

One inescapable conclusion emerges from this fortnight's burst of achievement: it was the result of a period of focused training, at least by the lights of that era, mixing speed and distance work. A teenager had repeatedly smashed the four-minute barrier, had lowered the record by four full seconds, and in the process had re-created the event to fit the quicker pace of the new century. When he ran through the tape at Harvard, the old European 1,500 looked recognizably modern.

Although Kiviat was the star attraction on the track, he was only one of many young athletes to excel during the afternoon's "spectacle of phenomenal performances." Of the eighteen winners of events, at least ten were twenty-three years old or younger. Indeed, sprinter Howard Drew (age twenty-one) and long jumper Harry Worthington (age nineteen) were still in secondary school. Drew of Springfield High School in Massachusetts, established himself as America's first great African American sprinter by defeating Ralph Craig, the acclaimed collegiate champion from Michigan, in a time that tied the Olympic record. Only the weightmen, the Irish Club's Pat McDonald and the NYAC's Clarence Childs (who won the hammer throw in the absence of Matt McGrath on police business) were older than thirty. Equally revealing, nine of the eighteen winners were either current students or recent alumni trained by the new professional collegiate coaches; the other half were the products of the big city athletic clubs. This was a clear departure from the past. The composition of the Stockholm contingent marked the beginning of a shift toward collegiate dominance of American track and field that would be the pattern for most of the century.[32]

Lawson Robertson's team was a disappointment. They managed only three firsts, three seconds, and two thirds. "On all sides after the games the principal topic among the New Yorkers present was the reason for the downfall of many of the Irish-American A. C. stars," the *Times* reported. In addition to Alvah Meyer, runners Jimmy Rosenberger, Frank Riley, and Harry Gissing did not qualify, nor did hurdler Jack Eller.[33]

On the following Monday morning, the Selection Committee held its final critical meeting at the Waldorf in New York. In addition to confirming the places on the Olympic team of the event winners in the regional trials, it also chose from the second- and third-place finishers. More difficult was the creation of a supplementary list of athletes who would be guaranteed spots, especially if they could find their own funding. Then, in an atmosphere that was the Progressive era's version of the current media circus surrounding the selection process for March Madness in basketball, James Sullivan, now wearing his official hat of U.S. commissioner to the Olympics, spoke to newspaper reporters about the team. All told, he had a list of 164 athletes, most of them in track and field. The committee's supplementary choices happily included the Irish Club's Alvah Meyer (whose parents would pay his way), Matt McGrath, Jack Eller, and Jimmy Rosenberger. For the 1,500 meters, the committee named nine runners, including Abel Kiviat, Norman Taber, Oscar Hedlund, John Paul Jones, defending champion Mel Sheppard, western trials winner Walter McClure of Oregon, and Louis Madeira of Penn, who had been a surprisingly close runner-up to Jones and Taber in the IC4A mile. Many writers commented at the time (and have done so since then) about the formidableness of this contingent of milers. Finally, Sullivan sent lettergrams to these athletes: "You have been selected a member of the American team. Report at Hotel Hermitage, New York not later than Wednesday morning, June twelfth to compete in Olympic fund benefit games to be held that day. Bring club or college flag for decoration of boat."[34]

By Tuesday, June 11, athletes began arriving at Olympic headquarters from all over the country. They were to participate the following day in a special track meet at American League Park, the home of baseball's Highlanders

(Yankees), arranged by Commissioner Sullivan as a final fund-raiser for his Olympic team. The idea was to enable New Yorkers to see the new Olympians in action just before they sailed for Europe, while giving the athletes an opportunity for a tune-up.

Rain interfered with a good idea, delaying the start of the meet and softening the League Park cinders. Nevertheless, about five thousand New Yorkers watched the Olympic team put on quite an exhibition. Led by Sullivan, AAU president Gustavus T. (Gus) Kirby, and team manager Matt Halpin, who was the flag bearer, all dapper in straw hats, the team paraded across the wet outfield grass in their club or college singlets and shorts, as a photographer caught their businesslike manner. We can assume they were beginning to realize the challenges that lay ahead. In an opening ceremony, the normally irascible Mayor William Gaynor spoke warmly to the team, encouraging them to continue the American tradition of success at the games. The athletes then showed the mayor and everyone else that they could not miss. The running events were deliberately set at three-fourths of the standard metric distances. Kiviat returned to the site of his high school baseball exploits and narrowly defeated Walter McClure of Portland in a 1,200-meter run in 3:08.4. His Irish Club teammates did well also.[35]

What captured the attention of athletes and spectators alike were the superior performances by the two men the *Times* called "Uncle Sam's wards from the Carlisle Indian School." Jim Thorpe and his teammate, the seasoned distance runner Louis Tewanima, a Hopi, beat the nation's best in the high jump and a 3,500-meter run, respectively. Tewanima sprinted past Tell Berna and George Bonhag, who was finally rounding into top shape, in the last hundred yards. Thorpe was more amazing: he cleared 6 feet 5 inches to triumph over the era's best high jumpers, Alma Richards of Brigham Young University and George Horine of Stanford, the inventor of the Western roll style of jumping. Yet no matter how outstanding the Native Americans were, some in the crowd could only see them through the received stereotype as "sons of the forest," in the words of the *Times* report.[36]

What was promising about this practice meet, both for the immediate challenge in Sweden and for the nation's athletic future, was the ability of the athletes from the Midwest and the Pacific Coast to compete on equal terms with the easterners. Assisted mightily by the recent advances in transportation and communications, Commissioner Sullivan and his associates had accomplished their objective of assembling the first Olympic team that would more closely reflect the new geographical and social diversity of the American nation.[37]

It was time for the team members to pack up and say their farewells. Like many of the out-of-towners, University of Illinois hurdler John Case made the most of his two days in New York, squiring a girlfriend to the theater and to Coney Island before parting. The chauffeurs and newsboys of Times Square presented their beloved traffic cop, Pat McDonald, "with a handsome silver loving cup" in a ceremony in front of the subway stop at Broadway and Forty-second Street. The Kiviat family had a different response. Although his parents were "starry-eyed" after reading in the Yiddish newspapers about his exploits in making the team, Kiviat remembered years later that their own experiences had made them understandably fearful about their well-known son's going to Europe. "They warned me, keep away from Russia."[38]

6

"Golden Stockholm Days"

ON THE EVENING before the Olympians were to sail for Europe on the S.S. *Finland,* the team had its formal organizational meeting at the palatial NYAC on Sixth Avenue. Of those in attendance, the majority—108 men— were members of the track team, including athletes who had not reached New York in time to compete in the previous day's meet. Col. Robert M. Thompson, president of the American Olympic Committee, gave a welcoming speech that had a real impact on his audience. A Naval Academy and Harvard Law School graduate, a world traveler and yachtsman who had made a fortune in copper and nickel, Thompson had raised substantial sums all over the country for the Olympic effort. For him, the games were both sport and a potent means of cultural integration that he believed the nation badly needed. In essence, he dreamed of a "sporting republic" that would help to restore a sense of national identity. Especially meaningful, therefore, was the presence in his audience of representatives of several different ethnic and racial groups. "We are going to Stockholm, boys, not as sports, but as sportsmen," he told them. "We are going to show the representatives of the forty nations [*sic*] with whom we will compete that we can take defeat with victory, and prove to them that, composite though we are, our forebears made no mistake in becoming a part of this great country. I want to say that I am proud to meet you all and I want to feel that I'll have reasons to be prouder when we come back from these great games."[1]

Did Jim Thorpe sit there thinking about his forebears and their devotion to the land long before the Europeans arrived? Although Kiviat has left no record of his feelings about Thompson's remarks, he might well have been struck by the irony of his finally being invited into the anti-Semitic NYAC's headquarters after all of his victories against them on the track.

But for sprinter Ralph Craig, who did not have such concerns, the Olympic Games "began to have a real meaning" that evening. "The mere fact of being with a large body of men and boys who had been picked from all over the country for the same purpose, who had been working, all unknown to one another, for the same thing, was an inspiration in itself, and where it had seemed work before, we began to see where it would be a pleasure to get out and train."

During the evening, the team was instructed about the sailing of the *Finland* the next day. Assignments of staterooms were also made. Kiviat learned he would bunk with Jim Thorpe. He received his dress uniform: "Blue coat, brass buttons," he recalled, with white flannel trousers and white shoes. "Only we had no caps; we had a fedora hat, a flat hat. They made us press it down. And we had a little blue band around with this, about a two-inch American shield . . . tied around the hat."[2]

S.S. *FINLAND:* A FLOATING OLYMPIC VILLAGE,
JUNE 14—JULY 5, 1912

Early the next morning Kiviat arrived at Pier 61, at the foot of Twenty-first Street and the Hudson River, to find what the *New York Times* called "a demonstration unrivaled in the history of American athletics." About five thousand relatives, friends, and sports enthusiasts, there to see the team sail, waved American flags and cheered from the docks as a National Guard band played patriotic tunes. Police reserves were called to keep order. A group of two hundred members of the Irish Club, the NYAC, and other local athletic clubs, including assorted Tammany politicians, carried little flags, "around the stick of which was entwined a ribbon with the slogan 'bring home the bacon.'" To Kiviat, it was "the same as if we were going off to war," which, in a sense, they were. At 8:55 A.M., five minutes before the *Finland* was to sail, Mel Sheppard became the last track star to board, much to the relief of the nervous officials.

The *Finland* itself was a scene of mass confusion, as the athletes, in their best suits and their Olympic hats, were busy having their pictures taken. Kiviat posed, relaxed and sitting on the deck, with Jim Rosenberger and Jim Thorpe. The ship was decorated in red, white, and blue, with flowers

10. The S.S. *Finland* sails from New York Harbor to Stockholm, June 14, 1912. Courtesy of Mary Honey.

everywhere. Mel Sheppard was embarrassed to receive a six-foot-high floral horseshoe from his fellow employees in the U.S. Customs Service. Col. Thompson, Commissioner Sullivan, and team manager Matt Halpin were busy helping "many of the boys from the Middle West, most of whom had never seen an Atlantic or any other type of liner," the *Times* reported with a touch of New Yorkers' condescension. As the ship steamed out to sea, the athletes were at the rail casting a last look at the Manhattan skyline.[3]

Kiviat unpacked and explored the ship with his teammates. A decade after her launch in 1902, the S.S. *Finland* of J. Pierpont Morgan's Red Star Line was still "one of the few transatlantic steamers flying the American flag." Yet as an observer of ocean-going vessels since childhood, Kiviat thought it was "a small 10,000 ton boat"—at least in comparison to the enormous hulk of its year-old contemporary, the 45,000-ton *Olympic*. But that did not detract from the adventure. The two-funneled *Finland* was actually larger than it appeared to Kiviat: at 12,806 tons, it was 560 feet long, 60 feet wide, with a promenade deck of 273 feet.

His roommate, Jim Thorpe, "was amazed by the fantastic machinery of the steamship"; he later told his daughter that during the voyage, "he climbed and crawled through every space on that ship."[4]

The *Finland* was unique. "I doubt if a more strangely equipped ship ever took to the water," was Mel Sheppard's reaction to the boat. Given the problems the Olympic Committee had experienced in transporting, housing, and feeding earlier U.S. teams, Col. Thompson had the idea of chartering a steamship, which, after landing in the harbor at Stockholm, would serve as a kind of floating Olympic Village for the American athletes throughout the games. In the era before such a village became a fundamental part of the Olympic experience, Thompson's idea was innovative—and he persuaded his executive committee to undertake the necessary fund-raising campaign. The colonel himself contributed $13,500. He also persuaded a number of wealthy sportsmen and their families to sail with the team on the *Finland,* which ultimately netted the Olympic Committee an additional $55,000. But the disaster of the *Titanic* in mid-April that year aroused great apprehension about the whole enterprise until the *Finland*'s far more solid security arrangements, including a large supply of lifeboats and rafts, became known. Making the ship particularly desirable to the committee were the athletic facilities already in place: a gymnasium below deck, showers, and rubdown tables.[5]

Before the *Finland* sailed, important additions were made. The Olympic Committee built a cork-coated, approximately 176-yard track on the promenade deck, with a long straightaway. Real sand pits were constructed on the deck below the promenade for the jumpers and pole vaulters to practice. To accommodate athletes in other events, the committee set up two canvas tanks for the swimmers on the lower deck; make-shift stationary bicycles for the cyclist team; and, at the stern, a wooden wall with a line across it, net high for tennis practice. Kiviat and Thorpe could see plainly this was intended to be a no-nonsense voyage.[6]

Although the committee's idea was to simulate a first-class urban athletic club, the *Finland* also had the elegance of a Red Star Line steamer. On his tour of the ship, Kiviat saw a saloon that doubled as a social hall, a gentleman's smoking room (closed to the athletes), and the first-class dining room, with its long tables, for the team's use.[7]

Team members enjoyed themselves that first day out and became better acquainted. Some played deck shuffleboard and quoits. Others, such as Norman Taber, "spent the afternoon lying around on deck and talking to different fellows." Kiviat found Thorpe to be "not very talkative at all, very quiet." It probably did not help the relationship that Kiviat was five years younger and, at this stage, almost as quiet as Thorpe. Kiviat rarely initiated a conversation, which he later attributed to his upbringing by immigrant parents. Characteristically, however, he remained relaxed in a situation where some might have been tense or uncertain.[8]

Although the Olympic Committee wanted to develop true team unity on the S.S. *Finland,* from the outset it was obvious that the athletes' behavior reflected contemporary social relations within American sport. The *Finland* was no melting pot: the men lived side by side on the boat for more than a month, but ethnic and class consciousness affected their relations. The privileged collegians stayed together; quiet Kivie hung out with other working-class club athletes.

One such athlete who quickly became his "buddy" was Howard Drew, the first African American sprinter known as the "world's fastest human." Drew was two years older than Kiviat, married with two children, but they were drawn together in part by their unusually disciplined approaches to overcoming the struggles of hard lives. Encouraged by his stepfather, the Reverend David St. Drew, Howard was still a student at Springfield High School, having enrolled at age twenty after working at odd jobs as a red cap at the railroad depot, a hotel bellhop, and an elevator operator. A compact and remarkably smooth runner at five feet seven and a half inches and 160 pounds, he burst on the national scene with his exceptional ability to pick up his speed early in a dash and won the Junior AAU championships in 1910 and 1911. He was introduced to the great Penn coach Mike Murphy, who told him to "keep it up. In a year or so you'll beat them all." In the Olympic trials at Harvard Stadium, he surprised everyone but Murphy with his victory in the 100 meters over Ralph Craig, the IC4A champion from Michigan, in 10.8.

"Howard and I got together almost by instinct," Kiviat believed, "a little Jew and a little colored man." Drew was a man of intellect as well as character: a gifted writer as well as a sensitive and quite modest person. The two young athletic prodigies would sit on the deck talking and reading. Drew admired his companion for representing "something more than mere athletic prowess." Kiviat stood out to him as one of the Olympians whose "mastery on the cinder path lies in the clean lives they live." "People must have figured that we were outcasts," Kiviat said later. Yet at the time he did not speak about this friendship, which meant a great deal to him. They had much in common: Drew, a native of Virginia who had migrated to the North, experienced the worst era of Jim Crow laws and racism. Kiviat grew up in an America of pervasive anti-Semitism. Jewish opinion makers, especially the Yiddish press his parents read so avidly, repeatedly and empathetically pointed out the historic parallels between the Jewish and black experiences. Like those editors, but in his own unsophisticated way, he may have gravitated to Drew from a similar unconscious motivation—as a means of dealing with his own ambivalence about WASP America. With Drew, he could be himself, without having to act out either Col. Thompson's or the Irish Club's versions of the melting pot ideal. In a fundamental sense, he was practicing the lessons of respect and affection for black people he had learned in Zelda Kiviat's home. The apple had not fallen far from the tree.[9]

The first day at sea ended with a banquet. Afterwards, tired athletes called it an early night.

The "magnificence" of the next morning surprised the athletes when they came out on deck to find a calm sea with "a gentle swell," as "the sun gleamed across the blue ocean." The training regimen began under the supervision of track coach Mike Murphy. No one had a better reputation: the Penn trainer had coached the Olympic teams in 1900 and 1908, and had won wide respect for his handling of elite athletes and his "scientific" approach to training. He had even studied medicine at Penn to increase his understanding of the human body. Still not fully recovered from his severe illness, "he came on our Olympic boat slightly sick," Kiviat reported. It was clear that assistant coach Lawson Robertson would have to play a significant role in guiding the team.[10]

Although Murphy was a man of few words, Kiviat thought he "was very nice and quiet—a typical Irishman. Looked 100 percent Irish. He looked like the brogue would come out of his nose, ears, and mouth. I never had any trouble because I didn't have a big mouth." His pal Drew had a closer relationship to Murphy, a sprint specialist, and a sharper view of the coach's complex personality. "Gifted with a great sense of humor, but absolutely settled in his opinions," Drew wrote, Murphy "was a mixture of congeniality and contrariness." The coach warned the men "on the necessity of being very careful to avoid getting leg-sore from the bounding of the boat." Murphy was particularly concerned about an athlete's diet and prohibited "eating between meals."[11]

For their workout that afternoon, Murphy had Kiviat and the other distance men run twenty laps, about two miles, on the cork track. Because Olympians did not have official warmup suits in that era, Kiviat ran in his "little green jersey with white stripes," the same Norwood Athletic Club outfit he had worn since his youthful play on Staten Island fields.[12]

The pattern was set for the two weeks at sea. Murphy insisted on daily workouts. According to Sullivan, "some of the men began to think they were being worked too much." In fact, the athletes said that, even with the cork track, "hard work was out of the question." The decks were simply too hard and the corners too sharp, producing sore calves and muscles. At times, the rolling of the ship made running at pace difficult. One afternoon the milers "ran about twelve laps, at an even gait," roughly about 1.2 miles. They received frequent rubdowns from the coaches on board, especially from the hard-working Lawson Robertson, who each night in his stateroom gave massages to as many as a dozen athletes. They also took long walks around the decks, mainly with their social peers. Norman Taber, for example, exercised with Wallace McCurdy, Coach Murphy's distance ace at Penn.[13]

A vicious myth created then and embellished by sportswriters throughout the century, claimed that Jim Thorpe, the "natural man," spent the voyage lazing in his bunk while others trained. His teammate in the decathlon and pentathlon events, Avery Brundage, flatly denied it. "'Certainly Thorpe trained and never missed a session! Even if he, or anyone else for that matter had wanted to loaf, our trainer Mike Murphy, would not have permitted it.'" In fact, Thorpe worked as hard as anyone on the *Finland*. So did Lt. George S. Patton Jr., a competitor in the modern pentathlon, a challenging new event of five military disciplines limited to soldiers. Patton was all over the *Finland*, exhibiting the intensity that

11. Kiviat wears his boyhood Norwood Athletic Club uniform on the S.S. *Finland*, 1912. Courtesy of Lucy Price.

would later make him a legend. Although Patton made no impression on Kiviat, Avery Brundage did—and it was not positive. "He wasn't liked at all," Kiviat recalled. "He was bossy and fresh. He had a habit of, you know, making room for himself. You had what's left over." Kiviat and others "avoided him as much as possible." Perhaps in that casual comment may be found the seeds of his roommate Jim Thorpe's later torment at the unforgiving hands of Brundage's AAU.[14]

Curfew each night was at ten, when the team's assistant manager, NYAC track coach Paul Pilgrim, would search with his electric pocket lamp for transgressors in every nook of the decks. One night he missed Jim Thorpe, who returned to the stateroom drunk and kicked in the door panel. The coaches quickly moved Thorpe in with the older fellows. Lawson Robertson's concern for his young protégé was evident here. However, Thorpe and Kiviat remained friends throughout the trip.[15]

Soon enough, the training seemed almost secondary to many of the young men for whom the *Finland* was their first experience of an Atlantic crossing. Despite the calmness of the sea on most days, there were rough passages. Norman Taber noted how one night he "would roll over and hit one side of my bunk with a thud and then repeat the sensation on the other side." Taber's fellow milers—Kiviat, Jones, and Hedlund—suffered from seasickness. "The terrible food . . . on heavy seas left Jones in bad shape," recalled fellow Cornellian Tell Berna. Hedlund became dehydrated and lost thirteen pounds. Kiviat's symptoms were less extreme. Many believed the seasickness ultimately affected his performance during the games, but he downplayed it, not wanting to make excuses. Characteristically, even with his distress, he was still a well-liked figure on the *Finland*.[16]

The athletes mostly relaxed in steamer chairs on deck, talking, reading, enjoying the sun, or having afternoon tea. Kiviat undoubtedly browsed Howard Drew's copy of the popular new novel *Stover at Yale,* which Norman Taber also borrowed and read. The relaxed style carried over to the dining hall, where the athletes, who were allowed to enter unshaved and wearing their track suits, brought their hearty appetites. Many, including Kiviat, gained weight quickly, to Mike Murphy's displeasure. Heavy eating, the coach knew, only intensified the distress of mal de mer.[17]

The weight throwers refined this shipboard lifestyle into an art form. Consider the poor steward "worn bowlegged carting food to them," Arthur Daley wrote. "No wonder the harrassed [*sic*] steward moaned: 'It's whales they are, not men,'" at that moment creating one of sports' memorable nicknames. Kiviat recalled: "We'd get a brick of ice cream. You know, that's about a half-inch thick? They'd get the whole can. . . . Fruit. Nuts. They'd get plenty. We'd get a couple of nuts, one piece of fruit."[18]

The concerts in the grand saloon, with Col. Thompson presiding, put on display the slightly richer ethnic and cultural diversity of this American team than its predecessors, at least by the lights of that era. Although the

Olympians were overwhelmingly of WASP and Irish Catholic origins, the minority representatives included three Jews (Kiviat, Alvah Meyer, and race walker Sam Schwartz), one Italian American (marathoner Gaston Strobino), three Native Americans (Thorpe, Carlisle teammate Louis Tewanima, and marathoner Andrew Sockalexis), one Hawaiian (Duke Kahanamoku), and one African American (Howard Drew). At the first concert, distance runner Tewanima, a member of the Hopi tribe, "sang an old Indian song," and swimmer Duke Kahanamoku "sang a Hawaiian song." After eating with Tewanima in the dining room a few times, Kiviat thought "he was a wonderful person." Duke Kahanamoku was even more exotic: "He was a strange person to us," Kivie said. "None of us ever saw a Hawaiian or Philipino [sic]. You know, what they look [like] except in pictures in the paper. So we were very respectful of him and he proved him [sic] to be a wonderful, a real chap. As good as any of us." However much he tried to relate to Kahanamoku as an equal, Kiviat's impression of him was built on the stereotypical views of Hawaiians as an exotic and primitive race. Toward the close of the concert, Abel's Irish Club teammate Jack Eller sang Irish melodies. Despite the heavy-handed, patronizing quality to the evening, it did show an awakening of multicultural awareness in elite amateur sport. In this context, historian Mark Dyreson's suggestion that the early Olympic leaders "sought to exclude other forms of ethnic identification" and to "create an entirely American entity" requires clarification.[19]

The officials made certain that, along with this appreciation of America's cultural heritage, the athletes had the inspiration of religious faith, Protestant style. On the first Sunday morning at sea, "a short church service was held at which Col. Thompson took the leading part," Norman Taber wrote approvingly. "He spoke of the test which the American representatives would be put to in a moral as well as a physical way for as we act so the whole United States will be judged by the 40 other nations which will be represented at Stockholm." Such an evocation of the values of muscular Christianity must have served only to remind Kiviat once again that despite his practiced pose of behaving like Norman Taber and his other teammates, he was different in a basic way.[20]

On June 24, the day after Abel celebrated his twentieth birthday, the *Finland* sailed past the windmills and dykes of the lowlands up to the great port of Antwerp. When the ship docked, "we ran so fast down the gang plank it nearly knocked some of us over," Kiviat recalled. For the next three days, team members "got rid of our sea legs" by touring the historic city, its famous cathedral and museums, and training at the Beershot Athletic Club.[21] On the first afternoon, they worked out on the grass of the club's polo grounds in a downpour. The milers ran over their distance, up to two miles, "at a medium clip," sprinting at the end. They discovered they had considerable work to do before the games. Back on the *Finland* at night, Mike Murphy gave them "a little call down," saying they "were good for nothing," and announced double practice sessions at Beershot for the second day. They felt the effects of a fast 880 the next morning but returned for an afternoon workout. Before departure on the third day, their two-hour practice included running "a good stiff mile." Both the athletes and their coaches reported they looked and felt better. Yet Kiviat was still far from his record-breaking form of only two weeks earlier, the evident result of the voyage. The men returned to their ship for "a magnificent farewell demonstration, thousands of people gathering on the quay and along the waterworks." The Americans again waved their little flags, and the band played the "Star Spangled Banner" as the *Finland* sailed at noon toward the North Sea and Sweden.[22]

For the last four days of the voyage, the tired Olympians were almost languid travelers, indulging their hearty appetites. Coach Murphy held only one formal practice session. On their own, the milers took occasional long walks or jogs "just to keep loosened up." The team did have daily drills on deck "to get in shape for the parade" at the opening ceremony. There were also the familiar nightly concerts and dances, but the final entertainment was different. As they approached Stockholm on Saturday night, Kiviat's fellow miler, lanky Louis C. Madeira III, teamed up with the little Chicago pole vaulter Frank J. Coyle for a troubling "Jeff and Mutt combination." Madeira epitomized Proper Philadelphia and its patrician values: the scion of a coal baron, himself the 1884 national champion miler, he had prepared at the exclusive St. George's School for his studies in mechanical engineering at Penn. He made the Olympic team, surprising his college coach, Mike Murphy, by finishing just behind Jones and Taber in the IC4A meet on June 1. For this final concert, "Madeira and Coyle blackened up as a couple of darkies and cracked numerous jokes much to the amusement of the audience," Norman Taber noted in his diary. It "was a great success." How did Howard Drew and Kiviat react to this caricature of African Americans? We are left to wonder in the absence of surviving documentation. We should keep in mind, however, the complex and contradictory roles of blackface in American black, Jewish, and majority cultures. Consider, for example, historian Hasia Diner's suggestion that by appearing in blackface, Jewish actors were demonstrating sympathy for African Americans while proving their own Americanism. Yet one can also grant Michael Rogin's insight that as prominent interpreters of blackface, they helped to perpetuate a racist image invented by the larger American culture. Nevertheless, Kiviat's experience with Howard Drew, informed by the teachings of his mother, Zelda, supports Diner's conclusion that in or out of blackface, immigrant Jews identified with African Americans.[23]

A far better experience was the "enthusiastic" reception when the *Finland* finally docked in front of Stockholm's Royal Palace at nine o'clock on Sunday morning, June 30. Thousands of Swedish athletes, Olympic Committee members, and sports fans were at the pier and serenaded the Yanks with popular American songs and loud cheers, led by their national track coach—none other than Ernie Hjertberg. The Irish Club's former coach had been in Sweden since 1910, doing his usual thoughtful and methodical job of preparing his native country for the Olympics. After the Swedes concluded with the singing of their national anthem, Hjertberg, Col. Viktor Balck, and J. S. Edstrom, the president and vice president of the Swedish Olympic Committee, boarded the ship for a formal welcoming ceremony. Col. Thompson responded and then threw open the ship, the largest ever to dock in Stockholm, to swarms of curious visitors who were fascinated by all things American. Late in the afternoon the *Finland* anchored out in midstream in order to assure some quiet for the athletes who would continue to live and eat on the ship during the period of competition.[24]

Although Swedish hospitality was unlike anything these Americans had ever experienced, Kiviat put aside the temptations of the magnificent city and prepared himself to compete. He was completely focused on the task at hand, he recalled, "because Robertson insisted on taking care of yourself, watch everything you do 'cause it will help you. A little slight difference, a trip or something, or grabbing the wrong rail going up or down you might get hurt, and naturally you couldn't run anymore." Robby, who was now functioning in all but name as head track coach because of Mike Murphy's worsening health, made sure Kiviat ran daily. Training rules were strictly enforced, and the chagrined athletes were prohibited from leaving the ship at night.[25]

Murphy and Robby held track practice at the recently renovated Ostermalm Athletic Grounds, located near the Olympic Stadium and used by most of the other nations. Ostermalm's track was a little more than 200 meters and very firm, Norman Taber noted. On Monday afternoon, athletes speaking numerous languages worked out, most of them eager to gauge if the Americans were really as good as they were cracked up to be. Howard Drew erased any doubts when Murphy timed him in 10.6 for 100 meters, while several other watches registered an unheard of 10.4. He had now established himself as the clear gold medal favorite. The American 1,500-meter men "ran a mile at a good fast pace," and they felt they were in fair shape. Then they walked over for their first look at the Olympic Stadium.

Years later, Kiviat tried to be blasé to an interviewer about his initial reaction to this building, but he didn't fool anyone: its powerful, almost medieval appearance and beauty deeply impressed him and all the young men. Architect Torben Grut had used gray-violet hand-made Helsingborg bricks, had erected two great clock towers on either side of the track's curve as well an arcade with great arches and vaults, and had placed the royal box in the center of the eastern grandstand. The horseshoe form seated twenty-two thousand, with the inclusion of a temporary wooden grandstand built across the open northern end of the arena for the games. However, Grut designed the permanent seats of reinforced concrete. Here was another dramatic creation of Stockholm's new "stone city" in the upper-middle-class neighborhood of Ostermalm—brick buildings evoking a romantic Swedish architectural style, but rationally planned. "The Stadium is a new structure and made according to the most modern methods of construction," Taber wrote in his diary. "The track is 383 meters around and has very broad turns. It seems very hard and will doubtless prove fast." Indeed, Kiviat himself admitted afterward "that the Stockholm track is the best in the world."[26]

The milers ran about two miles on the stadium track on Tuesday morning in a light rain before a large crowd of spectators. On Wednesday, they returned to the stadium for time trials at 1,500 meters. Taber did his with Wally McCurdy, and his notes were an indication of the milers' condition. "I set the pace and killed us in the first lap doing it in 51 or about 56 for the quarter. The next two laps we could scarcely move but I came in fairly strong on the last lap but only did 4:15 for the distance." The milers had now completed whatever hard training they and their coaches planned before their trial heats in the 1,500, scheduled for the following Tuesday afternoon. Mike Murphy expressed the consensus of feeling to Orton Tewson of the *New York Times* "that everyone is in fine shape and ready to do or die."[27]

Again, although the evidence suggested Kiviat was not in his best condition, he carried his own—and others'—high expectations of his success. In a revealing newspaper comparison of the results of the recent Olympic trials in the four leading nations—England, France, Germany, and America—Kiviat's performance stood out. His world record of 3:55.8 on June 8 was almost ten seconds faster than the "Foreigners' Best," by Henri Arnaud of France. It seemed obvious Kiviat's competition would come from his own teammates. Yet in a conversation with the *Times* correspondent, the experienced James Sullivan tempered his exuberance about the Americans' chances with the prescient comment that "there will be keen competition and some disappointments." Back home, such judiciousness was in short supply. "All eyes will be turned to Stockholm, Sweden, next week, and Staten Island fans are watching with added interest to see how Abel Kiviat, our 'native son,' fares in his specialty of showing the 'Furriners' how nice he looks from the back. There'll be not a few who will go down fish, hook and sinker on the stocky little Stapletonian," the *Richmond County Advance* remarked.[28]

Yet even Kivie's premeet concentration and the burden of high expectations could not completely dampen his natural interest in his surroundings. He began to make friends with a promising young Swedish miler, John Zander, a protégé of Ernie Hjertberg, and two Canadians, old rival Jack Tait and Mel Brock, who was Kiviat's age. The four middle-distance stars soon "became close." The pressure of the situation also did not blind Kiviat to the beauty of Stockholm. As a resident of an island, he appreciated this city of waterways, "the Venice of the North." He would explore it after he finished competing.[29]

During this final week of training, however, the American athletes were "high strung, like opera singers," wrote Tewson of the *Times,* and the

American officials wisely provided them with some relief. On Thursday, July 4, they organized an enjoyable celebration. For most athletes, it was their "first Fourth of July in a foreign country. A few firecrackers were set off on board after breakfast and the smell of powder brought back patriotic remembrances." In the afternoon, they extended an open invitation to the athletes and officials of the nations for a reception on the *Finland*. "Foreigners of every description were welcome and the whole affair seemed to be a success," Taber recorded. Fraternizing was again determined by social class. The American team had a special dinner afterward: "At each place was a box of candy, a roll containing a paper cap, and an acrobatic toy." Olympic veteran George Bonhag presented Col. Thompson with a loving cup from the athletes. The wonderful evening ended with fireworks on deck.[30]

Unfortunately, Kiviat's enduring memory of that week was less pleasant. One day he was idling in the area of the ship's dining room, almost certainly unshaved and dressed casually. Behind him, discus thrower Jim Duncan, who had been picking on him, moved quickly and called out, "Sheeny, get the hell out of the way," or words to that effect. Duncan was "a tough guy" and "was detested by everybody," according to Kiviat, who had first-hand knowledge because Duncan had joined the Irish Club that spring. Standing nearby were Kiviat's friends and protectors, Babe McDonald and Ralph Rose. They were truly whales compared to Duncan, who was much shorter and "weighed 225 stripped." Before Kiviat could respond, McDonald and Rose "grabbed" Duncan. "And they said, 'we'll break the porthole—we can't open it—and throw you out the porthole into the harbor.'" Duncan left him alone after that, but the incident remained fresh in Kiviat's mind for the rest of his life.

It was another reminder, if one was needed, that in a summer when New York's hotels posted signs "No Jews and no mosquitos," even Olympians were not immune from anti-Semitic harassment. Yet it also illustrated that Kiviat's skills in establishing warm interpersonal relations with fair-minded non-Jews usually served him well.[31]

THE OLYMPIAD BEGINS, JULY 6–8, 1912

When Kiviat went into Stockholm early on Saturday morning, there was movement everywhere on the sunlit, festooned streets. Some people, in open autos, waved their countries' flags; others packed into trolleys; and many walked—but all headed excitedly toward the stadium. Well-dressed women may have outnumbered the men. The American team gathered with the twenty-four other delegations at the Ostermalm practice field. At eleven sharp, led by Col. Thompson and Commissioner Sullivan, they marched into the arena between France and Greece (according to the Swedish spelling of countries' names) in columns four abreast and lined up in the infield facing the royal box. Kiviat thought "it was stupendous." Wherever he looked, there was bright color: the royal box, fringed with tassels, in stripes of white and gold; the flags of the nations flying from the arena's roof; and, at the back of the north grandstand, the host's twenty light blue-and-gold flags. What particularly impressed him were the king's guards in their light blue uniforms. "They were giants," he said. "All of them must have been seven-feet tall. They carried these big swords." The International Olympic Committee (IOC) officials were dressed formally in morning coats and top hats.

The one-hour ceremony had a more festive aura than its four predecessors in the modern Olympic movement, somewhat more artfully arranging "a congeries of ritual symbols" (sacred music, processions, flags, and so on), in the words of social scientist John J. MacAloon. First, the standing-room-only crowd sang in Swedish the Lutheran hymn "A Mighty Fortress Is Our God." Clergymen offered prayers in Swedish and English. After a brief speech by the popular crown prince, in which he expressed his belief that this Olympiad "will prove to be the greatest international trial of strength in the athletic field that our times can show," his father, the tall and elegant King Gustav V, formally opened the Olympic Games. That was the signal for trumpeters in medieval costume at the top of the watchtowers to play fanfare; the crowd cheered the king; and a male choir sang the Swedish air "Stand Strong You Knighted Guardian of Light." Finally, in the order they entered the stadium, the national delegations marched around the track past the royal box. "Gentleman" George Bonhag was the American flag bearer. Walking just behind him, in the front row, McDonald, McGrath, Rose, and Simon Gillis looked like "giants compared with most of the men on the field." Unfortunately, Kiviat's view of his Irish Club teammates was obscured by his position in the parade. The stylish and practiced Yanks turned in unison toward the monarch and covered the shields on their blue blazers with

12. The U.S. team marches in the opening ceremony at Olympic Stadium, Stockholm, 1912. Courtesy of Mary Honey.

their straw hats. As the bands played "The Star Spangled Banner," the Swedish crowd "joined the American spectators in shouting 'Rah! Rah! U.S.A.!'" Almost five hundred writers in the press section—far more than at previous Olympiads—were preparing to convey the excitement of this spectacle in front-page stories all over the Western world.[32]

Baron Pierre de Coubertin, founder of the IOC, experienced a transforming moment in his long and zealous struggle to institutionalize "Olympism." The baron believed prophetically that sporting events conducted with imaginative ceremony and ritual and informed by the arts would serve as "a kind of secular religion" for the emerging middle-class democracies. Athletics was originally one component of this cultured French aristocrat's broader educational theory developed in reaction to his country's bitter defeat in the Franco-Prussian War of 1871. His travels in England and North America reinforced and expanded his interpretation of sport in educational terms: its purpose was to cultivate a citizen who was moral, international minded, and physically accomplished.[33]

An 1890 visit to the Shropshire village of Wenlock in northwest England provided Courbertin with the means of achieving his ideal. Dr. W. P. Brookes had been holding annual Olympian Games there for four decades. As revisionist historian and classicist David C. Young has demonstrated, the country doctor's program of reviving the ideals of ancient Olympia, including the pageantry and symbols, and his proposal to stage international Olympics in Athens, became the determinative influences on the young baron's work. But if Coubertin essentially adapted what he saw in Shropshire to the circumstances of the new European generation, he was also a genius at public relations and organization. During the 1892 meeting of the French Union of Athletic Sports Clubs, of which he was the founder, he proposed the idea of an Olympiad. Two years later, the French Union held an international congress at the Sorbonne (ostensibly to discuss the issue of amateurism), and during the proceedings he "cast a spell over the seventy-nine delegates from twelve countries," who voted unanimously to revive a quadrennial Olympics. He created the IOC and awarded the first modern games to Athens in 1896 and to his own Paris in 1900. After the Greeks' modest success at the inaugural Olympiad, the baron's movement faced a series of crises in the first decade of the new century. Many considered the Paris and St. Louis Games failures, and only the somewhat better-organized, unofficial 1906 Athens Games and the official London Olympiad rescued the enterprise.[34]

"Of all countries," stated Coubertin at the IOC meeting in May 1909, "Sweden is at the moment best qualified to host a great Olympic Games." The sports-loving Swedes justified his faith. They chose a national Olympic Committee headed by Col. Viktor G. Balck, a charter member of the IOC, whose dynamism, organizational skills, and wide network of contacts were essential both for the development of Swedish sport and for the awarding of the games to Stockholm. His vice president was the aristocratic and energetic Sigfrid Edstrom, once a fine sprinter and at thirty-nine years old the president of the Swedish General Electric Company, a key institution in the transformation of Stockholm into a major industrial center. The SOC identified quickly its basic tasks, developed a comprehensive master plan, and implemented it with "efficiency and almost mathematical precision," commented decathlon man Avery Brundage.[35]

At the conclusion of the opening ceremony, the sprinters began gathering in the infield, and the highly organized track officials were readying things for the first event. The "start-criers" shouted "all out for the hundred" through their megaphones. Kiviat and his teammates went to watch in their reserved seats in the temporary stands.[36]

The 100 meters had a huge field, with seventeen heats. Kiviat's personal interest was in the ninth, which his Irish Club teammate Alvah Meyer won easily, and in the fifteenth, which Howard Drew took from a German sprinter in 11 flat. Drew looked very strong and graceful, with only a bandaged left leg revealing he had "caught cold" in his leg muscles during the week. He was a troubled young man on a mission: after suffering inwardly when he perceived Mike Murphy to be calling him "uppity" during a training incident the previous week, he wanted "to run my heart out" and show up his admired coach.[37]

When the sprinters returned about 4:00 P.M. for their second round, five Americans—Drew, Meyer, Don Lippincott of Penn, Ralph Craig of Michigan, and little Frank Belote of Chicago—and a South African won the six heats and advanced to Sunday's final. The consensus of European opinion was that Drew had "the best performance," leading by a full five meters at 50 meters when he "struck a piece of soft track" and suddenly felt the "muscles in the fleshy part of [his] leg give way." He "finished the heat hopping," he recalled later. The courageous effort finished Drew; he went into the locker room crying in pain. "My buddy was . . . the best sprinter we had on the team," Kiviat said sadly. "Was picked to win the sprints, 'til he pulled a tendon."[38]

On Sunday, in perfect summer weather, Kiviat's roommate, Jim Thorpe, won gold in the Pentathlon, taking four of five events and thrilling everyone with his all-around athleticism. A legend was born that afternoon.[39]

Forgotten today is a "false legend" created when Howard Drew hobbled in vain to the starting line for the final of the 100 meters "but had to be helped back" to the locker room before the starter's commands. A rumor circulated for years afterward—and still has a half life in Sweden today—that a racist American coach had kept him there to prevent the first great African American sprinter from winning. In fact, Mike Murphy came over immediately to Drew, whom he regarded as the fastest man he had ever seen, and told him: "I wouldn't have this happen for $500." With the prerace favorite incapacitated, Kiviat rooted for Meyer, with whom he identified as a fellow Jew. After seven false starts (there were no penalties for jumping the gun in these Olympics), Ralph Craig burst to victory by two feet over Meyer in 10.8, with Don Lippincott a close third. Three American flags were hoisted up the flag poles in the center of the northern grandstand, amidst frenzied yells of "Rah, Rah, Ray, U.S.A.M.E.R.I.C.A."[40]

With the trial heats of the 1,500 meters scheduled for Tuesday, Kiviat relaxed on the boat on Monday and missed a classic of Olympic history. In the debut of the 10,000-meter event in the Olympic program, Hannes "the Mighty" Kolehmainen of Finland joined Thorpe as a superstar of these games. He destroyed the field with the unexpected speed of his early pace in the long race. Just twenty-two years old, the always smiling and gracious Finn had learned an uncommonly tough-minded approach to training from his eldest brother Willi—which, ironically, Willi credited to the tutoring of Lawson Robertson during a visit to America in 1910. Of the other competitors, only Louis Tewanima of the Carlisle School ran within himself—that is, comfortably at his own pace—for the silver medal. In the stands, delighted Finns, then subjects of the Russian Empire, waved their country's forbidden flag, defying the czar. Through his achievement that afternoon, the Finn began to inspire a younger generation of his countrymen, "Kolehmainens of the imagination" in Peter Lovesey's felicitous phrase, to develop Finland's twentieth-century tradition of dominating distance runners.[41]

Kiviat did see the 800 final later that afternoon, which was also the stuff of legend. It would turn out to have a fatal impact on his thinking about his own 1,500 final later that week. Fearing the closing sprint of Hans Braun of Germany, Mel Sheppard decided spontaneously at the starting line to "set a terrific pace in order to perform the duty myself of running the German into the ground." His 400-meter split of 52.4 was "unheard of," but the formidable field of eight was still bunched together when they came into the final straight. "Then the schoolboy, Meredith, came from nowhere," Sheppard recalled graciously, "and with one of the most remarkable sprints I have ever seen, slowly forged to the front." In a dramatic finish, Ted Meredith, an inexperienced nineteen-year-old from Mercersburg Academy, beat Shep to the tape by half a meter, with Ira Davenport of the University of Chicago on the defending champion's shoulder. Meredith's time (1:51.9) broke the world mark Shep had set in 1908 and would endure until 1926. "We were all dazed at the results of the race, and none more so than Ted himself," Sheppard wrote in his memoir. For the second time in two days, three Stars and Stripes flew from the winners' flagpoles. What impressed Kiviat most, however, was how Shep had set a fantastic world record pace "only to get nipped at the finish," and he determined then and there *he would not take the chance of a similar experience.*[42]

WARM UP FOR GLORY: THE 1,500 TRIAL HEATS, JULY 9, 1912

Kiviat woke to a cloudy and threatening sky on the day of the 1,500 trial heats. Under coaches' orders, the milers "loafed around the boat all forenoon doing practically nothing." They were a cocky band when they left the *Finland.* "Of all the events on the program the 1500 meters was the one most generally conceded to the Americans," Norman Taber wrote. "They had in their ranks the greatest set of milers that have ever run in the Olympic Games. On paper no country had a single man who could touch at least three of them"—Kiviat, Jones, and Taber himself.[43]

Kiviat was very confident, despite his lingering malaise from the voyage. "I thought I'd win, and people sort of helped me think that way," he said later. He was in the third of seven trial heats, with two men from each qualifying for the next day's final. His competition included Henri Arnaud, the French champion, Jack Tait, his Canadian friend, and Neil Patterson of Chicago. He "took it for granted" that he was superior to them, and he did not push himself. Yet this was the fastest heat; Kivie led most of the way and won easily in 4:04.4, only a second off Mel Sheppard's Olympic record, with Arnaud second.[44]

Taber ran in the second heat and found the pace "terribly slow for three laps and then I let out on the last and passed the field," he wrote in his diary. Qualifying behind him was a seasoned British miler whom the Americans feared, Philip John Baker, a twenty-two-year-old graduate of King's College, Cambridge. Baker had been a brilliant student in economics, a member of a social circle with the likes of John Maynard Keynes, Hugh Dalton, and Rupert Brooke, and the president of both the prestigious Cambridge Union and the Cambridge Athletic Club. But he had a painful problem in Stockholm, a dislocated bone in his foot that he bound up with surgical tape. With great courage, he beat out a German for second place in the heat. Because of his experience and guts, Baker demonstrated that he might still be a factor in the final.[45]

Baker's countryman, rival, and close friend Arnold N. S. Jackson faced John Paul Jones in the fourth heat—both men the quintessential examples of the Anglo-American ideal of "gentlemanly amateurism." Handsome J. P. was the most well-liked man on the Stockholm track, as admired by the Olympians as he was feared for his record-breaking accomplishments. But the Americans knew little about Jackson, a six-foot-three-inch, twenty-one-year-old Oxford student who "has more the appearance of a poet than an athlete," wrote a reporter. He had come to Stockholm directly from the enclosed and intellectually vital ancient quadrangles of Brasenose College. An English public-school graduate, he had quickly established himself at college as a witty and thoughtful student of law and history as well as an all-around athlete—soccer and hockey, golf and rowing. One day in 1911 his uncle Clement Jackson, an Oxford don who once held the high hurdles record and was now the university's track coach, convinced Arnold to focus on running. His uncle's training regimen was extraordinarily casual. "I invariably had a bottle of Guinness for lunch and a nice bottle of Burgundy for dinner," he recalled. "Jacker" improved enough to win the mile in the 1912 Oxford varsity meet. Then, on March 23, his raw talent enabled him to win the Oxford-Cambridge dual meet in 4:21.4. Jackson impressed the experts with his "tremendous springy stride and a long, rangy build, just right for a miler," as one put it. His best weapons were his finishing kick and a rare mental toughness. If he was within twenty meters of the leaders at the bell lap, he knew he would catch them. Indeed, notwithstanding Kiviat's recent "series of remarkable performances," in Jackson's words, he made a bet of a shilling with a Brasenose teammate "that the United States would NOT win the 1,500." British officials selected him for the Olympic team despite his limited competitive experience—and much of that racing clockwise on Oxford's antiquated three-laps-to-the-mile Iffley Road track.[46]

On July 9, however, the luck of the draw pitted Jackson against the genial Jones, whom the Englishman called "undoubtedly the greatest runner of his day." "The thought of it gave me a twinge in my stomach," he wrote later. But he rested in bed for a day before the heat, and that did the trick. Although Jones led until near the end, Jackson went by him with daunting strides in 4:10.8. Many observers focused on Jones's beautiful running style, but Commissioner Sullivan, who knew better, saw "Jones wasn't in form. He has not been right since the trip upset him." The Oxonian did catch his eye, and he "realized that there was the man our boys had to beat. . . . I marked his name on my program, unconsciously selecting him as winner." Yet another enduring Stockholm legend was born: that of "the fabulous Jacker" of Oxford.[47]

Eight others made it through to the final: three Swedes, including national champion Ernst Wide, Evert Bjorn, and Kiviat's new friend John Zander; the German record holder, Erwin von Sigel; and four more Americans. The other surviving Yanks were defending champion Mel Sheppard, Oscar Hedlund, Louis Madeira of Penn, and Walter McClure of Oregon. It was tall, towheaded Wide, with his ability to unleash a sustained and powerful sprint on the last lap, who worried the Americans. As Coach Murphy said to Jones, "A good big man will beat the hell out of a good little man at any time."[48]

"THE GREATEST RACE EVER RUN," JULY 10, 1912

The milers rested on the ship during a rainy morning and ate their prerace meal about 11:30. As the weather cleared and they were preparing to depart for the stadium, they mulled over their strategies for the final. Taber talked with Jones, Kiviat with Sheppard. Since Shep realized "he had no hopes of repeating" his 1908 performance in this event, he agreed to Lawson Robertson's plan that he should serve as the rabbit for Kiviat, Jones, and Taber. Shep would set a slow pace, "the idea being that it could be won by sprinting"—which would be to Kiviat's advantage.[49]

Conditions in the stadium had altered dramatically since the morning. The afternoon was sunny but less intensely hot than on the previous days, with the biggest crowd to date in attendance for the much anticipated finals of the 1,500 and 5,000 meters. Even with his intense concentration and steely composure, Kiviat was still a patriotic young man whose eyes, he recalled, searched for the American flag "almost first when we came in the stadium with our bag on the way to the dressing room." To compete for the United States was "the most wonderful thing in life, particularly for a little Jewish boy" whose parents had escaped from the pogroms of eastern Europe. He was required to be in the locker room one-half hour before his race at 3:30, but his later comments suggest he went up into the stands at two o'clock to watch the finals of the 5,000.[50]

No one had ever seen a distance race like this before. Eleven men answered the starter's gun, with the Americans convinced that either George Bonhag or young Louis Scott, who had the year's best time, would give the great Continental rivals, Hannes Kolehmainen and Jean Bouin of France, all they could handle. Bonhag led briefly after two laps when Kolehmainen, with long, smooth strides and arms held high, moved into first place, followed closely by Bouin. The quick-striding, handsome Frenchman, who sported a Charlie Chaplin mustache and parted his hair in the middle, appeared to Kiviat "a little, stocky fellow, all shoulders. . . . And he ran so straight and chesty." Separating themselves from the field, the two Europeans began at this juncture, literally and spontaneously, to inaugurate the modern era in distance racing. Kolehmainen led through 1,500 meters in 4:17 when Bouin took over, running with a "metronomic tempo." They reached 3,000 meters in 8:46, which was just inside the world record for that distance. The field was soon half a lap behind them. Bouin was about 3 meters in front when they began their classic last lap duel, a series of surges and responses. But in the final 50 meters Kolehmainen somehow caught him and broke the tape by a meter. His time of 14:36.6 was fully twenty-five seconds under the existing world record.[51]

British miler Philip Baker, waiting anxiously for Kiviat and the other Americans to appear, went over to Kolehmainen and warmly congratulated him. Forced to represent the czar, the Finn "turned and pointed at the flag-pole and said: 'I would almost rather not have won, than see that [Russian] flag up there!'" Kiviat, who would later have his own memorable duels with Kolehmainen, admired Bouin. "The Frenchman's [a] great distance runner," he said.[52]

By 2:30, Kiviat was in the team locker room beneath the stands with the six other American 1,500 finalists. He put on his meet uniform—a thin white short-sleeved jersey with the national emblem in front and the white, almost knee-length shorts with red, white, and blue stripes down the sides. He taped his spikes and pinned on his number, 795. "We sat in the dressing room so we'd be together and [they] wouldn't have to go looking for [us] to go out in the race," he recalled. At about 3:15, the Swedish "start-crier" struck a gong in the locker room, alerting the milers it was time to go up to the field. Kiviat went from the locker room through the tunnel and entered the arena.

He proceeded to jog and stretch on the stadium track, warming up for the race. For the last time, he reviewed in his mind quickly the plan he had made with Robby. He knew the cinder track measured 383 meters to the lap, and he would have to race almost four laps. The race would begin at the top of the first turn and would finish near the end of the final or east straightaway. He was also fully aware that he had his work cut out for him: this was without doubt the best field of milers yet assembled anywhere for a competition. At least half of the fourteen finalists were capable of running 4:20 for one mile. He and John Paul Jones had run five seconds faster than that. Although the Yanks seemed unbeatable, track buffs worried there were too many starters for a fast race.[53]

Lap One. Kiviat had the rotten luck to draw the outside lane. The starter, Lieutenant G. Uggla of Stockholm, called the runners to their marks at 3:30. Then, moving a little behind the runners, he yelled the word *fardiga* ("ready" in Swedish), waited until the men were set, and fired his gun. According to plan, Mel Sheppard, who was on the pole, dashed into first place for a few meters; Arnaud of France quickly passed him, followed by von Sigel of Germany. Kiviat, who had to sprint from the extreme outside to get into the thick of the pack, tucked in behind Jones, with a small group of other Americans—Taber, Sheppard, and Hedlund— following closely. The Brits, Philip Baker and Arnold Jackson, were near the rear. Arnaud slowed down on the final straight and passed the first 400 meters in 65 seconds.[54]

Lap Two. Quickening his stride, Arnaud ran the second lap at a 63-second pace. This was still a very slow, tactical race, and the large field stayed well bunched, maintaining virtually the same positions as on lap one. Kivie was in third after they hit the back straight. He was clearly determined not to repeat Shep's mistake in the 800 final. There was one noticeable change, however. Ernst Wide, the feared Swede, moved up from the rear to seventh

13. "The Greatest 1500-Meters Race Ever Run." *The start:* Mel Sheppard leads; Kiviat is in the far outside lane. From Eric Bergvall, ed., *The Fifth Olympiad: Official Report of the Olympic Games of Stockholm 1912* (Stockholm: Wahlström and Widstrand, 1913), Plate 129.

place, in striking position. Running just in front of him in fifth place, Taber felt "it was anybody's race."[55]

Lap Three. Arnaud went by the 800-meter mark in 2:08. Watching each other warily, Kivie, Jones, and Taber began to take charge of the race at this point. As they went past Arnaud, the trio increased their speed. Taber was leading briefly when he passed the 1,000-meter mark in 2:39. Near the back of the pack and below the leaders' radar, Philip Baker signaled to his countryman, Jackson, and began to guide him around the crowded field ahead. With this maneuver, the Oxbridge team of Baker and Jackson probably ran fifty meters more than the other runners.[56]

Lap Four. When Kivie heard the bell ring for the last lap, he moved into the lead and picked up the pace even more, followed closely by Taber

14. *Lap two:* Kiviat in third place and moving up, just ahead of John Paul Jones. Courtesy of Mary Honey.

and Jones. He led around the first curve and down the backstretch, passing 1,200 meters in about 3:09. (His third 400 meters split was 61 seconds.) Uncharacteristically, his strike was not decisive. Kivie was so busy battling with his American rivals that all three were burning themselves out. Behind them on the backstretch, Philip Baker dropped back, but Arnold Jackson, who was in sixth place on the outside lane, revved up. His stride became even longer, his arms "swung like piston rods" as he passed Sheppard, while the defending champion tried gamely to stick with him.

Kivie took them sprinting through the last turn, holding onto his slight lead. Behind him in a bunch were Taber, Jones, Jackson, Shep, and the flying Ernst Wide of Sweden. Kivie remembered: "I heard him [Jackson] when he came off the turn. I was a little ahead of him, then, ten yards. . . . I heard a strange footstep. . . . [T]he teammates [Taber and Jones] were natural, 'cause I've heard them in the race for the last three laps. You get used to that. You understand that. You can tell when a man starts to sprint. The turn is hit harder. He's digging a little deeper to get a jump."[57]

The finish was very fast. Wide had waited too long to make his move. Jones simply did not have enough left. *Kiviat appeared to have won the race.* But Lawson Robertson, who was watching him anxiously, thought "Kiviat seemed to be running on his nerve and was wavering, but game."

Suddenly, Jackson passed Kivie. It was "the biggest surprise in life," Kiviat said, as Jackson seemed almost to leap in front of him to the tape. A step behind Jackson, Kivie and Taber finished together. "Each one believed himself the victor," wrote Lawson Robertson. "Their arms were thrown into the air almost at the same instant as they pushed their breasts to the finishing tape." In the stands, Commissioner Sullivan's "lips twitched," observed popular track writer Frank Albertanti, "his head sank forward and he was on the verge of falling into open space; his eyes moved restlessly and while a light breeze glided over his dome, he was choking a Svenska stogie to death. 'Gosh, that was a tough race to lose,' he exclaimed."

Kiviat said later, "[A] lot of spectators thought I did catch him [Jackson] at the tape—that it was a dead heat"—but that was his disappointment talking. He knew better. Taber had a different take: "I jumped Kiviat about a yard from the finish and finished second a foot ahead." He expanded his claim later: "Everybody on the American team said I finished second, and Kiviat who is one of the finest chaps you could meet, told me himself that he thought I beat him."[58]

The First Photo Finish. It was left to the officials to sort it out. "Kiviat and Taber were so close together the judges refused to trust their eyes to judge between them and waited for the development of photographic plates, automatically taken when the tape was broken," Coach Robertson wrote of the first use in track history of this new technology. "The photographs showed Kiviat was a shade ahead of Taber." Ever the proper gentleman, the Brown miler would not protest, even though he believed it was not fair. He mistakenly assumed a single photograph was snapped exactly when Jackson crossed the line, and he thought that in the next fraction of a second he had flung himself ahead of Kivie for second. He apparently did not realize that in making their judgment call, the officials had at hand *"a series of photos"* taken "as the runners passed the finishing line."[59]

15. *The first photo finish:* Arnold Jackson of England surges ahead in the final meters to defeat *(from left)* Jones, Kiviat, Ernst Wide of Sweden, and Norman Taber. Courtesy of Mary Honey.

Now heralds called out the results to the crowd in Swedish and English: first, Arnold Jackson, Great Britain, 3:56.8, smashing Mel Sheppard's Olympic record by more than 6.5 seconds; second, Abel Kiviat, United States, 3:56.9; third, Norman Taber, United States, 3:56.9; fourth, John Paul Jones, United States, 3:57.2; and fifth, Ernst Wide, Sweden, 3:57.6. Less than a second separated these five gallant runners at the finish of a remarkable Olympic race. With justice, then, Coach Robertson wrote, "[T]here was glory enough in the thing for everybody, though three expected points were kept out of the total tally of the United States."

Perhaps every bit as noteworthy as the performance of the first five men was the effort of Britisher Philip Baker, who, despite his painful foot, found the stamina and speed to kick in sixth. Behind him, Ernie Hjertberg's protégé John Zander, Walter McClure, and Mel Sheppard were seventh, eighth, and ninth, respectively. Oscar Hedlund, still ill from the voyage, was never a factor in the race and ended up a disappointing eleventh.[60]

Kiviat appeared relatively fresh after the race and had enough energy left to make a spontaneous gesture demonstrating what his coach, who was still watching him intently, called "the sportsmanlike spirit all his New York friends know is in him." When he ran over to shake Arnold Jackson's hand, Philip Baker had just picked up the almost unconscious Oxonian from the ground. Jackson's head was lolling from side to side, and he did not recognize Kiviat—who congratulated him with his standard "God bless you" greeting. Jackson pushed Kiviat's hand away, thinking it was a spectator's. Abel walked back to the American locker room. A few minutes later a message of regret came from Jackson to Kiviat and the American team. "Tell the Americans," Jackson's message ended, "that I shall be over to call on them as soon as I am myself again and shall apologize to them. I wouldn't have had that happen for the world." In turn, Kiviat and team manager Matt Halpin sent back their answer: "Tell Jackson it is all right. Tell him to stay right where he is, because it is up to the Americans to call on him. We take our hats off to him right here and now."[61]

In fact, Kiviat had been focused so intensely on his two American rivals that one of his first statements after he caught his breath apparently was, "Well, I beat Jones anyway." To Kiviat's chagrin, track writer Howard Valentine overheard the statement and reported it—as well as Abel's later denial. Although Valentine was an undisguised admirer of Kiviat throughout his career, he brutally blamed him in print "for the loss of the 1,500-metre race to England." So did the team's head coach. "The tongue lashing that Mike Murphy gave the Yankee trio after the race was worth going miles to hear," Valentine wrote, "but that didn't win the race."[62]

For once, Kiviat could not hide his emotions. He was deeply upset and disappointed. "It was just a stupid race on my part," he felt. In retrospect, he admitted he would have run it differently. He would have been less tentative in delivering a knockout blow to the field by starting his kick earlier. With his ability to sustain speed, he should "have sprinted the whole last lap." He also worried the loss was "a disgrace to my club, the Irish-American Club— getting beat by an Englishman, even if I am a Jew." But despite their strong nationalistic feelings, his Winged Fist teammates commiserated with him. Their words, "Hard luck" or "Sorry, Abel. . . . We know you gave everything you had," meant a great deal to him. Further consolation came from Sullivan himself, who told the newspapers that afternoon: "The loss of the 1,500-meter race was a terrible disappointment. We did not think there was any man living who could break up our wonderful combination of Sheppard, Kiviat, Taber, and Jones. . . . Still I think Kiviat is a greater runner than Jackson, which is proved by the fact that his [world] record is unbroken."[63]

Yet what has endured in our collective memory has been less about records—there would be other "miles of the century" subsequently, at much faster pace—than about the recognition that the Stockholm final was the prototype of a modern championship mile or 1,500-meter event. The steadfast application of a coach's grand design gave way to tactics under the competitive circumstances on the track. Consider the pace itself: successively quicker 400 meters of 65, 63, and 61 seconds, with a final 300 meters in 47.8, contradicted accepted strategic thinking. There was no long "float" in the middle of this race; these milers started slowly and edgily, then accelerated.

The result might have been different if Mel Sheppard had stuck to plan and served as a rabbit until the bell rang. He could have taken the weight of pace making off Kiviat and his countrymen—and the final spurt from Arnold Jackson. (A sensible alternative proposed by Howard Valentine would have been for either Lou Madeira or Walter McClure, neither of whom had a realistic chance, to set a fast pace for the first 800, leading to the same desired effect on the Englishman.) Then, as Ted Meredith remarked later, any one of the well-matched top five finishers might just as easily have come in first.[64]

Twenty years before the Stockholm Olympiad, William James pointed out in *Psychology* (1892) the paradox that ending up the world's second best boxer or rower can be the cause of personal disquiet and shame. Having learned to confront life's hard realities at a very early age, Abel Kiviat refused to blame others for his defeat. He accepted the fact that too much of his energy was spent sticking with John Paul Jones and not enough on making an extended and decisive last lap sprint. Yet he never fully came to terms with the experience of losing this challenge on the first great international stage of sport only days past his twentieth birthday. How could he know that this race would be how others would define him—and how, to some extent, he would define himself for the next eight decades? The painful memory would still disturb his sleep at age ninety-five, and he would remain very defensive about taking the silver medal from Norman Taber.[65]

Coach Lawson Robertson offered the wisest valedictory when he said all the medalists shared in the glory of this event. Tell that to the profoundly disappointed Kiviat, the toast of the world for the preceding months, but at this point and thereafter consigned to the company, in Sebastian Coe's sympathetic phrase, of the "nearly men" of Olympic sport.[66]

TEAMWORK, JULY 11–17, 1912

Abel Kiviat had guts, and he demonstrated it beyond a shadow of a doubt two days later. Despite being "so damned disappointed that nothing bothered me—didn't think of things," he ran one of the great races of his career in the heats of the 3,000-meter team event. Certainly, the nature of Olympic competition provided a powerful antidote to depression. The necessity to contribute to the success of his national team outweighed personal issues. Especially in light of the lofty expectations placed on the American track stars—to build a "sporting republic" at home and to showcase American superiority to the world—dwelling on personal failure would have been tantamount to committing an unpatriotic act.[67]

On Friday afternoon, Kiviat and Taber were the American entries with the nation's best distance runners—George Bonhag, Tell Berna, and Louis Scott—in the first of three heats of the 3,000-meter team race. This interesting event, discontinued by the IOC after 1924, had teams of five men traveling almost eight circuits of the stadium track and was scored like cross-country, with each nation's first three finishers counting in the scoring. The heat winners—the national teams with the lowest totals—would advance to the next afternoon's final. Given the inability of America's track stars to meet expectations in the 1,500 and 5,000 races, Taber noted "there was considerable doubt whether or not she would come out victorious" in the team event.[68]

The Yanks' sole competitor was Finland after the South African team scratched from the heat. This would be no cakewalk: in addition to the challenge of Hannes Kolehmainen, the Finns also entered Albin Stenroos, who had already placed third in the 10,000 meters behind Kolehmainen and Louis Tewanima. Kiviat was "under orders" from Robby to follow Kolehmainen when he heard the starter call *färdiga* and "to secure second place beyond question for the American team." Kolehmainen wasted no time going to the head of the pack, with Kivie on his shoulder and Stenroos close behind for the first two laps. Many in the big crowd were chanting *"Han-nes,"* but it was Kiviat who was about to create the excitement of the afternoon. When they reached the 1,500-meter mark, Kolehmainen and Kivie had opened up a twenty-meter gap over the pack. Kolehmainen looked unstoppable again, running "with beautiful judgement" of pace, commented a British reporter. "It is a debatable point," wondered the *London Daily Telegraph*'s correspondent at this juncture, "whether Kolehmainen's stamina will rob Kiviat of his speed." At the bell, Kivie was still drafting on the Finn's back as the pair led Tell Berna, now firmly in third place, by fifty meters. Kivie was able to stick with Kolehmainen on the back straight, and it looked to some observers as if he might make a close finish of it. But on the final curve Kolehmainen began to kick hard, and Kivie had nothing left with which to respond. Kolehmainen actually eased up during the last few meters before breaking the tape about fifty yards in front of his pursuer. Kiviat had done his job, however, leading Berna, Taber, and George Bonhag home in that order, thereby assuring the Americans' advancement.

Now the heralds shouted the surprising results of the heat into their megaphones: first, Kolehmainen in 8:36.9, lowering the unofficial world record for the event (8:46.6) by almost ten seconds; and second, Abel Kiviat in 8:46.3, which was also 0.3 second under the existing record set by Bror Fock of Sweden.

It was an extraordinary performance against the best distance runner in the world, particularly for a youth barely twenty who was competing way over distance. Although modern writers have forgotten Kiviat's role in this race, his contemporaries, including his teammates and rivals, were lavish with praise for his effort. "Abel Kiviat's wonderful running earned a place for the American team in the finals of the 3,000 team race," concluded the NYAC's *Winged Foot* magazine. Some now believed he had a great shot for individual honors in Saturday afternoon's final.[69]

Kiviat took it easy on the ship all Saturday morning. The final of the team race was at 3:30. On paper, it appeared that the two European finalists, England and Sweden, had too much experience and depth for the Americans. After all, only George Bonhag and the collegiate champion Tell Berna could be considered seasoned distance runners. Berna was encouraged, however, by his feeling that the five Swedish entrants were "all medium grade two-milers." The largest crowd yet in the stadium was unexpectedly treated to what many considered one of the most thrilling events of the 1912 games.[70]

For Kiviat, this event would be his fourth world-class race in five days—the heat and the final of the 1,500, his exceptional heat in and now the final of the 3,000. (He mused years later: "Is that enough for a school—ex-schoolboy, a few years out of high school? A shrimp?"—especially considering that he had not fully recovered from the recent ocean voyage, although he would not admit it.) He lined up for the start in the second row of the crowded field of fifteen, just behind Bonhag and Cyril Porter of Britain. As Coach Robertson urged, he went up with the leaders from the gun. Porter set a rather slow pace on the first lap, followed by Ernst Wide and Kivie. During the latter part of lap two, Bror Fock of Sweden, the former world-record holder, took over first and stepped up the pace, with Kivie right behind him in second place. Kivie stayed there on the third and fourth laps. When they reached lap six, Tell Berna made his move on the still bunched field. The blond-haired, long-striding Cornell man went by everyone into the lead, followed closely by Kiviat, Bonhag, and four Englishmen. Kivie was still in the hunt, but it looked like Berna's race. With the bell, Berna began a sustained sprint to the tape. That proved too much for Kiviat, who had finally run out of gas. "Kiviat," Orton Tewson of the *New York Times* reported, "after making all the running, was left behind on the last lap." He faded to the back of the pack. Meanwhile, on the final turn Thorild Ohlsson of Sweden began a long spurt of his own and nearly caught Berna at the tape. The officials had them in the identical time of 8:44.6.

When the heralds announced the individual places and times of the first eleven finishers, they did not include Kiviat's name. The final standing: first, the United States with 9 points (Berna, 1; Taber, 3; and Bonhag, 5), Sweden with 13 points, and Britain with a surprisingly high 23 points. A photograph taken of the winning team, including Kiviat, shows tired athletes, with mouths hanging open.[71]

Kiviat soon had more frustration. He discovered that whereas at home all five members of a winning cross-country squad received gold medals, the rules were different in Olympic team races. "First three, only," he recalled later of the experience. "I couldn't understand that. And that, while I didn't question any Olympic officials, but I questioned our men, particularly Mr. Dan Ferris, who was secretary treasurer and the brain of the Amateur Athletic Union." Perhaps Kiviat did complain, but there was little Dan Ferris could do. Although the thoughtful and soft-spoken Ferris was naturally diplomatic in controversial situations, he was only twenty-three years old and attending his first Olympics. Himself a sometime sprinter for the Irish Club, he had been secretary to Sullivan at the AAU since 1907 and, like his boss, was a stickler for the rules. Of course, he would have deferred to Sullivan about any decision to protest the awarding of only three medals. None was ever made.[72]

The failure to win a medal in the team race added insult to Kiviat's injured feelings from the 1,500. He remained "upset for a long while." Nevertheless, youthful exuberance enabled him both to participate in the concluding portion of the games and, finally, to explore Stockholm. He went to the stadium with his teammates on Sunday, July 14, to watch Jim Thorpe compete in the second session of the inaugural Olympic decathlon, then spread over three days. Thorpe won the high jump and a fast 110-meter hurdles race, and led the decathlon by 550 points at day's end.[73]

At nine o'clock that night, the Swedish Olympic Committee gave a memorable banquet for all the athletes and officials. Under the warm light of the Midnight Sun, about four thousand people ate at rows of long wooden tables set up in the infield of the stadium. Although the *Official Report* stated that only "non-intoxicating liquors" were served, Kiviat recalled that in front of each place was a "miniature keg with a spout and it was filled with Swedish punch." He and his friends quickly got high. The gates were opened afterward, and the Swedish public filled the grandstands for the entertainment: an all-male chorus of three thousand sang Swedish songs, and Baron de Coubertin touched his listeners with his brief address in Swedish. "We shall never forget Sweden," he said, "the Royal family, or the Swedish people. We leave with them a part of our hearts." From the tops of the two clock towers, an impressive fireworks display began, while the spirited athletes of the nations fraternized. (A group of Finnish weight throwers began the game of tossing their American counterparts in the air on blankets.) For the more international-minded young men, such as sprint champion Ralph Craig or the British miler Philip Baker, this event advanced the "transcendent purpose" of Coubertin's Olympic movement. For an unsophisticated lad such as Kiviat, it was more about sheer fun, although he grasped the real point of the event.[74]

Following this night of revelry and fellowship, Kiviat participated in the debut of baseball as an Olympic sport. He took his position as shortstop for the American team on a ball field laid out at the Ostermalm facility. The game had been arranged as an exhibition between Sweden's first baseball club, Vasteras, and some of the American track stars with experience in the sport. Conveniently, the S.S. *Finland* transported not only baseball uniforms and equipment, but also a distinguished umpire—elderly George Wright, once the star of the original Cincinnati Red Stockings. The Yanks were simply too speedy and too good for the Swedes. Indeed, there may never have been more world-record holders on a ball club, including a recovered Howard Drew and Fred Kelly, the hurdles champion, in the outfield, as well as second baseman John Paul Jones and shortstop Kivie as the keystone combination. Before a handful of spectators, they scored five runs in the first two innings, added eight more in the fifth, and won 13-3. Abel starred. He was flawless in the field, had two hits, including the game's only triple, scored two runs, and stole a base. Umpire George Wright called the game after six innings, but not before generously allowing the Swedes six outs in their final turn at bat.[75]

Kiviat spent Monday afternoon in the stadium watching what he realized was "real greatness"—Jim Thorpe in the final two events of the decathlon. After placing third in the javelin, Thorpe outran his rivals in the 1,500 meters with a personal record of 4:40.1. His middle-distance workouts with Kiviat and Mel Sheppard had paid off. Thorpe finished almost seven hundred points ahead of the runner-up, Hugo Wieslander of Sweden. His point score would endure for twenty years as a world record, until the Los Angeles Games of 1932. Olympic historian David Wallechinsky has remarked that Thorpe was so far ahead of his time that he probably would have earned a silver medal in the 1948 Olympiad. Small wonder Kiviat always maintained "that Thorpe was the greatest athlete that ever lived."[76]

As the afternoon waned, the medalists in all sports assembled outside the stadium for the awards ceremony and paraded in three columns toward three platforms placed on the infield before the royal box. In his dress uniform of blue blazer, white trousers, and white shoes, Kiviat was in the left column with the other "nearly men" who would receive the silver medal from the crown prince. The track and field prizes were presented first, with nearly one-half going to Americans. When the herald called "1,500 meters: Jackson, Kiviat, Taber," the three "went forward simultaneously to receive their prizes." Prince Gustav Adolph handed Kiviat his silver medal with a big blue-and-gold ribbon attached and congratulated him. However, Abel was still too disappointed to enjoy the moment.[77]

It took decades of maturation for him to be able to say, near the end of his life, "What's wrong with the silver?" "Most wonderful thing in life, particularly for a little Jewish boy," he said in 1984. He likened it to being awarded a medal at a White House dinner. Even more revealing, for this high school dropout, the medal ceremony had become a substitute for the Curtis High School graduation he had missed out on. "Just like graduating from school or college and walking up in a bench in your robe and getting a diplomy [sic], in high school you just got a diploma. And you had to walk up to the platform or stage." When viewers of Bud Greenspan's nationally televised special *America at the Olympics* heard Kiviat's vaguely Yiddish-sounding mispronunciation of "diploma," it may have seemed an aged character's charming eccentricity. It was in fact revealing of character: remembering at that moment his parents' pride in his Olympic fame, but also knowing how much more they valued intellectual prowess, he made the grandest moment of his life into a kind of simple if unconscious homage to their values.[78]

Moments after Kiviat received his medal, Jim Thorpe stepped forward for his prizes to thunderous applause. It was then that King Gustav uttered his famous words: "Sir, you are the greatest athlete in the world!" To which Thorpe apparently responded, "Thanks, King." A photographer then got Thorpe to pose for a group shot of ten young American champions, each crowned with a wreath for his performance. The five members of the winning 3,000-meter team look like young pashas. Standing next to a scowling Thorpe, little Abel, whose wreath covers the top half of his head, looks like an actor in a school play.[79]

16. The Awards Ceremony at Stockholm: *(from left)* Jim Thorpe, Abel Kiviat, Louis Scott, Norman Taber, George Bonhag, Tell Berna, and U.S. field event winners. Copyright © Bettmann/CORBIS.

That night it was time for youthful adventure. Kiviat walked with Thorpe and other buddies to the cafés "along the main street" and had "a beer or two," while observing all the "gorgeous-looking blondes." Because an open-air café usually had a bush in front, these Yanks would stick their hands through the bush to a table "and reach for the beer inside the bush without being seen." Thorpe, "who never had a nickel," according to Kiviat, always reached in for a glass of "Swedish punch." When a policeman answered the Swedes' call for help, the officer "would say, 'crazy American.' Wouldn't, never arrested us," Kiviat recalled. More than the horseplay and collegiality, the overall impact of Stockholm, with its elegant buildings, its parks, its waterfront, and its people, was unforgettable. "Nice land of the Swedish" was Kiviat's heartfelt summary phrase.[80]

Kiviat continued to have the time of his life for the next two days, interrupted only by a team photo shoot at noon on Tuesday and by a second baseball game that afternoon. He was at shortstop for the "Olympics," a team of easterners who played an exhibition against the "Finlands" of the western United States. This game drew a large crowd of curious Swedes to the Ostermalm field to see the easterners win 6-3. Kiviat's teammates this time included great ballplayers, catcher Charlie Brickley of Harvard and in right field Thorpe, who would later play six seasons in the National League. Jim was still "a bit tipsy" from celebrating, Kiviat remembered, but he "picked up a baseball and threw it 400 feet" from one end of the field to the other. Kivie had two hits, including a double, in three trips to the plate. He stole a base, scored a run, but made two errors in the field. He demonstrated conclusively that his athletic gifts were not limited to the cinder track.[81]

Although Kiviat and his teammates enjoyed the pleasures of Stockholm on Wednesday, June 17, a momentous event in the history of track and field also occurred that day that would permanently affect his reputation. At five in the afternoon, delegates from seventeen nations met in the columned and stately Parliament Building to form the IAAF, the sport's governing body. The federation was the brainchild of Leopold Englund, president of the Swedish Amateur Athletic Association, who realized track needed uniform rules for international competition and the standardization both of meet events and the resulting world records. Sigfrid Edstrom was elected as provisional president of the new IAAF, a position he held until 1945. The other two influential figures, James Sullivan, representing the United States, and a thirty-year-old German journalist and administrator, Carl Diem, joined with Edstrom in pushing for a second meeting, to be held in Berlin the following August. It was during the congress in Berlin that the IAAF ratified the first official list of world records, with Kiviat named as the first official holder of the 1,500-meter standard.[82]

GRAND TOUR, JULY 18–AUGUST 10, 1912

It was time for the *Finland* to depart. Most of the American party, including Kiviat, sailed for Dover, England, shortly after midnight. Others formed groups that planned to "combine sight-seeing with invitations to compete in meets in various countries." Two athletes Kiviat avoided, Jim Duncan and the domineering Avery Brundage, headed for Helsinki and czarist Russia.[83]

Lawson Robertson's athletes also had an invitation to Russia, but that presented a problem for Kiviat. For half a century, the anti-Semitic czarist regime had refused entry to Russian Jews naturalized in the United States who were seeking to visit their native land, nor were the children of these emigrants welcome. Meanwhile, the Jews of Russia had been experiencing "almost unrelieved gloom." Their lot in 1912 was one of "expulsions and restrictions, ritual murder, accusations, and arbitrary arrests." In response, the American Jewish community had been lobbying President William Howard Taft and the U.S. Congress to abrogate the 1832 Commercial Treaty between the United States and Russia, and this campaign was moving toward a successful conclusion that summer. Kiviat would not go to Russia, where, as he put it, there were "pogroms. They were killing Jews right and left."[84]

Ironically, it was the experience of Jimmy Rosenberger, his gentile teammate, that brought home how difficult Russia was for Jews. Rosie was sufficiently interested in a quick trip to Russia to apply for a passport from the Russian consul in Stockholm. The consul assumed Rosenberger was a Jewish name and refused to issue a visa. "Mr. Rosenberger declares that he is a more or less pious Christian and protests to the American consul at this indignity thus put upon him by being refused admission to a country professing to be of friendly disposition towards America," *The American Hebrew* reported. Although the Russian official relented, Rosenberger was no longer interested.[85]

Instead, the Irish Club athletes went from Dover to Paris with a group of twenty-one American Olympians. "We figured we['d] get a lot of free wine and stuff," Kiviat said. But there was more to his post-Olympic travel plans, he admitted to the Staten Island newspaper. "A fellow don't get a chance to see the world every day of his life, so I'm going to make the most of it this time."

The awakening of the French people's interest in sport after the turn of the century, including expanded press coverage, was part of the appeal of hosting these young American champions.[86] During the Yanks' first evening in Paris, they were taken on a tour of the music halls by the congenial Jean Bouin. As a memento of the occasion, the Frenchman "gave me a [gold-plated] cane, with his name on it, J-e-a-n Bouin," Kiviat recalled later. "I remember them kidding me when I carried it, and I remember the warm beer. We all got along swell."[87]

On Tuesday morning, July 23, accompanied by their ailing coach, Mike Murphy, they took an early morning train for the capital of the champagne region, Rheims, ninety miles east of Paris, with its magnificent cathedral. The marquis de Polignac initiated the visit and welcomed them with large carriages decorated with American and French flags, which took them to their hotel. After lunch and a brief rest, they went out to the Pommery Park, located on the outskirts of the city, to compete against French Olympians and provincial champions in front of a crowd of more than fifteen thousand. Jim Thorpe stood out, taking the 110-meter hurdles from the Olympic champion, Fred Kelly of the University of Southern California, in 15.6. Kiviat, who had clearly lost his sharpness, ran from the scratch mark with Henri Arnaud in a handicap 1,500 race. Although he led Arnaud home again, exactly as he had done in his heat and the finals at Stockholm, he could not catch another Frenchman who had started with a fifty-meter allowance. Compensating for his disappointing performance was the memorable exhibition of "'trick' flying" by airplanes circling over the stadium.[88]

The tourists returned to Paris for five more eventful days. They competed in the stadium at Colombes, where Kiviat captured the 1,500 meters in 4:06.8, his slowest time of 1912. He could not have imagined at that moment that his next 1,500 race at Colombes would be as a doughboy in military uniform.[89]

Abel and his buddies were a merry band, and they made a hit in France. Yet the Yanks' boyish immaturity confirmed for the French a lingering impression of a certain American coarseness and provincialism. For Kiviat, however, it was an eye-opening opportunity that came to few youths of his background. Jewish lads from struggling immigrant families were not ordinarily wined and dined by a marquis in Europe. His talent had opened up new vistas, although he was still too young and unsophisticated to benefit fully from the French experience.[90]

While sports officials in London talked about organizing a match race between Kiviat and Arnold Jackson, the Irish Club athletes traveled to Ireland for a two-day visit, where "they had the time of their lives. We didn't have to spend a damn cent; everything was free." That included quantities of food, Irish whiskey for the Whales, and "Guinnesses beer and stout" for Kiviat. As he floated through this brief stay, the island's troubles apparently escaped him. He never mentioned the political convulsions over home rule that were building up that August toward an inevitable climax.[91]

They left by train for Queenstown in Cork, the historic Place of Embarkation for millions of Irish emigrants. But there was a potential problem: "We had no tickets," Kiviat recalled. "I didn't have a damn cent in my pocket when I reached the ship. . . . Whoever invited us to Ireland paid our expenses." Most of the Irish Club party, including Kiviat and Alvah Meyer, boarded the steamship *Celtic* of the White Star Line on Friday, August 2, for the eight days' crossing to the United States. They found emigrants from all over Europe packed into steerage. From a place of comfort above, Kiviat observed for himself exactly what his parents had experienced in their own desperate passage twenty years earlier.[92]

A KNICKERBOCKER TRIBUTE, AUGUST 23–24, 1912

Kiviat was a celebrity on Staten Island, and normal life did not come easily. His parents hung out his Olympic jersey and running shorts in a spare room. "And, people would come in and see them—they'd always take them in there," he recalled.[93]

He still had the final reunion of the Olympic team. New York put the red carpet out, with a committee of prominent civic and AAU leaders arranging "a tribute from Father Knickerbocker, the like of which no body of athletes has ever been accorded before." On Friday night, August 23, about one hundred Olympians and officials attended a performance of the hit operetta *The Rose Maid* at the Globe Theater on Broadway at Forty-sixth Street, as the guests of the producers. The appearance of "a stunning rosebud garden of modish girls" in the cast held their attention.[94]

Kiviat gathered with his fellow Olympians early the next morning at the Irish Club house on East Fifty-ninth Street for the great parade in their honor. Sixty-five men were assigned alphabetically to thirty open automobiles, two or three in each. Kiviat was in the thirteenth car with his buddy, the hard luck distance runner Willie Kramer, whose leg injury had wrecked any chance he might have had against Kolehmainen at Stockholm. The parade that began at ten o'clock soon became, in Commissioner Sullivan's words, "a monster celebration." New Yorkers have always loved a parade, and to many in the crowd this one ranked with the city's reception in 1899 for the returning victor of Manila Bay, Admiral George Dewey, and the ticker-tape parade for Theodore Roosevelt in 1910. Fully twenty thousand people escorted the Olympic team along the route from Forty-first Street and Fifth Avenue to city hall. New Yorkers crowded rooftops and stood in open window frames or on the ledges of office buildings, and hundreds of thousands more lined up five deep on the sidewalks. In front of them, along the street curbs, more than ten thousand schoolchildren cheered their heroes with "the Olympic 'yell.'"

A photograph survives of Kiviat and Kramer seated in the back seat of an open-air car, dressed in the team's snappy outfit of blue blazers and skimmer hats. Riding directly behind them was the legendary Hawaiian swimmer Duke Kahanamoku. Jim Thorpe received a special honor: he sat "in solitary grandeur in a big car," preceded by another vehicle that contained only his Stockholm trophies. At that moment, the motorcade passed a huge sign advertising the recently nominated Democratic ticket of Woodrow Wilson and Thomas R. Marshall. News reports of the event singled out Abel Kiviat, Ralph Craig, Ted Meredith, Pat McDonald, and Matt McGrath as receiving "their share of applause from the crowd."

When the parade reached city hall, the athletes grouped around the reviewing stand, where Mayor William J. Gaynor warmly thanked them for their accomplishments. After the team cheered the mayor, Thorpe, McGrath, and McDonald were chosen to shake His Honor's hand.[95]

The weekend's concluding event was a gala dinner for five hundred guests at Terrace Garden. Supreme Court judge Victor J. Dowling, the Tammany politico and a former leader of the Irish Club, chaired the evening and spoke fervently for the cause of amateur sport. Commissioner Sullivan commented about Sweden's successful advancement of the Olympic movement and outlined briefly what he hoped would be the seminal role of the new IAAF in the continuing modernization both of the games generally and of track and field specifically. Finally, Col. Thompson reminded the assembled athletes how much the Olympic experience had advanced America's standing in the world. The assumption was that their athletic dominance confirmed the superiority of American civilization and its newer emphasis on world order through economic and cultural interdependence.[96]

More than most at Terrace Garden, scholarly Norman Taber understood Col. Thompson's message. His fellow track stars, having been recruited from throughout the widespread, heterogeneous nation, "formed a democratic team that had one common purpose and view; namely—to reflect credit on their country." If the Olympic team served the republic as a kind of super-heated melting pot at home and as an advance agent of American culture abroad, Taber read more into the experience. "On an equal basis the nations are brought into contact with one another and given an opportunity of becoming acquainted with the customs that prevail in other parts of the world than their own and of gaining a broadened point of view upon matters of international importance," he wrote. "These great Olympiads have been and should continue to be potent factors in the fostering of peace and union throughout the civilized countries."[97]

The rhetoric never pierced some aspects of reality, however. As grandly as Col. Thompson might orate about the role of athletics in the American-ization process, meaningful team unity remained an elusive goal. Despite a summer in which they all lived together, the social experiences of Kiviat and Thorpe, ethnic poor men, remained significantly different from those of Norman Taber and Ted Meredith, middle-class WASPs. A theoretical American sporting republic had limitations on the full rights of citizenship.[98]

OF GOLDEN LEGENDS

The parade and hoopla ended, but the memories of the games' "golden glamour" endured. For the next half century, Ted Meredith argued that "for management, good feeling and a general all round good time for the athlete it is my opinion that this was the greatest Olympiad." He bolstered his case by pointing out "that 1912 team was composed of athletes who made his-tory in American athletics and when any list of 'greats' is compiled you will find among them a number of the 1912 group."[99]

Of the finalists in the metric mile at Stockholm, Kiviat would compete often against Norman Taber, Mel Sheppard, and Oscar Hedlund in the years leading up to the Great War. Others, whose paths would not cross his again, burnished their reputations with sterling adult lives. For example, John Paul Jones's track career ended abruptly upon his graduation from Cornell—but not before this golden lad returned to form and lowered his own world mile record to 4:14.4 at the 1913 IC4A championships. Jones stunned the track world with a final quarter-mile split of 58.2. He went on to a productive professional career, founding a firm that provided the engineering for such significant projects as the Cleveland Museum of Art and the Ohio state capitol. Tellingly, he and Taber maintained lifelong friendships with Arnold Jackson, but not with Kiviat. For his part, Kiviat once remarked admiringly to Jones's daughter that J. P. remained for him the model of a great miler and a gentleman.[100]

Kiviat had no known face-to-face contact with his conqueror, Arnold Jackson, for another forty-four years, until they met at the 1956 Penn Relays. They had virtual meetings of sorts, however, through frequent press "postmortems" of their famous race. On one such occasion, Kiviat told Arthur Daley of the *Times:* "'It was the only conservative race I ever ran in my life and I had to pick the worst possible moment for doing it.'" After acknowledging the magnitude of Kiviat's achievement in smashing the 1,500 record thrice in two weeks (for which "'he never received quite the full credit he deserved'"), Jackson told Daley good-naturedly, "'I hate to think even in retrospect, that he was slackening on the job. The race has become a legend, and one might as well, at this date, try to upset King Arthur's Round Table.'"

In the long interval between their real encounters in Stockholm and Philadelphia, "the fabulous Jacker" became an Oxford legend. He remained a true amateur athlete: he continued to play hockey for his college, but ran only a few more big races. His last, almost a carbon copy of Stockholm, was a gritty anchor leg from fifteen yards behind in the four-by-one-mile event at the rain-swept 1914 Penn Relays, to give Oxford the narrowest of victories over the host Quakers. (Ironically, Jackson started off in a poor position because Oxford's third runner, Rhodes scholar Norman Taber, was beaten soundly by Louis Madeira of Penn, another of the Stockholm milers.) The guns of August 1914 stripped away the last pretense of gentlemanly casualness from newly commissioned Lieutenant Jackson. He used his "rare courage and will-power," wrote his old teammate Philip Baker, as "a specialist in trench raids—raids of extraordinary daring in conception, backed by lightning responses to any enemy resistance or surprise." Wounded three times and left with a permanent limp, Lieutenant Colonel Jackson received seventeen medals by 1918, including the Distinguished Service Order with three bars. His later accomplishments, after changing his name to Arnold Strode-Jackson, were no less remarkable. He was, in succession, a delegate to the Paris Peace Conference, a member of the British Olympic Council, a successful business executive in the United States, the director of the first Kentucky Derby Festival, an administrator of wartime antisabotage programs, a lecturer on art history, and a novelist. At his death in 1972, "the fabulous Jacker" was eulogized "as the Brasenose man of the century." Indeed, he seemed to many the personification of the ideal Olympian of the twentieth century.[101]

That honor might also belong to Jackson's lifelong friend, the sixth-place finisher at Stockholm, Philip Baker. Like Jackson, Baker was too tough-minded and experienced to buy the post-Olympic grouse that Britain was no match in competition for the overly professionalized American athletic apparatus. To remedy the situation, he argued persuasively, the English had to take a leaf from the Americans' "organizing ability and intelligence, supported by a reasonable amount of money." His message eventually had an impact.[102]

True to his Quaker faith, Baker was a noncombatant during World War I but served as a courageous and decorated ambulance driver in France and Italy. That experience dramatically shaped his later life. While a delegate to the Paris Peace Conference, he played a significant behind-the-scenes role in founding the League of Nations. He also returned to intensive training for the mile and won the silver medal in the 1,500-meters at the 1920 Antwerp Olympiad. Baker captained the British Olympic teams in 1920 and 1924. Thereafter, he was devoted to the cause of world disarmament. He served as a member of Parliament for four decades, a minister in the Churchill and Atlee governments (where some derided him as naive and injudicious), a U.K. representative to the United Nations, and chairman of the Labour Party. Throughout the century, he lectured and wrote on world peace. In 1959, he was awarded the Nobel Peace Prize, based in no small part on his magisterial study *The Arms Race*. In 1977, Queen Elizabeth made him a life peer as Baron Noel-Baker. He also remained passionately devoted to athletics and the Olympic movement. Upon his death in 1982, Sir Roger Bannister wrote that not only had Noel-Baker played a central role in placing sport on the agenda of the United Nations and other leading international agencies, but elite athletes had looked to him for advice and "for his unfailing personal interest in their progress."[103]

In the Stockholm final, Kiviat's Swedish pal John Zander finished behind Baker in seventh place. By 1917, he had matured into a great distance runner, and, with neutral Sweden still engaged in a normal athletic life, he took aim at his friend Abel's 1,500-meter world record. During the Stockholm Championships at the Olympic Stadium on August 5 that year, Zander went out fast but had enough left to break Kiviat's record in 3:54.7. He never came close to that time again. It remained the world standard until the advent of superstar Paavo Nurmi.[104]

In Kiviat's view, no one would ever measure up to the athletic standard of Jim Thorpe. Even in his nineties, he could tick off the Oklahoman's outsized achievements in football and baseball. He never wavered in his feeling that the AAU's decision in 1913 to bar Thorpe from amateur competition and to take away his medals and prizes because he had played briefly in the minor leagues was "awful." "A poor baseball player getting—what was it, a hundred dollars a month?" he asked sarcastically. The episode left Kiviat bitter about the shabby treatment of struggling athletes by the lords of amateur sport. He would shortly acquire first-hand knowledge of this treatment.[105]

Some Olympians were even less fortunate and paid the ultimate price during the Great War. Two summers after they returned from Stockholm with their imaginations fired by Coubertin's vision of a sixth Olympiad in Berlin in 1916, European athletes exchanged their track shorts and spiked shoes for army uniforms and bayonets. Both the silver and bronze medalists at 5,000 meters, the legendary Jean Bouin of France and George Hutson of England, were killed in the early days of the fighting. Leading his artillery corps over the top in an attack, Bouin was felled by a shell splinter, whispered "Vive la France," and died. Other Olympians, young men of exceptional promise, soon joined the two runners on the list of war casualties.[106]

On the eve of this nightmare, Philip Baker was not the only athlete to notice "the gathering storm clouds" in 1912. Hannes Kolehmainen evidently had had enough of Europe, especially with the increasing Russification of Finland. On September 1, he arrived in the port of New York in the steerage of the steamship *California* with his brother Willi, spent the night at Ellis Island, and, after admission to his new country, told reporters he planned to work as a mason. What he did not mention was that Lawson Robertson had recruited him to run for the Irish Club. Kolehmainen's arrival signaled the start of a new era for distance running in America. It also marked the beginning of the final phase of Winged Fist supremacy in track and field. Kiviat's competitive career would now be linked closely with the great Kolehmainen's.[107]

7

"The Most Versatile Runner in the World"

ON LABOR DAY 1912, New York's growing army of track fans, captivated by the reports from Stockholm, had a choice of attending five meets in the metropolitan area. The Irish Club's annual Tailtin Games at Celtic Park was the most attractive because in connection with it the AAU also held its national all-around championship. On a field turned into a virtual quagmire by heavy rains, Jim Thorpe was sensational. In the last major track competition of his life, he demolished his rivals and broke Martin Sheridan's three-year-old record for the ten events by ninety-one points. Sheridan himself was moved to tell a reporter: "Even when I was in my prime I could not do what he did today."

Kiviat had little competition in the handicap mile race and strode to an easy victory on the rain-swept cinders. Focusing on Thorpe and Kiviat, news reports from Celtic Park barely mentioned the appearance of the great Kolehmainen of Finland, who came directly from an ocean voyage and Ellis Island to be introduced to the scattering of wet fans and to run three laps as an exhibition. The beat writers missed a story of long-term consequence. Although a few Continental track stars had run in America after the London Olympiad in 1908, Kolehmainen was setting the pace for a post-Stockholm invasion of athletes and officials who would begin to internationalize the daily lived world of athletics. Concurrent with the lofty discussions among the elite leaders of the IOC and the IAAF in European capitals, this brief prewar movement provided American trackmen with real glimpses of the far wider stage on which their athletic clubs and schools would perform in the future.

Lawson Robertson deserved some of the credit. He did more than supervise milers and shot-putters at Stockholm. He used his reputation, quiet charm, and commanding presence to recruit distance runners from the Scandinavian national teams for the Irish Club. Others would soon follow Kolehmainen to New York, including athletes and officials from Asia and central and eastern Europe.

The ships sailed both ways. When several European nations decided to reach a higher level of performance in preparation for the Olympiad scheduled for Berlin in 1916, the lesson of Ernie Hjertberg's success in Sweden was not lost. The Europeans began contract negotiations with Robby and other leading American coaches. The best American athletes also were encouraged to compete all over the world. This spontaneous global initiative lasted only a few years because the Great War intervened. During the 1920s, the trend would prove irresistible again, setting the structure for the globalization of track and field in the twentieth century.

These developments inevitably had a direct impact on Kiviat's career. His coach would make plans to leave the country for a plum of an overseas assignment. Kiviat himself would be invited to join an all-star tour of the then-remote Australasia. He would also have the opportunity to duel Kolehmainen in memorable match races, thereby sharpening his skills at longer distances. In the process, he helped to refute the unjust European criticism post-Stockholm that America's elite athletes were narrow, overtrained specialists. These competitions with Kolehmainen, together with his striking successes at a variety of middle distances, would earn Kiviat a well-deserved reputation as the era's most versatile runner.[1]

Still a person of quiet bearing at this time, Kiviat nevertheless reveled in the limelight. As he reached physical maturity and the height of his success on the track, he was fulfilling his deep-seated need to act the successful leader. The oldest Kiviat child in an education- and success-minded family, he became "the great little miler" who had overcome his frustrating failure as a student in the school system.[2]

The price of this renown was his increased vulnerability to the overt and subtle attacks by bigots. At a moment when his sport was pursuing an intensive globalization initiative in the name of international comity, young Abel experienced his own society's inhumanity. Much as he always downplayed its impact, anti-Semitism would shadow the climactic phase of his career.

DIEGES & CLUST

When Kiviat returned to New York from Europe, he had a job waiting for him at Dieges & Clust. Capt. Charles J. Dieges knew a good thing. Kiviat was an excellent hire, given his three years of solid experience as a salesman, his practiced and pleasant public manner, and his shrewd use of his contacts in the sports world.[3]

He was quite familiar with his new boss. Capt. Dieges, a well-known AAU and MAL official, had timing as his hobby and his passion, and he approached it as an art form. For the previous two decades, he had seemed to be ubiquitous, holding a stopwatch at all manner of contests involving automobiles, horses, or men. However, track and field in its strictly amateur construction was his sport.[4]

Born into the ethnic enclave of Little Germany on the Lower East Side in 1865, Dieges developed into a "strapping" fellow and a natural athlete who specialized in weight-throwing events for the Pastime Athletic Club. He learned his trade as an apprentice with a New York jewelry firm and became a talented designer. In 1898, he joined with Prosper Clust to found the firm of Dieges & Clust, which developed into one of the country's leading manufacturers of medals, trophies, plaques, and class pins and rings. The same warm and enthusiastic personality that made Dieges so popular a figure in athletic circles was a significant factor in his successful business.

To his legion of friends and admirers, Dieges was an inveterate joiner in the interconnected turn-of-the-century male society of leading fraternal and athletic organizations, the National Guard, and Tammany politicians. "Captain Charley," the *New York Times* once remarked about his boosterism, "did not come to this country wearing wooden shoes." On the contrary, he was the proverbial "well-met and friendly person," a former president of Dieges & Clust recalled.[5]

Kiviat's work environment was as dynamic as his boss. The offices of Dieges & Clust were on John Street, a few yards from Lower Broadway, in the center of the city's lively jewelry district. Around the corner was the

Singer Building, a beautiful and ornate forty-seven-story skyscraper, then the second-tallest building in the world. Wall Street was nearby.[6]

Captain Dieges paid Kiviat modest wages. His salary, Kiviat recalled, "was never up enough. Never reached over thirty-five dollars a week." He held onto the job because Dieges allowed him time to train and to skip work for competitions. Nevertheless, his family was impressed and grateful for this excellent source of support. "He sold medals and trophies to all the schools because of his connection in athletics; he had connection with all the schools," his brother Harold remembered with pride. "That was a big job in those days." Kiviat had to hustle constantly to cover a sprawling territory, which included northern and central New Jersey. "All the towns in Jersey ran big track meets," he remembered. "Singer [of Elizabeth] used to have one every year. I supplied the prizes. Helped run it."[7]

DUELS WITH KOLEHMAINEN, FALL 1912

Kiviat had little time to rest on his Olympic laurels. Recruited by an Olympic teammate, distance runner Harry Smith, who functioned as a kind of early underground sports agent, Kiviat went upstate to Troy on Sunday, September 8, and ran in a track meet sponsored by Our Lady of Mount Carmel Church of Watervliet. Although he impressed the unsophisticated spectators with his "remarkable mile" in "the wonderful time of 4:35," he would live to regret the experience. According to a later statement by one of the parish priests, the Rev. M. L. Galanti, Smith had arranged with Roscoe Campbell—the same local AAU official who had allegedly paid Abel and his fellow "Invincibles" $125 the previous winter—to give Kiviat the sum of $25 for his appearance. Kiviat, of course, denied the allegation. However, the practice of track stars' receiving appearance money for giving exhibitions to eager fans was not uncommon. Despite the athletes' self-righteous denials to AAU officials and the press, this murky business of under-the-table payments helps to explain in part how Roscoe Campbell and Harry Smith could promote successful events week after week all over the East Coast.[8]

By Tuesday, Coach Robertson had reassembled the team at Celtic Park to prepare for the national championships in Pittsburgh. Kiviat was starting to get sharp again, and Robby pushed him harder. He made no secret of his "ardent designs" on John Paul Jones's unofficial world record for the mile. To ensure the proper conditions for setting records, the host city's AAU officials announced their intention of having the specially prepared quarter-mile track at Forbes Field in top condition. For a second year, however, the athletes dug their spikes in and found a heavy surface with loose cinders.[9]

Once again, too, a large and enthusiastic crowd was on hand when Kiviat went to the starting line on September 21 to defend his national title. The field lacked the depth of either the Olympic trials in June or the final at Stockholm. His principal opponents were familiar—the BAA's Jim Powers and the NYAC's Dave Noble. George Kimball of the BAA was the rabbit, and he took off from the gun "at a '400' pace," with Kivie sticking close to him. At the half-mile mark, Kimball and Kivie were one hundred yards ahead of Powers. They continued to increase their lead on the backstretch of the third lap. A few of the well-meaning Whales standing on the infield grass "shouted for [Kiviat] to take his time. He slowed down into almost a jog," the *Times* reported. When Kimball, the unexpected rabbit, completed three laps, he walked off the track. Now Kivie "was told he could establish a world's record if he tried." He began a prolonged lift, sprinting into the homestretch far ahead of Powers and Noble while normally staid officials and thousands of fans shouted "'Come on Kiviat.'" He broke the tape in 4:18.6, lowering his own year-old meet standard by a full second, and received an extended ovation.

Observers concluded unanimously afterward that this was a unique opportunity gone awry. The NYAC's *Winged Foot* magazine commented that if Kiviat had had competition on the last lap, he would have undoubtedly broken Jones's record of 4:15.4. The *Times* had a more accurate analysis and placed the blame where it belonged. "Had he been coached *in the third quarter*," the paper concluded, "it is thought he would have established a mile record." Nevertheless, his sterling race was the focus of Sunday's newspaper coverage nationwide.[10]

Robby's athletes outdid themselves in other events. The Irish Club won eight (of eighteen) events in various disciplines and outscored the NYAC sixty-seven points to thirty-four. They would have had more points, but Kolehmainen, who won the five-mile run easily, was still required by the

AAU rules to compete unattached for a six-month period. It was all sweet justification after the club's several disappointments at Stockholm.

That feeling was particularly true for two of Kiviat's buddies. Alvah Meyer had the race of his life, the fastest 220-yard dash yet run around a curve. His winning time of 21.8 tied the American record and, given the quality of the track, was considered "phenomenal." Perhaps most gratifying to Kiviat, Howard Drew, still representing Springfield High School, took the 100 from Meyer, the Olympic silver medalist, and became the first "school-boy" to win a national senior championship.[11]

One week later, Kiviat went up to Montreal for the Canadian national meet and smashed one of Canada's oldest records—set in 1892 by former Olympic champion George Orton—winning the mile in 4:20.6.[12] With the year's championship season completed, Kiviat finally settled into a routine in New York. While he resumed his business career, shrewd Lawson Robertson started him immediately on running longer distances. He was ready for it, as his impressive 3,000-meter contest against Kolehmainen in Stockholm had demonstrated.

He faced an immediate and major challenge. Coach Robertson entered him in a two-mile race against Kolehmainen at Celtic Park on Columbus Day. Track fans looked forward to the distance race of the year in America, and the Olympians delivered.[13] Koley (as the Irish athletes nicknamed Kolehmainen) went out from the starter's gun and set a fast pace, with Kivie tucked in behind him for the first seven laps. The pair entered the backstretch of the bell lap together. Was Kolehmainen remembering how he had smoked Kivie at this juncture of their 3,000-meter duel at Stockholm? At the least, he "underestimated Kiviat sadly." Kivie burst past the surprised Hannes and tried to steal the race. He quickly opened up a five-yard lead and tried desperately to maintain it to the finish, but Koley made up the deficit during the final hundred yards. In the excitement of the finish, one of the judges dropped the tape, and the officials called the race a tie. Given the condition of the track, the time of 9:24.6 was excellent—only two-tenths of a second slower than the unofficial American outdoor record.[14]

During the month's interval before their next race, Kolehmainen acclimated himself to board tracks through regular workouts and predicted a winning time of at least 9:32. Kiviat, in contrast, trained only four times indoors. For the first time, he acknowledged publicly a worsening—and potentially devastating—problem for a man whose strong suit was indoor track. "The little Staten Islander suffers from 'indoor sickness,' and has to limit his work on the board floor on that account," Howard Valentine reported to readers of the *New York Globe*. "Every time he runs hard indoors Kiviat becomes nauseated and remains that way for perhaps an hour after his effort." Despite that surprising revelation, Kiviat was confident he could compete successfully against Kolehmainen and his own Olympic teammate, Louis Scott of Patterson, in the feature two-mile event of the games of Brooklyn's St. Agnes Athletic Club.

A Brooklyn movie house stoked interest during the days before the race by showing the new film of the Stockholm Olympic meet to large crowds. They were "said to be the most perfect set of sport films ever made." Many of the paying customers were Finnish Americans who cheered lustily when Kolehmainen appeared on the screen entering the stadium on his way to winning gold in the 8,000-meter cross-country race.[15]

The meet on Saturday night, November 9, was in the Fourteenth Regiment Armory in Brooklyn's grand Park Slope neighborhood. The feature event started with a bang, as Kolehmainen led Kivie and Louis Scott around five laps of the 220-yard oval. The Americans had the advantage of extensive indoor experience and passed Kolehmainen on the wide first turn of lap six. Kivie, following a plan laid out by Coach Robertson, took over now, moving quickly and passing the mile in 4:34.2. Robby was at trackside giving him lap times "and thus kept him going at a steady pace all the way." Scott stayed right behind him until the mile-and-a-half mark and then made his move to the front. The Patterson man's lead did not last long; Kolehmainen sprinted past him. Kivie was still full of running, however, and in turn retook the lead from the Finn.

By the gun lap, the race had settled into an extended two-man sprint between Kivie and Scott. Reviving the script he had used to perfection in the previous winter's Baxter Mile against Oscar Hedlund, Kivie "made four distinct jumps in that last circuit, and each one kept Scott from coming up on even terms." He was in full control, even glancing behind him as he neared the finish. Kivie broke the tape by two yards, with Kolehmainen another ten yards in the rear. The winning time on the armory floor was 9:20.2. It was the second-fastest two-mile yet run indoors, exceeded only by George Bon-hag's questionable 9:14.2 in Buffalo almost three years earlier.[16]

Kolehmainen appeared fresh when he walked into the locker room, but had trouble breathing. "He don't like the hot air or the board floor, but he'll run some more, and maybe he'll learn to run in the house, like you Ameri-cans," his brother Willi remarked. Kiviat, the young man "who handed the great Finn the very first defeat of his career in a scratch race" and "showed a brand of running that was nothing short of wonderful," was again sick to his stomach for an extended period.[17]

In time, Kolehmainen did become virtually unbeatable indoors at long distances. Yet three decades later, in the midst of World War II, sports writer Lawrence Robinson would recall this series of "two-mile tests with Kiviat" as Kolehmainen's "greatest races" in this country. They offered a rare insight into the world of elite distance running of the future. Before long, successful athletes would not only borrow a leaf from Kolehmainen and train daily and single-mindedly, but also need Kiviat's innate ability to race at sprinter's speed.[18]

Kiviat had a breather of two weeks before his next round of intense competitions, but he kept himself razor sharp. On Thanksgiving Eve, at his regiment's indoor meet, he took the then-popular 1.5-mile handicap race in record time.[19] Less than forty-eight hours later, Coach Robertson walked into the Dieges & Clust office unexpectedly on Friday afternoon and said: "'Hey, Kivie, we may need you for the fifth man on the cross-country team at Van Cortlandt Park to-morrow. Be sure to bring your suit with you.'" Robby was referring to the *national* AAU meet for which Kiviat had not trained at all. As Kiviat recalled the event eight decades later, "'I had never run it [cross country]. We had to stop at someone's house to borrow a uni-form and shoes.'"[20]

The 6.2-mile race at the park in the Bronx was more like a local cham-pionship. Only thirty starters from four New York clubs were on hand, most tough hill-and-dale veterans. Everyone in the large crowd of specta-tors assumed Kolehmainen would win, *with all kinds of wagers backing that sentiment.* But after Hannes dropped out shortly before the midway point with a stitch in his side, Willie Kramer, who had recovered from his injury at Stockholm, won easily. To the onlookers' amazement, Kivie had enough left to finish first for the Irish and fourth overall in 35:01. Following Kiviat at regularly spaced intervals, Robby's men finished with twenty-one points, overwhelming the runner-up NYAC, which had a team score of fifty-six.[21] Kiviat's fellow runners now spoke to the press about his "truly wonderful exhibition of all-around running" in races from the mile to cross-country. Still twenty years old, he had revealed more fully his stunning potential.[22]

Attaining the age of discretion would be another matter, especially if he maintained both his endless schedule of competitions against the world's elite runners and his drive to shatter existing records in his best event, the mile. Despite repeated assertions by Kiviat himself and by leading interpreters of track in later years that he ran only to defeat his competitors, the fact was that he had records on his mind at this time. Robby did him no favor by encouraging this frenetic approach.[23]

The year 1912 belonged to history, and the experts stepped forward to evaluate Kiviat's achievements and prospects. James Sullivan named him his all-American miler, displacing Jones, the previous year's selection. Howard Valentine of the *Globe* recalled that not only was Kiviat the first ever to defeat Kolehmainen in a distance race, but that he ran consistently fast miles, with his 4:15.6 during the Olympic trials the year's best mark "barring none." And Valentine, who knew first-hand the traditions of the sport, penned the fullest appreciation. "Such running as Kiviat has shown this year is seen only when a Conneff or a George comes along." Any notion that the equally gifted Kiviat or Jones was superior to the other was "nonsense," he asserted. "Should they be brought together again—each fit to run the race of his life—either is likely to win, and the time will be around 4 minutes and 10 seconds." Yet Valentine could be unforgiving, and he called the defeat of Kiviat and his fellow American milers at Stockholm ("because of personal ambition"), the year's "greatest disappointment."[24]

AN UNMATCHED FEAT, WINTER 1913

On the heels of such recognition, Kiviat launched the most productive stretch of his career slowly and carefully. At winter's end, he ran a series of brilliant races in a brief period of time that largely earned him his place in the USA Track & Field Hall of Fame. Nevertheless, he would pay a high price for an excess of competition.

Repeating the formula that had worked well the previous winter, Robby had him prepare for the major indoor events by concentrating on speed work. Kiviat ran both on relay teams and in individual events at shorter distances. His leg as third man for the Irish quartet in a losing mile relay against the BAA on a flat armory floor was the fastest 440 of his career (50.6).[25]

Kiviat now moved into the serious phase of the winter campaign, with his focus on the Hunter and Baxter Mile races and the nationals at Madison Square Garden. Robby had him use the three-quarter-mile handicap event at the Knights of St. Anthony meet as a final tune-up. His winning time of 3:08.6 broke his own world indoor standard by two-tenths of a second.[26] Then, in the Hunter Mile against Oscar Hedlund, Kiviat won the slow two-man match on the difficult boards of Boston's Mechanics' Hall. This was his second successful Hunter Mile; if he were to win a third, the handsome trophy would be his permanently.[27]

Shortly after returning from Boston, he faced the first sign of an insidious campaign by the NYAC management that eventually tarnished his career. With the booming interest in indoor track, promoters took a leaf from baseball and scheduled "a double-header" on Lincoln's Birthday—a meet sponsored by the Thirteenth Regiment in its armory in the afternoon and the annual NYAC meet in the Garden at night. Kiviat of course had no choice but to spend the holiday with his regiment. The NYAC had planned splendid games and worked hard to sell out the Garden, albeit unsuccessfully, and was therefore angry that its cross-town rival, the Irish Club, did not enter its stars in the meet. When Kiviat turned down the invitation to go against Hedlund and Norman Taber in a special handicap mile race at night, he became the scapegoat for the NYAC's failure. With the AAU's case against Jim Thorpe now fresh on everyone's mind, the NYAC cited Kiviat as an egregious example of "flagrant professionalism" for trying to "hold up the Club for appearance money." It called on the AAU's Registration Committee to clean its house of this "nauseating" condition. For its part, the AAU demanded proof.[28]

Kiviat wasted little time in responding to the insinuation that he was an "athletic grafter." On Monday, February 10, he spoke candidly to Howard Valentine:

> Yes, I was asked to run against Tabor [sic]. Mattie Halpin [of the NYAC] called me up and asked me to run. First he offered me a box in the Garden on the night of the games. Then a special prize, besides the medal up for the race. I told Mr. Halpin, and I repeat now, that I have entered the mile and a half race at the Brooklyn-Seagate games in the afternoon and did not want to run two hard races on the same day. Furthermore, as a matter of club policy, I do not see why the Irish-American A.C. athletes should fall over each other entering the New York A.C. meet. There was a most noticeable scarcity of New York A.C. talent from our games last Wednesday evening.[29]

Alleging Kiviat was on the take evidently did not stop the NYAC from offering him a box for six people at the Garden worth fifteen or twenty dollars—a considerable sum in 1913. Not coincidentally, the NYAC, with its policy of discriminating against Jews, had self-righteously singled out Kiviat as the exemplar of the grasping athlete.

In characteristic manner, Kiviat put the unpleasant incident and its overtone of anti-Semitism and class bias out of mind. He interpreted the situation as resulting from athletic club "rivalry between the Irish and New York." Years later, Kiviat's would-be challenger, Oscar Hedlund, recalled that Kiviat was in a box at the Garden that night to watch him run away from Norman Taber in the handicap mile race with a new world indoor record of 4:18.8. It seems unlikely, though, that Kiviat had the chutzpah to be present in the nearly "half empty" arena.[30]

Kiviat did have a point to make, and three nights later he had the right occasion to make it—the Baxter Mile, the most important race of the season, which he had dominated for the past three years. He walked confidently to the starting line with Hedlund, Taber, and Mat Geis of Buffalo. From the outside lane, he sprinted immediately into the lead and stayed there for the ten laps around the Seventy-first Regiment Armory's flat floor track. He took them through the 440 in 61.6 and the 880 in 2:08.2. Taber, Hedlund, and Geis followed him in single file, each about a yard apart. With two laps to go, Hedlund and Taber "were still sticking close to Kiviat," but then Taber began to tire and fade. It was a two-man contest at the sounding of the bell when Hedlund made his move. "The answer that Kiviat gave Hedlund settled the race right there," Howard Valentine wrote. Kivie pushed hard through the final 176 yards, leaving Hedlund twenty-five yards back and Taber out of sight. The timers had him in 4:18.2, breaking Hedlund's three-day-old indoor record by six-tenths of a second. The new world standard would last until 1917, when John Overton of Yale broke it by more than two seconds. It endured as the Baxter record until 1925. Perhaps most remarkable, only in 1938—a quarter-century later—would Glenn Cunningham be the first to run a faster mile on a flat armory floor.

Yet to those who watched him put on his sweater and take deep breaths, Kivie appeared, except for a sweaty face, to be comparatively fresh. "Does Abel Kiviat know what fatigue is?" wondered Howard Valentine aloud. Kiviat certainly showed no outward signs of his terrible "indoor sickness" afterward, even though the air in the armory bothered other runners. At that moment, he seemed to the astute Valentine "two seconds faster for the mile this winter than he was last year at this time." If the Baxter had "been run on the fast track in Madison Square Garden there is small doubt but that he would have done as fast as 4:17 for the mile." Kiviat agreed with him. Clearly recalling this race eight decades later, he lamented having had to wear "flat shoes" rather than "spikes, which makes an awful difference for your speed."

His prospects seemed limitless. Valentine, the best of the track beat writers, was again impressed enough to call Kiviat "one of the greatest runners in the history of the cinderpath" under a banner headline in the *Globe*. Valentine picked him to better John Paul Jones's unofficial world outdoor record of 4:15.4, and he noted that both Kiviat and Coach Robertson were "anxious" to make the prediction hold up during the coming summer.[31]

Kiviat was ready for prime time at the Garden and defense of his national indoor titles at 600 and 1,000 yards. In 1912, for the only time in American history, including years of war, there had been no indoor championships to provide him the opportunity. The AAU now drew on the enormous reserve of enthusiasm generated by the Stockholm experience to plan an innovative meet for 1913. It would serve appropriately as a finale to the indoor campaign instead of, as in the past, taking place in the early winter. It would also be a one-night event rather than being spread over the traditional two. James Sullivan and his championship committee therefore decided to hold the 1,000-yard run at the start of the evening and to bill the 600 as a special feature near the end, which would enable Kiviat to attempt the double with an adequate interval of rest. Entries from American and Canadian Olympians poured in for the March 6 meet. The *Times* declared grandly that this meet "inaugurates the campaign for the Berlin Olympics" of 1916.

With three weeks following the Baxter to prepare, Kiviat went down to Philadelphia and Washington, D.C., for indoor meets, and the crowds greeted him as an "Olympic celebrity." These unnecessary trips testified to his psychological need to be constantly in front of the nation's track fans. Realizing at last that this spasm of activity had involved "hard work" and that he was a little "fine," he did next to no training for the ten days before the nationals. His coach's thinking was even more of a puzzle. At this early stage in his coaching career, Robertson appears to have allowed his best athletes to compete to the brink of physical and mental exhaustion and then to ban all training for a week or more preceding the season's championship event.[32]

Shortly after the fans settled into their Garden seats on the evening of March 6, Kiviat went to his mark with the other competitors in the 1,000-yard run, including Eugene Marceau of the BAA and Homer Baker of the NYAC. To many in the packed arena on Madison Avenue, the bloom disappeared from this race when they discovered that the big farm boy, Olympian Dave Caldwell, did not make the trip down from Cornell to challenge Kiviat. Homer Baker, the nineteen-year-old protégé of Coach Bernie Wefers, was no lightweight, however, although his great promise in the middle distances was partially offset by an as yet undetected problem with his vision. He simply could not see well indoors. (Only years later would Baker realize that he suffered from "lack of pigment.") But he had enough natural talent to ensure an interesting race, with or without Caldwell.

Marceau of Boston took the lead from the start and held it for the first five circuits of the 176-yard track, with Kivie and Homer Baker tucked in behind him. There was a great deal of bumping throughout the race, and the inexperienced Baker in particular was buffeted repeatedly. Kivie, in contrast, was beautifully controlled and tough-minded. He and Baker waited until the final 100 yards and jumped Marceau. Kivie kept on going for a commanding 10-yard victory over Baker. As easy as he made it seem, he nevertheless had lowered his own world indoor record to 2:15.8. In the excitement of that moment, one veteran writer thought James Sullivan was about to dance the popular "'turkey-trot'" to ragtime in celebration. To a more detached Howard Valentine, it was "no exaggeration to state that Kiviat can break 2:15 for the distance on the Garden track" whenever "the occasion required."[33]

Kiviat had about forty-five minutes to recover before the widely anticipated 600. During that interval, the Irish and NYAC teams were in a close fight for the point trophy. The contest would likely hinge on Kiviat's success in the shorter race. He had a far greater challenge ahead of him this time, even with the disappointing news that the Olympic silver and bronze medalists at 800 meters, Mel Sheppard and Ira Davenport, would not start. Shep had a legitimate excuse: he had been involved in a serious train wreck earlier that week, and the trauma resulted in "the only nervous breakdown" of his life. He was recuperating quietly down at the Jersey shore as Kiviat was preparing to go back out on the Garden track against a field that still had exceptional depth. With Olympic champion Ted Meredith, Tom Halpin of Boston, and Ray Bonsib of the NYAC on the starting line, "'Kivie' can hardly be expected to win," wrote Howard Valentine.

Kivie made the prediction look accurate for the first 500 yards of the race, staying in last place behind Meredith in the tight pack. With about 220 yards to go, he began to move on the outside lane, and Meredith and Tom Halpin went with him on the inside. Just after the bell, with Meredith leading the bunched runners on the first turn, little Kivie "squeezed his way to the pole, glided to the shoulders of Meredith and the two went at it for all they were worth," wrote Francis Albertanti in the *New York Evening Mail*. The Garden crowd was really into it now. Kivie edged slightly ahead on the backstretch and stayed there around the last turn. Howard Valentine left his own enthralled account of the final chase:

> Meredith went after the great little miler like fury and at the head of the homestretch was but a stride to the bad. Down the straight they went to the greatest finish of the night: Meredith gaining by inches, and Kiviat not

weakening a whit, but being outsped by those same inches. Abel hit the tape not more than three inches in front of the world's 800-metre champion. It was the kind of finish that rouses frenzy, and the crowd poured out on the floor to get a close look at the two greatest middle-distance runners in the world.[34]

The protracted ovation echoed in Stanford White's Garden and its successors throughout the twentieth century. In 1963, on the occasion of its Diamond Jubilee, the AAU singled out Kiviat as the outstanding middle-distance performer in indoor track history. Four years later, in his history of the Millrose Association, Fred Schmertz reported a conversation he had had years earlier with Lawson Robertson in which the coach said Kiviat's defeat of Meredith, Halpin, and Baker in the two races was "the greatest feat in indoor track history." Toward the end of the century, Kiviat's remarkable double was again featured prominently in the program for the one hundredth anniversary of the indoor nationals at the Garden. No other runner has ever matched his accomplishment in a one-day national championship.[35]

At the moment of its completion, however, the principal importance of the double was to put the Irish Club over the top for the team championship. Led by Kiviat and Pat McDonald, who had two wins in weight events, the club finished the night with thirty points to the NYAC's twenty-five.[36]

After the rousing finale to the indoor season, Kiviat had two encores. Only forty-eight hours later he was the proverbial good soldier and led his Thirteenth Regiment to victory in the MAL championship meet at the Twenty-third Regiment Armory. Looking wan from his intense effort at the Garden, he nevertheless won a 440/880 double. By scoring ten of his regiment's thirty-four points, Kiviat handed Coach Robertson his second national team title in two days.[37]

Robby's next move once again raised serious questions about the young coach's judgment. When Abel could not resist the lure of a final curtain call, an invitation to Buffalo on the following Saturday night for a three-quarter-mile handicap event on the fast Seventy-fourth Regiment Armory track, he let him go. It proved to be a serious mistake in more ways than one. Kiviat lost the race to smooth-striding Joe Driscoll and much more. As Robertson confided to Howard Valentine, "Kiviat did too much racing in too short a space of time." Each of the "four championship victories over fast fields in forty-eight hours," followed by the Buffalo excursion, had "taken its little bit of Kivie's racing vitality." He would not recover for an extended period, and, in truth, he never again reached his full potential.[38]

Finally, after the damage was done, Robby called a halt. "Abel Kiviat will do no more racing this season," the *Globe* reported. While he watched others run, well-deserved honors came his way for his extraordinary season. The *Times* praised his record-breaking 1,000 at the indoor championships. It continued: "With three-quarters of a mile in 3:08 3-5, and one mile in 4:18 1-5, the running of [Kiviat] . . . appears to entitle him to the top position among runners from half a mile to one mile, as he has defeated men who have at various times outrun him from a time standpoint, and shown consistency which has caused him to be hailed as the best all around runner in America."[39]

THE END OF ATHLETIC INNOCENCE

Others inevitably began to develop plans for Kiviat that reflected the changing circumstances of his universe. Boston's energetic and athletically minded Mayor John F. ("Honey Fitz") Fitzgerald told reporters that he and a group of sportsmen connected with the BAA had "almost consummated a deal" for a one-mile race between Kiviat, John Paul Jones, and Norman Taber at Harvard Stadium on June 21. The potential for sponsoring "the greatest pedestrian event ever held in the world between amateurs" was not lost on the enterprising James Sullivan. He used a lengthy trip around the country in April to convince the regional AAUs to support the idea of holding the national outdoor championships at the fast Harvard track, with the mile race as its centerpiece. His trump card was to bring over from Oxford the 1912 Olympic gold medalist, Arnold Jackson. "Such a race would decide once for all the question as to who is the greatest miler in the world, and who is entitled to hold the world's record," wrote Howard Valentine. Given Kiviat's and Jones's performances that winter on cramped board tracks—J. P. had run 4:19.8 at Ann Arbor in March—the experts believed one of the pair was capable of winning in 4:10. When Jones asked his perceptive coach if he thought breaking the 4:10 barrier (then "the goal of the great milers," in

Jones's words) was humanly possible, Jack Moakley replied: "'Within three years, and some day four minutes will be beaten.'"[40]

The race never occurred. Oxford postponed Jackson's voyage for a year; Jones set a new world record (4:14.4) at the IC4A meet on May 31 and announced his retirement from track. Eager to pursue his engineering career, "the Cornell captain told the newspaper men that he will not return to the cinderpath to race Abel Kiviat or any one else." However, the episode illustrated how the sport's administrative leadership was thinking more imaginatively and boldly under the spell cast by Stockholm.[41]

Meanwhile, the AAU's Sullivan was intrigued by another scheme floated by William Unmack of the Pacific Athletic Association in San Francisco. Acting on the invitation of Australian sports officials, Unmack, a native of Brisbane but a longtime American citizen, proposed to organize a competitive tour of the island continent and New Zealand for a few of America's most versatile trackmen. Sullivan approached the jumper Platt Adams and Kiviat to be the delegation's East Coast representatives. Kiviat expressed interest, but he was understandably dubious about "taking one 'middle distance' runner to compete in all events from 880 yards to five miles." In the end, Capt. Dieges would not grant his employee an extended leave of absence, anyway, and Kiviat was "compelled to refuse" the opportunity. If Kiviat felt anger about being deprived of an exotic overseas voyage, he left no record of it.[42]

There was something distinctly modern about these ventures. Although individual American track stars had competed in Australia previously— indeed, in 1887–88 the first elite American Jewish runner, the great professional Lon Myers, had raced there—an *officially* sponsored tour Down Under was new. During the coming outdoor season, other American delegations would plan to join these stars on the high seas. In August, the nation's leading AAU and Olympic officials—Sullivan, Gus Kirby, Col. Thompson, and Joseph McCabe of Boston—were delegates to a critical IAAF meeting in Berlin. During this visit, Sullivan discussed sending an American team to an off-year (and unofficial) Olympics in Athens in May 1914. The American team would then compete in Berlin, the designated site of the 1916 Olympiad. When the Athens games were cancelled owing to the Greek organizers' failures, the alert athletics federation of Holland invited Irish Club athletes to participate instead in an international meet in the new Amsterdam stadium.[43]

If heightened worldwide interest in track sent Americans abroad in 1913, other nations decided to see for themselves the conditions that made possible the Yanks' spectacular successes at Stockholm. During the summer and fall that year, visiting foreign officials disembarked at New York harbor on fact-finding expeditions. For example, members of the Imperial German Olympic Commission, led by its thirty-one-year-old administrator Carl Diem, spent five weeks studying American facilities and training methods. A highlight of their tour was a visit to Celtic Park, where they especially enjoyed watching Lawson Robertson supervise his athletes' workouts. Soon afterward, Sullivan and his aide, Dan Ferris, hosted Dr. Otto Herschmann of Vienna during his three-week study mission on behalf of the Austrian Olympic Committee.[44] Sullivan also received assurances from at least six European track federations of their countries' commitment to participate in the important Panama-Pacific International Exposition scheduled to take place in San Francisco two years hence.[45]

In this dynamic environment of international exchange and cooperation, a twenty-one-year-old star of the world's leading athletic club had unmatched opportunity. However, Kiviat's condition would prove to be a serious hindrance. *Why, then, did he race so often?*

If the energy generated by the success at Stockholm provides part of the answer, long-standing factors were also determinative in pushing Kiviat and his peers into a year-round schedule of competitions. There is good reason to point to baseball, then at the height of influence as the national pastime, with its model of daily games for at least seven months of the year. Yet even by the lights of 1913, few assumed that the physical demands of playing center field for John McGraw's Giants were equivalent to running world-class middle-distance races week after week. The science and culture of the era offered surer clues regarding this regimen.

Many physicians in 1913 still believed that the extreme exertion necessary in middle- and long-distance running caused "serious heart disease" (the so-called athlete's heart). Even some reformers argued that overtraining was deleterious and urged the athlete to rest before competing. More accurate studies by physiologists and medical scientists were changing that approach, however, demonstrating that "cross-country and track races were the most beneficial components of a schoolboy's physical (and moral) education." As early as the mid–nineteenth century, the pioneering British physician and physical educator Archibald Maclaren had written that the typical three-week preparation for a race was insufficient. Nevertheless, as sport historian Roberta Park has reminded us, even the most informed coaches—she discusses Mike Murphy and mentions Ernie Hjertberg, but it is equally true of their disciple Lawson Robertson—"continued to rely heavily upon observations of successful athletes and little that was more 'scientifically' exact." Particularly compelling, therefore, was the testimony of Hjertberg that "two and three races a week" during a long season and the hard training for them might "dull the mental edge" but cause no other "harmful effects." Hjertberg's credo: "Punish your body SENSIBLY all the time. Endurance is of most value."[46]

Broader cultural attitudes overlay these seasoned trainers' theories. As historian Gail Bederman has written, this period was a time when American men were struggling with traditional ways of understanding their "male bodies, male identities, and male authority." The inherited Victorian concept of civilized "manliness," as personified by Theodore Roosevelt, was being challenged by a newer fascination with more primal forms of "masculinity." Just as boys like Kiviat had absorbed Roosevelt's ideals of "the Strenuous Life" at the turn of the century, his younger siblings were now enjoying the potboiler *Tarzan of the Apes* (1912), with its images of "physical strength and perfection." According to Bederman, these seemingly contradictory notions were explicable as twin ideological components of civilization's ineluctable advance toward "a higher race and more perfect manhood."

This cultural obsession played itself out on the track and the field. They were venues, on the one hand, for developing the WASP's highly disciplined approach to "vigorous, manly" games. Yet, on the other hand, as Stockholm had demonstrated in bold relief, they were also theaters where America's most talented immigrants and other minorities (in particular Jim Thorpe) could reach unimagined physical heights. Middle America's reaction to these disadvantaged athletes was highly ambivalent, alternating between fascination and repulsion, but fans nevertheless lined up everywhere to watch them smash records.[47]

The fans also came to the arenas to wager. Although mostly kept from public exposure by the colluding print media, the thrill of gambling on the new amateur prodigies stoked fan interest. The betting on Hannes Koleh-mainen at the 1912 cross-country nationals offers a quick glimpse of this widespread phenomenon. In unguarded moments, Kiviat himself remarked on his peers' propensity to bet.[48]

Some top athletes also defied the rules of amateurism and accepted excessive appearance money to perform. Here was a true vicious circle: the stars' acceptance of illegal payments resulted in packed arenas, which only encouraged them to race more often than was good for them.[49]

In that athletic universe, where Kiviat brought a special combination of speed, stamina, and versatility, he was always being invited to compete. His normal desire to take trips with his buddies and have fun, as well as his abnormal psychological need for the limelight, predisposed him to accept too often.

HARRIER, SUMMER–FALL 1913

Having absented himself from the track most of the spring, Kiviat was con-fident that with a few early races and hard workouts three times a week for a month, he would recover from any lingering ill effects of the indoor season and be ready for the nationals in early July. He made no secret of the fact that he wanted the mile record John Paul Jones had set in his final race on May 31. Encouraged by Robby that he was in condition to reach his goal, Kiviat trained hard in June and ran a fast mile at the NYAC's Spring Games (4:20.2).[50]

The AAU national championship was another matter. Because Jim Sulli-van had been unable to close the deal on the Harvard Stadium site, the meet was held in killing afternoon heat on a poor track in Chicago's Grant Park, with the wind from Lake Michigan blowing clouds of dust on the athletes. Kiviat was never a factor in the mile. Taber tucked in immediately behind the pace-setting Jim Powers of Boston, caught him on the backstretch of the gun lap, and sprinted away from him on the final turn to win by ten yards. Although Taber's time was only 4:26.4, he had the "sweet satisfaction" of finally taking the measure of Kiviat, beaten into third place.[51]

Kiviat returned to New York a sadder but seemingly wiser young man. He had failed to defend the national outdoor mile titles he had won in 1911 and 1912. "Not a few of his friends are a bit worried over the prospect of seeing Abel interred in an early athletic grave, and his name posted up on the board in the clubhouse as gone but not forgotten," Howard Valentine reported. Lawson Robertson scoffed at this assessment. The defeats were symptoms of physical and mental fatigue; the cause was excessive competition during the winter, exacerbated by Kiviat's psychological tendency to become "quite easily upset by little things at times." The coach's prescription was "a rest, and a good long one." His protégé had not had a complete and extended break from running since he joined the Irish Club in 1909. Even when Kiviat had planned to take a break, Robby acknowledged, "an important relay in which club or regiment needed him badly, or a trip to Boston, Buffalo, or some other place that promised some fun with the other fellows, as well as a nice prize, has drawn Abel out to race."

On June 23, Kiviat reached the age of majority, making him at last eligible to vote for his Tammany patrons. He faced a more pressing personal question: Would he also vote with his feet and save his brilliant career? In the final analysis, however, his coach would have to accept equal responsibility for any outcome, too.[52]

Coach Robertson failed him at this critical juncture, allowing Kiviat to run several sprint races during the summer before he won the Senior Mets championship mile at Travers Island on September 20 in a slow 4:26.8.[53] His points helped his Irish Club mates to take the measure of the NYAC again in the team competition, seventy-four to sixty-eight points.[54]

The glow was short-lived. His essentially unproductive summer concluded with a terrible encounter. "Kiviat Knocked Out by Gang of Toughs" ran the headline in the New York Globe. He was returning from his office in Manhattan one night and was getting off a Staten Island trolley about a block from the Kiviat home on Broad Street when "several boisterous fellows," to whom he had previously "paid no attention," shoved him. "'Kivie' remonstrated good naturedly, and then, to use the champion miler's own words: 'The first thing I knew I knew nothing.'" He had no idea what hit him. When he regained consciousness and managed to get home, the family summoned their physician, Dr. Lucey of nearby Tompkinsville, "who sewed his head up and sent him to bed." Characteristically, he did not mention the story afterward, but the four stitches over his right eye bore witness to the island's pervasive anti-Semitism—or so his younger brother always believed. "They waited for him with baseball bats at the ferry. . . . [T]hey didn't want a Jew getting all the honors," was Harold Kiviat's vivid memory near the end of his long life. Despite Harold's excitability and tendency to exaggerate, his belief was plausible: at that moment, the wide press coverage of two notorious trials raised the specter of riotous anti-Semitic reactions. In Kiev, the czarist government was attempting unsuccessfully to convict Mendel Beilis of the ritual murder of a gentile youth. In Atlanta, a jury found businessman Leo Frank guilty of the brutal murder of a young girl who worked in his pencil factory. That September, the publicity surrounding the Frank case spurred the formation of the Anti-Defamation League of B'nai B'rith. After the initial headline in October, Kiviat chose to push his experience out of mind.[55]

He had other matters to occupy his attention following the Irish Club's banquet for its champions at Terrace Garden. The fifty athletes in attendance elected Mel Sheppard to succeed the recently retired Frank Riley as captain of the track team. Deeply honored, Shep decided to reorganize the team by decentralizing administrative responsibility. He appointed six teammates as "lieutenants" in the sport's several disciplines. Kiviat was his choice for the middle distances. The Irish Club gave Kivie life membership and a small, engraved sterling-silver plaque.[56]

For the first time in a half-year, Kiviat resumed serious training. He worked out frequently with fifteen Winged Fist distance men over the Van Cortlandt Park cross-country course, led by Hannes Kolehmainen and newcomer John Eke, Sweden's Olympic bronze medalist in the 8,000-meter cross-country race. Coach Robertson's crew looked invincible for the hill-and-dale competition at the Senior Mets on Saturday, November 15, and for the nationals three weeks later. Although Robby had outdone himself by corralling from Scandinavia the 1912 Olympic gold and bronze medalists in this event, it was Kiviat who drew repeated notice in the New York newspapers for his return to top form in practice. His progress was due in part to the individual workouts Robby tailor made for each member of the squad.[57]

Nevertheless, Kiviat had a disappointing performance in the Senior Mets, fading to tenth place, nearly two minutes behind Kolehmainen's record pace. However, he did help the Irish capture the championship banner before a crowd of five thousand spectators, a number that today seems unimaginable for a cross-country event.[58]

Although the praise Lawson Robertson received for this triumph was gratifying, of greater value to him was the essential stamina his runners acquired for later success on the track. By 1913, this approach was the conventional wisdom about cross-country imparted to Robby by his own coaches, Ernie Hjertberg and Mike Murphy, and with which he trained Kiviat. Yet based on what Abel would accomplish only three weeks later, we can infer that Robby's protégé was thinking less about the sport's instrumental role than in preparing to win its national championship and restore his reputation.[59]

The national event took place in perfect conditions on Saturday afternoon, December 6. Going in, several factors made Kiviat a legitimate dark horse for the title: the absence or questionable health of the nation's best distance runners, the small number of entries, and a revamped course well suited to his skills. His chances appeared realistic given Kolehmainen's badly strained thigh muscle, defending champion Willie Kramer's uncertain recovery from a congested lung, and 1912 runner-up Harry Smith's decision not to enter. Only twenty-eight men representing four greater New York–area athletic clubs and a scattering of unattached athletes warmed up for the race. The Van Cortlandt course mapped out by AAU official Fred Rubien emphasized running on the flat, leading to much subsequent criticism, but making it ideal for a miler moving up to a longer distance. By the strange luck of the draw, Kiviat pinned number 13 on his Winged Fist singlet during his warm-up for this 1913 championship. "The hoodoo did not worry 'Kivie' one bit," noted Howard Valentine about Kiviat's cool demeanor in approaching the competition.[60]

The starting pistol sent Willie Kramer quickly to the front of the pack on cross-country's classic field of dreams. The tough-minded defending champion initially did not show ill effects as he led the harriers across the polo field, past the Van Cortlandt mansion, up the steep hill over the golf course, and across Gun Hill Road to the old Croton Aqueduct. Having covered about one mile of six at this point, Kivie was running easily in ninth place, "within striking distance of the pacemaker." He stayed there during the run along the Aqueduct and downhill to the flat. Kramer began to struggle. As the pack moved across the polo field at about 2.7 miles, there was "a general closing up of the men of the first dozen." Kramer dropped back to third place behind Tom Barden of the Irish Club and Sid Leslie of the Long Island Athletic Club, the national junior cross-country champion. Kivie, finding the moderate pace "just to his liking," moved up into fourth place easily, a stride behind the faltering Kramer.[61]

About twenty seconds after the four leaders began their second three-mile loop of Van Cortlandt, Kramer was undone by his labored breathing and stopped. Kivie had a green light now and found he had plenty left. He surprised his rivals by lifting his tempo and charging into the lead during the second run up the hill over the golf course. Only Sid Leslie still offered him a serious challenge as they raced along the aqueduct, but Kivie pulled away from him when they started downhill at the 4.75-mile mark. "Once on the flat it was all over except the shouting as far as the winner was concerned," the *Times* reported, "as Kiviat, a marvel in his ability to sustain a long drawn out sprint, had it comparatively easy taking care of the challenge of Leslie." Kivie beat him to the line by about one hundred yards in 33:52, fully forty seconds faster than Willie Kramer's championship record of 1912.

His success, he liked to say in later years, was a "big surprise"—but not to Howard Valentine, who had been impressed with Kiviat's two months of solid training for this race. "Looks as though the Staten Islander has hit his stride at last. He looked like the old Kiviat last Saturday," commented the track writer.

The Irish Club did not follow his lead and could only tie the NYAC for the team championship, with thirty-two points apiece. In a Solomonic decision, James Sullivan, who was on hand as meet referee, announced that the first five men on both teams "should receive championship gold medals."[62]

Kiviat never raced cross-country again, but the successful chase for gold over Van Cortlandt's hills and dales underscored both his versatility and his resilience. Like Caesar's Gaul, his 1912–13 track campaign was divided into three parts: a six months' trough of fatigue and frustration from April to September, the result of an excess of competition during the winter, separated two periods of high-level accomplishment. "Despite the fact that numerous experts agreed Abel Kiviat to have reached the pinnacle of success and had him backed for a quick and rapid slide," wrote old chum John Drebinger, "'Able Abel' once more set the athletic world agape with his wonderful performance" in the autumn.

Honors poured in. The *Times,* in its annual review of sport, highlighted Kiviat's world indoor record set in the Baxter Mile. The newspaper also named him to its all-American track team in the cross-country event. James Sullivan, more impressed with his performance at the indoor nationals, selected him as his all-American at 1,000 yards. If further proof were needed of his ability "to give a good account of himself at any and all times," it came in the announcement by Capt. Mel Sheppard that Kiviat was the Irish Club's leading point scorer in 1913. His total of 165 points far outpaced the likes of Sheppard, Alvah Meyer, Babe McDonald, and even Hannes Kolehmainen. Only McDonald equaled Kiviat's total of 22 points in the championship meets.

To sum up, Kiviat had won three national titles—600 and 1,000 yards indoors and cross country—as well as the mile in the outdoor Senior Met championships. At one point in the winter of 1913, he held the world indoor records for at least five events (600 yards, 1,000 yards, 1,320 yards, the mile, and 1.5 miles), an unprecedented achievement. He had also established a new standard for the U.S. cross-country championships at Van Cortlandt Park. This was, by any measure, an all-American year.[63]

In the end, however, Kiviat's star status did not shield him from the common experiences of other second-generation Jews in 1913—anti-Semitic innuendo, physical attack, and harmful exploitation of his skills (albeit with his cooperation) by the captains of the burgeoning sporting industry. These problems would become exacerbated in 1914–15, ultimately destroying his career.

8

An "Up-and-Down Life"

KIVIAT WAS SICK AT HOME and facing a minor surgical procedure on Sunday, January 25, when President Pay Jay Conway and the Winged Fist leadership welcomed 1914 by holding a grand reception for the club's champions, past and present, in its new headquarters at 159 East Sixtieth Street. The move to a less expensive building in the neighborhood enabled the board of governors to announce to its members that annual dues would be reduced from twelve dollars to six and that all past debts would be forgiven. The growth in membership over the next few years would attest to the shrewdness of the decision, but it could not hide the cracks already beginning to appear in the Irish Club's foundation. Weight throwers Pat Ryan and Emil Muller became enraged by perceived slights from management and threatened to leave the organization. Then Captain Mel Sheppard made the surprise announcement that he was leaving the Irish Club for the Millrose Athletic Association, the athletic club of the John Wanamaker store in New York. Shep claimed he switched affiliation after eight years "because the Irish A.C. seemed to be rapidly losing interest in track-and-field athletics." Although dynamic recruitment of established athletes by the Millrose Club—the so-called "Athletic Federal"—was drawing comparison to similar practices by baseball's new Federal League, Shep was in fact motivated by anger. When it became public knowledge that Lawson Robertson was a candidate to replace Mike Murphy as the University of Pennsylvania track coach, Shep asked President Conway "to consider him as a successor" and was rebuffed. The worst blow to the club was when Robby, who was himself being heavily recruited by American and overseas track teams, signed a six-year contract to coach the Hungarian Olympic team.[1]

190

Although the guns of that August would change Robby's plans abruptly, Kiviat was beginning the climactic phase of his running career in an altered environment. Moreover, the refreshing winds of cultural and athletic change that had begun to shake the sport after Stockholm were being deflected in part by prevailing tendencies. The leadership of the Metropolitan AAU, through its powerful Registration Committee, was even more draconian in its efforts to impose its rigid and moralistic requirements of eligibility for amateur competition. Woe to the runner who took an extra pittance of expense money or failed inadvertently to follow proper registration procedures for a race! Unfortunately for Kiviat, his Jewish identity as well as his standout talent were red flags to the AAU purists. In the process, he, like others of his athletically elite but socially disadvantaged peers, suffered the consequences.[2]

"KILL KIVIAT," WINTER 1914

Coming off his unexpected victory at Van Cortlandt Park, Kiviat had every reason to anticipate another triumphant indoor season. How could he miss? His objective for 1914, he told Howard Valentine, was "to take another fling at the world's record for the mile before quitting. He . . . planned to train through the early summer with the record in view, and after making one or more attempts at Jones's mark to hang up his shoes for good."[3]

His personal experiences both provided support for his immediate ambition and stirred him to begin thinking about life after track. His career with Dieges & Clust was going well, and his relationship with his girlfriend, Yetta Schimansky, was intensifying. Both were now twenty-one, and Yetta, after completing her studies, was pursuing her own career as a fashion designer. She had landed an exciting job as a sketch artist for a costume company. Discussing this moment long afterward, Kiviat would become embarrassed and assume the era's air of primness. He recalled having a kosher dinner at the Schimansky home surrounded by Yetta's sisters and her brother. As close as they were becoming, Kiviat claimed in his oral memoir that he was a "virgin" when the couple married. In reality, however, Abel and Yetta were advancing to an active sexual relationship that winter.[4]

His training strategy on the track also reflected a new maturity. He planned to set limits on himself this year, running "one race a week" indoors before going all out after John Paul Jones's outdoor record in June. He looked forward eagerly to a two-mile match race with Kolehmainen on January 24 that he had proposed to highlight the games of his National Guard unit. Kiviat took the challenge seriously. "'He's had his heart on this race for weeks,'" his boss, Capt. Dieges, commented, "'and has trained harder for it than he did for the national championships last summer.'"[5]

Then, on Saturday night, January 17, Kiviat developed "a cold, bronchitis, and an inflamed nose" that bothered him enough to require a visit to Dr. Lucey's office in Tompkinsville on Tuesday. His condition worsened, with the match against Hannes only three days ahead. On Thursday, Dr. Lucey lanced his nose and saw him again on Friday and Saturday. The doctor advised him not to race. Even with the treatments, Kiviat was unable to sleep on Thursday and Friday nights. On Saturday morning, he "came to the office so sick," and Capt. Dieges "strongly advised him not to run, but he would start."[6]

Upon arriving at the Brooklyn armory in the evening, Kiviat reported to his captain "that he had been ill and did not feel that he could give a good account of himself in the race with Kolehmainen." Capt. Robert Aikman proposed informing the fans that the event had been postponed due to his illness. Kiviat would not hear of it, "saying 'that people would not believe it, and that they would think I am afraid of getting beat, so I will run and do the best I can.'"[7]

Kiviat's response was completely understandable, given the advance publicity about this race and the large crowd in attendance.[8] Howard Valentine and thousands of other stunned track fans witnessed a "fiasco," as the world's most accomplished distance runners appeared to be "reeling along like a couple of 4 A.M. drunks," he told his readers. Indeed, they were running the second mile in 5:17.8. Valentine could not believe it when Kiviat did not try to pass the Finn, who was overweight and had a sore leg, after the bell clanged for the final circuit. Kivie somehow summoned the strength to pull even with Kolehmainen about one hundred yards from the tape, and the pair went across the line together like novices "dying away in the last few strides."[9]

A blast of raucous boos and cries of "'fake and frame-up'" greeted them from the galleries all around the armory. The memory of the runners' controversial tie at two miles on Columbus Day of 1912 was still fresh. After the announcer confirmed the race was a tie in 10:05.8, the crowd began another sustained uproar. Here was Kiviat's first hard lesson on the down side of modern athletic celebrity, but he was too sick to care. "Standing within six feet of where Kiviat came to a dead stop," Valentine wrote, "I could see that he was purple faced—almost unconscious on his feet." Taken to the locker room, he lay in misery for an hour, and a doctor on duty administered a local anesthetic, undoubtedly the newly popular Novocaine, to relieve his pain. On Sunday, Dr. Lucey lanced his nose again. By Monday, January 26, his body was healing, but his real troubles were only beginning.

Suspicious officials assumed the worst. That night the registration committee of the Metropolitan AAU announced that it would begin an immediate and thorough investigation of the incident. The committee held a closed-door meeting at the midtown St. Bartholomew's Club on Monday night. Chairman Jacob Stumpf sent letters to Kiviat and Kolehmainen afterward, notifying them they "were suspended" due to the "suspicious circumstances" of their race. Stumpf instructed the pair to appear before his committee on February 4 at St. Bartholomew's. The session, the *New York Times* remarked, would be a trial in all but name.

Reaction was swift. Kiviat became "so upset" that he told reporters "he would go into the investigation, clear himself, and throw his running shoes into a bonfire." Capt. Dieges, who knew how sick his employee had been, was enraged about the charge. "'If I thought Kiviat had taken part in a 'framed' race I would throw him bodily out of my shop,'" the former shot putter declared. "'I wouldn't bother opening the door, either, I'd chuck him right through the plate glass window. But I'll bet my life that Kiviat tried his best to win that race.'" The unaccountably silent Coach Robertson finally stated forcefully to a *Brooklyn Eagle* reporter that "'[a]nyone who says that Kiviat did not try on Saturday night is a liar. . . . Had I known his real condition, I never would have allowed him to start.'"[10]

Cold reality was setting in for Robby and Kiviat. The Millrose Games would be held for the first time at Madison Square Garden two nights later, and the ambitious coach wanted his suspended stars to run in the featured two mile. Robby had Kiviat write a letter to the Registration Committee applying for temporary reinstatement. It contained a heartfelt statement "that he had been badly treated by the committee because he had not been given an opportunity to clear himself from any charges which might have been brought against him." A subsequent plea to Chairman Stumpf by a Millrose official fell on deaf ears.[11]

By the weekend, the Irish Club's board of governors had retained John T. Dooling as counsel for the two runners. Already established as a shrewd legal adviser to the sachems of Tammany Hall, the forty-three-year-old Dooling had also built up a successful practice as a civil and criminal attorney. His strategy, based on his evident confidence in the case, was to let the hearing take place and in the unlikely event of an unfavorable decision to go to court and secure an injunction against the AAU's action. There was precedent for this approach in past Irish Club battles with the governing body. Dooling clearly helped to restore his client's own confidence and sense of purpose: two days before the hearing, Kiviat resumed training for the coming indoor cup races.

As expected, the lengthy hearing at the St. Bartholomew's Club proved nothing. Kiviat, Kolehmainen (through an interpreter), and a dozen other witnesses—Dr. Lucey, officials at the Thirteenth Regiment meet, and journalists—testified to the facts that already had been circulated widely in the press. In the end, the Registration Committee lifted the athletes' suspension but censured the meet officials for letting the pair compete in their condition without notifying the committee members in attendance.[12]

Why, then, this demeaning and unnecessary process? Although some argued that the committee was only doing its job, the backgrounds of its members would suggest a predisposition to sympathize with Kiviat and Kolehmainen. They were mostly savvy lower-middle-class urbanites who could have dismissed the case with dispatch—that is, if the powers in the AAU had so signaled. At that moment, however, James Sullivan and his president, Alfred J. Lill of Boston, were disseminating a redefined code of strict amateurism that was in part a response to a radical proposal floated by immediate past president Gus Kirby for limited joint competitions between professionals and amateurs.

Perhaps Mel Sheppard provides a more penetrating insight into the tactics of the Registration Committee. He comments in his memoir about his own experience several years earlier:

> [T]he registration committee of the A.A.U. was suddenly seized with one of its periodical and hysterical attacks of righteousness. It set about once more to make the amateur athletic world a safe and pure place for the rising generation of the country's youth. The exact reason for these outbreaks is never known, but in order to make them as spectacular as possible, it is customary to select as the victims the most prominent athletes available.

Of course, the job was made easier in 1914 if the targets were an "alien" Jew and a Finnish-speaking immigrant.[13]

The strain of two weeks of abuse by the track world was evident in Kiviat's defense of his titles in the Hunter and Baxter Miles. He did defeat Oscar Hedlund in a slow (4:28) Hunter race to take permanent possession of the trophy. (It turned out to be his final indoor battle against Hedlund, who went on to coach the MIT track team for a generation and to run a successful insurance firm.)[14] The Baxter, which Kiviat had owned since its inauguration in 1910, was another matter. He was outfoxed by a clever twenty-year-old unknown, Willie Gordon of Yonkers, who grabbed the lead before Kivie started his kick and beat him by three yards. In a sense, Kivie was still in a state of suspended animation.[15]

Kiviat appeared to regain his presuspension form over the next three weeks as he prepared in a solid manner for the indoor nationals, where he was seeking an unprecedented "three-peat" at the Garden, having won the 600 and 1,000 events in 1911 and 1913.[16] He delivered, running two excellent races and helping the Winged Fist to win decisively what many said was New York's best indoor meet to that date. In the 1,000, Kivie glanced back quickly on the final turn of the bell lap and, seeing Homer Baker sprinting furiously behind him, showed the Garden crowd his old kick in the fifty yards remaining to the tape. He defeated Baker by three yards in 2:15.4, thus lowering his own meet and world indoor record by two-tenths of a second. His achievement, Howard Valentine wrote, was due to "the best noodle [brain] as well as superior speed." An hour later, though, he fell short in his defense of his 600 crown, unable to catch Tom Halpin, who finished a brilliant performance seven yards ahead of him in the new indoor record of 1:13.4.[17]

Far less satisfying was Kiviat's experience two weeks later, the MAL championships at the Seventy-first Regiment Armory on Park Avenue. While he waited for the mile relay, he had the pleasure of watching his friend Tommy Lennon, still a senior at Curtis High, run away with the 220-yard dash. Both Kiviat and Lennon must have felt sick, however, when they looked up in the stands. "Some athletic rooters with a streak of saffron right up the middle of their backs hung a sign over the balcony railing at the Military A. L. games, reading '*Kill Kiviat*,'" reported Valentine. "This is the same bunch that hisses Kivie every time he appears in a race. Several members of the Long Island Athletic Club climbed up and tore the offending sign down." Because there is no other report of contemporary track stars having had such an experience, we can assume what these fans really meant was "Kill the Jew." As extraordinary as this incident was, it should not have been unexpected. Historian Leonard Dinnerstein has reminded us that the leading popular magazines of 1914 were publishing venomous articles about Jews that "expressed what much of America was thinking." These spectators at the armory were simply acting it out. We can also assume that Abel and Tommy said something about the incident on the ferry ride home to Staten Island. But because denial was a familiar coping mechanism for Kiviat, he never referred to it afterward.[18]

Forty-eight hours later Kiviat demonstrated anew his steel-like inner drive when he took the measure of the world's best middle-distance runners, including Homer Baker, Ted Meredith, and Mel Sheppard, in the "Jasper Special" three-quarter-mile race at the Sixty-ninth Regiment Armory. Were a few art lovers recalling the famous Armory Show at this site the previous winter and wishing for an equally transforming event in modern athletics? Kivie waited until there were 330 yards (one and a half laps) left and went through on the pole and opened up a sprint that carried him to an eight-yard victory over Baker. Olympic champions Meredith and Sheppard were left far behind. Kiviat's time of 3:07.4 was an indoor record for the metro New York area and was likely a world's best, given the problematic nature of the Buffalo track on which the existing record had been set.

At the conclusion of Kiviat's somewhat inconsistent campaign, Howard Valentine wrote: "It's been a sort of up-and-down life with Abel this winter. He's been licked more than he relishes, no doubt, but it's a matter of record that every man who has beaten the great little Staten Islander has got it back quickly with interest." The Jasper would be his last race for five months. The interval from competition gave him ample opportunity to reflect on his recent successes as well as the bitter experiences he had had—being suspended and subjected to a humiliating hearing, booed and threatened with bodily harm in arenas—largely because he was Kiviat, "the Hebrew runner."[19]

CAPTAIN OF THE IRISH, APRIL–DECEMBER 1914

On April 4, 1914, the *Times* reported that Kiviat would stop training until shortly before the AAU nationals in September. He acknowledged that he "has not been in his best form for some time, and he believes that it will do him good to take a rest." It was a particularly good time to pull back, given the situation at the Irish Club. Sheppard had quit, Kolehmainen was preparing to sail for Finland without being certain of returning, and Coach Robertson was in conversation with the Hungarian Olympic authorities about a multiyear contract. Despite Pay Jay Conway's promise of a five-hundred-dollar raise in salary for his coach, the handwriting was on the wall at Celtic Park. Then, in early May, Kiviat was sprinting to catch a subway train at the Hudson Terminal station during the evening rush hour when he tripped on the concrete floor and lacerated his left thigh severely enough that he had to be taken to a surgeon. He compounded the problem by twisting his ankle a few days later. His season was ruined.

"How much longer will Kiviat last? And who will Staten Island have to take his place?" wondered *Richmond County Advance* sports columnist John Drebinger. "Famous athletes come to a community of the size of Staten Island about once to the generation and sometimes longer." Abel, Drebinger reassured island readers, was "still in his prime and all the calamity howl of the impending gloom of Kiviat passing is entirely premature." Indeed, Drebby predicted Kiviat would be a member of the 1916 U.S. Olympic team in Berlin, as would his best friend, Tommy Lennon, who was to enroll at the University of Pennsylvania in the fall.[20]

At this time, dramatic developments in Kiviat's personal life were demanding his attention. In his oral memoir (1984), he claimed he married Yetta Schimansky in March 1914, and their baby was born within the year. His statement reflected both his inherited sense of propriety and, undoubtedly, a desire to protect his family. The facts, however, were otherwise. Abel and Yetta were "planning to get married during the summer," the *New York Times* announced on April 4. Weeks later, Yetta informed Abel that she was pregnant. The practical lovers decided to get married in a civil ceremony. Although in later years Yetta would tell friends a fanciful tale about eloping on the Staten Island ferry, in fact Abel arranged for a Tammanyite Manhattan alderman, John J. Riordan, to officiate at city hall on June 24.[21]

The news must have shocked their religiously observant families, who quickly planned to make matters kosher. Two weeks later, the bride and groom stood under the traditional bridal canopy at the Schimansky home in New Brighton as "the Rev. Goldsmith, who is a city alderman, performed a ritual ceremony." Then the Schimanskys issued a statement to the *Richmond County Advance* that the Jewish wedding had been preceded by "a secret" civil ceremony "on April 3." When the reporter asked about Kiviat's prospects, "a relative of the bride last night denied the report that Kiviat was to retire from the track."

Abel and Yetta left for a honeymoon at the Pines Hotel at Sacandaga Park in the Adirondack Mountains, a popular riverfront resort. Although the riverbank once had a sign reading "No Jews or dogs allowed," by 1914 a large percentage of the resort's thousands of visitors were Jewish people from Gotham. The newlyweds strolled the hotel gardens and the huge Midway hand in hand and enjoyed well-known vaudeville acts at the Rustic Theatre. They spent about two weeks there before returning to the city. It was probably the only truly happy time in their marriage.[22]

The young couple rented an apartment in a townhouse at 18 West Twelfth Street on the edge of Greenwich Village—another practical decision because the house was located midway between Dieges & Clust and Yetta's old office on Thirty-first Street, but also much more. In that prewar period, "Greenwich Village was a Mecca" for gifted and rebellious poets, artists, and writers, wrote the Progressive reformer Frederick C. Howe, who lived near the Kiviats. Although their wedding notice stated, in the manner of the time, that "Mrs. Kiviat formerly was a maker of theatrical costumes," Yetta's ambition and talent unquestionably meant she would resume her artistic career after she had the baby. The Village was therefore for her a congenial milieu, with its stirrings of serious feminism adding to the neighborhood's appeal. Indeed, it was "not merely a neighborhood. It was also a state of mind," Lloyd Morris once remarked. Abel was out of his element.[23]

When he went back to the familiar world of the Irish Club at the end of July, he learned that in his absence Lawson Robertson had agreed to a six-year contract at an annual salary of five thousand dollars to coach the Hungarian Olympians. This figure was impressive for that era, "greater than this club, and, we think, any club or college in the United States, could afford to pay him," a dispirited Pay Jay Conway told reporters. As a further inducement, Robby was promised use of a special Olympic fund "of not less than one million dollars" established by the Hungarian government. The Irish Club was planning a farewell dinner for him at Terrace Garden; Robby and his family were to sail for Budapest on August 12. In the meantime, Conway admitted "he was at a loss to know who would train the Irish-American A.C. athletes after Robertson's departure." His first choice, his former distance star George Bonhag, turned him down because of the demands of his engineering career.[24]

The outbreak of war in Europe during the first days of August changed Coach Robertson's plans abruptly. He unpacked his belongings and immediately began preparing his Winged Fist athletes for the outdoor championships scheduled for mid-September, the nationals at Baltimore, and the Senior Mets at Celtic Park. Even before Robby opened the training table on August 10, Kiviat showed his old natural speed in a sprint relay race, with no evidence of the injury that ruined his spring. Regaining world-class form at middle distances would take longer, yet with exactly one week to go until the AAU nationals, his coach had great confidence in his miler. Robby predicted "that Kiviat would win the mile, even if he was not at his very best, because he had a better 'noodle' than the men that would start against him." Other experts were less certain and believed he would have a struggle with six world-class milers in the feature event of the championships. The general assumption was that the winner would have to break Kiviat's two-year-old meet record of 4:18.6 and that J. P. Jones's world record was at risk.[25]

Kiviat found Baltimore in a patriotic fever awaiting the Star-Spangled Banner Centennial celebration on Saturday, September 12, of which the AAU meet was to be the finale. The meet would take place at Homewood Field on the new Johns Hopkins campus, whose track was reportedly the fastest in the country. The Irish Club was the favorite to retain the team trophy, largely because of the Whales' dominance in the field events. They would have to do it without crucial points from sprinter Alvah Meyer. The wealthy Olympian had been on his way to a Long Island weekend in August when his chauffeur crashed into a tree, throwing Meyer from the vehicle. He escaped with fractured ribs and facial bruises, but would not be at his best for the championship meets.

Heedless of the cold and wet weather on Saturday morning, an esti-mated half a million people lined the parade route from downtown Balti-more to Fort McHenry, which was dedicated as a public park at noon. But to the great disappointment of the officials and athletes, only about a thousand Marylanders paid their way into Homewood Field. Too many free celebra-tions were going on around town that afternoon.

The best race those thousand paying spectators saw was the mile run. For the fifth time in as many years of his competing in these championships, Kiviat discovered again that the hype about the quality of the track far out-paced the reality. The cinders were heavy, and the weather did not please the talented milers who went to their marks: Kiviat, Norman Taber, on vacation from Oxford, Jimmy Powers of the BAA, Willie Gordon of the NYAC, and twenty-year-old Joie Ray from Illinois. A distance man of exceptional prom-ise who had already run 4:20, Ray had been the subject of much comment in the press. Built like Kiviat at five feet five inches and only 118 pounds, crew-cut "Chesty" Joie was a muscular lad. He led from starter Hugh McGrath's gun and stayed in front through the early stages of the race. On lap two, the race developed into a tactical struggle, with several men jockeying for the lead. Kiviat, realizing he was not yet at his best, stayed back, wisely running within himself if he was to have a chance. Ray, Taber, and Gordon faded by lap three, and after the bell it became a battle between Kivie and Powers. The two men began to sprint on the backstretch, racing abreast around the turn and into the final straight. "Down the line it was nip and tuck, and it was anybody's race right down to the finish, when Kiviat managed to get across first by inches," reported the *Baltimore News*. Kiviat had made his coach a prophet by the way he had "outgeneraled" Jim Powers in the final 220. Although Kivie's time was only 4:25.2 on the slow Homewood track, Robby believed that it "was good for better [*sic*] than 4:18" on first-class cinders. This was Kivie's ninth and, as it would turn out, his final national title. The stereotypes about his innate intelligence aside, Kiviat's capacity to overcome his recent personal circumstances and perform with rare mental toughness epitomized his career.

Coach Robertson had also calculated that his Whales would score thirty points; they "delivered to a point," as the Irish Club doubled the team total of the second-place NYAC. The powerful Chicago and Boston athletic associations made even lower scores.[26]

Forty-eight hours later these results were suddenly of less consequence to track people. James Sullivan returned to New York from Baltimore, became severely ill with an intestinal problem, and died following emergency surgery. He was only fifty-two. Although he had built the AAU into the world's leading sports organization, he took particular pleasure, his eulogist noted, in his supporting role in organizing the PSAL for children and youth. Perhaps because of Kiviat's overnight transformation from obscure schoolboy athlete to world-record holder, Sullivan had admired him and was clearly fond of him. Yet that respect provided Kiviat with little protection from the AAU's arbitrary, elitist, and moralistic decisions.

Worse trouble was in store for him. The day after Sullivan's funeral, Justice Bartow S. Weeks of the state supreme court and a longtime power in AAU affairs, successfully nominated Fred Rubien to take over the presidency of the Metropolitan AAU. Many athletes liked Rubien, according to Howard Drew, for his "never-failing good humor" as an official. But for all of Rubien's quarter-century of experience as a civil servant in the sophisticated metropolis, he remained, in his midforties, a limited and malleable man. His bald, bespectacled, moon face, atop a shirt with stiff collar and round corners, conveyed the impression of an earnest and ambitious clerk. A distance runner in his youth, this native New Yorker had founded the Church Athletic League in a reformist effort to prevent the growing problem of juvenile delinquency on the city's multicultural streets. What Drew did not know about Rubien in September 1914 but would discover with other

Americans during the crisis of the 1930s was that his "optimistic smile" hid a deep-rooted anti-Semitism. Two months later, Weeks's proposal of Rubien to succeed Sullivan as secretary-treasurer of the national AAU met with unanimous acclaim. Within a year, these two men would set out deliberately to destroy Kiviat's career.[27]

Out of respect for their deceased president, the leadership of the Metropolitan AAU postponed the Senior Mets until October 3, giving Kiviat the additional training time he needed to try and regain peak condition.[28] He was ready and ran away from his opponents in an excellent time of 4:20.8 for the Celtic Park cinders. No other miler would come close to his new mark for the metropolitan championships until 1930. His dominating race was a key factor in the Irish Club's outscoring the NYAC by nine points. That night, at a victory dinner held at the Chalet restaurant in Long Island City, his teammates and coach expressed their appreciation by selecting him as their captain to succeed Mel Sheppard. Did you think "it was funny that a Jew should be captain of the" Irish Club? his oral historian asked him in 1984. His forthright response had the ring of truth: "I never gave it a thought as a Jew." It speaks volumes about the Irish Club's role in the social history of American athletics.[29]

"Capt. Abel Kiviat," as he was now called in the press, immediately faced difficult personnel problems in his new role, but he had to set them aside and prepare himself and his team for the Irish Club's annual meet in the Garden on November 28. Kiviat's own entry was in the invitation McAleenan Cup race at 1,000 yards. The race attracted much advance media attention because of the established rivalries between the five top-flight entrants—Kiviat, Meredith, Baker, Gordon, and Powers. According to Howard Valentine, "Kivie was conceded a chance to 'place,'" but no more.[30]

"Poor old Abel Kiviat, who isn't anything like the runner he used to be, gave a remarkable demonstration of the dead coming to life at the Irish-Americans' athletic carnival," Valentine wrote afterward. Kivie surprised everyone by going to the front immediately. He recalled the situation seven decades later: "We didn't have any rabbits [pace-setters] like they do today. Can you imagine going up to Ted Meredith, who was a great runner at the University of Pennsylvania, and asking, 'Would you pace me in the half-mile?' Your eyes wouldn't look the same for a month." Instead, Kivie's front-running strategy burned off everyone but Meredith. On the fifth lap, Homer Baker moved to within three yards of Kiviat; Meredith was ten yards back in third place. The gun sent Kivie's two pursuers into high gear. The lanky Baker, whose "great stride is not suited to the sharp turns in the Garden," according to Valentine, "broke up completely when he hit that Madison avenue turn in the middle of his sprint to take the lead." At that moment, Meredith went into overdrive, passed Baker on the backstretch, and appeared to be catching Kivie. With the Irish fans screaming their heads off, "Kiviat's tremendous strength enabled him to last just long enough to shove his chest against the tape in front of the fast-coming Meredith by the narrowest of margins." Kiviat's winning time of 2:15.2 was without question the fastest that the 1,000 had yet been run indoors. The AAU declared it the world record for an event in conformity with the new IAAF rule that a track had to be built twelve inches from the pole, instead of the traditional eighteen. Because this meant Kiviat had to run an additional five yards, his performance translated to 2:14.5 under the old rule.

He had more than an hour to recuperate until the evening's final event, the intercity mile relay. Only two teams, the Irish Club and the BAA, went to their marks. The Winged Fist's first three quarter-milers held a small lead over their Boston competitors. Then, it was little Abel's turn against Long Tom Halpin, who had fresh legs for his only race of the night. Kivie remained in front for the first one and a half circuits. With the firing of the gun, Halpin sprinted up to Kivie's side. "'It's all over now!' howled the athletic bugs, standing up in their seats to see Halpin sweep that long stride of his to one more triumph," wrote Valentine. He continued:

> To the amazement of every one Kiviat dug up a jump, too, and in desperation Halpin flung himself forward to reach the turn first. This superhuman effort on Halpin's part caused his undoing. He reached the turn ahead of Kiviat, quite true, but he was going so fast when he struck the curve that he could not hold to the pole, and Kiviat, running like a madman, came through on the pole and thus got the lead away from the tall Bostonian by perfectly fair running. Up the back stretch they had it out again, but this time Halpin, who is not the Halpin of last winter, had shot his bolt, and

Kiviat, running stronger and faster with every stride, held the great Boston sprinter off to win by two yards.

This was Captain Kiviat's night of triumph, leading his Irish team to a smashing success in its own games. For what proved to be the final time in his prewar career, he used all his skills—a miler's strength and a sprinter's speed, courage and brains ("noodle" in the headlines)—to become the toast of the Garden.[31]

Aggravation from the AAU quickly replaced the thrill of his captaincy. In mid-December, the Registration Committee threatened to suspend twenty-three Irish Club athletes for nonpayment of their entrance fees for the autumn NYAC meet. Although the athletes complained that they had expected their club to pay automatically, Kiviat had had the administrative responsibility to ensure the smoothness of the process. The Irish Club paid up, but Alvah Meyer, for one, was so angry he threatened to quit the team.[32]

The close of 1914 also brought Kiviat well-deserved honors, notably selection by the AAU as the miler on its all-American track team. His most tangible and meaningful recognition was being elected track captain during the last standout year for the great Irish team. Six national and metropolitan team titles attested to the club's dominance of the sport. In a larger sense, these accomplishments headlined the public's keen interest in track and field: an estimated *half a million spectators* attended track meets in the United States during the year. Yet Capt. Kiviat and his colleagues had to confront two significant events that shadowed the sport. The first, of course, was the terrible reality that "the splendid youths who would have tried out each other's prowess on track and field are now killing each other with bullet and bayonet on the blood-soaked field in France, Russia, and Belgium," in Howard Valentine's words. The second, although it paled in contrast, was the sudden death of James E. Sullivan. Many feared a decline in the sport's fortunes at home and abroad, especially in the all-important councils of the IAAF, without Sullivan's forceful leadership. Although Kiviat did not know it then, he himself had cause to fear: despite Sullivan's arbitrary treatment of him in the past, his passing removed the final possible breakwater against the AAU storm that would sweep over Kiviat in 1915.[33]

PORTRAIT OF A MARRIAGE

A more pressing source of anxiety and anticipation in Kiviat's life that December was his marriage. The painful differences that eventually separated him and his wife may have been clear already when Yetta went into labor on Christmas Day of 1914 and delivered a baby boy just after midnight.

The timing of Arthur Lewis Kiviat's arrival was the cause of much joy and some hilarity in the Kiviat family. "Some relatives joked that the baby was a Catholic Jew," Abel remembered. Arthur was circumcised eight days later and during the ceremony given a traditional Hebrew name that his proud father could not "even pronounce."[34] In the joy of the birth, Abel allowed family responsibility to take precedence for a brief time over his obligations to the Irish Club. But issues at home would continue to impede his full-hearted participation in track during the coming year.[35]

One source of tension was over Yetta's role in the family. One of a pioneering group of young professional women then being trained in distinctly modern schools of design, she was eager and well prepared to resume her career. Yetta's two years of study at the New York School of Applied Design for Women had emphasized courses in fashion design. The faculty also included the illustrator and naturalist Dan Beard, who taught figure and costume illustration, and the renowned designer Alphonse Mucha. It was her responsibility, the school instructed—and she, in turn, would preach to younger designers—to "learn every phase of designing before [the] attempt to design." Like many other alumnae, she was determined eventually to have a successful business of her own. In the meantime, she began to work as a sketch artist for costume houses specializing in theater and had immediate success. "You can name any Broadway show from 1915 into the 1920s and she designed the clothes for the women," Abel once bragged.[36]

At the time, however, he had a real problem in dealing with her professional ambitions. Yetta hired a nanny to care for the baby and threw herself back into her career. Arthur later remembered Yetta telling him that "she was very busy all the time" when he was a baby. As a consequence, Abel, long used to being catered to as a superstar and as the son of a traditional Jewish mother who had devoted herself to her family's needs even while working long hours in the store, began to react in a hostile manner to Yetta's absorption in her career. He wanted things the way he wanted them at home, and she did not have the time to pamper him.[37]

It probably did not help matters when Yetta took the then-unusual and dramatic step of changing her professional name to "Kiviette." Nevertheless, Abel made an effort to be the loyal husband. He went up with her to Albany for a play's final out-of-town tryout before Broadway. He also agreed with her proposal to move to a roomier apartment at 580 St. Nicholas Avenue in Harlem, then a large Jewish neighborhood.[38]

Further enhancing this picture of a successful young couple, Abel and Yetta bought their first car. Rather than going with the Ford Model T, Abel chose one of the General Motors cars, probably the new and popularly priced "baby Oldsmobile." It "had a California top, you could take down and ride in the open," he recalled.[39]

Unfortunately, the Kiviats' marriage portrait stressed artifice rather than realism. Abel and Yetta were simply very different personalities going in different directions. She was an artist and an intellectual, with a real interest in society. His life centered on athletics and his job as a salesman. Some who knew them well believed she was attracted to him principally because of his celebrity. His younger brother Harold probably reflected accurately the Kiviat family's bitter feelings when he said eight decades after these events: "She was a hustler. She married Abe when he was at the height of his fame, and she had the name 'Kiviat.' 'Kiviette.' That's why she married him."[40]

A PSYCHOSOMATIC DISORDER, WINTER–SPRING 1915

The tensions from his marriage had a destructive effect on Kiviat's running career. That is the most plausible explanation for the rapid change in his track fortunes during 1915, although he left us transparent clues. He returned to racing in mid-January, looking sharp enough in minor races on armory boards to augur another solid year. Yet for the first time he tellingly decided not to run in the winter's major cup races that he had dominated, the Hunter and Baxter Miles. He began to experience acute stomach pain. This was not the manageable albeit miserable "indoor sickness" of years past, but an incapacitating problem that would force him to seek medical treatment by the end of the season. In the meantime, he ran on gamely.

His next opportunity came at the end of February when he agreed to replace Mel Sheppard as the featured performer of the Kansas City Athletic Club meet. Shep had injured himself badly when he crashed through a loose board on the Garden track during a race earlier in the month, and the great champion finally realized it was time to hang up his spikes and devote himself to coaching his Millrose team. Kiviat made the trip to Kansas City and won a very slow 1,000-yard handicap race. Why did he submit himself to such a long weekend's railroad journey, one wonders, given his stomach problems and the necessity to leave his wife and infant son in New York? Was the still powerful lure of the West a way to escape briefly from the psychosomatic cause of the illness, the tense relationship at home? In fact, such escape would recur.[41]

As the Irish Club captain, he had to push aside his personal distress and focus on his team's readiness for the upcoming indoor nationals. "Among the beauties of track and field," the writer Frank Litsky has reminded us, "is that it changes its character" for national championships. "What is essentially an individual sport becomes the ultimate team experience." Kiviat worked hard with Robby that week to prepare the Irish Club. He himself went into Madison Square Garden seeking his fourth straight title in the 1,000-yard race. Although enthusing that Kiviat was "the most wonderful all-around runner in the world," the *Times* noted this meet would be Kiviat's first major competition since his exciting McAleenan Cup victory. Indeed, Kiviat was uncharacteristically tentative from the starter's gun against Dave Caldwell of the BAA and five lesser middle-distance men. Worse, he had nothing to give when the big Bostonian sprinted away from him on the final circuit to win comfortably by six yards. At that, he was lucky to hold second place. Something was obviously wrong: this was not the aggressive Kivie track people knew. However, if there was one consolation for the track captain, his runner-up finish helped the Winged Fist take home the team trophy again with thirty-five points to twenty-three for the BAA and fourteen for the NYAC.[42]

Stubbornly, he refused to give in to his worsening health and "made a miserable showing" in two meets during the following fortnight. On March 17, Kiviat finally saw his physician, who advised him "to give up athletics for at least two months and perhaps longer."[43]

For once, he listened and stopped all workouts until late May. When he returned to Celtic Park, he indicated clearly that "this may be his last season in competition" and that he planned "to make it his best." That claim was wishful thinking, given his draining marital problems. He trained for a month for the Senior Mets. The carrot for the Irish athletes was the promise of an all-expenses paid trip to Boston for the AAU's Eastern Trials on June 26 if they were successful at the Mets. Sometime during a final week of hard workouts, Kiviat pulled a tendon in his left leg. He was "in bad shape" when he lined up at Travers Island for the mile against a field headed by Mike Devanney and Willie Gordon. Although Kivie managed to push the pain out of mind for most of the race, Robby had instructed him to ease off in the final lap. Remarkably, he finished second, twenty yards behind Gordon. His courage inspired his teammates to dash the NYAC's hopes again, ninety-two points to seventy-one.[44]

Kiviat's leg responded rapidly during a week of preparation for the Eastern Trials. His ability to give a close race to Gordon on one good leg certainly suggested that he might yet have another great mile in his body. On Saturday afternoon, the atmosphere in Harvard Stadium was reminiscent of the Olympic trials as strong showings would qualify the athletes for a trip to the national championships at the Panama-Pacific International Exposition in San Francisco. The major obstacle in Kiviat's path to California and defense of his national championship was a familiar face. Norman Taber of the BAA had returned from England only two weeks earlier to take a position as a financial officer in Providence. Despite the virtual discontinuance of athletics at Oxford with the start of the war, Taber's former coach at Brown, Eddie O'Connor, had kept in touch and had convinced his protégé he could still set a world record for the mile if he would make an "all-out effort." As fiercely determined as ever, Taber had begun months of training on Oxford's Iffley Road track during the winter, and when he went to the starting line at Harvard against Kivie, the seasoned internationalist was at the top of his game.[45]

Most of the experts in the crowd expected the race would be between Kiviat and Mike Devanney. Taber, the thinking went, had been away for too long and was not ready for such high-powered competition. But ready Taber was, surprising everyone by taking the early lead, relinquishing it to his BAA teammate, Phil McGrath, but drafting on McGrath's back as they passed the 880 in 2:07.2. The pace was more than two seconds faster at this point than the one Taber had set at Harvard in 1913 when J. P. Jones had passed him to set his world mile record. Unobserved by most in the crowd, Kivie moved from seventh to fourth on lap two, just ahead of Devanney.[46]

Now Taber demonstrated that he really was in peak condition, his mechanical stride as deceptive and powerful as ever. He "shot into the lead, closely followed by Kiviat, and with the third lap but half completed there began a duel for the honor position that seldom has been equalled," wrote one Boston reporter. "Kiviat stuck to Taber's shoulder, threatening at every moment to pass the latter, but finding the task too much for him." Unexpectedly, here was the wonderful summer of 1912 redivivus.

Out of nowhere at the bell came Harry Mahoney of the BAA. He sprinted by Kivie on the first turn and caught up with Taber. As if on signal, Kivie gathered himself once again and "tore past" the Bostonian to reach Taber. The same Boston writer described the denouement: "The young Hebrew unloosed a sprint that seemed to bode ill for his competitor. Hardly had he done so when Taber also cut out, and chewing off the final 300 yards in sprinter fashion. His unexpected dash took Kiviat completely by surprise, and before the latter realized his position the Brown man had a good 15-yard lead, which he increased by five more before he reached the tape."

The winning time was 4:15.2, second fastest ever in the history of amateur miling. Some pointed out correctly that Taber was very close to Jones's 4:14.4 record because the new IAAF rule for measuring tracks forced Taber to run an additional five yards. In any event, the conclusion was much different than Kiviat and his coach had anticipated.

Still, Kiviat walked off the Harvard cinders knowing that, as good as Taber now was, his own performance on a recovering leg meant that he would have a legitimate chance to catch him in San Francisco if—and only if—he prepared himself to run the race of his life. Unhappily for Kiviat, others were concluding that with the right conditions Taber was ready to break Jones's record, *"but there is no one in the country capable of pushing him to his limit. The mark will have to be made in a handicap contest."*[47]

Taber did the next best thing. On July 16, the BAA organized a time trial for him at Harvard Stadium, with three clubmates given substantial yardage allowances as pacemakers. Eddie O'Connor had prepared a precise time schedule for Taber en route, and the dogged runner stuck to it throughout the race. He reached the three-quarters mark in 3:13 and ran the final lap in 59.6. His 4:12.6 not only broke Jones's record by nearly two seconds, but was 0.15 seconds faster than W. G. George's professional record set twenty-nine summers earlier in 1886. It was, as Taber himself later typed out on a sheet of paper, the "fastest ever recorded by mortal man." At that moment, however, as Taber modestly walked off to the locker room with Coach O'Connor, observers remarked that he looked surprisingly fresh. Coach Johnny Magee of Bowdoin College spoke for many in the crowd when he said that Taber "should make his present remarkable record look sick."[48]

PANAMA-PACIFIC EXPOSITION, SUMMER 1915

If anything, the new record should have made Kiviat feel sick, but, perhaps mercifully, he had other matters on his mind. The day before Taber's time trial, he had left for San Francisco with Lawson Robertson and a lively party of eight athletes. Joining the Irish Club's stars for the long train ride to the Panama Exposition were Ted Meredith and Frank Albertanti (pen name "Francis"), the *New York Evening Mail*'s outstanding track writer. A trip across the country was no small journey before World War I; it took five days at best. Robby, who was a masterful organizer of such trips, made sure his team departed well before others to allow for stopovers for workouts and also time to acclimate to the coast. (Robby originally had the nostalgic notion of booking passage on the S.S. *Finland* when she made her maiden voyage through the Panama Canal to California, but the sailing date of July 3 was too early.) In effect, Robby had planned this cross-country expedition as a domestic "Grand Tour" for his best athletes. He sought also to fulfill a larger Irish Club objective: to use sport as "a means to encourage and express Irish nationalism." At a climactic moment in the struggle for an independent Ireland, his Winged

Fist athletes would be the guests of and perform for Irish associations in several cities.

Ultimately, though, the purpose of this trip was to win the AAU meet in its most spectacular setting yet. Before James Sullivan died, he had worked hard to create an international track meet of Olympic caliber at the Panama Exposition. Even without the participation of the European nations because of the war, Sullivan's AAU successors still planned to hold a top-notch Olympic-style meet that would demonstrate the nation-wide dissemination of elite track and field athletics. "Like Jason, who led the Argonauts in search of the Golden Fleece," wrote sports columnist George B. Underwood, Coach Robertson was "leading a band of stalwart athletes westward to the Pacific coast, where they hope to capture the titles in the annual national championship games which will be held under the shadow of the Golden Gate."

This once-in-a-lifetime trip was too good for Yetta Kiviat to pass up. She decided to accompany her husband to the West. The handsome and well-dressed young couple posed beaming for a photographer outside Grand Central Station prior to departure. At the end of the day, however, Yetta was no Medea, and her presence, far from improving their relationship, appears to have inhibited Kiviat's quest to prove something to Taber and the sporting public.[49]

A highlight of the Kiviats' travel by rail was the scenic route across Montana, with the observation car offering unforgettable views. They reached the copper-mining center of Butte late on the night of July 22, and the Winged Fistites were touched by a tumultuous reception from two hundred members of the Robert Emmet Literary Association (RELA), the local chapter of the revolutionary Clan-na-Gael. Pat Ryan had barely stepped down from the train when "his well-wishers crowded around him and nearly tore his arm off in handshakes," Albertanti reported. The heroes were escorted to specially decorated automobiles and driven to the historic Finlen Hotel.[50]

The spontaneous response to Pat Ryan, native of County Limerick and strongman, was understandable in a city that was fully 25 percent Irish. Moreover, the radical nationalists of the RELA faced the twin challenges of

17. Abel and Yetta Kiviat ready to board a train for the Panama-Pacific Exposition in San Francisco, 1915. Copyright © Bettmann/CORBIS.

supporting the struggle for a free Ireland (the Easter Rising would occur in nine months) and dealing with unpromising changes in the demographics of the Butte Irish. The appearance of the Irish Club therefore meant something to the hosts, and they demonstrated it by arranging a splendid three-day weekend, including time for workouts. While the RELA took the club members down the copper mines, to the Anaconda smelters, and on other sightseeing trips, the press played up their presence in town. They were the biggest athletic news in Montana in years. But this trip went far beyond fun and publicity: Robertson held disciplined team workouts, as a result of which he confided to Frank Albertanti that "he believes deep in his heart Kiviat will trim Taber."[51]

At an impressive farewell banquet for 120 guests at the team's hotel, Senator Henry L. Myers spoke to an appreciative audience of Irish nationalists in support of American nonintervention in the Great War.[52] The Winged Fist party left Butte on Monday morning for additional stops in Missoula, Spokane, Seattle, and Portland. At Astoria, Oregon, Abel and Yetta boarded the coastal steamship *Northern Pacific* with the rest of the athletes and arrived in San Francisco on Wednesday afternoon.[53]

They received "a royal reception." Members of the Olympic Club, the city's leading sporting association, acted as hosts to the visiting athletes, accompanying them to their hotels in taxis and afterward opening up their clubhouse on Post Street as their social headquarters. The visitors explored the energetic city that had been rebuilt only a decade after the disastrous earthquake and fire of 1906. Amidst all the natural and manmade beauty, nowhere was the city's energy more evident than at the Panama-Pacific International Exposition, where they went for a luncheon. It was built on reclaimed land east of the Presidio to celebrate completion of the Panama Canal and was a marvel to visitors. From the moment they entered the fairgrounds through the arch at the base of the 430-foot Tower of Jewels, the architecture and statuary and the striking exhibits—the Palaces of Machinery, Agriculture, Mines, Transportation, and Fine Arts—were a feast to their eyes and their imaginations.[54]

Not to be overlooked, the new exposition cinder track laid out by Dad Moulton, the University of California at Berkeley coach, was being hyped as the fastest ever constructed. Kiviat and his teammates worked out on Wednesday afternoon and claimed they were "delighted with the track" but dubious about the weather, especially the cold wind, which chilled them.[55]

Overall, the scene was reminiscent of Stockholm in 1912, with enthusiastic San Franciscans covering the city with banners and posters to whip up interest in the meet. Sprinter Joe Loomis of the Chicago Athletic Association wrote home that the projected match between "the famous Kiviat" and Taber was "arousing the greatest interest." However, Taber had been focusing on the 880 in practice and told Loomis he was more interested in trying to break Ted Meredith's world record for that event. Taber's physical status was also a question mark because he had picked up a debilitating virus upon arriving in the West. A seasoned observer of afternoon practice at the expo track assumed Taber would run the mile, but he was more impressed with Kiviat's workouts. "Norman Taber, world's record holder for the mile, will have no cinch in his race against Abel Kiviat, the Irish-American A.C. miler, who is running in fine style just now," wrote AAU secretary Fred Rubien. "It would not startle me to see Kiviat leading the Oxford boy home in the mile run. At any rate, the Winged Fist representative will give Taber a hard race." Perhaps—unless his prolonged interaction with Yetta during the trip proved once again to be an enervating factor.[56]

Twenty thousand spectators cheered excitedly when the milers lined up for starter John McHugh's commands on Saturday afternoon. The wind whipping across the bay ensured that the race would be a slow, tactical one. Eugene Marceau of the Chicago Athletic Association went to the front immediately, and the others—including Kivie, Taber, and tough little Joie Ray of the Illinois Athletic Club, by now a 4:16 miler—were content to let him do the early work. At the approach of the half-mile mark, Taber took over the lead, with Kivie and Ray following closely. Fighting his cold as much as the field, Taber was still there when McHugh fired his gun for lap four. As the Rhode Islander put into motion his plan for an extended quarter-mile kick, Kivie stayed only a yard or two behind him, still in the hunt to retain his national title. To the untutored eye, Ray looked in trouble at this point and trailed even little-regarded Ivan Meyers of Chicago. Joie knew exactly what he was doing, though, "being smart enough to let Taber and Kiviat break the strong wind on the backstretch." However, longtime Kiviat-watchers such as Fred Rubien could tell that there was something wrong with their man, that he seemed to be "lacking the fighting spirit which we of the East have often admired in him." When the milers came off the final turn into the straightaway, Ray suddenly became a pint-sized version of Arnold Jackson at Stockholm. "He tore to the outside of the track and sprinted by the field as though they were going backwards," wrote Joe Loomis. Kivie's last look at the barrel-chested twenty-one-year-old was from the rear. While Ray was upsetting Taber convincingly by eight yards in a slow 4:23.2, Kivie faded into fourth place behind Ivan Meyers. Noting this dismal finish from his spot as chief field judge, Rubien went out of his way to write to New Yorkers that Kiviat "ran one of the most disappointing races of the meet." The end of Kivie's career appeared to be in sight.[57]

As the captain went, so went his team. The Irish Club lost the team championship to the host Olympic Club by six points, thirty to twenty-four. Alvah Meyer's defeats in the sprints, especially a narrow one to Joe Loomis in a disputed 100, made the difference. Meyer's disappointment paled in comparison to that of Kiviat's friend Howard Drew. The University of Southern

California sprinter said he "was bothered with my legs a great deal today in the race," failed to place in the 100, and announced his retirement from competition. So powerful was the impression he had made, however, that two decades later a newspaper reported Olympic coach Lawson Robertson's comment that Drew was "the one sprinter who, at his best, could beat the supposedly invincible Jesse Owens."[58]

The old order was fading quickly, but Abel and Yetta still managed to enjoy themselves at several sightseeing excursions and banquets arranged by the Olympic Club after the competitions.[59] On August 10, the couple headed east on the late night train. As they prepared to board, Fred Rubien preempted the news of what Kiviat was contemplating with his special report to the *New York Times* that "Kiviat may announce his retirement from athletics upon his return to New York."[60]

LAP THREE

STAYING THE COURSE

9

Ordeal

The AAU v. Kiviat

KIVIAT EVIDENTLY RECONSIDERED RETIREMENT while traveling and told Lawson Robertson he would enter several races in New England and Canada before he "quit competition." Neither man could have imagined the devastating consequences of this decision; however, there were portents of Kiviat's tragedy in a sudden bitter flap between the Irish Club and Fred Rubien. His problems began when Robby complained to reporters that the team had lost the national title only because meet officials in California failed to pick Alvah Meyer and Pat Ryan as the deserved winners of their respective events. That claim was too much for Rubien, who felt the Irish Club "was guilty of unsportsmanlike tactics." Both parties sought quickly to smooth over the ugly public spat, but bad blood remained.[1]

Kiviat was barely at home in Harlem when he began making new travel plans. Sometime after August 26, 1915, he had a discussion—its exact content and form hotly disputed in coming months—about running a special three-quarter-mile race with Taber and Meredith in the AAU's Eastern New York Athletic League meet at Schenectady on September 18.[2]

He never made it to Schenectady, but soon enough Schenectady found him. On Tuesday, September 28, Frank Albertanti dropped a bombshell into the middle paragraph of his evening column. Under the heading "Two Stars May Be Canned," he reported—with one major factual error—that Roscoe Campbell, the AAU official from Troy, had been spreading a story that "two prominent runners will be brought up on charges for demanding 'appearance money' to compete at" the Schenectady meet. Albertanti had discovered that distance runner Harry Smith and Kiviat were "the alleged grafters" who had "demanded in writing $40 and $75, respectively," but he refused to print their names until Campbell made a full report to the newly elected Registration Committee. If the accusation were true, the two would have violated a recently introduced national AAU rule—drafted, it should be noted, by a special committee chaired by Justice Bartow S. Weeks, with assistance from Gus Kirby—reducing an athlete's traveling expenses to five dollars a day. Thus began unobtrusively what Albertanti would later call "the most sensational episode that has marked amateur athletics since it was found that Jim Thorpe was a technical professional." Kiviat would shortly find himself trapped in a web of fanatical amateurism woven together with ethnic and social class prejudice by the AAU mandarins.[3]

JUSTICE WEEKS'S "SQUARE DEAL," AUTUMN 1915

At this initial stage, Kiviat and his Irish Club supporters had every reason to assume the case would be resolved in his favor exactly as had his earlier run-ins with the AAU brass. The new composition of the Registration Committee was one source of optimism. Only two of the five members, George Matthews of the Long Island Athletic Club and Charles Elbert of Jersey City, were holdovers; of the three new men, Charles Ericksen of the Scandinavian-American Athletic League and John J. O'Hara of Newark had won their seats with the support of the Irish Club. Stephen Byrne was the crucial swing vote. As a twenty-nine-year-old competitive race walker in the Church Athletic League and a Catholic, he seemed on paper to be positively predisposed toward the club.[4]

The same could not be said of the committee's new chair, George Matthews, whose candidacy the Irish Club had vigorously opposed. A week later, after Roscoe Campbell did not respond to Matthews's letter to him demanding written evidence and after AAU commissioner James P. Eaton of Schenectady had resigned, Matthews took the unusual step of traveling upstate by himself on a fact-finding mission, apparently—although he disputed this assertion—without consulting with the four other committee members. When Campbell indicated he was having second thoughts and wanted to drop the matter, Matthews pressured the ambitious Troy official, whose term had just expired and was seeking reappointment, "to make good or else President Rubien will apply the boot." Here was the first clear indication that Matthews was a mere tool of hostile higher powers within the AAU.[5]

Kiviat did not yet realize the gravity of his situation. While Matthews was upstate on his fishing expedition, Kiviat participated in an invitational track meet inaugurating Lehigh University's new stadium. Once again, he was a pale reflection of his old self and gave an embarrassing performance in a special three-quarter-mile race with Lehigh's track captain Jimmy Burke.[6]

The AAU began to turn up the heat a few days after his return from Pennsylvania. On October 11, 1915, Matthews sent letters to Kiviat and Smith that revealed the lengths to which Fred Rubien, in his capacity as president of the regional association, and Justice Weeks were prepared to pursue this matter. After first formally charging them with "demanding excessive expense money" to compete in Schenectady, Matthews in the next breath summoned the runners to an *investigative* hearing only three days later. Kiviat gave his letter to Terence Farley, the Irish Club counsel and track chairman, and himself the immediate past vice president of the Metro-politan AAU. Farley, age forty-eight, had been a capable litigator for years in the office of the city's Corporation Counsel, and he recognized "suspicious circumstances" when he saw them. That night, enraged, he dictated a blunt and incisive statement to Frank Albertanti describing the proposed process as illegal and unfair, and, for good measure, as an act of spite by Matthews. "Under the A.A.U. rules," Farley argued, "if charges are preferred the prac-tice has been in the past to have a copy of the complaint upon which charges are based served upon alleged delinquents. Such charges as in the present instance have not been served. If this is a mere investigation of the amateur status of an athlete the rules provide that the accused athlete shall have thirty days notice. Such a notification has not been given." Farley also questioned why the upstate officials who claimed to have seen the incriminating letters from the athletes had not brought them promptly to the Registration Com-mittee. The lines for Kiviat's defense were drawn.

For that role, the Irish Club retained as counsel John T. Dooling, who had successfully defended Kiviat and Kolehmainen in their 1914 hearing. Joining him on the defense team was Congressman Murray Hulbert, a physi-cally imposing Tammanyite, who, at age thirty-four, had begun representing his district of Harlem and the South Bronx only seven months earlier. Kiviat would be well served.[7]

As the parties prepared for the hearing on October 14 at the American Express Company offices on Madison Avenue, Matthews denied this action was a personal vendetta. His behavior suggested otherwise. His unhappy fellow committee members apparently were unaware of the upcoming hearing until they read about it in their morning papers on October 12. He claimed to Howard Valentine that he had "tried unsuccessfully to get into touch with" them, noting several unanswered phone calls to Charles Ericksen from AAU headquarters. Even more hypocritically, he submitted that it was these committee people (through a majority vote) who would be the real decision makers. "I am nothing but the little detective who brings in the evidence." Not surprisingly, therefore, many in the sports world believed the case would be thrown out the first night.[8]

They did not account for the zeal of Rubien and especially Weeks, which many attributed to longstanding prejudice against the Irish Club. His patrician appearance topped by a dramatically full beard, Weeks was a scion of a Civil War hero and of families prominent in the revolutionary era as well as the embodiment of the old Knickerbocker society. Following his graduation from the Columbia Law School in 1883, he had used his considerable talent, social connections, and close ties to Tammany to forge a career as a leading real estate and criminal lawyer. Like others of his circle in the nineteenth century's closing decades, he was an avid bicyclist and yachtsman. His sporting interests found a congenial home in the NYAC, where he hobnobbed with the likes of the Roosevelts, the De Peysters, and the Belmonts. He became a central figure in the club, honing and ever after preaching a straightforward, genteel philosophy rooted in beliefs in amateur athletics, morality, church, and family. By the 1890s, anti-Semitism had also become a cardinal tenet of Weeks's enclosed world. The NYAC, like other elite social institutions in the city, locked the doors to Jewish candidates, however qualified.[9]

As Weeks matured, the AAU and its allied American Olympic Committee offered new channels of fulfillment. After 1900, he was a close adviser to Secretary Sullivan, who entrusted him with major responsibilities in building up the nation's amateur athletic enterprise. Indeed, to Weeks belonged much of the administrative credit for the success of the American team at

Stockholm. Following Sullivan's death, he even assumed his friend's managerial duties on an interim basis until Rubien was selected. And in spite of having been appointed by New York governor William Sulzer to the state high court in 1913, the new justice still managed to devote time to his beloved AAU. In the end, that factor would prove Kiviat's downfall.[10]

Rubien conferred with Weeks at every step. In addition to summoning a number of track officials and writers to testify at the hearing, Rubien secretly went to Troy on Columbus Day, October 12, and had Campbell write out a summary of his past transactions with Kiviat and Smith. Rubien's motivation for this unprecedented trip, he said shamelessly, was "just to satisfy myself that everything would be done either to clear Smith and Kiviat of the charges made against them or to prove the allegations true." When Pat Conway learned about the trip, he concluded Rubien was "afraid that Matthews and his associates would fail to perform their supposed duty."[11]

Kiviat was not the first great track star the AAU had charged with professionalism. As Robert Korsgaard has demonstrated, a slew of similar cases had been adjudicated since the 1890s, notably that of the great sprinter Arthur Duffey of Georgetown, who was banned for allegedly accepting excessive expense money in 1902. Other prominent cases had followed, highlighted by Jim Thorpe's. In the months before Kiviat's ordeal, sprinters Don Lippincott of Penn and Harry Heiland of New York's Xavier Athletic Association, his Olympic teammates, were charged with competing "in a fixed professional race" in upstate New York. Lippincott was exonerated, but Heiland was barred permanently. Then Alma Richards of Cornell, the high-jump gold medalist at Stockholm, was suspended for an expense account violation, but was ultimately reinstated. A cynical Roscoe Campbell was therefore correct when he told the *Troy Times* that the Metropolitan AAU was "well aware of the practices of prominent athletes in New York demanding exorbitant expenses for their appearance in out-of-town meets." Rubien's denial, claiming the practice was limited to a "few undesirables," rang hollow. Consider, too, that in each instance of accusation, athletes representing the Ivy League establishment got off, but those from minority ethnic or religious institutions—Carlisle, Xavier, Georgetown—fared less well.[12]

Viewed in one way, the AAU's exposure of graft and corruption in track and field was simply another face of the era's muckraking. Like a Lincoln

Steffens or a Ray Stannard Baker, the AAU leaders claimed they were seeking to create "a square deal" in sport. But whereas the muckrakers were idealistic Progressives and meticulous researchers, Fred Rubien and his associates were narrowly conservative men intent on manipulating the facts in order to preserve a dated ideology and way of life.

The hearing two nights later confirmed the Irish Club's worst fears that this exercise was really a vendetta against Kiviat and his club (as well as against what they represented in the new urban America, although this connection went unstated). The proceeding was quasi-legal, with all the trappings of a court trial. While attorneys Dooling and Congressman Hulbert, assisted by Terence Farley, questioned witnesses and debated procedures and evidence with Chairman Matthews for more than four hours, there was no question about who was really calling the shots for the Registration Committee. Seated beside Matthews and Rubien was the August presence of New York Supreme Court justice Bartow Sumter Weeks.

When Congressman Hulbert asked, "Is [this proceeding] in the nature of an investigation or the hearing or charges?" George Matthews answered (after consulting with Justice Weeks), "An investigation which might possibly be made the basis of some future charges."

With Matthews turning constantly to Justice Weeks for counsel and rulings, Dooling objected to the process. "Judge Weeks exclaimed: 'I am chairman of the law committee of the metropolitan association, and in that capacity I have the power to act as I see fit. I want to see every one in this case get a square deal. But I think amateur athletics should be purified, and unless the sport is purified I'm through with it.'" In effect, as the Irish Club people realized, Weeks had just "declared that there was no doubt in his mind about the present matter." This virtual pronouncement of guilt at the outset meant the burden was on Kiviat and Smith to prove their innocence. Spectators in the crowded hearing room applauded.

Weeks listened intently as Harry Smith took the stand and denied that he had printed the postscript "It will have to be 40 bucks," in a letter to Roscoe Campbell about his own appearance in the Schenectady meet. Then, it was Kiviat's turn. Prompted by Justice Weeks, Matthews asked Kiviat about having inserted "a typed yellow slip in a letter to Campbell, sometime between August 26 and September 3, which read: 'I will run in the three-quarter-mile race in Schenectady, but must have $75 for expenses.'" Kiviat flatly denied writing it. At that point, Matthews placed in evidence the document Campbell had written for Rubien on October 12 claiming that Kiviat had in fact demanded the expense money. Since Campbell was not present, citing the demands of his position as a postal official in Troy, Matthews noted for the record Campbell's statement "that he was unable to find the slip with the demand for money on it, but that he would make further search for it."

Next, Matthews questioned Kiviat about supposedly receiving $25, or one-fifth of the total payoff, for running with the "Invincibles" relay team at the Troy Armory in February 1912. He "replied, 'I don't know.'" Using Campbell's information, Matthews then asked if he had received twenty-five dollars from Our Lady of Mount Carmel Church to run the mile at Troy in September 1912. Kiviat denied that accusation also.

Frank Albertanti thought Kiviat and Smith made credible witnesses. "They stood their ground well, and expert counsel assisted materially," he wrote. "They denied in as strong terms as they could apply implications in Campbell's expose."

Matthews now called to the stand erstwhile Commissioner James P. Eaton of Schenectady, who testified that Campbell had shown him the yellow slip on which Kiviat had demanded seventy-five dollars. During cross-examination by Dooling, however, Eaton had to admit he was not there when Campbell opened Kiviat's letter with the yellow slip. Even more damaging to the AAU case, Eaton stated that at a later time he merely gave the slip a cursory glance. That was enough for Pay Jay Conway, who was incredulous at the "utterly ridiculous manner" in which a justice of the New York Supreme Court allowed circumstantial testimony to be admitted.

There were additional witnesses, but none was more dramatic than Fred Rubien with the disclosure of his secret meeting with Roscoe Campbell in Troy forty-eight hours earlier.

By midnight, it was evident that there could be no closure to this case without cross-examining the athletes' principal accuser. Chairman Matthews therefore announced a continuance until October 23, when the Registration Committee would hold a second hearing with Campbell present, possibly in Troy.[13]

As if to confirm the Irish Club's suspicion that something was rotten in Troy, the following day a brazen Campbell sent a letter to a friend seeking "the assistance of local athletes in procuring the position" that was open on the New York State Athletic Commission. The *Troy Times* reported "he has enlisted in his campaign hundreds of his friends around Troy, Albany and Schenectady, and believes he has a splendid chance of getting the position." After again expressing second thoughts about initiating the case against Kiviat and Smith, Campbell reassured his friend "'that everything would come out all right.'"[14]

Kiviat still held an AAU Registration Card, although it was cold comfort. As he had continued to train during the ordeal, he decided to run in the mile handicap race at the James E. Sullivan Memorial Meet on October 17. This meet was a major sports event, a fund-raiser in honor of the old chief, and nearly fifteen thousand spectators packed the reservoir field in Jersey City on a bright and warm Sunday afternoon. What better way for Kiviat to demonstrate to the sporting public a positive attitude toward himself and his cause. It quickly became a two-man race between Kiviat and Willie Gordon, with Kivie a distant second until the gun lap when he "attempted one of his famous sprints in the dash for home." A crowd of men in bowlers and their Sunday best leaned over the curb of the cinder track and urged him and Gordon on, but Kivie failed to catch Willie, who won by a few yards in 4:30.8. It would be Kiviat's last competition for three years.[15]

Off the track, the Registration Committee and Kiviat's lawyers jockeyed for advantage. George Matthews told reporters the date of the next hearing would be moved up two days to Thursday, October 21, when Campbell would come down to New York to testify, possibly accompanied by another witness for the AAU, Father Galanti of Our Lady of Mount Carmel Church. In turn, John Dooling requested a postponement until the following week because of a conflicting court appearance. Matthews and his patrons, Weeks and Rubien, turned him down. Most likely, they suspected that Dooling wanted additional time "to get the statements of witnesses in Troy that Campbell had told them that he knew nothing about this matter and that it was all newspaper talk." Dooling and Congressman Hulbert also had obtained information "that Campbell, very much against his will, was forced, under threats of losing his job in the post office, to come down here and testify. Who was powerful enough to make such a threat?" The Irish Club finger pointed squarely at Justice Weeks.[16]

With this legal maneuvering off stage, the second hearing turned into a fiasco. The defense lawyers kept their clients away, probably in protest, and only Congressman Hulbert appeared midway through the session to make a formal request for a postponement owing to the unavoidable absence of his colleague John Dooling. Chairman Matthews leaned over to Justice Weeks, who whispered "no," and then denied the request. In the audience, Pat Conway thought Weeks had made Matthews into his mouthpiece. Congressman Hulbert, who knew a kangaroo court when he saw one, dramatically exited the hearing.

That was of little concern to Justice Weeks, who had already held the essential part of the session without the defense. Weeks had Matthews call his star witness, Roscoe C. "Rocky" Campbell. The nickname fit: the thirty-three-year-old Campbell's unpolished appearance reflected his experience as a small-time hustler. The son of the Troy Police Department's chief of detectives, he had been a Democratic Party ward heeler and a postal worker but had made his reputation as a sports promoter who could deliver famed track stars for Troy armory meets, with Kiviat's name at the top of the list. On the stand, Campbell identified the typed letter in which Kiviat and Smith had allegedly demanded extra money to race in Schenectady on September 18, but he was forced to confess that he did not bring his smoking gun, the enclosed yellow slip, because it no longer existed. Campbell stated that when President Rubien visited his home and demanded the yellow slip, Mrs. Campbell informed him that she had destroyed it, unaware that it amounted to anything significant. Could there have been a better opening for John Dooling to cross-examine and damage the witness's credibility? But Weeks had made sure that the defense counsel had not been invited to the table.

Campbell now told Matthews that he had had another unexpected visitor in Troy—Abel Kiviat, who "asked Campbell to hush up the matter, as it would endanger his candidacy for Congress on the playground platform." (Loud laughter from the audience; Chairman Matthews banged for order.) Continuing his story, Campbell "told Kiviat that he need not worry, and said he could go back to New York satisfied that he would not 'squawk.'" Indeed, Campbell "promised he would" carry out Kiviat's request "to destroy the now famous yellow slip."

Next, Matthews took Campbell back to 1912 and reviewed with him his two other allegations. Campbell testified to a letter written on September 8 by the Rev. M. A. Galanti in which the priest said he witnessed Roscoe Campbell paying Kiviat $25 and additional expenses to Harry Smith. Campbell also confirmed that he wrote to Smith in February of that year asking him to compete in the Troy indoor meet and to secure the "Invincibles." When the Winged Fist relay squad arrived at the Troy Armory, Lawson Robertson, who was to be the starter for this race, "insisted on 'seeing' him," Campbell stated. The promoter testified that he had no choice but to obtain $125 from his treasurer and give it to Robby then and there.

For his final witnesses, Matthews called Captain John Livingston of Troy and James Eaton of Schenectady, who verified the details of Campbell's testimony. The chairman announced afterward that the Registration Committee would go into executive session. The ensuing debate was lengthy and evidently acrimonious. The committee returned a split decision, three to two, with AAU veterans Matthews and Charles Elbert of Jersey City and young Stephen Byrne supporting a permanent ban, but John O'Hara of Newark and Charles Ericksen of the Scandinavian-American Athletic League voting "to acquit the accused athletes," according to the *New York Times*.

His mission accomplished, Matthews made a public announcement that Harry Smith was barred from amateur sport. Then he made the following statement:

> The committee having investigated the facts and circumstances in connection with the charge that Abel R. Kiviat asked for expenses in excess of the amount allowed an athlete under general rule 4, section 10, to appear at the games of the Eastern New York Athletic League held at Schenectady, N.Y., September 18, 1915 are not satisfied with the explanation given by him, and find that he did ask for the sum of $75 for such appearance and that such a request was a violation of said rule and he rendered himself ineligible for further competition in amateur athletics and his registration card is therefore cancelled.[17]

Throwing more salt in Kiviat's wound, the vindictive Matthews quickly ordered him to return his prizes from the Lehigh University and Sullivan Memorial meets, both of which had occurred after the AAU brought charges. And without in any way acknowledging either the closeness of the vote or the personal toll it would take, Matthews, looking delighted, made himself busy shaking hands all around for the next twenty-four hours. President Rubien was also beaming in satisfaction. At this moment of triumph for the AAU purists, some were even suggesting that Rubien would reappoint his trio of upstate "informers"—Campbell, Eaton, and Livingston—"because of the good services rendered in the tossing out of Kiviat and Smith."

Reached late that night by reporter Howard Valentine, Kiviat would not comment, but the officers of the Irish Club did. Immediately after the hearing, they met to discuss Kiviat's options. Some said he was finished; others, more optimistic, argued for mounting further appeals within the AAU system or, failing in that, taking the organization to court. The club's successful 1904 lawsuit against the AAU in a similar circumstance was still fresh in memory.[18]

While sports fans across the country awoke to headlines announcing Kiviat's disgrace, his legal team began preparing a lengthy notice of appeal to the board of managers of the Metropolitan AAU. It spelled out in blistering language why they believed Kiviat and Smith had been denied due process; indeed, in their view "the Registration Committee was illegally constituted." Central to their argument was the contention that they had notified the Registration Committee in advance of Dooling's unavailability for the second hearing. They also mocked the honesty of the AAU's witnesses and stated bluntly that Justice Weeks had predetermined the runners' guilt "and virtually ordered the committee to bring in this verdict." This process was in stark contrast, the defense lawyers pointed out, to a 1914 case when Weeks showed "not the slightest concern for the 'purity of amateur athletics'" as Olympic champion Platt Adams of the NYAC was exonerated of the charge of selling his prizes.[19]

A day later the Irish Club's institutional response came through President Conway. Although taking a softer approach than the lawyers' statement, Pay Jay minced few words in reiterating the major points of the Irish Club's rebuttal. From the outset, he said, the club believed:

> that if any charges were to be made in the future these boys would be given an ample opportunity to answer them and to defend themselves.
>
> We charge, therefore, that the registration committee has been guilty of the grossest bad faith in acting as it did in cancelling the registration cards of the accused without preferring [*sic*] any charges against them.
>
> . . . . When we view this situation as a whole we are firmly convinced that these boys have not had a square deal, and that it is our duty to proceed further and see that they get it.

Subsequently, the Registration Committee made a pretense of polling the athletic clubs in the Metropolitan AAU about reopening the case but claimed the response was negative. Then, President Rubien announced that the full AAU Board of Managers would meet on November 9 to consider an appeal. Kiviat's attorneys were much more upbeat about their chances of convincing the board to reverse the decision or grant him a new trial. Although Murray Hulbert would be unavailable for the appeal hearing because of his congressional duties, he played an active role in the preparation. Four days before the hearing, he and John Conway, Pat's son and the Irish Club secretary, sat for an interview with Frank Albertanti. "The matter was rushed to suit those higher up, and it is pitable [*sic*] the manner in which the committee disposed of the case," the congressman said. "When the evidence is read to the managers they will see for themselves that the men are not guilty, but that the upstate officials told lies, and they in turn should be expelled and made examples of."[20]

However, in order to persuade the full board, the defense counsel would have to deal again not only with Justice Weeks, but also with the district president, Fred Rubien. In the past, John Dooling knew where he had stood when he faced Jim Sullivan. "Compare Rubien with him," Pay Jay Conway reminded him bitterly, "and you have the reason why the newspapers and the sporting public are so fond of the A.A.U." One troubling element of Rubien's personality that became clear in the 1930s was his anti-Semitism and xenophobia, which strongly suggests he was not predisposed to support Kiviat during his 1915 trial.[21]

Neither were the overwhelming majority of the fifty-seven voting members of the board of managers who attended the hearing in the Seventy-first Regiment Armory. From the moment President Rubien called them to order until they concluded after midnight, four and a half hours later, the atmosphere in the regimental theater was electric and partisan. Even the reading of the complete record of the first two hearings by the association's secretary Andy Tully, which took fully one hour and forty minutes, kept the delegates in their seats. (Some thirsty wags estimated they could have crossed the street to the bar of the Park Avenue Hotel "seventeen times.") At last, Rubien rapped for John Dooling to present his case. Dooling began by requesting a postponement, arguing that his clients were barred without a real opportunity to prove their innocence. He also insisted that the AAU had to produce "the oral or written evidence" of their guilt. Justice Weeks (again at the right hand of the presiding officer) challenged him: "Are you trying to question the validity of the findings of the previous meeting? This is no place to bring up the question of the rightfulness of their suspension." To which Dooling replied: "Does my friend Justice Weeks not wish to hear the truth? I appeal to the managers and country. This is a free country and a man is considered innocent until he is proved guilty." Rubien consulted with Weeks and denied the request for a postponement.

Dooling now turned to a more pressing objective: to introduce for the record significant new affidavits he had obtained from Father Galanti and attorney James J. Flood, an Irish Club loyalist who had conducted fact-finding for him in the Troy area. In one affidavit, Father Galanti disavowed his letter of September 8, 1912, introduced at the second Registration Committee hearing. The priest now swore "that his signature to such a statement was given between confession time when he was extremely busy with his priestly duties. He said that the statement was read to him and he did not remember anything in it about Kiviat receiving money." Another affidavit demonstrated that Campbell "was decidedly irregular" in paying the bills for track meets. Dooling expected the board to infer that Campbell "'held out' the coin that was supposed to go to Kiviat." With the backing of Terence Farley and the fair-minded Judge Jeremiah T. Mahoney of the NYAC, Dooling argued forcefully to be allowed to present these documents. Unmoved,

Rubien called the question, and the Metropolitan AAU's board voted forty-six to eleven to deny the admission of this evidence.

The decision sealed Kiviat's fate. Keeping his composure, Dooling launched into a lengthy summation of his case that some in the audience considered "masterful."

He was outshone by Justice Weeks, who, using all of the skills he had acquired during his years as a celebrated trial lawyer, summed up briefly but with impact. He began by insisting his membership in the NYAC was irrelevant to this case; his interest was only to "purify amateur athletics." Specifically, "he believed all those who testified against Kiviat at the trial had told the truth, and that he really believed him guilty." He concluded with the dramatic plea "that if these two athletes were not banished from the amateur ranks the great organization built up by Jim Sullivan would crumble and that the little clubs and the really pure amateurs would suffer and that there would be no such thing as amateurism in athletics in America."

The extended applause that followed this oration was ominous. ("The judge's few words alone were worth the price of admission," one board member said to Howard Valentine.) Rubien finally let the clapping die after a few minutes and called for a decision. By fifty to six, the board of managers voted to uphold the Registration Committee.

This was all too much for Dooling. He immediately told reporters he would appeal to the national AAU, scheduled to convene in New York early the following week and, should that fail, to the New York State Supreme Court. But he also told them he was so appalled by the lack of due process that he was "forever through" with the AAU. Perhaps someone finally heard him, although cynical New Yorkers said the only reason the local Registration Committee suddenly proposed to consider Dooling's new affidavits was to remove any grounds for an eventual appeal to the high court. Chairman Matthews did hold a session forty-eight hours later, but, after Dooling presented the new evidence, his committee tabled the matter. The chairman apparently also heard Lawson Robertson's appeal to clear his name and his team's. Matthews called Harry Gissing to testify about his cut of the alleged $125 payoff of the "Invincibles" at the 1912 Washington's Birthday event in Troy. Gissing stated "he had never received a cent or heard of any money being paid for the team." From that moment on November 11, local jurisdiction in this case ended.[22]

FINAL APPEAL

At this critical juncture, Frank Albertanti stepped back and reviewed what had transpired so far. His essential point to his readers was that justice would be served only if Rubien and his Metropolitan AAU dismissed the three upstate officials "who banded together to 'crucify' the athletes." After all, he commented, they were guilty of violating the code of amateurism by offering the track stars appearance money. His choice of language was apt, even if, as a man who made his living covering the AAU, his outlook was shortsighted. Crucifixion was not a word normally found in the *New York Evening Mail*'s sports page; but in the haste of a deadline, "Francis" unconsciously spoke volumes. Yet Roscoe Campbell and his associates were mere legionaries useful to ideologically committed governors when a hustling, naive, talented Jewish lad stumbled into their path.[23]

Kiviat characteristically managed to maintain his sure footing in his area of excellence. He continued to train hard in the hope that the national AAU would reinstate him in time to run the McAleenan Thousand race in the Irish Club indoor meet on November 27. "He has his heart set on winning" it, Albertanti reported, "as by so doing he will gain permanent possession of the cup which goes to the athlete who wins it three times." This race would be his swan song, and Coach Robertson believed his time trials signaled a great victory against a world-class middle-distance field at Madison Square Garden.[24]

The final phase of Kiviat's appeals process began at the national AAU on November 15. After George Turner of Baltimore was elected as the organization's new president, his first significant task was to deal with the Kiviat-Smith affair. Because John Dooling asked the national governing body for a postponement, Turner met with the professional, Rubien, and decided to appoint a blue ribbon committee—Edward E. Babb of Boston, Gus Kirby of New York, and himself—to hear the appeal on November 27.

The Irish Club leadership felt that the selection of three successful businessmen so experienced in the governance of athletics would at last set matters aright. Turner was a heavyset, pleasant, and shrewd forty-one-year-old insurance executive who had rowed for the championship Ariel Club crew. The Irish Club should have seen a red light flash at Celtic Park, however: Turner had sought to ban Howard Drew as a "Colored man" from the 1914 AAU meet in racially segregated Baltimore. Was it not plausible that he regarded the Jewish athlete as a complementary object of disdain? Babb, age fifty-six, earnest looking and mustachioed, ran a school supply company and was a past president of the national AAU. But Turner's key selection was for the panel's chair: Gustavus T. Kirby.[25]

Chairman Kirby was something of a renaissance figure, with a reputation, in Allen Guttmann's words, for being "a fair-minded man of remarkable good will." However, research by John Lucas has revealed the complexity of Kirby's personality: he offended many people by his "pompous" manner and opinions grounded in his certainty of his own rectitude. Tall, bald-headed, and aristocratic looking at age forty-one, he was a Columbia-trained engineer and lawyer, but in 1915 serving full-time as a partner in his father's art gallery, the American Art Association. From his mother's side, a descendant of proper Philadelphians, including the flag-maker Betsy Ross, he was also a sensualist and had an irreverent sense of fun, with much of his interest and energy since childhood devoted to amateur sport. He claimed repeatedly (without corroborative evidence) that as an undergraduate in 1893 he had arranged the fateful introduction of Baron de Coubertin to James E. Sullivan. Thereafter, he became another of Sullivan's key right-hand men, serving as president of the AAU in 1911–12 and as a mainstay of the American Olympic movement.[26]

For years, Kirby had watched Kiviat's record-setting performances up close. We can infer that his view was filtered through his cultural heritage. Although twenty years later, during the controversies over the Nazi Olympics, he would write courageously to Avery Brundage about "the democracy of sport, the freedom of all to compete, irrespective of race or color or creed," he never lost the ambivalent attitude of his class toward New York Jews. Indeed, he once wrote to Iphigene Hays Sulzberger, wife and daughter of *New York Times* publishers, that although he had "the highest regard" for the Jewish contribution to civilization, "there are so many of what the Jews, themselves, call 'kikes.'" (This pejorative word for Jews was already in common usage in New York in 1915 and was certainly well known to Kirby at the time of Kiviat's trial.) Nor did Kirby ever entirely overcome the racism of his social milieu. Once, while broadcasting sprinter Ralph Metcalfe's race at Madison Square Garden in the early 1930s, he blurted spontaneously into the microphone: "'That big nigger is certainly plowing up the boards.'"[27]

The Kirby committee met on Saturday morning, November 27, at the Hotel Astor. Murray Hulbert and John Dooling focused their remarks on Roscoe Campbell's dishonesty, in the course of which they revealed that Campbell supposedly had additional "incriminating" correspondence from some New York athletes. Kirby ordered Campbell to hand over these documents at a second session on Sunday, when counsel for the defense would, at long last, be given an opportunity to cross-examine him. Nevertheless, the attorneys and their clients had little grounds for optimism. Kirby delivered a preliminary opinion that the decisions of the local Registration Committee and board were fully justified by the evidence, "either direct or circumstantial." But Kirby did maintain that the appellants had the right "to produce any new witnesses or evidence" they wished, as did the Metropolitan AAU. Until then, his panel would not issue its ruling. Dooling advised that Father Galanti would come down from Troy to testify on behalf of Kiviat and Smith. The ubiquitous Justice Weeks announced he might produce "a witness who would be an unpleasant surprise for the defense."[28]

There was one major disappointment for Kiviat. Dooling and Pay Jay Conway had talked about seeking an injunction to enable him to run in the McAleenan Thousand that night, but the continuance of the case until Sunday persuaded John Dooling not to go to court. Captain Kiviat had to watch his own Irish Club meet from the Garden stands with Harry Smith.

The final session of the Kirby committee the next day was strangely brief. The upstate trio of AAU witnesses was present, but Dooling called only Captain John Livingston to the stand. The witness handed over his account book of the 1912 Washington's Birthday meet at the Troy Regiment Armory, after Kirby, with advice from Justice Weeks, ruled that it would be admissible. Then, in a surprise move, the book was taken out of evidence after one item was investigated. Although we have no documentation of why this occurred, reporters covering the hearing hinted this action prevented another big scandal, affecting the colleges in particular.

Perhaps not coincidentally, Gus Kirby was chairman of the IC4A. The additional "incriminating" letters in Roscoe Campbell's possession were also removed from scrutiny because Dooling never called him or James Eaton. Then, Dooling and Congressman Hulbert asked for a brief recess to consult with their clients. After five minutes, Dooling made a startling announcement to Chairman Kirby and his committee that his clients were willing to plea bargain. They would discontinue their appeals if the special committee recommended to the national AAU Board of Governors to change the athletes' punishment "from expulsion to suspension." Congressman Hulbert cited as precedent a similar case in the Middle Atlantic AAU involving an Olympian who was suspended temporarily then reinstated. The committee's counsel would have none of it. Weeks exploded "that if Smith and Kiviat are guilty the rules of the A.A.U. must be upheld, and they must suffer the full measure." Cooler heads prevailed. After a long discussion about whether suspension was permissible under the AAU constitution and by-laws, Kirby requested defense counsel to submit briefs by January 3, 1916, justifying their plea of the athletes' innocence. The chairman announced that his committee would make a decision by mid-January.

Not surprisingly, Justice Weeks was unhappy about this further delay, especially because Kirby stated candidly he felt the behavior of the Metropolitan AAU had been "a little high-handed" and "over-jealous [sic]" and that Roscoe Campbell's conduct was "unbecoming an official of the A.A.U."[29]

Shortly afterward, Secretary Rubien announced far-reaching decisions emanating from the Kiviat scandal. As president of the Metropolitan AAU, he would not reappoint Campbell and Livingston to their positions. Instead, he would redistrict the upstate area, "rewarding" Commissioner James Eaton of Schenectady—"who aided in the conviction of Kiviat and Smith"—with increased responsibility. Even more astonishing was a little noticed item in the *Troy Times* that Rubien would name "Rocky" Campbell as a member of the Metropolitan AAU's prestigious District Championship Committee, under the chairmanship of the popular secretary Andy Tully. Rubien's rationalization of Campbell's appointment was that "He has been a good official, and would not have done what he did except that he was forced to do it. I think he is a good official despite the fact that he is accused of violating the A.A.U. rules. The fact that he gave testimony that convicted Kiviat and Smith is sufficient reason for my appointing him."[30]

Kiviat and Smith received less merciful treatment. Early in the New Year, the Kirby committee sent its twenty-three-page report to Rubien upholding the Metropolitan AAU's guilty decision. The committee did not consider the athletes' pleas for a brief suspension but declared the pair "ineligible for further competition" and cancelled their AAU registration cards. Rubien, in turn, sent the Kirby report to the sixty-eight members of the national AAU Board of Governors, with the request that they vote whether or not to affirm it. On February 3, he announced that, by a vote of fifty-three to one, Kiviat and Smith had lost their last appeal.[31]

"A BLACK MARK" RECONSIDERED

Were Fred Rubien and his associates solely responsible for this travesty of justice, or did Kiviat bear some measure of guilt? Abel kept silent about this chapter of his life for the next seven decades. Then, in a stunning revelation near the end of his long life, he "reluctantly admitted" to a reporter for his old hometown paper, the *Staten Island Advance,* that something had occurred. "I had been running in a race in upstate New York and after I won this guy comes up to me and wants to know how much I wanted for running." The occasion had to be Kiviat's winning mile at the September 1912 meet of Our Lady of Mount Carmel Church, and "this guy" was of course Roscoe Campbell. "I thought he was kidding . . . I didn't think . . . so I said a number. I don't remember if it was $25 or $35." In his tale, he had made himself into the innocent victim of another man's artifice. He conveniently omitted both the fact of his having an agent, Harry Smith, and the suggestion from Rev. Galanti's testimony that some sort of negotiations may have occurred in advance of the meet. His conclusion to the story, however, was accurate. "The AAU found out about it and, even though I denied taking the money, to them it didn't matter whether I did or not, so they threw me out." Without a pause, he confided to Philip Russo of the *Advance* that "I've never talked about it since, but it's been a black mark on my heart."[32]

A year later, in his oral memoir (1984), Kiviat recounted a more sanitized version of his 1912 encounter with Roscoe Campbell. He admitted that he "asked them to take care of me. You know what that meant?" he asked the interviewer. After all, he had been doing "all the dirty work—training—suffer[ing]," for which he received little from the AAU beyond medals and an intangible celebrity. But, he admitted, "that was against the rules. I didn't come out and ask them for money or mention any amount or anything. And they caught me. I didn't deny it. So they suspended me." The "they" that stuck in his mind all those years as the culprit was not Justice Weeks and Rubien, but Gus Kirby. Old habits die hard, however, and Kiviat continued to express his commitment to the strict rules of amateurism inculcated in his youth by the AAU mandarins.[33]

In the final analysis, whatever Kiviat's degree of culpability, the treatment and punishment he received did not fit the infraction. Many leading track stars in Kiviat's heyday were charged with accepting "appearance money" and, as in the cases cited earlier, most of them, especially those representing the WASP establishment, were quickly reinstated. However, athletes representing minority ethnic or religious teams and themselves belonging to a minority group faced unequal justice. In the court of amateur athletics, Kiviat's fate was preordained; he was, after all, the perfect scapegoat for the establishment. As Gordon Allport observes in his classic study of prejudice, "Scapegoats need not be lily-white in their innocence, but they always attract more blame, more animosity, more stereotyped judgment than can be rationally justified."[34] Driven to conserve a fading social order and fueled by ideology and prejudice, the AAU leaders spun a web around "the Hebrew runner," the captain of the Irish Club, in order to displace their aggression. His career appeared to be at an end.

10

From Doughboy to "Wonder Man"

ABEL KIVIAT WAS A YOUNG MAN IN TROUBLE IN 1916–17. The Winged Fist, which had been a central source of his identity and his prestige, was gone from his life. Indeed, the organization itself now existed virtually in name only. Hannes Kolehmainen quit the team and competed "unattached" before returning to Finland, for whom he won the 1920 Olympic marathon race. With Lawson Robertson's move to Philadelphia to begin an outstanding coaching career at Penn and America's entry into the world war, Pay Jay Conway's organization began a period of "voluntary idleness" from which it never recovered. Kiviat did keep his hand in the sport by coaching his younger brother Sam, a senior at Curtis High and the unexpected runner-up in the 1916 citywide PSAL cross-country championships. He told a reporter that when Sam reached physical maturity, he "will prove the sensation of the athletic world." Through Abel's intervention, Sam received a scholarship to run for Lawson Robertson's track team after being heavily recruited by New York–area universities.

Kiviat himself received and "declined inviting offers to turn professional." In spite of everything that had transpired, in his own mind a track career still meant competing as an amateur athlete. He therefore began to search for a job that would pay more than his modest salary at Dieges & Clust. And, to complicate an already unhappy marriage, the ambitious Yetta now wanted a home that would make a statement. "We moved to 910 Riverside Drive in Manhattan," Kiviat remembered of their relocation to this recently developed street along the winding western slope of the island. Twenty-five years earlier Riverside Drive had been mostly scrubby and wild land; by 1917, builders were beginning to attract "middle-class tenants with upper-class pretensions" to their new apartment houses. "That's when the

Jews thought if you said 'Riverside Drive,' that meant you were on the way up," Kiviat said. His family and friends back on Staten Island were certainly impressed by the couple's new address.[1]

Abel's life continued to sour, however. His wife was increasingly involved in her career and even less interested in him. Yetta had her first big break designing gowns with Henri Bendel, a trendsetter in fashion, for the hit Broadway show *Odds and Ends of 1917*. The army offered him an escape route.[2]

American athletes began enlisting. Tommy Lennon, who had trained as a pilot the previous summer, left Penn to join the army's Aviation Service and was soon flying in France. Kiviat's great rival, John Paul Jones of Cornell, attracted wide notice by enlisting in the navy. His role models, Mel Sheppard and Lawson Robertson, joined the colors, too, as physical training instructors. Although soldiering on the Western Front was of a different order of escape than a train trip to Kansas City or Buffalo, Kiviat's old pattern of fleeing from personal and marital conflict through travel now seemed a viable solution to his current problems. Of course, Kiviat was not unique: many other young Americans viewed service in France as a release from domestic constraints. Near the end of the year, word of his intention began to circulate in athletic circles.[3]

OVER THERE, DECEMBER 1917–JANUARY 1919

Kiviat enlisted in the U.S. Army on December 14, 1917. After passing the required physical examination, he was ready to report for duty. He was not shy about announcing his action to old friends in the press, and they put him back in the headlines as a hero. One telephone call went to Frank Albertanti at the *New York Evening Mail*: "'It may surprise you to learn that I have just enlisted in my old company of the Thirteenth Regiment, now known as the Fourth Company, Coast Artillery,'" Francis quoted him. "'It's me for Fort Hamilton next week and then for France to help make the world safe, etc.,' he continued. 'I'm glad to be back with my old pals, and believe me I'm happy to be able to be of assistance to Uncle Sam at this time. I am leaving a wife and baby at home to pick up a gun and go chase them Huns.'" In fact, he admitted later, he enlisted over Yetta's objections.

Because the AAU had just passed a special wartime rule allowing its amateur athletes to compete against professionals in military meets, Kiviat planned to organize a track team at Fort Hamilton in Brooklyn. "'I will defy the A.A.U. to stop me from running,'" he told Albertanti, while confessing he still hoped that organization would reinstate him as an amateur.[4]

Kiviat was assigned to the Supply Company of the Fifty-ninth Artillery Regiment, most of whose eighty-eight enlisted men came from his old National Guard unit. He reported to the barracks at Fort Hamilton, an early-nineteenth-century post of 155 enclosed acres with a commanding view of the Narrows. Although his unit's goal in France would be to keep the combat forces at the front supplied with the required ammunition and equipment, Private Kiviat and his fellow soldiers were trained for combat duty during the coldest recorded winter in New York history. In his spare time, Kiviat also began working out on the track with a group from the Fifty-ninth. Although he had run little since his suspension, he had kept himself in good shape. He actually weighed less than he did in his final 1915 competitions, and it quickly showed. On Friday night, December 28, he ran a half-mile time trial in 2:05. The next day he made a rush telephone call to the Millrose Games officials requesting entry blanks for his track team of about thirty men.[5]

Given the reality that so many collegiate and club athletes had enlisted already, the Millrose Club made the sensible decision to focus their January 23 meet on events for military personnel. All receipts would be donated to the War Department's Commission on Training Camp Activities for the purchase of athletic supplies. Established track stars converged on New York from army bases and naval training stations from throughout the eastern half of the country. Many in the capacity crowd of six thousand, including Mayor John F. Hylan, had not yet taken their seats when Kiviat went to the starting line at Madison Square Garden for the first time in three years. This competition was a special 1,000-yard race for military personnel. An unwieldy field of thirty runners crammed together for the gun, among whom was his old nemesis, Willie Gordon, now based at a naval station. Kivie held back in fourth place for about 400 yards, made an unsuccessful move on the third lap, and then, on the next circuit, sprinted away from Gordon to the front. According to Frank Albertanti, Kivie "thrilled the spectators with a little of his old-time speed." In his rustiness, however, he was momentarily uncertain on the bell lap and, mistaking the finish line, slowed down. He quickly recovered and defeated Gordon by twenty-five yards in the slow time of 2:24.2. The crowd stood and expressed its appreciation for the still popular runner. His reception, commented the *New York Times,* "was one good result of the war."[6]

Being in that electric atmosphere again whetted Kiviat's appetite. The Hunter Mile was to take place at the BAA meet ten days later, and Kiviat, who had already put that event's first trophy in his personal collection, let the press know of his interest in pursuing the second. The influential Albertanti presented Kiviat's case for him, bluntly reminding his readers about the reservations he had long held about Kiviat's lifetime suspension. "If the A.A.U. really wants to make a hit with athletic followers it should allow this sterling little Fort Hamilton soldier to start in the Hunter mile at Boston, Saturday." Not surprisingly, Fred Rubien and his board remained unmoved.[7]

Kiviat now had no choice but to forget track and focus on getting ready for service on the Western Front. Early on the morning of March 27, 1918, the regiment went to the docks in Manhattan and boarded a troop transport ship, the former SS *Olympic.* There was apparently a miscommunication with the Kiviats, and no family member was at the pier. At 10:00 A.M. on March 28, Kiviat sailed for France.[8]

The trip across the Atlantic took eight days. The weather was mostly cold and rainy, and Kiviat, who "was worried" that he had "left a wife and baby," suffered from seasickness. As they neared port, a convoy of destroyers and airplanes protected them from the ever-present danger of German submarines.[9]

The Fifty-ninth disembarked in the harbor of Brest on the morning of April 5 and were ordered to march three miles uphill to the Pontanezen Barracks. The filth and smell at the barracks were overwhelming, he remembered. The soldiers couldn't settle in for their first decent sleep "until it was washed, scrubbed and clean." When they lay down on "their 'couchettes'— wooden frames filled with springy slats or wire netting"—they "understood why calling Pontanezen a 'rest camp' was one of the favorite jokes of the A.E.F. [American Expeditionary Forces]."[10]

Most of Kiviat's spring and summer were spent in and around the graceful medieval city of Limoges, training for the great battles to come.[11] Perhaps from sheer boredom with the routine, which included guard duty and kitchen police, he acquired the lifelong habit of smoking "Optimo Admiral" cigars. Ironically, despite this break from years of nearly obsessive devotion to Lawson Robertson's training rules, Kiviat turned to running again as a release from the life of a buck private. Indeed, the army provided the incentive for him to begin training a bit whenever he had time.

During World War I, the commanders of the AEF supported a remarkably wide-ranging sports program in the belief that it would train obedient and loyal soldiers who were ready for combat. They hoped it would also correct the serious deficiencies discovered in the physical fitness of a significant percentage of draftees, leading to a substantial improvement in the doughboys' overall health and morale. AEF commanding general John J. Pershing turned to the athletic experts of the YMCA, believers in "muscular Christianity," to create a program at domestic and overseas military posts. Within a year, the Y had three hundred athletic directors on duty in France, some behind the front lines. "Every man in the game" was the Y slogan. Ball fields, running tracks, and basketball nets appeared throughout the theater and engaged hundreds of thousands of the doughboys, a veritable "army of athletes."[12]

Nevertheless, the Y organizers recognized from the outset that even a mass movement needed a showcase. At a meeting in Paris on May 17, 1918, they made final plans with the AEF for their first big athletic event, a track meet to be held at Colombes Stadium on Decoration (Memorial) Day. "Let this be the great American Day," they proclaimed and promised big bands, delicious refreshments, and a tour de force of elite American athletes. The event received wide advance publicity and attracted several hundred entries, including a few marquee names from the prewar worlds of American and French track and field. "Somehow the news leaked out that I was a runner of exceptional merit back in the States," Kiviat recalled, "so the authorities prevailed upon me to run [the mile]." He secured a precious leave to Paris.

Six summers had passed since Kiviat, barely twenty, had raced 1,500 meters on the cinders of Colombes during his grand tour of 1912. A few familiar French faces were present from that occasion, but among the many missing young men was Kiviat's friend, the irreplaceable Jean Bouin. The afternoon weather was perfect, and the stadium was packed with thousands of soldiers and civilians when he lined up for the mile against a field of more than thirty runners. The best was Phil Spink, who had excelled in the 880 for the University of Illinois before the war. Meet rules forbade wearing spikes; Kiviat borrowed a dark singlet and had on white shorts cut off above the knees. "On my feet I wore low-cut army shoes, from which the hob nails had been pulled out," he recalled. "I wasn't trained for a grueling race, but fortunately Zink [*sic*] assumed that the event was in his pocket."

Kiviat described running the bell lap tucked in behind Phil Spink:

> He loafed along for a half a mile, setting a slow pace that didn't take much out of me. When he cut loose I was right with him, a stride behind. He was surprised and chagrined, but no doubt expected to leave me behind in the stretch. I timed my spurt just right and managed to nip him at the tape. I never saw such a picture of utter amazement as Zink [*sic*] presented when I broke the worsted. It doesn't pay to take anything for granted in running.

It was most likely during his train ride back to base in Limoges that he realized, based on his success at Millrose during the winter and now at Colombes, that he wanted to compete again after the war. "Those two impromptu races gave me the idea that I could return to the game with credit to myself," he once told sportswriter George Trevor. "I would rather run than eat—and I like eating."[13]

The St. Mihiel offensive precluded his participation in several Y-sponsored meets.[14] Late on the night of August 25, Kiviat's supply company left camp and traveled for five nights by trucks over muddy roads to Jaillon, the site of the new regimental headquarters, about ten miles due south of the St. Mihiel salient's base. While his supply company was performing useful service at Jaillon, three battalions of heavy artillery barraged the enemy and made a valuable contribution to the successful closing of the salient. By the evening of September 13, the battle was over.[15] This duty prevented Kiviat, for one of the few times in his life, from observing the High Holy Days. The newly formed Jewish Welfare Board arranged worship services at several sites in France and secured leave for Jewish soldiers, who composed more than 5 percent of the AEF. Kiviat drew comfort from his belief "that the war wouldn't last much longer" and that he would be "home before the spring."[16]

Kiviat had a more pressing assignment. General Pershing expected his divisions, complete with support companies, to move northward quickly from the St. Mihiel salient to their new battle positions for the Meuse-Argonne campaign. The men settled into the wooden shacks of Camp Dubiefville and prepared for the offensive that would take place on extraordinarily difficult terrain, between the Meuse River and the heavy growth and steep ravines of the Argonne Forest. The Germans had been entrenched there for four years. Pershing's ultimate goal for the offensive was to push north to Sedan in order to cut the all-important rail lines that supplied the German troops.[17]

The U.S. Army wasted little time. At 2:30 A.M. on September 26, battalions of the regiment began intense bombardment of the German forces in the Argonne Forest. One observer described it "as the sound of the collision of a million express trains." Then, at H hour, the regiment provided the foot soldiers three hours of protection with "a rolling barrage" of fourteen hundred shots. By nightfall, the army's First Corps had penetrated the German first position about a mile into the Argonne Forest.

After this initial attack, the Fifty-ninth Regiment was not involved in operations for another twelve days. Then, as the artillery battalions moved north on October 6 and 7, Kiviat had the difficult job of hauling ammunition across the devastated landscape to new positions near the villages of Very and Cheppy. For the next week, battalions fired hundreds of rounds at enemy positions during the bitter fighting on the Germans' vaunted Hindenburg Line. By October 14, key positions of the Hindenburg Line were in American hands.[18]

The doughboys participating in this offensive perforce lived with fear, and Kiviat freely admitted, "I wasn't a hero." This war was terrifying, "no matter how far back" from the front you were, he said. "We were with these big howitzers . . . [a]bout half a block long." The nightly bombardments with the British howitzers made rest impossible. "Geez, the nights to sleep were brutal," he clearly recalled decades later.

Once, on a day off, he drove up to the front, "and I got the scare of my life. Shells almost bouncing next to me, smoke covering the car." He couldn't tell "whether it was a mine or a shell."[19]

Fear was also a constant in the lives of the families on the home front awaiting news of their loved ones. The daily press reports from France only increased anxieties. Abel's younger brother Harold watched his beloved mother become "very sick while Abe was in France; she got shingles and worried about—when is the next letter coming. . . . You know, in those days they sent officials down to tell you your son died, such and such about. And that's all she worried about. And she got all kinds of nerve, neurotia [*sic*], shingles, burning pains in her back," Harold remembered.[20]

For the two weeks beginning on October 17, the Fifty-ninth Artillery battalions were constantly on the move and helped to deliver the coup de grace to the enemy. They fired a virtual nonstop barrage on targeted German defensive positions in the villages north of Romagne. "For miles and miles no signs of any Huns," Abel noted in a letter home. "They had no heart in their fighting." However, supplying these units was extremely difficult because of congested traffic on the crumbling roads. On the night of October 30, it was Kiviat's turn to drive ammunition to the front. Another member of the Fifty-ninth, an Irish lad named Bill Lewis, offered to switch places and was "killed by direct hit [of the] ammunition truck he was driving through Romagne," according to the regimental history. Private Lewis was the regiment's only casualty while carrying out the supply function.[21]

Abel Kiviat's war was essentially over. On the day of his fateful near miss, the AEF captured the final entrenchments of the Hindenburg Line. The sudden eerie silence at eleven o'clock on November 11 meant the armistice had taken effect. At that moment, he felt deeply that the sacrifices had been worthwhile. "The Germans of the future will never annoy anything related to America and Americans," he wrote to his brother. The doughboys had earned for the nation the respect of "the entire World."[22]

The following weeks were a blur of drills, broken up only by good meals and wine offered by grateful French villagers. Homecoming could not come "any too quickly for me and mine," Kiviat wrote. At last, early on the day of embarkation, January 8, 1919, the regiment marched with heavy packs on their backs down to the pier at Brest, whence they had arrived as green recruits nine months earlier. After going aboard the USS *Louisiana,* they lifted anchor at 2:00 P.M.

Kiviat was at sea for two weeks, arriving at Hoboken at noon on January 24. "Abel got back from France," his brother Sam noted with joy in his calendar book. Following a week at Camp Upton on Long Island that included a farewell party for his supply company, he was honorably discharged. For the last time, he marched with his fellow doughboys to the Riverhead railroad station, where they broke ranks on the platforms and headed home.[23]

For the rest of his life, Kiviat pointed with pride to his military service overseas. However, at times he exaggerated his period of duty into "twenty months in Europe." And, in his final years, he expressed bitterness about "most of the politicians" for denying veterans of World War I the pension and other benefits later given to the GIs of World War II. Perhaps not unsurprisingly, his most distinctive contribution to the war effort came through retooling his extraordinary athletic talents. His two races for military personnel at Millrose and at Colombes were cited then and afterward as highlights of the AEF's successful athletic program.[24]

DIVORCE, 1919–1922

On the surface, Kiviat's life in New York soon had more in common with the struggles and disillusionments of returning German soldiers in Erich Maria Remarque's postwar novels *Three Comrades* and *The Road Back* than with the real experiences of many of his fellow doughboys. It began pleasantly enough, however, with "the first family reunion in several years." The Friday after his return, the Kiviat clan gathered with Abel on Staten Island for a traditional Sabbath dinner. A relieved Zelda must have outdone herself cooking Abel's favorite gefilte fish. He spent the next day touring in Manhattan with brother Sam and a friend and seeing a matinee of the Broadway musical comedy *Little Simplicity* about, of all subjects, an American soldier in the trenches.

He was thrilled to present his four-year-old son with a sailor suit he had brought home with him from Europe. "I remember that, giving him a French sailor suit," he reported in his oral memoir. "Oh, with a whistle and everything. Which we kids wore when we were young, like that." Harold Kiviat always remembered how handsome his little nephew looked in it.[25]

As late as that spring, there were occasions when Abel was still enjoying himself.[26] One afternoon, a dozen or so of his former Irish Club teammates, including Pat McDonald and Matt McGrath, and a few athletes from the NYAC went out to Ebbets Field in Brooklyn to watch Jim Thorpe play the outfield for the Boston Braves against the Dodgers. Lawson Robertson came up from Philadelphia for the reunion. They "asked an usher before the game started to tell Thorpe we were there," Kiviat recalled. Thorpe snubbed them. "And they said, 'The hell with 'em.' Yelled out loud so that everybody could hear it. . . . He changed evidently, something or other." What Kiviat did not know was that after Thorpe's little boy had died from polio the previous year, his personality changed drastically. Kiviat never saw Thorpe again.[27]

The pleasure of those experiences faded quickly when Yetta confronted him with a painful reality: she wanted a divorce. While he was overseas, she had been having a love affair with Dr. Herman Pomeranz. Already a successful physician at thirty-five with a practice largely serving artists and writers, the doctor was Kiviat's polar opposite. He was an accomplished student of languages and literature, medical history and folklore. Yetta wanted to marry him.[28]

Because adultery was then the sole legal grounds for dissolution of a marriage in New York State, Yetta concocted a plan to catch Abel in a compromising situation. Although the court records in this case are sealed until 2019, it is a safe assumption, based on their later repetition of this behavior, that Yetta's brother Al was her partner in this scheme to exploit the loneliness of her rejected husband. Long afterward, Harold Kiviat was emphatic in recalling the details of his big brother's humiliation: "Yes! That's how it was. She framed him with a Ziegfield girl. She paid the Follies girl to play the part of a hooker. And then she married Pomeranz after she got rid of Abel. He was a doctor. . . . Anything to progress her, her career."

Kiviat claimed later that he did not fully understand Yetta's real motivation during that spring and summer. She said "she had good reasons. I found out after what they were. Weren't very good," he said in his oral memoir. He decided not to contest the allegations. Yetta was granted the divorce and custody of Arthur in the New York Superior Court on October 18, 1919.

Although Kiviat saw himself as the accommodating party, he felt Yetta was vindictive. "She took—she wanted everything. Took the son. The car I think was gone by then." Despite his matter-of-fact pose in dealing with this trauma, he was in fact cut to the quick and never really got over the loss of his teenage sweetheart. His family's culture surely added an additional layer of discomfort: divorce among Jews was a rarity in the early twentieth century. In his 1984 oral memoir, he called this episode one of the major sorrows of his life. Yetta quickly married Dr. Pomeranz, and the lovers became known in their Broadway milieu "as [having] 'the ideal marriage.'" To add to Kiviat's problems, his ex-wife kept him completely away from his son for the next decade. The boy had no knowledge of him. Even worse, she began to call the boy "Arthur Pomeranz," and she let him grow up assuming that the doctor was his real father.[29]

Cast adrift, Kiviat went to live with his parents on Staten Island. The family had recently moved. "We moved to [a] higher class, New Brighton, in a big house, fourteen [rooms]," Harold Kiviat remembered. A local writer visiting Abel at his new Oakland Avenue residence noted it was "adorned with trophies, certificates and other evidence of his victories."[30]

About this time, his parents realized they had had enough of their long-troubled marriage and began to live apart. Morris, who had alienated his sons, moved into his own apartment in the St. George neighborhood. He remained to the end of his life a decade later (1930) a maladjusted Talmud student in the strange New World. Abel therefore began to help his mother in the family store on Broad Street before taking a job as a life insurance salesman.[31]

Sport became his release from the mess in his life. It took him out of his parents' house and into the community again. He was a vigorous twenty-seven-year-old, but still barred by the AAU from resuming his amateur track career, so he spent his energies in other pursuits. Basketball was "the sport of the Jews" in the 1920s, engaging the children of eastern European immigrants in the great cities of the Northeast and Midwest, many of whom were no taller than Kiviat. He began to play basketball with the Wilco Athletic Association.

The name "Wilco Athletic Association" was a derivative of the W. S. Wilson Corporation, a successful hardware firm at 155 Chambers Street in the city hall district of Lower Manhattan. The company president, Hugh Hirshon, had run on relay teams with Kiviat at both the Irish Club and the

Thirteenth Regiment, and they had remained friends. With the demise of the Irish Club after the war, Hirshon decided to organize his own club as an offshoot of his business. Kiviat accepted his friend's invitation to join and play basketball. When he took the floor for the Wilco quintet, he had a noticeably more mature appearance than in his youthful glory days. He sported a mustache now. He had also "filled out a lot": he weighed more than 150 pounds, his chest was "deeper and broader," and the added strength complemented his speed of foot and mental agility in athletic contests.[32]

In the spring and summer of 1920, he played baseball for the Staten Island Elks. Semipro baseball was in its heyday on the island. Dozens of good teams enjoyed the sponsorship of island businesses and drew big weekend crowds to Sisco Park in Port Richmond. Kivie was at home again in his second sport—but his first love—and he quickly stood out as an outfielder and at the plate.[33]

On autumn Sundays, he served as a referee for semipro football, whose playing conditions were primitive by today's standards. A club he officiated for, the Staten Island Stapes, continued in operation after he moved on and by the end of the decade evolved into one of the pioneering teams of the National Football League.[34]

Refereeing semipro football or playing centerfield for the Staten Island Elks was not quite the same as straining at the tape to win a national championship in world-record time in Madison Square Garden. Kiviat realized how much he missed competing in track: "running gets a grip on a man that he can't shake off," he told a sportswriter. By late 1922, he had recovered sufficiently from the traumatic experience with Yetta to begin rebuilding his life. In October, he decided to apply to the AAU for reinstatement as an amateur athlete. At that moment, circumstances at the AAU were propitious.[35]

COMEBACK, 1923–1924

The Registration Committee of the Metropolitan AAU acted favorably on his application, as well as on that of his former "agent," Harry Smith, and forwarded their names for final approval to the national AAU convention in New York. Newspaper reports reflected the popularity of the decision, and one—the *Times*—even revised recent track history by claiming "Abel was never disqualified, or even cautioned, for unethical conduct during his competitive career prior to the fatal Troy incident. A desire to remove this blot on his record is advanced by Kiviat as the cause for his application for reinstatement." Finally, on November 20 Kiviat received good news from the national AAU.

"What did they say to you when they restored your amateur status?" his oral historian asked him in 1984. "Well, they were glad to have me back," he responded. "Was a different bunch in, you see . . . [a] lot of new men. . . . May have seen me run. New president—more democratic, you know. A new vice president. New chairman of the Registration Committee." Kiviat was accurate as well as concise. The "new men"—who were in fact old friends—helped to turn around his life.[36]

In retrospect, the first surprise was the Registration Committee's action, given its brutal treatment of Kiviat before the war. It was evident that in the AAU of the 1920s, staff secretary Fred Rubien, who still harbored hostility to Kiviat, had nowhere near the decision-making power of his predecessor, James E. Sullivan. Kiviat had another important supporter in independent-minded Judge Jeremiah Mahoney of the NYAC, a delegate at large. Perhaps most important, by this date Justice Bartow Weeks had passed from the scene. Thus, the underlying bigotry that had bedeviled Kiviat and was a powerful—if latent—factor in his lifetime ban was not an issue, despite the alarming increase in anti-Semitism among middle- and upper-class Americans during the postwar years.

Kiviat was on even firmer ground at the national AAU meeting. The organization's president was William Prout, the former BAA runner who had competed against Kiviat. Prout chose Murray Hulbert, Kiviat's defense counsel during his 1915 trials, as his new first vice president and heir apparent. Hulbert, who was now the powerful acting mayor of New York and president of the New York Board of Aldermen, took advantage of his position to right an historic injustice.[37]

How far was Kiviat prepared to take his reinstatement? Was this effort principally a successful attempt to remove from his résumé the stigma of a lifetime ban? Or was it, as some track experts argued, an opportunity to revive a championship career, provided he got himself into peak condition? Kiviat was clear about his motivation: "I never deluded myself into thinking that I could attain my 1912 form," he told George Trevor of the *Brooklyn Eagle* during his comeback, "but I do believe that I am good enough to give the topnotchers a run for their money." After a seven years' absence from the indoor circuit, he hoped to hold his own "at distances from the half mile to two miles."

What Kiviat was attempting to achieve was rare. He would have to challenge the traditional assumption that only the young had the requisite speed or suppleness for most track events. True, good marathoners were often in their midthirties, as were several of the weight throwers. However, in 1923 the prototypes for middle-distance runners remained John Paul Jones, who gave up the sport immediately after college, and Norman Taber, who competed for a couple of postgraduate seasons before devoting himself to profession and family. Kiviat was now past thirty years of age.[38]

Some fundamental aspects of the world of track and field had altered by the time Kiviat returned to it that winter. During his absence, the world war had cancelled one Olympiad, but a second, the modestly successful Antwerp Games of 1920, had both renewed global interest in athletics and called forth a new generation of outstanding individuals and teams. Increased attendance at major meets and new levels of performance offered hard evidence of a return to normalcy. Track writers of the early 1920s filled endless columns with fact and speculation about the phenomenal Finnish distance runners, successors to Kolehmainen, Paavo Nurmi and Willie Ritola. The grim-faced Nurmi especially captivated the world press with his demanding and varied training regimen and his ever-present stopwatch in hand to monitor his record-breaking times. Yet in early 1923, American track stars still held world records in thirteen of the twenty-two events comprising the standard Olympic program.

One trend just emerging in Kiviat's day had since become irreversible: the leading collegiate teams, not the athletic clubs, were now the backbone of America's track elite.[39] This rich and seemingly limitless human resource presented the AAU and American Olympic Committee leaders with a creative opportunity. Abandoning their prewar agenda to use sport as an antidote to the perils of rapid immigration and modernization, these men now developed a new mission for their movement. In the interwar era, comments Mark Dyreson, they "used the Olympic Games to promote the export of American culture." Marketing sporting goods abroad rather than emphasizing their use in civic renewal at home became, in their minds, the basic purpose of the Olympic sports. For a shrewd and battle-hardened man such as Abel Kiviat, success in this bottom-line athletic universe also held the promise of job opportunities.[40]

Those who knew Kiviat best were realistic about what kind of performance to expect. John Drebinger revealed to readers of the *Staten Island Advance* that his old friend had been working out secretly for years on the hilly roads of Staten Island. Although Drebinger cautioned fans not to expect their hero to "start right off in his championship stride," he predicted prophetically that before long "he will be fit to give the best in the game a run for the laurels he once held." Kiviat's initial period of training seemed to bear out Drebinger's contention. His speed work at shorter distances began to produce "astonishing results," culminating in a solo time trial of two minutes flat for the half-mile. Buoyed by the effort, Kiviat announced that the first race of his comeback, representing the Wilco Athletic Association, would be in the Metropolitan half-mile championship at his club's indoor games on Saturday night, February 10, 1923. Track writers evoked the image of the renowned "Kivie" and declared him a legitimate contender for the Wilco meet's Meritorious Trophy.[41]

The headline in the Sunday *Times* was unmerciful: "Kiviat's Comeback Fails." He was simply not ready for the eight young club runners who lined up with him at his old haunt, the Thirteenth Regiment Armory. The crowd of eight thousand was in his corner and "yelled its encouragement" to the veteran runner with the inimitable, "peculiar, almost awkward 'shuffle.'" He ended up in fourth place in 2:02.4, about eight or nine yards behind the winner. It was not quite the meritorious performance of his dreams.

During the next ten days, he ran four more slow races at assorted distances, finishing second twice. This comeback business was much harder than it looked to the casual fan, and Kiviat "battled with disappointments and discouragement." He missed his old killer instinct, "the indefinable feeling that I could count on myself to deliver at any stage of a race," he said. "I felt like a novice—as if I were breaking into the game for the first time."[42]

The revival of his track career led to an unexpected opportunity when another old friend approached him with a proposal. Elmer Ripley, once his Curtis teammate and now a fine basketball player for the Fort Wayne club in the fledgling professional game, was also developing into a first-rate coach at Wagner College. He invited his former schoolmate to help coach the track team on a volunteer basis, and Kiviat accepted. This move was a shrewd one by Ripley, who was well aware of Kiviat's reputation as a keen student of the sport.

The Wagner campus had been located on the Cunard estate atop Grymes Hill on Staten Island for only five years. The college, whose mission was to prepare young men for the Lutheran ministry, had moved from Rochester in 1918 with sixteen students, one professor, and a small library. When Kiviat drove up to Wagner's magnificent site overlooking New York Harbor and the Manhattan skyline in the spring of 1923, the school had an enrollment of seventy-three students and a small faculty, but did not yet have accreditation from the New York State Board of Regents. The college's board of trustees was busy buying up nearby estates, including Captain Jacob Vanderbilt's, and constructing new buildings. The sixteen youths who reported to Kiviat and Dr. H. T. Weiskotten, the head coach and a faculty member, were enthusiastic. However, the coaches faced almost impossible challenges. The limited number of available athletes meant they had to double or triple in events against fresh competitors. Relay teams were out of the question. Equally problematic was the lack of a home track for workouts.

Undaunted, Kiviat held practices twice weekly for the two meets scheduled that spring. He also recruited his own schoolboy mentor, Chief Barkley, to join him on the coaching staff. The boys responded immediately to Kiviat. Distance runner John Futchs recalled seven decades later that all the athletes liked him. The Green and White won their meet with Curtis High in April and repeated it in May. Five of Kiviat's boys earned a varsity letter. Judging by a writer's laudatory comments in the 1924 *Kallista* yearbook, Kiviat taught more than running skills.

> To choose from a school of but seventy-three students a track squad that will defeat the teams of schools of two thousand registration is a record of which any coach would be justly proud; and Abe Kiviat is proud of his work at Wagner. But even if Abe's record was not such a splendid one, yet Wagner men would admire him for the fine example of hard, loyal, active service which he set before them. To see Abe run is a pleasure, but to have him run alongside of one, advising one how to remedy one's faults, and encouraging one to fight is an experience that would put a back-bone in a jelly fish.

Kiviat coached at Wagner for only one season. The increasing demands of training, once he decided to prepare for the 1924 Olympic Games, coupled with the need to make a living, prevented him from continuing as a volunteer coach. He never again received an offer to coach collegiate track, leading one sportswriter to argue that Kiviat was "probably the best coaching bet that has been overlooked by colleges and clubs throughout the land." Because anti-Semitism, a visceral feeling of being engulfed by "the Jewish problem," was pervasive—and increasing—on campuses nationwide in these years, discrimination in academic employment hardened. A similar pattern of barring Jews was the rule in elite social clubs. Although many of Kiviat's peers from the Irish Club and elsewhere secured attractive coaching positions, even a well-prepared Jewish athlete had little chance of doing so.[43]

Coaching at Wagner kept him happily occupied that spring, but he continued to train and to pursue "in real earnest" a dream of making the U.S. team for the 1924 Olympic Games in Paris. He examined his prospects realistically and decided to focus on the 3,000-meter team race, for which four Americans would be selected at the Olympic trials in June 1924. In Kiviat's mind, only the great Joie Ray was a serious threat in the team event. Some of the AAU brass evidently encouraged this line of thinking.

In October 1923, he began a program of regular workouts on Staten Island roads and, whenever time permitted, at the Columbia University board track. He faced considerable skepticism as well as "some good-natured 'kidding,'" Howard Valentine reported. By early January 1924, he was making significant progress, running a comfortable time trial for one mile in 4:29.4. But this effort required more than the casual training of his youthful heyday, he told a reporter. "A comeback isn't child's play. You've got to make heavy sacrifices. Only the hardest sort of training enabled me to regain a measure of my old form. I didn't spare myself, watching my diet rigorously and practicing four days a week. The only way to develop your running muscles is to run. Believe me, I've done enough running in training to satisfy even a glutton for work like Paavo Nurmi."

He also claimed to return to his strict personal habits of 1911–13—no smoking, no drinking, no sex, and early bedtime.[44]

Kiviat had a modest payoff from this intense effort, but he did not suddenly metamorphose into a Paavo Nurmi or even return to his old self. The training regimen seemed only to solidify the pattern of the previous winter: he was sharper at shorter distances, but he lacked the stamina to close out elite races at 1,500 meters and greater. Altogether, he ran thirteen races during a long board season, beginning with a disappointing two mile in the Millrose Games at Madison Square Garden on January 29. His victories came in shorter-distance events.

He still had some of his ability to maintain an extended sprint. The Metropolitan AAU three-quarter-mile championship was the feature of the Seventy-first Regiment Armory Games on February 11, and he drew headlines by defeating a field of eleven seasoned runners that included Olympian Mike Devanney, his prewar rival. The fact that Kivie's winning time, 3:15.4, was fully eight seconds slower than his personal record was irrelevant. The essential point was that he had his first major victory since his defeat of Ted Meredith in November 1914, in what seemed another world. Kiviat would have "to be seriously considered when Uncle Sam comes to pick his Olympic team" was the surprising lead in the *Brooklyn Eagle*'s account of the meet. The *New York Telegram and Evening Mail*'s headline was less judicious: he was simply "[t]he Wonder Man."[45]

His performance in March encouraged him more. On the evening of the fifth, Kiviat lined up for the national AAU 1,000-yard championship against a classy field: Lloyd Hahn of the BAA, the recent winner of the Baxter Mile; Ray Buker and Ray Dodge of the Illinois Athletic Club; and George Marsters and Willie Sullivan of Georgetown. Few in the crowd of five thousand at the Twenty-second Regiment Armory gave Kivie a chance. He surprised them, however, sprinting from sixth place to third on the gun lap, passing the awkward-striding Hahn as well as Buker and Dodge. Kivie barely missed catching the fading pace setter, Willie Sullivan, for second place. Sullivan's Hoya teammate, George Marsters, had come from nowhere to win in 2:17.6. With accuracy as well as pride, Kiviat could say long afterward: "I came close to winning the national championship in the 1,000 yards in 1924."[46]

Perhaps the sense of being restored did the trick, for a few nights later Kiviat had his first big victory at Madison Square Garden in years. He won "the Thousand" in the Metropolitan AAU's indoor championships, holding off a field of thirteen. He "felt that the 'old stuff' was there again. My muscles responded the way they did when I was beating all comers." He won by five yards in 2:18.4 and had "plenty left."[47]

The New York newspapers now referred to him as "the talk of the athletic world," but in truth he was a shadow of his youthful self. A writer for Henry Ford's anti-Semitic publication the *Dearborn Independent* could not resist remarking that Kiviat was "making a none too pretentious comeback."[48] He had already received blunt advice from the newly appointed head Olympic coach Lawson Robertson to change his plan about running the middle distances and to "make his bid for a place on the American Olympic team in the 3,000-meter steeplechase event." According to Howard Valentine, Robby "told Kiviat plainly" that he lacked the speed to stay with the younger stars in his former events.

Kiviat made the serious mistake of rejecting his old coach's advice and stuck to his original plan to try for the 3,000-meter team race. This was the first time that he had intentionally disregarded the words of a man who was as much a father figure as a trainer. Even more curiously, during the weeks when other Olympic distance hopefuls were devoting themselves single-mindedly to training, Kiviat spent precious time and energy as the regular centerfielder for the Elks baseball team.[49]

Perhaps in the final Olympic trials hope would still triumph over his recent experience. Kiviat, however, seemed determined to block his own success. A week before the meet, he played a doubleheader at Elk Park. Three nights later, less than seventy-two hours before the trials, he starred in centerfield again for the victorious Elks. Then he caught the train for Boston.[50]

The program at Harvard Stadium on Saturday afternoon, June 14, listed Kiviat as "competitor 333" in the 3,000 final, which was scheduled to start at 4:55 P.M. He never made it to his rightful place at the starting line. His Olympic experience had ended more than an hour earlier in embarrassment in the 3,000-meter *steeplechase*. What occurred in the interval remains open to interpretation. Late in life, Kiviat claimed repeatedly that "about five minutes before the [steeplechase] race, one of the assistant managers"—Olympic distance coach Tom Keane of Syracuse—informed him they were switching him from the 3,000 flat race to the steeplechase. Keane told him there were enough "experienced men" entered in the 3,000, including Joie Ray (whom Keane had switched there from the 1,500 moments earlier), but only eight

starters in the steeplechase. "I looked at him," Kiviat recalled, feigning innocence, "but what could I do? I had never hurdled in my life and didn't know
how to go over the water jump." Again, one can conclude that Kiviat paid
dearly for not heeding Lawson Robertson's advice.[51]

The water hazard on every lap was only the beginning of his problems;
there were also the four hurdles, three feet high and twelve feet wide. A
steady rain over the stadium made them appear even more formidable. A
photograph in the *Boston Globe* showed Kivie trailing the field as they took
the first water jump. He claimed later that in trying to clear the barrier and
pit "like a V," he "wrenched my ankle" and "fell on my face." By the time
Russ Payne of Ohio State passed Rick Marvin of the NYAC on the last lap
for an upset, Kiviat had long since gone into the dressing room for "a massage, and an ice pack and all that." In a postrace interview, he admitted to
the *Boston Globe*'s veteran track writer John J. Hallahan that he "withdrew,
as he felt the youngsters of the present day were too much for him."[52]

Kiviat embellished his steeplechase story over time. He claimed variously
to have been "laid up for three or four weeks" to as much as "eight weeks"—
"with a cane." Yet there is no mention of his sustaining a severe injury in contemporary news reports. On the contrary, the following weekend he was in
his customary spot in centerfield for the Elks. Kiviat's tale drew on the painful fate of steeplechase finalist Basil Irwin, who was in fourth place when he
tripped and fell "prostrate" going over the final barrier of the race and required
medical attention. It seems clear that in order to cope with the profoundly
disappointing experience at the 1924 Olympic trials, Kiviat—remembering
Basil Irwin—converted his psychological pain into a more acceptable physical
symptom. Perhaps, too, lingering guilt over disobeying the wise counsel of
his beloved father figure played its part in this conversion reaction.

Although he refused to label his coaches' decisions "anti-Semitism" in
his 1984 oral memoir, he did suggest the possibility to historian William
Simons in 1986. "In later years they sometimes tried to keep Jewish runners
out. Makes you wonder," he commented. Kiviat well remembered when U.S.
officials pulled Marty Glickman and Sam Stoller from the 400-meter relay
at the last minute during the Berlin Olympiad of 1936. Coincidentally, the
head coach for the U.S. teams in both 1924 and 1936 was Lawson Robertson. Despite remaining close to Robby, did Kiviat thereafter hold a corner

of doubt in his mind about his former coach? If so, he did an injustice to his mentor. Unlike the incident in Berlin, when Robby deferred to the bigotry of his fellow Americans Avery Brundage and assistant coach Dean Cromwell, as a first-time Olympic head coach in 1924 he was guilty only of constantly juggling his lineups to produce the best results. Ambition, not bigotry, was his motivating factor in switching his athletes from one race to another.

Kiviat refused to watch the 3,000 race later that afternoon, upset that he had lost his "chance to be on the '24 team. I would have made the 3,000-meter team because we had no one besides Joie Ray." He was not being realistic, though. In a field of good collegiate distance runners, Ray won a close race in 8:43.9. Based on Kiviat's recent performances, he would have been left far behind.[53]

Having outlasted almost all of his contemporaries, Kiviat should have ended his running career then and there, but he found it impossible to call it quits. Stubbornly and rather ineffectually, he continued to race indoors for the next two seasons. He did manage a few second- and third-place finishes against local runners, but he was no match for elite athletes. His last race was not the way a great champion should have gone out. On February 13, 1926, in the 1,000-meter event of the Wilco Games at the Thirteenth Regiment Armory, he was buffeted on the backstretch of the first lap and "tumbled down on the drill shed while the flying heels of his rivals trampled over him," reported the *Times*. "He regained his feet and started twenty yards to the bad, pluckily continuing until near the end of the fourth lap, when he withdrew and limped to the track side." Like a Chaplinesque character in silent films, at once pathetic and unconquerable, he had reached his personal finish line.[54]

The finality of his situation was underscored by the demolition of Madison Square Garden. In late 1924, promoter Tex Rickard and his financial backer, circus king John Ringling, built a new Garden on the site of a trolley barn at Forty-ninth Street and Eighth Avenue. Although Kiviat's youthful achievements would forever be linked with Stanford White's great arena, his popularity in track circles soon enabled him to fashion a part-time career as an AAU official in the new Garden that would sustain him through the next half-century.[55]

11

"A Runner Whom Renown Outran"

IN 1926, A. E. Housman's popular poem "To an Athlete Dying Young" touched the hearts of readers with its ode to a great runner's fleeting glory. Better a premature passing, Housman wrote, than to be

> Of lads that wore their honors out
> Runners whom renown outran
> And the name died before the man.

Housman's lovely and succinct stanza partially described Kiviat's fate, but there is greater nuance to the story than previous writers have suggested. When he limped off the track at the Thirteenth Regiment Armory in 1926, already thirty-four, he had sixty-five more years to live. Having been set apart by what the poet called "that early-laurelled head," Kiviat would by no means be forgotten. His part-time career as an AAU official kept him before the public. The press quoted him frequently during the interwar years as an authority on middle-distance racing. As a *Jewish* sports personality, he remained an important figure to his fellow second-generation American Jews, but he ran into problems again with anti-Semitic leaders of the AAU that gave him unwanted public notice. Increasingly, though, as the memory of his youthful accomplishments faded during the second half of the century, he "lived in relative obscurity."

In his private life, he played many social roles: as employee, husband (again) and father, son and brother. He enacted those roles through seven dynamic decades of New York, Jewish, and track history. In the process, he experienced significant failures as well as successes, and at times he exhibited idiosyncratic behavior. In short, he developed into a great character, a quintessential Jewish New Yorker. Later, during the final chapter of his life, the world at large would rediscover him as an ancient Olympian and return him briefly to front-page renown.[1]

THE BACHELOR

At first, in the midst of the boom of the mid-1920s, Kiviat lived a lonely and desperate existence on Staten Island. After the failure of his Olympic bid, he continued to reside in his mother's large and comfortable home on Oakland Avenue. He was unemployed, had few friends, and, his brother Sam claimed, developed a "bad reputation" because of "scandal." His behavior "worried" his mother constantly, turning her into "a mental wreck." At home, he was "always yelling," Sam noted, with "never a kind word for Mom." Although he was unable to express "affection," his need for her attention was consuming. He refused to let her have a life of her own. He interfered whenever she and his sister Anne wanted "to go visiting, to city or to movie." In the summer of 1925, he even "spoil[ed] Mom's first vacation in years."[2]

Sam believed his big brother was also making a public "jackass of himself," as evidenced by Abel's employment record, his last gasps on the track, and his semiprofessional baseball career. Sam was soon proved wrong on all counts. Abel found meaningful employment. He commuted daily to Lower Manhattan, where he worked as a bond salesman for the investment banking firm of T. H. Rhoades & Company. He was fortunate to land this position at a time when nine out of ten white-collar openings were reserved for non-Jewish New Yorkers. According to his brother Harold, who later interned there, "He had a name. They used him as a stooge to bring in business. Kiviat. Kiviat. Everybody wanted to see the great . . . Kiviat." In fact, Abel worked hard to make a success of his new career.[3]

He also demonstrated his managerial skills on the ballfield. As happened to his childhood hero Honus Wagner and to many other professional ballplayers of that era, Kiviat's playing days ended where they began, on the sandlot of his earliest neighborhood. Given his legendary reputation for keen sports intelligence, the semipro Rosebank Pioneers of Staten Island hired him as their new manager and centerfielder at the start of the 1925 season. For the next three seasons, he successfully turned around a failing and unpopular team by emphasizing fundamental plays and his own drive to win.[4] He also somehow found the time to replace his pal, Wagner basketball coach Elmer Ripley, as the college's part-time volunteer baseball coach for two seasons. His supervisor at Rhoades & Company allowed him to leave the office before the New York Stock Exchange (NYSE) closed, and a student would pick him up at the St. George ferry terminal at 3:30 and drive him to the college. As in his previous stint coaching the Wagner track team, he took a small squad with few seasoned ballplayers and turned them into skilled winners. His 1927 varsity team won nine of eleven games, and the players credited him with their success.[5]

Following the 1929 stock-market crash, Kiviat left Rhoades and secured a position as a recreation supervisor with the NYSE at 11 Wall Street. For almost a decade, the NYSE had been creating an outstanding athletics program for young men working on the exchange. It offered recreational opportunities in nine sports, including baseball, basketball, track, and cross country. Kiviat remained on staff there for four years.[6]

He was also now living the bachelor's life in a large apartment on the island. He drew unwanted headlines in November 1931 when Henry Joblin of Port Richmond named him as corespondent in a messy divorce action against his wife, Ruth. Joblin, who had already filed for separation, "was 'shadowing' his wife" and caught Kiviat "filandering [sic]" with her in a car on Todt Hill.[7]

While Abel lived carefree, his more entrepreneurial younger brothers were busy creating the Kiviat family's modest fortune. First, his brother Israel (Izzy) opened Kiviat's Bathhouses on the rebuilt boardwalk at South Beach.[8] Far larger revenues that would provide lifelong support for several family members resulted from an idea inspired by Zelda in the early 1920s.

Her fourth son, Sam, was a student at Penn Dental School after receiving a bachelor's degree from Wharton. It was apparent, however, that Sam's gifts lay elsewhere. In addition to competing for Lawson Robertson's track team and lettering in varsity lacrosse, he had been a head counselor at an exclusive camp in the Berkshire Mountains. He was a "driven" young man, in his grandson's words, eager for upward social mobility. This son of Polish immigrants "wanted to re-invent himself as a self-made German Jew." Hobnobbing with Zeta Beta Tau fraternity brothers Ben Gimbel of the department store family and Bill Paley, the future builder of the CBS network, gave him his role models. Zelda gave him the means when she asked him: "'Why don't you start a camp once you graduate?'" as Harold Kiviat remembered the conversation. Sam began searching for land "to create a WASPy summer camp for Jews."[9]

His timing was excellent. New England educators of the post–Civil War era had invented the idea of summer camping for wealthy adolescents. Their successors had introduced it to the broad middle class, with the American Jewish community particularly receptive to its lure. In the autumn of 1923, Sam discovered an "ideal" site, an old farm of 250 acres on the shore of a large lake in the hilly resort region near Kent, Connecticut.[10] He began modestly with forty boys and signed up family members as his staff. His mother supervised the cooking and made some of her memorable dishes, especially latkes (potato pancakes). Izzy, Harold, and Charles Kiviat also had year-round jobs. Their sister, Anne, a partner, served as the recruiter, interviewing the parents of prospective campers. Sam's social connections brought in well-off Jewish families. The roster of Ken-Mont for boys and Ken-Wood for girls, which he added later, included at various times the Sulzbergers of the *New York Times*, Estée Lauder and Charles Revson of the cosmetics industry, the Tisches of the Loews Corporation, builder William Leavitt, and real estate developer Leonard Wien. Despite the success of the enterprise, Sam's "autocratic" leadership style soured his relations with his siblings.

Sam was not shy about using Abel's athletic fame in marketing the camps. In fact, he had always traded on his older brother's name. He also went out of his way to recruit Abel's pal Elmer Ripley as his sports counselor. Abel, already leery of Sam's condescending attitude toward him since his postwar maladjustment, did not like it a bit. Although he visited Ken-Mont for Zelda's birthdays and maintained "cordial" relations with Sam, "there wasn't much love lost" between the two brothers.[11]

Once in 1931 the Kiviats did function harmoniously to assist Abel. Sam had stayed in touch with Abel's ex-wife and now sought to renew the friendship in behalf of his brother. By then, Yetta's costume designs for leading Broadway musicals—*Girl Crazy, Three's a Crowd*, Ethel Merman's gowns in *George White's Scandals*—had brought her wide notice.

Sam convinced her to let Abel meet the son she had taken from him more than a decade earlier.[12]

The lad, Arthur Louis Pomeranz, had entered the Peddie School in Hightstown, New Jersey, in September 1929 after completing his elementary studies at Columbia Grammar School in Manhattan. Unlike most prep schools in that era, Peddie did not discriminate against Jewish boys. Fifteen-year-old "Pommie," as he was nicknamed by his chums, was very happy there. He was handsome, bright, and confident, having been raised by gifted parents whom he and everyone else believed had "the ideal marriage." He joined the dramatic club and the tennis team. But suddenly the protective wall around his privileged and innocent youth began to crumble. In March 1930, his mother ran off to France with a lover and cabled Dr. Pomeranz asking for her "freedom and peace." The physician was distraught, he told the *Staten Island Advance,* and turned to his son. With Pomeranz's evident coaching, Arthur radioed back: "'Horribly hurt. Mother, please reconsider, Arthur.'" In the meantime, Yetta reverted to her old form. While she was in Europe, she had her brother Al hire a Broadway showgirl to entrap Pomeranz in a tryst in a midtown hotel. After lurid media publicity, Yetta secured her divorce. Despite being a pawn in this ugliness, Arthur managed to complete his senior year at Peddie and to gain admission to the Wharton School.[13]

Sometime during his final months at Peddie, Arthur finally learned that Abel, not the departed Dr. Pomeranz, was his real father. There are several versions of the reunion, but Abel's is the most authentic. Sam, Anne, and Yetta "made a date for me to see him. So they brought me up to my mother's house," an apartment next to the original Stork Club on West Fifty-eighth Street that Zelda and Anne shared with Sam after he moved his office to Manhattan. "And I came in the room, and I see this kid in a corner, all dressed up neatly," Abel recalled. "And we hugged and kissed automatically. Then I became friends. I used to visit him down at Peddie. When he went to Pennsylvania, I almost visited him every week." Arthur formally changed his name to "Kiviat."

Abel did the best he could to make up for his absence during Arthur's childhood and for the shock of his reappearance. When Arthur pledged the Phi Sigma Delta fraternity, Abel arrived at the house in Philadelphia with ping-pong balls and racquets. He drove some of the boys over to

Cherry Hill for a good dinner. However, Abel sabotaged his effort by his boisterous behavior in restaurants. He made loud, crude comments about waitresses and other patrons ("she's fat"), conduct he continued intermittently for the rest of his life. He unintentionally embarrassed and alienated his sensitive son.[14]

Continuing hostility between Abel and his ex-wife further complicated his relationship with Arthur. According to Abel's sister-in-law Esther Kiviat, Yetta "poisoned Arthur against Abel. And Arthur never had any feeling for his father at all." The situation was too much for Arthur, who became depressed, withdrawn, and deeply unhappy at Penn.[15] With time, he pulled himself together and received a degree in marketing from Wharton in June 1936. He returned to New York and worked for his adoring mother, "but he wasn't built for that work," observed Berenice Kaufman, who was a protégé of the great Kiviette on Broadway. Arthur quickly married and divorced the first of his five wives and then went out to Hollywood, where, through his mother's connections, he found work in a studio office. With his considerable personal charm, he hobnobbed with young stars such as Ronald Reagan, Jane Wyman, and Audrey Totter. In a final cut to his father, in August 1940 he changed his name for a third time—to "Arthur Kiviette." By then, he was serving in the army at Fort Davis, North Carolina, prior to being shipped out for duty at Pearl Harbor. He would have little to do with Abel for the next half-dozen years.[16]

THE PRESS STEWARD

A decade after the humiliation of a lifetime's banishment from amateur sport, Kiviat's rehabilitation by the AAU bureaucracy had begun on July 4, 1924, when he served as assistant director of a large track meet for Staten Island's youth. Two summers later he organized successfully the borough's first annual track and field championships at the county fair grounds. Shortly afterward, he assumed the position of AAU commissioner of Staten Island.[17]

Although his serving as a volunteer official was "a labor of love," it took only a brief time before an ancient problem caught up with him. On June 21, 1927, the leadership of the Metropolitan AAU, with the active support of the organization's national president, Murray Hulbert, planned to reappoint Kiviat as a commissioner, but the recommendation drew immediate protest from Hulbert's own secretary-treasurer. Fred Rubien told him "he had had a good deal of trouble with Kiviat in the past, but found that Kiviat was a hard worker," according to a newspaper report of the meeting. The reappointment was tabled for two weeks, and then Kiviat was back on the job. He directed with dispatch and precision the island's second annual track championships in mid-September, and even Rubien joined in the chorus of praise for the meet's organizer. Kiviat was in part a pawn in a messy personal struggle between Rubien and Hulbert that led to Rubien's resigning as the national AAU's secretary-treasurer in 1927. Equally obvious, however, was that Kiviat was again a victim of Rubien's anti-Semitic animus.

Their long-run, two-character drama spotlighted on the athletic stage the intensified effort by the American middle and upper classes to disassociate themselves from the emerging generation of American Jews. During the interwar period, narrow-minded men such as Rubien feared that these children of eastern European immigrants would establish themselves in key institutions governed by the Protestant establishment. To cope with their anxieties, they issued endless accusations against Jews' character and claims of their alleged wrongdoings. Kiviat was once again a convenient target.[18] Nevertheless, he continued to serve as borough commissioner through 1928, with his tenure noteworthy for increasing the popularity of track meets. Kiviat was asked to serve next as press secretary for the major metropolitan track meets, following his volunteer work as an assistant to chief press officer Dan Ferris. He took to the work immediately. When Ferris moved up in the organization, Kiviat succeeded him.

It was a busy, demanding job in an era before sophisticated communications technology. Whereas today's reporters covering major events expect a steady flow of information and results delivered instantly to their wired places in the press box, Kiviat recalled how in the late 1920s "I would gather the data from the officials and yell it up to the newspaper reporters." In those early days at the new Madison Square Garden at Forty-ninth Street and Eighth Avenue, he had a table in back of the finish line that gave him a clear view of the runners crossing the line. But to ensure accurate results, he had to run back and forth between the two groups—the timers, led by Charles

Dieges, and the judges at the finish line, including the chief judge Dan Ferris. A complicating factor was the imprecision of some timers with hand-held stopwatches. The position of press steward therefore required great tenacity to get accurate information about the races and also the field events on the Garden infield. In the heyday of a fiercely competitive and abundant press, especially after the introduction of tabloids such as the *New York Daily News* and the *New York Mirror,* a cluster of reporters would await his words.

In the 1930s, his job expanded with the diversification of the media and the growing national interest in the sport, especially in the big-time indoor meets. Dressed in a tuxedo, he worked far above the Garden floor in "a little squirrel cage in front of the mezzanine press box." From all accounts, the writers found him indispensable and admired his selfless devotion.

Kiviat's schedule as an official went far beyond the Garden meets on successive winter weekends. He traveled year-round to high school and AAU handicap events as well as to national championships, the Penn Relays in late April, and the annual Princeton Invitation meet in June. He was always "the able and willing Abel," Arthur Daley commented in a "Sports of the Times" column devoted to Kiviat's career as an official. "At schoolboy and novice meets he is constantly chasing place-winners to pry loose their first names so that the track writers can continue to seem omniscient," Daley wrote. "His job would exhaust the patience of a saint and the fortitude of a marathon runner."[19]

Yet he thoroughly enjoyed it, especially the track lover's moveable feasts at Penn and Princeton, where he served with Tommy Lennon, who had become a skilled timer in his spare moments away from a highly successful career on Wall Street.[20] Historian John Lucas has rightly called the Princeton series "a jewel" in the crown of historic international athletic events.[21] It was the take-off point for huge broadcast media interest in track and field. Much of the credit belongs to pioneering sports announcer Ted Husing, who convinced the new CBS radio network to carry these races live from Palmer Stadium. According to Husing's memoir, his Princeton broadcasts "made radio track-conscious." He was not wrong, especially if one also factors in his many broadcasts of the Millrose Games and the Penn Relays.[22]

By 1930, Americans were using about eighteen million radios. Kiviat played his part in reaching the sports fans among them. A photograph shows

Husing at the announcer's table calling a race, with Kivat seated nearby in dress shirt and tie, vest, and an official's cap. Far more modestly than Husing, considering the historic significance of their collaboration, Kiviat simply said: "I broadcast radio with Ted Husing when he'd broadcast with that [portable short-wave] transmitter on his back."[23]

Kiviat had developed into a full-fledged character and delighted in reminding his captive audience in the press box that he had been "'the Jewish star of the Irish-Americans.'" The Jewish community certainly never let him forget it. In the winter of 1934–35, he accepted an appointment to the new American governing board for the Second Maccabiad, the Jewish Olympics, to be held the following April in the emerging city of Tel Aviv. The chairman of the board was Benny Leonard, former lightweight boxing champion; other members included basketball immortal Nat Holman and Irving Jaffee, 1932 Olympic speed-skating champion. Unfortunately, most Jewish sports enthusiasts of the era did not share Kiviat's commitment to the Maccabiah movement.[24]

When a battle royal broke out in the AAU over American participation in the Berlin Olympiad of 1936, Rubien and his colleagues continued their vindictiveness against Kiviat. Although Kiviat favored a boycott of the games, he was not a significant activist in the campaign. He was neither a delegate to the Metropolitan AAU meeting in October 1935 that refused to support a boycott nor a delegate at the union's stormy national convention in December that tabled a resolution calling on American athletes to boycott. That resolution was the work of the AAU's courageous president—and Kiviat's longtime supporter—former New York State Supreme Court judge Jeremiah T. Mahoney. A champion athlete in his youth, Mahoney had been a law partner of Senator Robert F. Wagner and was an influential figure in Tammany Hall, labor union, and Roman Catholic circles. Making common cause with Mahoney were prominent Catholic, liberal Protestant, and Jewish spokesmen as well as the leaders of similar campaigns in Canada, Great Britain, and France. To Mahoney's well-founded concerns about Jewish athletes being expelled from German training facilities, banned from competition with other Germans, and, ultimately, excluded from the German Olympic team, American Olympic Committee chairman Avery Brundage had a ready response. Kiviat's erstwhile Olympic teammate, now a millionaire sportsman, suggested "the reports of discrimination against Jews were untrue in sport, no matter what they might be in other fields." Moreover, Brundage insisted erroneously that the American campaign had been concocted by a "radical element" of Jews and Communists. (Fred Rubien famously announced that "the Germans are not discriminating against Jews. The Jews were eliminated [from the German team] because they are not good enough athletes.") In the end, the Mahoney coalition lost the key votes, the judge refused "in good conscience" to seek reelection, and the AAU chose Brundage unanimously as his successor.[25]

Despite Kiviat's minimal involvement in the boycott movement, the Metropolitan AAU dropped him and Max Silver, another Jew, from its list of officials for its indoor championships on February 29, 1936. An explanation of sorts came from Secretary Charles Elbert. "'If Kiviat and Silver are not among the officials,' Elbert said, 'then they were accidentally overlooked, yes, accidentally overlooked, this is all.'" Twenty years earlier, Elbert had been one of the Met board members who had voted to ban Kiviat for life. His partner in that affair, Fred Rubien, was now the meet director of the Met championships. Rubien told the *New York Herald Tribune*'s Jesse Abramson that "he knew nothing about the 'accidental' dropping of Kiviat and Silver. He could not understand, he said, how it happened." However, other track officials had more candid off-the-record conversations with Abramson, interpreting the decision to drop the two leading Jewish officials as a "purge" in the wake of the boycott struggle.

Kiviat did not comment publicly. He simply did not occupy his desk at the championships. Max Silver did show up for the meet in the Thirteenth Regiment Armory and officiated at the high jump. Rubien and his associates said afterward that they had not singled out Kiviat and Silver and claimed that several other unnamed officials were accidentally overlooked in drawing up the list of officials for the meet. Kiviat thus suffered one more insult in silence and shortly thereafter returned as the AAU press steward.[26]

He was not done with the boycott drama, however. Behind the scenes, Judge Mahoney and his top associate Charles Ornstein were planning to add a final act, and they tapped Kiviat for their best supporting actor. Ornstein had once been a sprinter on the New York University track team during Kiviat's heyday and was now the manager of the Paramount Hotel near Times

Square. He also served as the representative of the Jewish Welfare Board to the executive committee of the American Olympic Committee, from which a vindictive Avery Brundage had dropped him. In late spring, Ornstein announced that Kiviat would join a number of prominent and independent-minded AAU and labor leaders, including Dan Ferris and Mel Sheppard, on a committee for the first annual World Labor Athletic Carnival, an anti-Nazi olympics at the city's new Randall's Island Stadium in mid-August. Honorary chairmen included Judge Mahoney, Mayor Fiorello La Guardia, Governor Herbert Lehman, and William Green, president of the American Federation of Labor. The meet was to be the domestic version of a similar undertaking in Barcelona in July that had been called off because the Spanish Civil War had erupted on the scheduled opening day.

The purposes of the New York labor games were to oppose American participation in the Berlin Olympics and to encourage workingmen's participation in amateur sports. Mahoney's plan included open events for all-stars and a few competitions for working-class athletes. He and Ornstein found the necessary support in the new Jewish Labor Committee, composed mainly of union leaders in the garment trades.

Ornstein ran the meet. He gave Kiviat the crucial job of handling the entries and set him up in an office in the Knickerbocker Building at Times Square. Kiviat obviously felt an obligation to Mahoney for the judge's support during his 1915 AAU trials and his reinstatement bid in 1922. Ornstein became so close a pal that track writer Arthur Daley called Kiviat the hotelman's "fidus Achates," referring to the trusty friend in Virgil's *Aeneid*. Because Kiviat grew up with his parents' stories of Jewish persecution in Poland, the cause was also fundamental. He therefore grasped the opportunity and labored for two months to produce an entry list of more than five hundred trackmen from thirty athletic clubs and twenty-two colleges. He signed up topnotch people who failed to make the U.S. Olympic team, including pole vault world-record holder George Varoff of San Francisco and sprinters Eulace Peacock and Ben Johnson. On the Sunday preceding the meet, his efforts earned a banner headline in the *Times:* "World Athletic Carnival at Randall's Island Draws Brilliant Entry." Noteworthy, too, was that many of his entries had Jewish names, which Anglo-Jewish newspapers such as the *B'nai B'rith Messenger* (Los Angeles) and the *Jewish Times* (Baltimore) highlighted.[27]

The actual results at Randall's Island were somewhat less impressive. Attendance was only about seventy-five hundred each day, leaving 80 percent of the seats empty. The athletes' performances were below the Olympic standard. Nevertheless, the *Times* reporter concluded that the meet had been well run and "interesting," "despite the fact that not a single [world] record was broken." Kiviat had reason to be pleased with his effort, especially in light of his recent humiliation by Fred Rubien and others in Avery Brundage's coterie.[28]

Other aspects of Kiviat's life were less pleasing. Having lost his job at the Stock Exchange on December 31, 1932, he faced the same periodic unemployment and economic insecurity common to New York Jews in the Depression, especially those without his prominence or contacts. Lacking a high school diploma and other formal credentials, he bounced around and took what jobs he could find. For a time, he served as the coach of the Seventy-first Regiment track team in its imposing armory on Park Avenue. Stints as a salesman for two jewelry companies located near his prewar Dieges & Clust office, Drilling & Company on Nassau Street and Shiman & Company on Maiden Lane, lasted only a couple of years. In 1937, at age forty-five, he accepted a position as a salesman for Surrey Buick Company in Long Island City. When this job ended after only eight months, Judge Jeremiah Mahoney became a pivotal figure for him.[29]

Kiviat now applied for a Social Security number under the terms of the recent federal legislation and wrote on the form that he was "unemployed." But, tellingly, he also filled in "N.Y. Democratic Hdqtr's, 1440 Broadway—J. T. Mahoney" as his former employer. Indeed, it was probably at this juncture that Mahoney and his Tammanyite AAU colleague Murray Hulbert urged Kiviat to stand for the state assembly. At one level, it made sense. New York Jews had become fiercely loyal to Franklin Roosevelt's party and his New Deal. The practical Mahoney, who had bucked Tammany and supported FDR against Al Smith in 1932, realized Kiviat was still a popular sports hero with a salesman's charm. He might prove useful to the Democrats by serving a neighborhood Jewish constituency, then a basic institution of New York politics. But Kiviat wisely decided against politics.[30]

While Mahoney and Hulbert, whom FDR had appointed a federal judge for the Southern District of New York, sought a permanent government position for Kiviat, he had the pressing problems of food and shelter. Like other Jews who faced unemployment or financial reverses in the Depression, he looked to his family for support. Zelda and Anne had moved to a comfortable new apartment at 180 East Seventy-ninth Street, so Abel moved in with them.[31]

His appearance belied such problems. To John Kieran, the learned *Times* sports columnist in the late 1930s, Kiviat was the same "slim, brisk and black-haired" fellow he had been at Stockholm, and he "still looks as though he could go the distance." His year-round involvement with track, including regular workouts of his own, was surely a major factor contributing to his robust health.

The writers turned to him as an authentic voice from "the so-called 'good old days' of American track"—the era of Sheppard, Meredith, and Jones—and therefore able to provide a unique perspective for a new generation of track lovers. His views about the modern evolution of running the mile, especially about the possibility of doing it in less than four minutes, received wide notice and even stimulated thoughtful letters to the editor. Perhaps most indicative of this recognition, he either was the subject of or received prominent mention in no less than eight "Sports of the Times" columns by Kieran and Daley between 1938 and 1950. Most were about the legendary Olympic 1,500-meter race at Stockholm.

The publicity jogged the memories of New York's sports fans. In the winter of 1944, while the Allied forces in Europe prepared for D-Day, the War Finance Committee for New York conducted a poll to determine the most popular American sports heroes. Voters had to purchase a Series E bond for twenty-five dollars. On February 13, the *Times* reported that Kiviat had received 524 votes, placing him twenty-first among 134 sports figures. His enduring popularity was an eye-opener. It spoke in part to an era's valuing of track and field. Other Jewish sports stars received votes from the city's huge Jewish population, but only quarterback Sid Luckman of the Bears and baseball's Hank Greenberg outranked Kiviat.[32]

By then, through the patronage of Judges Mahoney and Hulbert, Kiviat already had launched a career in the federal bureaucracy. Shortly after Pearl

Harbor, he joined the staff of the U.S. Marshals as a bailiff in the court for the Southern District of New York, where Hulbert had his seat. He began to reconstruct his life in the august courthouse on Foley Square, its colonnades and golden pyramid roof a city landmark. His duties included producing the prisoners in court from the Federal House of Detention on West Street, yet like many other New York Jews, he had every reason to be grateful to his friends in Roosevelt's New Deal circle for offering him the opportunity of a government job.[33]

This position prepared him for long-term service as a court clerk. On November 16, 1944, he was sworn in for his final and most important job, as deputy clerk in the same court where he had been serving the marshals. His base salary was $1,440 per annum. However, this position was to be only temporary until the soldier whose job he had taken returned from military service. He made friends with Bill Connell, an experienced clerk of court, who broke him in. Several months later his job performance earned a rating of "excellent" and a small increase in salary. He continued to impress his supervisor, and at war's end he was appointed a permanent deputy clerk.

He had a variety of administrative support duties, made more interesting because, unlike today, deputies rotated assignments among the sitting judges, which presented a constant challenge, given the judges' diverse approaches to work. Kiviat quickly made himself indispensable. Behind the scenes, Kiviat recalled later, "I ran the court for the judge until he sat down. . . . [I]f the judge wanted to know about a certain case, when, where, and how, I got the papers on it." He also went out of his way to be helpful to the attorneys, including those with bad tempers. In effect, he often had to act as go-between.

During trials, most of which had a jury then, the deputy made announcements to the court, assisted the jury, handled the evidence, and swore in the witnesses. As one attorney commented, Kiviat's "sense of decorum and especially his distinctively solemn administration of the oath lent an added sense of dignity to the court room and made a lasting impression on all of us."[34]

Although he was in his early fifties, he threw himself into the work and for the next quarter-century served the court well. His new environment was far different from the car dealership or the jewelry houses where he had scrambled for his living. As the "mother court" of the federal system, it was the venue for landmark cases decided by leading members of the judiciary—men of the stature of chief judges John C. Knox and Harold R. Medina. Early in Kiviat's tenure, which coincided with the start of the Cold War, Judge Medina presided over the lengthy and controversial 1949 trial of eleven American Communist Party members for sedition in violation of the Smith Act *(Dennis v. U.S.)*. Kiviat also served as Judge Medina's clerk for *U.S. v. Morgan,* a major antitrust trial that dragged on for nearly three years. When Medina finally dismissed the charges, several of the attorneys wrote unsolicited letters to the court praising Kiviat's performance.[35]

With better prospects, Kiviat could rethink his living arrangements. The death of his beloved mother in March 1946 after a yearlong illness was an additional stimulus to let his sister, Anne, who had been caring for Zelda, have the family apartment to herself. Kiviat moved into his own place at 250 West Eighty-second Street. Having avoided marriage during the economic crisis of the Depression, he was finally in a position to consider it. His opportunity soon appeared. One day he excused a man from jury duty. As he told the story decades later, "'I used to smoke a cigar after lunch on a bench outside' [the federal courthouse] and the grateful non-juror approached him to say, 'I have a young lady I'd like you to meet.'" The man's name was Zelig (Charles) Solomon, and the woman was his daughter, Isabel. Kiviat invited her to lunch at a Chinese restaurant.[36]

Isabel Solomon was forty, petite, single, with a family history similar to his. Born in Pennsylvania in 1905 to Yiddish-speaking parents who had emigrated at an early age from Poland and Bessarabia, she was the oldest of their three children. When Isabel was about five years old, the Solomon family settled in the town of Beaver Falls, near Pittsburgh, where other family members had already established themselves in the junk business. In the classic immigrant pattern, her father opened a candy store in the home and had success. Isabel left Beaver Falls in the 1920s to attend college and then a business course in Syracuse. After moving to Manhattan, she became a skilled executive secretary with her own apartment, which she shared dutifully with her widowed father.[37]

Like everyone else who knew her, Kiviat was taken with Isabel's sweet and gentle manner. She was also thoughtful and "level headed," with a serious commitment to Jewish life. At fifty-three, Abel fell in love. "'One word led to another,' later there was 'some hugging and kissing,' and he said, 'let's get married.'"[38]

The wedding took place in April 1948, and Abel moved into Isabel's apartment on Broadway across from Columbia University. For the first time in decades, he began to enjoy a stable lifestyle. Fortunately, Isabel hit it off with Virginia Lennon, Tommy's wife, whose late father, Isadore Freeman, was an immigrant Jew from Russia. The two couples became close. Tommy decided to hire Isabel in his brokerage house, Delafield & Delafield, at a time when anti-Semitism was still a factor on Wall Street. She assisted Lennon until his death in 1967 and was "the greatest secretary my father ever had," according to Lennon's daughter, Lucy Price.[39]

Between Isabel's excellent salary and Abel's yearly merit pay raises, they had a middle-class income. With Isabel's skill in managing their finances, their bank account gradually increased. Although middle-aged, childless, and occupied with their careers, they nevertheless developed a satisfying social routine in the great city. Isabel would leave her Wall Street office at the end of the workday and take a taxicab to meet her husband at the courthouse. "When we went out to eat, [we'd] just withdraw so much money for theater, good meal, couple of drinks," he remembered. "And come home in a taxi."[40]

Kiviat was not the easiest man to have as a husband, though. "He was pretty rough" with her at times, Harold Kiviat remembered. "Sometimes he was crude," especially when his athlete's ego took over his behavior and tried Isabel's patience. However, she never seemed "to lose her temper," even though she admitted in later years that she "put up with" a lot from him.[41]

Life with Isabel required Kiviat to participate more actively in his faith. Visible symbols of Judaism were inescapable in Isabel's apartment: from a mezuzah fastened to the apartment's outer entrance to Sabbath candles. Although he was not one to embark on a reflective religious journey of return, he did alter his behavior. He accepted again some obligations of being the oldest son: specifically, he began to attend services in order to say the Yizkor (memorial prayers) for his parents on the major holidays. He was in good company because at that time many of his peers, the children of the eastern European immigrants, were also renewing their ties to Judaism.

Indeed, according to Arthur Hertzberg, nearly 60 percent of American Jews affiliated with synagogues in the postwar years of Truman and Eisenhower.

Kiviat joined the Orthodox Civic Center Synagogue, located across Foley Square from the courthouse and founded in 1938. Its six hundred members were mostly court employees, attorneys, and judges as well as men in the textile business. They worshiped in rented office space above a bar and grill. Kiviat would often receive a telephone call to help in making a minyan for the daily morning service, and he would be there at 7:30. "I couldn't read [Hebrew]," he said. "I read the English part." He occasionally received the honor of carrying a Torah scroll during the scriptural reading portion of the service. However, he worried that he would be called on to recite a Hebrew prayer and would embarrass himself. "And I tell them, 'I can't read anything.' Suppose they ask me to say something? What am I going to do?" The officers reassured him: "'No, you don't have to say anything.'" When the synagogue members dedicated a new shul nearby in 1969, an imaginative and flamboyant structure that was part of the largest building boom in the history of American Jewry, Kiviat purchased two memorial plaques for his mother and father.[42]

THE SENIOR CITIZEN

During the second half of his career as an official, Kiviat moved back from the press box to the track level as chief press steward.[43] The postwar generation of officials and reporters had little knowledge about his place in the sport's tradition. In 1946, the future documentary filmmaker Bud Greenspan was a young reporter covering school sports for the *New York Mirror* and had a floor pass for the five winter track meets at the Garden. He saw Kiviat scurrying around doing his job. "I was always wondering who this little guy was, how he got the job," he recalled half a century later.

> And they told me who he was. And I was amazed, particularly since he didn't look like an athlete, the Jewish silver medal winner. He always greeted me like I was his son or something. It was like—he had an incredible memory. He used to tell me a lot of jokes all the time that weren't particularly funny. It was like going to a Broadway theater being with Abel because he gave us

story after story. . . . Basically, he was just a very *haimisch* [unpretentious] guy—he said what he thought and he never gave any questions about what he had to say. . . . He was just a very basic man. A gentle man, you could never get upset with Abel. . . . He reminded me so much, like the politicians of the Lower East Side that used to stand on street corners. He was a very real person.[44]

Other track people had very different encounters with Kiviat. Consider the story of Stan Saplin, a longtime public-address announcer and public-relations man. He was a twenty-nine-year-old sportswriter for the *New York Journal-American* serving in the navy in 1943 when he met Kiviat at the Millrose Games. Saplin secured a night's leave from the service in order to work with the media. "I was at the Garden handling the press box upstairs and Kiviat was on the floor," Saplin remembered. "And he was a plain pain in the ass cause he just came to glad hand. And I'd have guys from the *Times* or the *Trib*, Jesse Abramson or Arthur Daley, yelling 'Well, goddamn it, can't we find out?' And I'd call Abel, and he would say" (Saplin imitated a growl here, "'I haven't got time' or 'I gotta keep this record.' And I never got anything out of him. You know, we became friendly but he was impossible."[45]

On most occasions, the force of Kiviat's personality enabled him to make and retain friends among the fraternity of track officials and journalists who, in turn, provided meaning and structure to his life. His wife encouraged this connection and frequently attended meets with him. At midcentury, Kiviat received long overdue recognition for his career as an official. The Metropolitan Track Writers Association presented him with its Outstanding Service Award.[46]

Kiviat's real prize was an up-close view of the extraordinary development of his sport in the period from the 1940s through the 1960s. Several factors were at play, especially the much greater number of young people participating on American school or club teams. These athletes, generally taller and stronger than their predecessors, therefore faced stiffer competition and produced higher-quality records. They learned better techniques and training methods, based in part on advancements in sports medicine and exercise physiology. Their materials also improved, including

18. The AAU's chief press steward *(left)* at Madison Square
Garden, ca. 1955. Courtesy of Lucy Price.

the tracks and circles, implements and equipment. When Kiviat had time
to reflect on all these changes, he wisely refused to compare the record
breakers of his competitive days and their successors. However, he still
maintained that "the top athletes of my day would win today. They'd run
much faster. They'd train harder."[47]

Kiviat was himself occasionally thrust back into the Garden spotlight.
In March 1963, to highlight the AAU's Diamond Jubilee Celebration,
the organization selected him as one of its "Big Six"—the half-dozen all-
time leading track and field stars in the national indoor championships.

He joined Glenn Cunningham and hurdler Harrison Dillard among runners and field events' immortals Valery Brumel, Bob Richards, and Parry O'Brien as the honorees—august company, indeed, for a man whom the AAU had once banned for life.[48]

By 1968, when he was serving as the press steward in the fourth Garden, a circular structure atop Penn Station, television coverage and corporate sponsorship of meets had transformed the track world that he had inhabited for nearly three-quarters of a century. It was but a short step to the professionalization of the sport in the 1970s. Kiviat had lived long enough to see young athletes break the century-old grip of the AAU and its once inviolable ideology of amateurism.[49]

As his long career as track's colorful press steward wound down, other interests helped to sustain him. He continued to enjoy his career in federal court and had no interest in leaving when he reached the mandatory retirement age of seventy in June 1962. With the approval of the amiable new chief judge Sylvester J. Ryan, a Democratic politician who remembered Kiviat's track feats for the Irish Club, he was given a one-year extension. During the following decade, he received six more eighteen-month extensions, which was quite unusual.[50]

After World War II, he renewed his relationship with his son, Arthur, who had returned from the European theater with the rank of captain, a sterling reputation for his service as a quartermaster, and his fourth wife. Arthur had met beautiful, twenty-year-old Litzi Friedman, a Viennese Jewish refugee, in Cannes in the winter of 1944. He brought her to New York as a war bride on the *Queen Elizabeth* in 1946. The couple settled in Greenwich Village, surrounded by a circle of writers, artists, and actors. Kiviat visited them often, especially after the birth of a grandson, and Litzi recalled vividly that he was generous and intelligent. He was still a regular recreational runner after the war, and he tried to get his daughter-in-law to join him in his workouts. But Arthur's bouts of depression and alcoholism, coupled with his unhappiness away from the discipline of military life, doomed the marriage. Following the divorce, he had little contact with his father for almost a decade.

By 1964, Arthur had remarried for a fifth time and secured a position with Robert Moses, president of the New York World's Fair, as head of security. Upon learning that his father was visiting the fair at Flushing Meadows, Arthur had his guards detain Abel and take him to the security headquarters. "And this was his way of getting to see him," according to his son, Dennis. After the close of the controversial fair, Arthur continued in Robert Moses's employ, serving as an administrator at the Coliseum on Columbus Avenue until his retirement in 1986. Although Arthur and his father now stayed in frequent contact, Abel's grandson was a victim of the continuing hostility between Arthur and Litzi. She obtained a court order to stop Arthur from seeing his son and, in an eerie repetition of Arthur's own childhood, changed the boy's family name to that of her new husband, attorney David Goldner. For the next two decades, Abel had no contact with Dennis. During four of those years, from 1967 to 1971, Dennis was an undergraduate at Columbia and lived across the street from his grandfather's apartment house, although neither was aware of this fact.[51]

With advancing age, Kiviat became closer than ever to Tommy Lennon. They traveled together on weekends all over the East and Middle West to officiate at track meets. "I'd stop in every day to see Tommy," Kiviat remembered. "Tommy and Mrs. Lennon would have me and my wife over [for] dinner." The fact that Lennon was Isabel's boss on Wall Street did not interfere with the close personal relationship. But Kiviat took advantage of his friend's generous nature and the fact that Lennon "always felt sorry for him because he wasn't making much money." He regularly let Lennon pick up the checks, or he simply took handouts of clothes or cab fare from him. The clearest explanation of his behavior came from Harold Kiviat: Abel had "developed an ego," a sense of entitlement, from his athletic fame. Tommy, ever loyal, overlooked it. When the Lennons moved from their Park Avenue apartment to Toms River, New Jersey, Abel and Isabel stayed with them frequently. Lennon died of throat cancer in 1967. Passing over many of his accomplishments on Wall Street and in the bureaucracy of amateur sport, his *Times'* obituary mentioned prominently that he had once run on a schoolboy relay team with Abel Kiviat and John Drebinger.[52]

The years finally caught up with Kiviat on June 30, 1971. At age seventy-nine, he had to retire from the court. It was not easy after twenty-nine years of service at Foley Square marked by a nearly spotless attendance record. He would miss it, and to compensate for his loss, he created another legend about himself. He claimed frequently in the latter part of his life that "I had to retire from a job that I worked forty-one years."[53]

A year later Abel and Isabel decided to move from New York to Cedar Glen West, a retirement community in Lakehurst, New Jersey. During their visits to the Lennons in nearby Toms River, they had discovered that Lakehurst, once a posh resort when Kiviat was a boy, offered the attraction of affordable home ownership. They purchased a small one-story house on Lark Street, which included a nice lawn and shrubbery, for $13,500. Their neighbors in nearly identical houses on Pheasant, Mallard, Heron, Quail, Oriole, and Cardinal Streets were a congenial mix of seniors of various nationalities and religions.[54]

In a sense, Abel had come full circle. Unlike so many second-generation Jews, he had grown up in a remote portion of the great city, a place with plentiful open land. Having exchanged that life for a half-century of apartment living, he again had a private home with a plot of grass. Yet like his fellow migratory Jews, he had also left behind a familiar synagogue and all the other pervasive associations of New York's Jewish world. "But moving into the suburbs," writer Irving Howe pointed out at the time, "required that people decide whether or not they wanted to declare themselves as Jews."

Kiviat claimed in his memoir that he and Isabel tried on several occasions to join an area synagogue, but they were turned off by the staff's treatment of them. Nevertheless, they retained a keen sense of their Jewish identities in this new setting. Whether through visits from his family members with whom he had reconnected, Isabel's volunteering in pro-Israel activity, or their financial and moral support of Jewish causes, their neighbors knew where he and Isabel stood.[55]

In case they also might miss Kiviat's growing need for self-aggrandizement, he transformed his small Lakehurst home into a virtual Abel Kiviat museum of track immortality. He received an unexpected boost from Jess Silver, the sportswriter for the Jewish Telegraphic Agency, who wrote a widely circulated piece arguing that Lon Myers, the legendary nineteenth-century runner, and Kiviat were the "two great names in track history"

19. Abel, Arthur, and Isabel Kiviat in Lakehurst, N.J., ca. 1975. Courtesy of Lucy Price.

produced by American Jewry. "Will we ever see their like again?" wondered Silver.[56]

Such pleasant reflection suddenly seemed beside the point in January 1981 when Isabel suffered a stroke. She lingered for three days in the hospital before succumbing. At eighty-nine, Kiviat faced a lonely life in South Jersey.[57]

LAP FOUR

SPRINTING TO THE FINISH

12

Folk Hero

ELEVEN MONTHS of profound if mostly inarticulate grief ended unexpectedly for Kiviat in early December 1981 when he had the pleasure of being inducted into the Public Schools Athletic League Hall of Fame with his friend Elmer Ripley. The *Staten Island Advance*'s coverage of the event at Antoine's Restaurant in Queens Village included photographs of the now aged Curtis teammates of 1909. Although Ripley looked very old and would die within five months of the dinner, the eighty-nine-year-old Kiviat appeared not a day older than seventy.

Such robustness struck Stan Saplin, Kiviat's one-time assistant press steward, now a publicist for the New York Road Runners Club, sponsors of the New York City Marathon, and he broached an idea to its president, Fred Lebow. Why not honor Abel Kiviat, "America's oldest living track and field Olympian, the only surviving member of the 1912 track team," and a native New Yorker, to boot, on the occasion of his ninetieth birthday, next June 23? As it turned out, Kiviat was not the oldest surviving Olympic track star because two of his elder teammates, long jumper Harry Worthington and sprinter Donnell Young, were very much alive. But Kiviat could legitimately claim to be the nation's oldest living Olympic *medalist*.

Lebow, a Holocaust survivor from Romania, had given up his flourishing garment company and during the past five years had transformed the Road Runners Club into a pivotal institution in the creation of "the running boom." The key to his revolution was to attract corporate sponsors and network television by opening up road racing to young, upper-status participants. A tireless promoter with a seemingly unlimited supply of theatrical gimmicks, he used personal appearances by well-known runners to appeal to the urban baby boomers. Who better to market to them than "your 'Old Abel,'" in the grandfatherly Kiviat's words? "His achievements as a runner were outstanding," Lebow said. "He is an inspiring figure today for his good health and longevity. It would not surprise me if he could still run a fast mile."

Kiviat's vitality was also of great interest to his own contemporaries, the eighty-five and older population, which was the fastest-growing age group in the United States. In 1980, more than two million people were in that group, according to the U.S. Census Bureau. Without hesitation, Lebow put Saplin in charge of organizing an award ceremony at the club's headquarters on East Eighty-ninth Street. At that moment, the direction of Abel Kiviat's final decade turned 180 degrees from suburban anonymity and despair to renewed celebrity.[1]

"HAPPY 90TH BIRTHDAY, ABEL KIVIAT"

If the converts to leisure-time running wanted a role model for vigorous longevity, Kiviat was their man. His new physician, Dr. Richard Yeager of Toms River, was surprised at his "robust" health and "jovial" spirit for someone of his age. During the eight years Yeager treated Kiviat, he would record nothing more serious on Kiviat's chart than common colds or bronchitis. He was "a strong guy, strong willed." Yeager claimed he never saw signs of the gruffness and nastiness that marked some of Kiviat's personal encounters over the decades. Small wonder Saplin and Lebow were so enthusiastic about Kiviat's potential as a symbol of their movement.[2]

The preparations for the Road Runners' event renewed the widower's spirit. He began lively discussions with Saplin and agreed to his request "to run a few steps, 25, 30, up to 50" at the event. But he admitted, "I am nervous about all this, you arranged for me a 90 yr. old goat, and I'll be in your hands. Keep in touch with me about all this," he urged, including instructions about the proper dress for the occasion.[3]

Shortly before noon on Wednesday, June 23, 1982, the nonagenarian stood before a podium with a battery of microphones at the Road Runners Club on East Eighty-ninth Street and received the impressive, newly executed President's Medal for distinguished service. In his Transylvanian accent, Fred Lebow praised Kiviat both "as the greatest runner ever produced in any of the five boroughs of New York City" and for the example of his life. To a room crowded with track officials and coaches, media representatives, former Olympians, including Marty Glickman, the distinguished sportscaster, and family members, Kiviat, though understandably overwhelmed, was more than up to the challenge of a response. He regaled his listeners with stories about his ancient triumphs and his famous Stockholm defeat, about Jim Thorpe, and about the training methods of his youth. "At one point, when he was reminiscing about former rivals and became aware of the blank expressions around him," Jay Price reported to his *Staten Island Advance* readers, "he laughed. 'Isn't there anybody old here?' he asked."

As he cut his birthday cake for an awestruck audience, a forgotten star was rediscovered. He changed into a Road Runners' T-shirt, running shorts, shoes, and a cap, and walked outside to Fifth Avenue for what was to be a short ceremonial jog. "'Are they going to serve beer at this race?'" he asked the waiting photographers and reporters. He got down expertly into the sprint crouch he had learned seventy-three summers before at Celtic Park. "Then, at the command, he bolted off down the block, running—*running*—away from Road Runners' president Fred Lebow, who was supposed to be his jogging companion and now scrambled to catch up, and past the startled photographers and television cameramen, who were overrun before they could get off a shot," Price wrote. After Kiviat repeated the run more slowly to oblige the media, he announced: "'I wanted to show them I could still get off the mark.'"[4]

The sports world began to take regular notice of him again. He was an honoree at several sports banquets, most notably in December 1983 at Gallagher's Steak House in midtown Manhattan, when he and famed sprinter Wilma Rudolph received the Vitalis Award for Sports Excellence. Reporters and Olympic historians contacted him in Lakehurst; business opportunities suddenly materialized. Even more incredibly, according to the *New York Times'* outstanding track writer Frank Litsky, "he has turned down offers from two marketing concerns because he does not think he should take money for speeches or appearances relating to amateur sports."[5]

One of the Olympic historians who contacted him that winter was Sydney Thayer, an assistant to documentary filmmaker Bud Greenspan, Kiviat's friend of forty years. Greenspan was planning a film to be broadcast on CBS just prior to the coming summer's Los Angeles Games in which eight or nine Olympians would return to the sites of their famous triumphs. When Thayer telephoned Kiviat, the oldest of these athletes, with an invitation to accompany him to Stockholm in late April, Kiviat "was very excited about it." There was a problem, however: "Abel had never been out of the country since World War I, and had never had a passport in his life." The enterprising Thayer lobbied the passport services in Washington, D.C., collected the necessary family information from Kiviat and his sister, Anne, and within a week secured his first and only valid passport.[6]

After they settled in at Stockholm's luxurious Grand Hotel, Kiviat toured a little with Thayer and visited with Ture Widlund, the Swedish Olympic scholar, who would later publish a definitive account of the 1912 Games. He also went out to the Olympic stadium for the first time in seventy-two years. He did an interview there with the *Expressen,* an evening newspaper, in which he told the reporter, "I did not remember that the stadium was so big." It "seemed smaller when it was filled with spectators." Shown a yellowed 1912 photograph of himself about to start a run, he sighed and said: "I did not think then that I would be standing here one more time and that I would be so ancient." As if to disprove the statement, however, he demonstrated to *Expressen* that there was "still strength left in his legs" by jogging on the track in his overcoat, hat, and dress shoes. Afterward, looking like a geriatric Rocky, he beamed broadly and held up his arms in a victorious salute, while the watchtower of his youthful glory hovered behind him.

The following day Thayer took him back to the stadium to film his lengthy interview. Although Thayer and his crew had to nudge a dozing Kiviat several times, the interview went beautifully. All sorts of memories came back, only a small portion of which ended up in the final film. For an encore, Kiviat went to a Stockholm television station for an interview that was featured on the local news that night.[7]

Ten days after his return from his exhausting European adventure, he performed again in a public setting that brought him to the attention of millions of people with little interest in athletics. For that, he had Peter Ueberroth and his organizing committee for the 1984 Los Angeles Olympiad to thank. Ueberroth believed a nation still reeling from the war in Vietnam, the Iran debacle, and the other international crises of the final phase of the Cold War "needed, or wanted, a spectacle, some grand display of American pride and attainment." His proposal was an Olympic Torch Relay of 4,200 runners that would cover thirty-three states, from New York to California, in eighty-two days. When the Los Angeles Olympic Committee invited the grandchildren of America's greatest Olympic heroes, Jim Thorpe and Jesse Owens, to light the first torch from the Olympic flame, Saplin and Lebow lobbied successfully for Kiviat to receive it from them and to run the second leg. "'I think it's a wonderful idea, and I appreciate their sponsoring me,' Kiviat said." He would represent not only the Road Runners, but the very old. "'We aren't the fastest runners in the 1984 Olympics,'" he told *Modern Maturity* magazine, "'but we are part of the Games and that's important.'" Asked whether he would walk or run the kilometer distance, he responded: "'I'll do whatever I want to do.'" Well before he had departed for Stockholm, he had begun to prepare "by running in place and doing other warm-up exercises," as well as "walking a little fast to the mailbox."[8]

Readers of the *New York Times* awoke on May 8 to find a front-page photograph of Kiviat holding an Olympic torch, which he would carry a kilometer at the start of the cross-country relay. Dressed in his Road Runners shirt and cap, he looked remarkably fit. Later that morning, he waited in a steady rain and wind at Fifty-seventh Street between First and Second Avenues while the opening ceremonies took place a half-mile away on the United Nations lawn. After two torches were lit from the Olympic flame, which had just been carried to New York by chartered plane from Olympia, Greece, Thorpe and Owens's grandchildren ran with them for the first kilometer. Then they passed the flame to a torch held by Kiviat. The torch weighed "three or four pounds" and was "heavy" to hold, he admitted. He "jogged some and walked some," wrote Frank Litsky. "For one stretch, he carried the torch in one hand and a tiny American flag, given to him by a spectator, in the other hand. For a while, an accompanying escort runner carried the torch." Approaching Fifth Avenue, Kiviat lit the torch of a twelve-year-old boy who had won the honor in a raffle, and told him, "'carry on.'" To Litsky, Kiviat "seemed melancholy. 'Is it over so soon?' said Kiviat. 'I was just getting warmed up. I wasn't walking because I was tired. I was just trying to get something going.'" Like an ancient Jewish patriarch, his voice was still the voice of a youthful champion, but his body was the body of very old age.[9]

Astonishingly, he had enough energy left to fly to Los Angeles with his torch for an appearance on the Johnny Carson show the following night. NBC paid his expenses and an honorarium. Kiviat was a hit. Carson asked him about "having the same job for so many years. Yes, I said to him I had one of the longest jobs known in the history of the federal courts, 41 years. The same place, the same building. And I kept my job because my mother, God bless her, told her children never say no and she added you'll never get a bloody nose or a black eye if you do the right thing." Carson loved it and gave him his favorite Dewar's scotch on the rocks. What Stan Saplin had initiated two years earlier as a publicity stunt for the world of runners had now taken Kiviat to national celebrity.[10] Bud Greenspan's new documentary enabled an even wider audience to catch Kiviat's act. *America at the Olympics* was broadcast on CBS as a prime-time special on the Fourth of July. Kiviat's segment from Stockholm aired for nine minutes. Sydney Thayer had captured a charming character; the critics praised the film.[11]

One good thing led to another in Kiviat's high-flying world. A five-year campaign by Sam Kiviat to get his brother into the International Jewish Sports Hall of Fame finally succeeded. Sam had been lobbying longtime acquaintances, including Hall of Fame members Nat Holman, Benny Friedman, and Sid Luckman, in behalf of Abel. He persuaded his fraternity brother Sam Friedland, the wealthy supermarket chain founder, to write a moving tribute to Abel's athletic prowess. In mid-June, Abel received a letter from Dr. Uriel Simri of Netanya, Israel, informing him that he had been inducted into the Hall of Fame, located on the campus of the Wingate Institute for Physical Education and Sport since 1981. Simri wrote that Kiviat was a unanimous selection and that he was "now one of 83 inductees from all over the world." Kiviat was obviously touched, as his note of "deep appreciation" to the Wingate Institute made clear.[12]

As the sport was rediscovering Kiviat, he discovered anew—for the first time in six decades—that fame had its price. Being sought after for interviews, he told an interviewer, "drives me crazy sometimes. People whispering; all of a sudden you turn your back and walk away, and they start talking again. That's him! That's him!"[13]

Aging also exacted a heavy toll. His brother David had died of brain cancer in 1976. In 1984, Izzy, three years Abel's junior and in some ways the most troubled of the brothers, passed away.[14] But age did not appear to slow down Abel. He enjoyed spending time with the Lennon women in Toms River, especially during holidays. He was in regular contact with his sister, Anne, who at ninety remained the center of the surviving family. Although Arthur also telephoned his father frequently, Abel's hostile treatment of his daughter-in-law, Dolly, put a serious damper on their visits.[15]

He had been lost without Isabel, but he developed a structure to his life. His routine included a daily lunch at the nutrition center where he and Isabel had served as volunteers. "The van brings me to the door for a quarter," he told historian William Simons in 1985. He smoked a cigar after lunch, and, daily, he enjoyed a scotch on the rocks. "Do you still exercise?" Simons asked. "Not really," he responded. "I get around doing things you do in the normal life without purposely exercising. Every other Tuesday I walk to the recreation center. That's a mile away. And being Jewish I move my hands when I talk," he added.[16]

His daily routine also included keeping track of the invitations that kept coming along with his growing celebrity. The one that meant the most was the telephone call from Berny Wagner, chairman of the selection committee for the National Track and Field Hall of Fame, informing him that the nomination of him had been favorably acted upon. Administered by The Athletics Congress (TAC), the successor to the AAU as the sport's governing body in the United States, the National Track and Field Hall of Fame was located then in a wing of the Hoosierdome in Indianapolis. In a distinguished class that included sprinter Mel Patton and high-jumper John Thomas, Kiviat had received the most votes.[17]

He had Stan Saplin to thank again. Saplin made Kiviat's election to the Hall of Fame a major project. He prepared a meticulous dossier of recommendation and lobbied Wagner in person when they attended a track meet in Madison Square Garden.

There was a certain irony here. The leaders of amateur athletics had hounded and humiliated Kiviat at regular intervals until middle age. Longevity now paid a dividend that some of his gifted contemporaries did not receive. Whereas Mel Sheppard and Ted Meredith were members of the

Hall of Fame, John Paul Jones and Norman Taber, who had passed away earlier, were not.[18]

In early December, Kiviat flew to Houston with his New Jersey neighbor and fellow track official Sanford (Sandy) Kalb for the TAC convention and his induction into the National Track and Field Hall of Fame. With his charm and charisma, he was the hit of the ceremony. "'Thanks, folks, for being so kind to me,'" he told more than eight hundred people crowded into the ballroom of the Hyatt Regency. As they applauded, he said: "'I didn't know you knew me that well.'"

With performances like that, people began comparing him to another long-lived Lower East Side native and contemporary, celebrated comedian George Burns. The entertainer with the trademark cigar was still charming America and demonstrating that someone in his nineties could be alert and effective. A poll of professional comedians picked Burns as "King of Comedy." To many, Kiviat seemed his mirror image on the athletics stage.[19]

Everything in Kiviat's life was not all comedy, of course. Sam Kiviat died eight weeks after the Houston induction ceremony. Whatever bitter feelings Abel had about his younger brother earlier in life, Sam was the sibling he had bragged about most to interviewers in recent years. Sam, the Wharton man and Penn track star who had followed his path to glory under Coach Robertson, the great "dental surgeon," was how Abel exaggerated his most successful brother's career. He said little about Sam's real claim to fame and fortune—his summer camps—because that did not fit Abel's need to glorify the family past.[20]

At this juncture, Kiviat signaled that his own physical skills might be in decline. Although he insisted on keeping a car and driving himself around Cedar Glen West, one day he knocked over twelve mailboxes. "'The people at the motor vehicles department thought because I was 94 I should be tested again, and that my eyesight wasn't so good,'" he complained. In fact, he failed the test several times, knocking over cones in the process. He accepted the decision with a version of his mother's

20. An athletic prodigy at ninety-five: Kiviat runs on Fifth Avenue to celebrate his birthday. *From left:* Fred Lebow of the New York Road Runners Club, Ray Lumpp of the NYAC, Abel Kiviat, and Howard Schmertz of the Millrose Games. Courtesy of Esther Kiviat.

old philosophy: "'What's the use of arguing?'" The loss of independence bothered him more than he revealed.[21]

Yet with others happy to chauffeur him, he kept up a demanding schedule of appearances. He posed for a photograph with gymnast Mary Lou Retton at a New York preview of Bud Greenspan's new film about the 1984 Olympics.[22] He basked in the publicity of the New York Road Runners Club's ninety-fifth birthday party for him. During the party, someone asked Kiviat "if he had any goals. 'Yeah,' he said," sounding like George Burns, "'that I can come back in 1992, for my 100th birthday.'"[23]

Groups as diverse as schoolteachers, sports promoters, charities, the Special Olympics, retirement communities, and Jewish organizations all wanted him at their events, and he almost always obliged them. Perhaps his most memorable appearance was at Madison Square Garden for the 1988 U.S. indoor championships in late February. At this centennial of the meet, TAC staged an exhibition relay of past champions. Fifteen thousand track fans stood and cheered lustily "at the end of the relay, when Glenn Cunningham, the four-time indoor national mile champion, handed the baton to 95-year-old Abel Kiviat, who once won the 600- and 1,000-yard championships on the same night," the *New York Times* reported. Twelve days later Cunningham died of a heart attack at his farm in Arkansas. Kiviat, however, seemed just to be getting warmed up.[24]

The pursuit of fame now took over his life. "You know he ate up the adulation," sister-in-law Esther Kiviat remarked. "He lived for it! And he loved being flown places, as he got older, and being invited to officiate at track meets." Indeed, he had become a very old man who "would not refuse an honor." Yet his need was by no means unique. As historian Leo Braudy pointed out in 1986, for great amateur athletes of the early twentieth century such as Kiviat, celebrity status resulted naturally from their inspiring performances. When Braudy published his historical study of fame, "self-display" itself had become "the biggest theme" of sports stars. Paradoxically, then, whereas the media presented Abel Kiviat as a throwback to a lost world of sport for its own sake, his own drive was for celebrity itself.[25]

With that drive came his unabated need to attract women, according to Lucy Price, who was taken aback by his flirtatious behavior with her younger friends. USA Track & Field's Hal Bateman was one of many who were struck by how women, in turn, were attracted to Kiviat's charisma and charm. "The women couldn't stay away from him," Bateman observed.[26]

Now, midway in Kiviat's final decade, Glenn Kasper took over Stan Saplin's role and managed him. Kasper was serving as an assistant to the executive director of the New Jersey Governor's Council on Physical Fitness and Sports. When they met, Kiviat stated his terms for a public appearance: "'pick me up, feed me, and take me home.' Those were his conditions, and he'd go anywhere. A Damon Runyon character."

When Kasper asked about his Olympic medals, Kiviat said that "'he hadn't seen them in fifty years.'" (Kiviat simply maintained the fiction that he had won gold in the 3000-meter team race.) Glenn Kasper had a sudden inspiration. Because he was the New Jersey Council's representative to the New Sweden Commission, charged with developing plans for commemorating the 350th anniversary of Swedes landing in the Delaware Valley, he decided to present Kiviat with duplicate medals of the ones he had received at Stockholm. Happily, the current king of Sweden, a great-grandson of Gustav V of 1912, was scheduled to attend the commemoration in Trenton.

With only six weeks to pull this off, Kasper discovered the maddening problems of dealing with sport bureaucracies. Frustrated by the U.S. and the Swedish Olympic Committees, he wired a persuasive letter to IOC president Juan Antonio Samaranch in Lausanne requesting permission to replace the medals. Samaranch wired back his approval. The Swiss medal maker, Hugenin Medailleurs, accepted a rush order to cast 1912 medals from the original molds in its possession. Kasper called Kiviat with the news. "'Oh Glenn, that's great but what about the chocolate chip cookies that Nabisco [an Olympic team sponsor] promised me?' You know, when you're ninety-five years old, your values change," Kasper commented philosophically.

On Thursday, April 15, 1988, Kiviat received his medals at the State Museum in Trenton, surrounded by the Swedish royal couple and Governor Tom Kean. Dapper, smiling, and still looking decades younger than his age, Kiviat was for once speechless. "'I can't say anything except thanks, thanks, thanks.'"[27]

Glenn Kasper's next project was even more ambitious. Early in 1989, Kasper wrote to President George H. W. Bush requesting a meeting between the president and Kiviat. Kasper received a telephone call from the White House inviting him to bring Kiviat to the Oval Office. Kiviat was initially unenthusiastic: "'Well, to tell you the truth, Glenn, I'd rather not go.' And I tell you my heart almost came through my throat," Kasper recalled. Kasper raced over to Lakehurst and discovered that Kiviat "didn't want to spend the money to have the clothes cleaned" for the trip to Washington. Kasper took care of that detail and prepared a plaque containing a *Parade* magazine article about Kiviat by Bud Greenspan to present to President Bush.

It was raining hard on May 16 when Kiviat entered the White House, "kissed the hands of a few female receptionists along the way," and waited outside the Oval Office. "They came and got Abel," Kasper remembered. He "was out of his chair like a shot out of a cannon, walking down the hall," followed by the New Jersey officials. The meeting with the president was brief: a photograph, the presentation of the autographed plaque, a few words. But

21. King Carl XVI Gustaf of Sweden, great-grandson of Gustav V, presents Kiviat with replicas of medals from the 1912 Olympics, Trenton, N.J., 1988. Courtesy of Glenn A. Kasper.

Bush was intrigued when Kiviat told him he had shaken Teddy Roosevelt's hand in 1908.[28]

Soon after the White House meeting, Kiviat accepted an offer from the JCPenney Company to serve as a fashion model for its new line of recreational apparel licensed by the U.S. Olympic Committee. For the retailer, it was a shrewd way to market appealing merchandise to a booming senior market. For Kiviat, who suddenly reversed the philosophy of simon-pure amateurism he had been espousing since his reinstatement by the AAU in 1922, it underlined how much he was caught up in a campaign of self-promotion. As one fashion editor remarked, "The proverbial loneliness of the long-distance runner is not likely to hit Kiviat soon."[29]

A CHAMPION AT NINETY-NINE

Kiviat did nothing to disprove the fashion editor's assertion during his final two years.[30] At ninety-eight, he entered and won a 100-meter dash in New Jersey's Senior Games, defeating Orlando Bernabe, a ninety-six-year-old. Dressed for his final race in a Curtis High T-shirt, gym shorts, and baseball cap, Kivie recorded a time of 47.70 to the loser's 49.20. When Kasper said to him: "'Abel, it looks like it was awful close,' Kiviat responded: 'God, I could have kicked his ass, but I didn't want to embarrass him.' He didn't like to lose," Kasper concluded the story.[31]

Jim Reisler noted Kiviat's "fighting spirit" and commitment to sports programs for youth in incisive portraits for the *New York Times* and the *Asbury Park Press,* mentioning that the venerable runner had accepted an invitation to carry the torch during the opening ceremonies of the Barcelona Olympiad.[32]

Approaching the century mark, Kiviat remained an alert and lively companion. He was no "senile grandfather" in Kasper's care, but someone who kept up with world affairs and remained "entertaining and charming"— except to his son, Arthur, whose relationship with his father at this late date was still "like oil and water," Kasper observed. They had frequent disagreements, and during one of Arthur's monthly visits to Lakehurst he confided to Kasper that his father was a hypocrite about his unhealthy dietary practices, his statements to the press notwithstanding. Arthur might have done better to take his father aside and persuade him to see Dr. Yeager again. The old man had been complaining to Lucy Price for some time about symptoms caused by a prostate problem, yet he waved off her expressions of concern.[33]

During the winter of 1991, Kiviat's thoughts turned to planning with Stan Saplin and Fred Lebow for his ninety-ninth birthday celebration. The fact that he had outlasted all of his teammates and was now legitimately the oldest living American Olympian gave the printed invitation for Sunday,

June 23, a special poignancy. However, the pain in his back and legs was becoming severe and intrusive. On Memorial Day weekend, he drove to the cemetery on Staten Island with Price, and she could see that "he could barely get out of the car" to walk. She made an appointment with Dr. Yeager, who referred him to a urologist, and Kiviat received the grim prognosis: he had an advanced case of prostate cancer. He had simply waited too long to attend to it. Undeterred, he went ahead with plans for the birthday party. Encouraged by Arthur, who gave permission to Stan Saplin, he even decided to run a few yards for the press. This decision deeply upset his brother Charlie.[34]

Glenn Kasper took Kiviat into New York for the event and stayed with him at a hotel as guests of the Road Runners Club. When they went down for breakfast, Kasper saw that the old man was in agony and asked him: "Abel, what's the matter? 'My back, I hurt all in here,'" was the response. "Then, it struck me, it must be cancer," recalled Kasper. Only three people— Price, Arthur, and now Kasper—shared his terrible secret as Kiviat accepted an award from Fred Lebow and regaled an audience of a hundred people at the Road Runners Club. When the inevitable request came from a photographer to "run, Abel, run . . . one more time," he stunned Price by consenting. He changed into a sweatshirt, fluorescent green shorts, and running shoes, and jogged a half-block on Fifth Avenue with Lebow. "It had to be the most painful thing in the world for him to do," Lucy remembered. "His bravery and courage at the end was an inspiration to anybody."[35]

Kiviat collapsed after returning home, and he was soon a patient in the Toms River Hospital. The attending physician then made a catastrophic error, recommending prostate surgery. Arthur agreed to the operation, and Lucy therefore had no choice but to sign the consent form. Other family members thought it was a great mistake, given his age. The surgery was a disaster. Kiviat "became incontinent" and suffered terribly during the next eight weeks. Adding to his misery, his grandson Dennis recalled, "he was mentally alert until the end."[36]

On Saturday afternoon, August 24, Lucy Price stroked his face and body, said prayers, then left the house to keep a pressing business appointment. Moments later, Kiviat passed away. It was as if he had waited for her to depart, she felt, wanting to spare Tommy Lennon's daughter the pain of observing his death.[37]

Abel's siblings, Harold, ninety, and Charlie, eighty-eight, the last surviving children of Morris and Zelda Kiviat, seemed more upset about having to
face each other at Abel's funeral than with the inescapable fact of his passing.
"If that son of a bitch brother of mine is there, I'm not going," Harold told
Lucy. Charlie, in turn, told Lucy that "you're going to have [to have] a cop
there because I'm going to kill him if he's there." In the end, Charlie decided
it would be best if he did not attend the service.

During the final rites, Stan Saplin spoke about the old man he had rein-
vented a decade earlier. A saddened Fred Lebow announced the establishment of the Abel Kiviat Award, to be presented annually to the oldest man
to complete the New York Marathon. The cortege then took Kiviat's remains
back home to Staten Island, where he was laid to rest next to Isabel and his
parents in the Baron Hirsch Cemetery.[38]

IN THE LONG RUN

What makes a great runner's enduring reputation? Success in track and field
is measured in seconds or inches. The ability to reach the finish line of an
event faster than anyone else has previously marks an athlete's place in the
chain of tradition. Records provide the scaffolding of the sport. Often less
well remembered but more compelling than the record is the defeat of one's
peers in the chase itself. In middle-distance running, judgment and intelligence are as important as raw speed in carrying an athlete to a championship.[39] Abel Kiviat had a rare combination of those qualities. He secured
his place in history as the first official holder of the world's 1,500-meter
record, but he took greater pleasure in recalling closely fought duels with
the likes of John Paul Jones, Norman Taber, Oscar Hedlund, and Hannes
Kolehmainen. These first modern superstars set a fast pace for all the middle-
distance runners who followed them and led the way in the Americanization
of the Victorian-era sport of the British Isles.

In running, as in life itself, the ability to hang in no matter the pressures of mind, body, or circumstance often enables a participant to achieve
a desired result. Having usefully given back to his sport for decades as a volunteer official, Kiviat's persistence and devotion reaped unexpected rewards.
In December 1995, he was inducted posthumously into the inaugural class

of the Staten Island Sports Hall of Fame. His friend Lucy Lennon Price cooperated with Anne McAuliffe of the Curtis High School alumni association to create a permanent display of Kiviat's medals and memorabilia at the entrance to Curtis, named the school's track after him, and organized an annual Kiviat memorial meet on it. More posthumous acclaim at the national level followed.[40]

An extraordinary personality was a factor in this enduring recognition of human greatness. Initially a reserved and unassuming lad who let his feet speak for him when he reported to Coach Lawson Robertson in 1909, he developed into a voluble personality at Celtic Park. Mingling with working-class Irish athletes and assimilating their version of American culture prepared him to pick his way through all the twists and turns of eighty years of adulthood that lay ahead. His life was therefore a case study of Americanization *through* an ethnic athletics association.

Yet at the core of his personality was the inherited culture of his parents, the Yiddishkeit of eastern Europe. From it, he built a public persona as the "Hebrew runner," a strong and proud Jewish champion. He became a hero to young sports fans in serried city tenements because of his prowess as "a Jew who could beat goyim" at their own game, as one of them later put it. Over the course of his long life, he increasingly made his Jewish identity central to his status as a Hall of Famer. Like many others in the second generation of American Jews, he moved from a strong desire for assimilation to a more balanced perspective that bespoke the possibilities of cultural pluralism in life and sport. In the process, he helped to move track and field from its narrow and constricting mentality to an outlook more appropriate to a democratic society. Unintended or not, that contribution may be the true mark of his greatness.[41]

APPENDIX

NOTES

BIBLIOGRAPHY

INDEX

Abel R. Kiviat's Records

WORLD RECORDS

0.67 mile	2:47.6	Asbury Park, N.J.	Aug. 7, 1909
0.5 mile (indoors)	1:57.8	New York, N.Y.	Apr. 1, 1911
600 yards (indoors)	1:14	New York, N.Y.	Dec. 27, 1911
0.75 mile (indoors)	3:08.9	New York, N.Y.	Feb. 12, 1912
1,500 meters	3:59.2	New York, N.Y.	May 26, 1912
1,500 meters	3:56.8	New York, N.Y.	June 2, 1912
1,500 meters	3:55.8*	Cambridge, Mass.	June 8, 1912
1.5 miles (indoors)	6:48.2	New York, N.Y.	Nov. 27, 1912
0.75 mile (indoors)	3:08.6	New York, N.Y.	Jan. 29, 1913
1 mile (indoors)	4:18.2	New York, N.Y.	Feb. 15, 1913
1,000 yards (indoors)	2:15.8	New York, N.Y.	Mar. 6, 1913
1,000 yards (indoors)	2:15.4	New York, N.Y.	Mar. 2, 1914
0.75 mile (indoors)	3:07.4	New York, N.Y.	Mar. 16, 1914
1,000 yards (indoors)	2:15.2	New York, N.Y.	Nov. 28, 1914

*First official 1,500-meter world record accepted by the IAAF.

WORLD RECORDS AS MEMBER OF IRISH-AMERICAN
ATHLETIC CLUB RELAY TEAMS

Medley (220, 440, 880, 1 mile)	7:44.4	Boston, Mass.	July 24, 1909
4 miles (4 by 1 mile)	18:08.8	New York, N.Y.	Oct. 9, 1909
2,400 yards (4 by 600)	5:06.2	New York, N.Y.	Feb. 5, 1910
2 miles (4 by 880)	7:53	New York, N.Y.	Sept. 5, 1910
Medley (220, 440, 880, 1 mile)	7:43	New York, N.Y.	July 10, 1915

U.S. NATIONAL CHAMPIONSHIPS

1911   600 yards (indoors), 1,000 yards (indoors), 1 mile (outdoors)

1912   1 mile (outdoors)

1913   600 yards (indoors), 1,000 yards (indoors), cross country (6.2 miles)

1914   1,000 yards (indoors), 1 mile (outdoors)

Notes

ABBREVIATIONS

AAU Amateur Athletic Union

AOC American Olympic Committee

BG "Abel Kiviat/Olympiad," unpublished text of interview by Bud Greenspan, May 31, 1975, Cappy Productions, New York

CF "Abel Richard Kiviat," unpublished text of interviews by Lewis H. Carlson and John J. Fogarty, 1986

EK Esther Kiviat Papers, Rhinebeck, N.Y.

GK Glenn Kasper Papers, Eufaula, Ala.

HDS Howard Drew Scrapbooks, Washington, D.C.

HED Oscar Hedlund Scrapbooks, Little Compton, R.I.

I-AAC Irish-American Athletic Club

JPJ John Paul Jones Papers, Tucson, Ariz.

LC Library of Congress, Washington, D.C.

LR Lawson Robertson Scrapbooks, Garden City, N.Y.

NA National Archives, Washington, D.C.

NB Unpublished text of Abel Kiviat interview by Nancy Beffa, Apr. 27, 1984, Cappy Productions

NT Norman Taber Papers, Rhinebeck, N.Y.

NYDT *New-York Daily Tribune*

NYEM *New York Evening Mail*

NYG *New York Globe and Commercial Advertiser*

NYH *New York Herald*

NYHS New York Historical Society

NYPL New York Public Library

NYT *New York Times*

NYTEM *New York Telegram and Evening Mail*

OH Interview with Abel R. Kiviat, May 23, 1984, American Jewish Committee Oral History Collection, Dorot Jewish Division, New York Public Library, Astor, Lenox and Tilden Foundation

SIA   *Staten Island Advance*

SIJHS   "Interview with Abel Kiviat, July 3rd, 1984." Unpublished text, Jewish Historical
           Society of Staten Island, New York

SK   Samuel Kiviat Papers, Rochester, N.Y.

SS   Stanley Saplin Papers, New York

TL   Thomas Lennon Papers, Potomac Falls, Va.

UP   University of Pennsylvania Archives and Records Center

WS   William Simons, "Abel Kiviat Interview," *Journal of Sport History* 13, no. 3
           (winter 1986): 235–66.

PROLOGUE: STOCKHOLM 1984

1. See *America at the Olympics,* CBS Television Network, July 4, 1984, a Cappy Productions video.

2. Lewis H. Carlson and John J. Fogarty, *Tales of Gold: An Oral History of the Summer Olympic Games Told by America's Gold Medal Winners* (Chicago: Contemporary Books, 1987), 4, 7–8; *New York Evening World,* July 10, 1912; "Abel Kiviat," Mecca Cigarettes Series of Champion Athletes, 1911.

3. Interview with Sydney Thayer, New York, July 24, 1995 (all interviews are by the author unless otherwise indicated in the list of abbreviations or in the notes); *Stockholm Expressen,* Apr. 27, 1984; Sydney Thayer to Rosanne Pool, Passport Services, Washington, D.C., Mar. 26, 1984, papers of Cappy Productions, New York; Cappy Mailgram to Ture Widlund, Stockholm, Apr. 22, 1984, papers of Cappy Productions, New York.

4. NB, 1, 4; Erik Bergvall, ed., *The Fifth Olympiad: Official Report of the Olympic Games of Stockholm 1912* (Stockholm: Wahlstrom and Widstrand, 1913), 229–41; Cordner Nelson and Roberto Quercetani, *The Milers* (Los Altos, Calif.: Tafnews Press, 1985), 21.

5. Nelson and Quercetani, *The Milers,* 22–23; James E. Sullivan, "The Fifth Olympiad," in *The Olympic Games, Stockholm 1912,* edited by James E. Sullivan (New York: American Sports, 1912), 71; Bergvall, *The Fifth Olympiad,* 84, 178–79, 186, 364–65; the Rt. Hon. Philip Noel-Baker, "V Stockholm 1912," in *The Olympic Games,* edited by Lord Killanen and John Rodda (New York: Collier Books, 1976), 40. In reconstructing this race, I have been influenced by both the approach and the information in Bob Gilmore, "Four Laps to Glory," *San Diego Running News* (Oct. 1982), 10–12.

6. Norman Taber, untitled manuscript of a 1912 essay, 2–3, 15, NT; Bergvall, *The Fifth Olympiad,* 345; *NYT,* July 11, 1912; Sullivan, "The Fifth Olympiad," 69; B. Gilmore, "Four Laps to Glory," 11; NB, 3.

7. Lawson Robertson's description is in *New York Evening World,* July 10, 1912. For a full description of the 1,500 race and brief comments about the subsequent fates of the principal competitors, see chapter 6.

8. For the late-nineteenth-century background, see Edward S. Sears, *Running Through the Ages* (Jefferson, N.C.: McFarland, 2001), 80–162. Mark Dyreson's *Making the American Team: Sport, Culture, and the Olympic Experience* (Urbana: University of Illinois Press, 1998) is a landmark study of Kiviat's generation of athletes, full of important insights. For additional information, see Philip Baker in *The Outlook* (Oct. 19, 1912); NB, 3, 7; John Allen Krout, *Annals of American Sport* (New York: United States Publishers, 1956), 185, 204; and Fred G. Jarvis, *From Vision to Victory: America's Role in Establishing the Modern Olympic Games* (New York: United States Olympic Committee, 1996), 93–94. For a first-rate analysis of recent track history, see Joseph M. Turrini, "'It Was Communism versus the Free World': The USA-USSR Dual Track Meet Series and the Development of Track & Field in the United States, 1958–1985," *Journal of Sport History* 28, no. 3 (2001), 446–57.

9. OH, 44; WS, 247; conversation with Jean Drew Lightfoot, Aug. 26, 2000, Washington, D.C.; Norman Taber, Olympic diary, June 13–July 17, 1912, NT.

10. Melvin W. Sheppard, "Spiked Shoes and Cinder Paths: An Athlete's Story," *Sport Story Magazine* 3, nos. 5–6 and others unknown (1924), part X, 51 (collected into one volume by the Sheppard family, a copy given to the author). Although Norman Taber did not mention the incident in his Olympic diary, Sheppard's detailed account, in the context of his accurate reporting of other incidents, rings true.

1. STATEN ISLAND BOY

1. Bernard Bailyn, *Education in the Forming of American Society* (Chapel Hill, N.C.: Vintage Books, 1960), 48, for the Margaret Mead quotation. Recent historians have revived with substantial modifications the "classical model" of assimilation developed by Milton Gordon in *Assimilation in American Life: The Role of Race, Religion, and National Origins* (New York: Oxford Univ. Press, 1964), 60–83. See, for example, Ewa Morawska, "In Defense of the Assimilation Model," *Journal of American Ethnic History* 13 (1994): 76–84; Russell A. Kazal, "Revisiting Assimilation: The Rise, Fall, and Reappraisal of a Concept in American Ethnic History," *American Historical Review* 100, no. 2 (1995): 437–72; James R. Barrett, "Americanization from the Bottom Up: Immigration and the Remaking of the Working Class in the United States, 1880–1930," *Journal of American History* 79, no. 3 (1992): 996–1020. Taken together, their insights provide part of the framework for a narrative of Kiviat's life.

2. OH, 3–4; CF, 1; "Morris Kiviat," Standard Certificate of Death, Registered No. 811, Bureau of Records, Department of Health of the City of New York, State of New York, Apr. 28, 1930; M. Sirota, "Torah Institutions" (Yiddish), in *The Bialystoker Memorial Book* (New York: Bialystoker Center, 1982), 52–55; Awrom Szmuel Herszberg, "One Hundred Years Ago" (English), in *The Bialystoker Memorial Book*, 6–9; Arnold Zable,

Jewels and Ashes (New York: Harcourt Brace, 1991), 118–19, 139; Gedalyahu Alon, "The Lithuanian Yeshiva," in *The Jewish Expression,* edited by Judah Goldin (New York: Bantam Books, 1970), 448–64; conversations in 1997 with my father, Rabbi Harry W. Katchen, New York City.

3. Anne M. Kiviat to David Zabludowski, Apr. 14, 1969, Erik Kiviat Papers, Annandale, N.Y.; *Piesk & Most: A Memorial Book* (Tel Aviv: Irgun yots'e Pyesk u-Most be-Yisra'el vehatefutsot, 1975), 11–32, 48–52 (English), and 23–28, 407–24, 478–79, 597 (Hebrew); "Morris Kiviat," Standard Certificate of Death, Apr. 28, 1930.

4. Herszberg, "One Hundred Years Ago," 6–9; I. Shmulewitz, "Bialystok—A Historical Survey" (English), in *The Bialystoker Memorial Book,* 3–5; Pejsach Kaplan, "Recalling Our Proud Past" (English), in *The Bialystoker Memorial Book,* 21; David Sohn, *Bialystok: Photo Album of a Renowned City and Its Jews the World Over* (English and Yiddish) (New York: Bialystoker Album Committee, 1951), 14–16, passim; "Byelostok," in *The Jewish Encyclopedia* (New York: Funk and Wagnells, 1907), vol. 3; "Bialystok," in *Encyclopedia Judaica* (New York: Macmillan, 1971), vol. 4; Zable, *Jewels and Ashes,* 45–49, 118–19.

5. CF, 1; Sirota, "Torah Institutions," 53.

6. According to A. S. Hershberg, in 1880 an Abraham Zabludowki of Bialystok, who may have been Zelda's father, founded a textile mill employing eleven people in Bransk, fifty-seven kilometers to the southwest. See A. S. Hershberg, *Pinkos Bialystok* (Yiddish) (New York: Aroysgegebn fun der Gezelshaft far Geshikhte fun Byalistok, 1950), 2:59. See also Anne M. Kiviat to David Zabludowski, Apr. 14, 1969, Erik Kiviat Papers; telephone conversation with Dr. Erik Kiviat, Annandale, N.Y., June 19, 2004; CF, 1; WS, 237. Birth certificate of Zelda Zablutsky [*sic*], Kolno, County Kolno, Poland, 74, July 18, 1865, Bruce Conrad-Reingold Papers, Rochester, N.Y.; "Zelda Naomi Kiviat," Certificate of Death, Certificate No. 5736, Bureau of Records, Dept. of Health, Borough of Manhattan, Mar. 7, 1946; "Abel Richard Kiviat," U.S. Social Security Act, Application for Account Number, Oct. 21, 1938, Social Security Administration, U.S. Dept. of Health and Human Services; Hershel Kolinsky, "Our Kolno" (English), in *Kolno Memorial Book,* edited by Aizik Remba and Benjamin Halevy (Tel Aviv: Rozhan and Sigalit, 1971), 13–14; Simcha Shkoloniwitz, "History of Kolno and Its Jews" (Hebrew), in *Kolno Memorial Book,* 4–5; Akivah Fett, "Akibah Rubenstein of Blessed Memory" (Hebrew), in *Staviski: Yizkor Book,* edited by Yosef Rubin (Tel Aviv: Tenu'at moshve ha-'ovdim be-Yisra'el, 1973), 144–46; Alter Trus and Julius Cohen, *Brainsk: A Memorial Book* (Yiddish) (New York: Braynsker Relif Komite in Nyu York, 1948), 132; Shmulewitz, "Bialystok," 3. On the education of young women in eastern Europe, see Sydney Stahl Weinberg, *The World of Our Mothers* (Chapel Hill: University of North Carolina Press, 1988), 44–49. During an interview I had with Harold Kiviat in Fort Lauderdale, Florida, on January 28, 1996, he said that his mother had informed him that his maternal grandparents, Avram and Maty Zabludowski, died tragically at the hands of Polish neighbors. I have been unable to confirm this allegation.

7. Anne M. Kiviat to David Zabludowski, Apr. 14, 1969, Erik Kiviat Papers; Herszberg, "One Hundred Years Ago," 6–9; Zable, *Jewels and Ashes,* 161.

8. OH, 3–4; WS, 238; SIJHS; CF, 1; Anne M. Kiviat to David Zabludowski, Apr. 14, 1969, Erik Kiviat Papers; interview with Harold Kiviat, Jan. 28, 1996; Mordechaj Pogorelski, "Pogroms in the 19th Century" (English), in *Bialystoker Memorial Book,* 15–16; David Sohn, "The Pogrom Against the Jews" (English), in *Bialystoker Memorial Book,* 16–18; John D. Klier and Shlomo Lambrozo, eds., *Pogroms: Anti-Jewish Violence in Modern Russian History* (Cambridge, U.K.: Cambridge Univ. Press, 1992), especially 237–38; Lucy Dawidowicz, *The Golden Tradition* (Boston: Holt, Rinehart and Winston, 1967), 30; Moses Rischin, *The Promised City* (Cambridge, Mass.: Harvard Univ. Press, 1962), 19. In 1906, fifteen years after the Kiviats arrived in New York, a violent Bialystok pogrom killed two hundred Jews and injured seven hundred others.

9. OH, 3–4; interview with Harold Kiviat, East Windsor, N.J., Oct. 9, 1995. For the ocean crossing on the *Italy,* see "Passenger Lists of Vessels Arriving at New York, N.Y., 1820–1897," Micropublication M237, Roll no. 95-576, List no. 1448, NA; N. R. P. Bonsor, *North Atlantic Seaway: An Illustrated History of the Passenger Services Linking the Old World with the New* (Prescott, U.K.: T. Stephenson, ca. 1975), 207; Philip Taylor, *The Distant Magnet: European Emigration to the U.S.A.* (New York: Harper and Row, 1971), 127–28, 145–66. The name on the ship's manifest, "Moses Kwat" of Russia, was undoubtedly a misspelled version of "Moishe Kwiat." Moishe gave his age as eighteen rather than twenty-three, probably because he feared any detection as an escapee from the czarist military. For background on the Kwiats' arrival in New York, see *NYT,* Jan. 31, 1897; David Sohn, "The First Bialystoker in America," in *Bialystoker Memorial Book,* 165–67; Gerard R. Wolfe, *New York: A Guide to the Metropolis* (New York: McGraw-Hill, 1973), 17; Irving Howe, *World of Our Fathers* (New York: Harcourt Brace Jovanovich, 1976), 26–63; Hasia R. Diner, *Lower East Side Memories: A Jewish Place in America* (Princeton, N.J.: Princeton Univ. Press, 2000), 7.

10. The Kiviat children in New York were discouraged from pursuing inquiry about their relatives in Bialystok. Interview with Esther Kiviat, Rhinebeck, N.Y., Mar. 30, 1997; interview with Harold Kiviat, Jan. 28, 1996; OH, 2, 7–8; CF, 2; "The Bialystoker Synagogue in New York," in *Bialystoker Memorial Book,* 172 (English), 343 (Yiddish); Howe, *World of Our Fathers,* 67–84, 96–101, 116–17; *American Magazine* material from Rischin, 77–83; Wolfe, *New York,* 107–8, 112–13, 115–16, 127; Adam Bellow, *The Educational Alliance* (New York: Educational Alliance, 1990), 9–11, 82–83; David Von Drehle, *Triangle: The Fire That Changed America* (New York: Atlantic Monthly Press, 2003), 99. There are no references to the Kwiats (Kiviats) of Allen Street in the Manhattan directories for the years 1891 to 1893 at the New York Historical Society.

11. Shimon Feiginoff, "Son of Bialystok Rabbi, Renowned American Sportsman," *The Bialystoker Stimme,* no. 342 (Apr. 1988): 26–27; Carlson and Fogarty, *Tales of Gold,* 5; WS, 236; Rischin, *Promised City,* 55–56; Howe, *World of Our Fathers,* 77–80.

12. Abel R. Kiviat Passport Contact Sheet, 1984, Cappy Productions papers; Anne M. Kiviat to Passport Office, Apr. 2, 1984, Cappy Production papers; OH, 17–18, 20–21; CF, 2; Jacob A. Riis, *Children of the Tenements* (New York: MacMillan, 1903); Howe, *World of Our Fathers*, 256–63; Clifton Hood, *722 Miles: The Building of the Subways and How They Transformed New York* (New York: Simon and Schuster, 1993), 53–55, 127, 272; Erica Judge, Vincent Seyfried, and Andrew Sparberg, "Elevated Railways," in *Encyclopedia of New York City*, edited by Kenneth T. Jackson (New Haven, Conn.: Yale Univ. Press, 1995), 368.

13. Anne Kiviat to Sam Kiviat, Oct. 13, 1980, SK; interview with Harold Kiviat, Oct. 9, 1995; *Staten Island: A Resource Manual for School and Community* (New York: n.p., 1964), 1–2, 92, 106–12, 133–34; Dorothy Valentine Smith, *This Was Staten Island* (Staten Island, N.Y.: Staten Island Historical Society, 1968); Charles L. Sachs, *Made on Staten Island: Agriculture, Industry, and Suburban Living in the City* (Staten Island, N.Y.: Staten Island Historical Society, 1988), 11, 111; Charles L. Sachs, "Staten Island," in Jackson, 1112–14.

14. Sachs, *Made on Staten Island*, 11, 67; Robert W. Venables, "A Historical Overview of Staten Island's Trade Networks," *Proceedings of the Staten Island Institute of Arts and Sciences* 34, no. 1 (1989), 22; Sachs, "Staten Island," 1115.

15. OH, 3. *The Standard Directory of Richmond Borough, 1897–1898*, Staten Island Museum, listed "Morris Kiver [*sic*], peddler, 7 Henry S." The naturalization records at both New York's Varick Street branch of the National Archives and Staten Island's Borough Hall— including the indexed handwritten ledger books "Petitions of Naturalization" and the actual certificates, 1891 to 1910—have no references to the Kiviats. For origins of the Staten Island Jewish community, see *SIA*, Mar. 25, 1961, Nov. 6, 1963, May 8, 1976, Sept. 6, 1983, Nov. 25, 1984; Jenny Tango, *The Jewish Community of Staten Island* (Charleston, S.C.: Arcadia, 2004), 19–24.

16. Anne Kiviat to Sam Kiviat, Oct. 13, 1980, SK; SIJHS; WS, 238; CF, 2; "David D. Kivat," Certificate of Birth, New York City Department of Records and Information Services, Municipal Archives; *Church of Saint Mary, Rosebank, S.I., 1852–1952* (privately printed), 19; *Staten Island: A Resource Manual*, 65, 142–43, 147–52, 263; David C. Hammock, "Consolidation," in Jackson, 277–78; Howard Weiner, "Rosebank," in Jackson, 1022. My telephone conversation with Staten Island's county historian, Richard Dickenson, on January 20, 2005, helped to confirm the location of the Kiviat family residence in Rosebank.

17. WS, 238; interviews with Harold Kiviat, Oct. 9, 1995, Jan. 28, 1996.

18. OH, 8–9; WS, 246; interview with Esther Kiviat, Mar. 30, 1997; "Israel Kiviat," Official Registration Card, P.S. 13 archive, New York City Department of Education; records of David, Samuel, Harold, and Charles Kiviat, P.S. 14 archive, New York City Department of Education.

19. OH, 11–14; WS, 245–246.

20. OH, 8–10; SIJHS; Feiginoff, 26–27.

21. OH, 19; WS, 239; Alice Austen House, *A National Historic Landmark* (Staten Island, N.Y.: Friends of Alice Austen House, 1993).

22. CF, 2; "Abel Kiviat" and "Israel Kiviat," Official Registration Cards, Sept. 1, 1898–Sept. 9, 1901, P.S. 13 archive; *Fifth Annual Report of the City Superintendent of Schools, Dept. of Education, the City of New York* (New York: New York City Department of Education, 1903), 346; David Tyack, *The One Best System* (Cambridge, Mass.: Harvard Univ. Press, 1974), 229–55.

23. The files of the New York City Department of Buildings indicate that the 101 Broad Street of 1900 is today's 188 Canal Street. *Standard Business Directory of Richmond Borough, New York, 1906,* 382, Staten Island Museum; U.S. Bureau of the Census, *Thirteenth Census of the United States: 1910 Population Stapleton* (Washington, D.C.: National Archives and Records Administration, 1910), Richmond Borough, New York: Enumeration District Nos. 1318, 1319, 1320; "An East Shore Village Revisited: Stapleton, from 1890 to 1920," *Staten Island Historian* 29, no. 4 (1968): 26–36; Rosalie Mord Litinsky, "Stapleton's Harrison Street Revisited," *Staten Island Historian* 3 (new series), no. 2 (fall 1985): 18–20.

24. David C. Hammock, "Consolidation," Barnett Shepherd, "Stapleton," and Charles L. Sachs, "Staten Island," all in Jackson, 277–78, 1111, 1112–18; Sachs, *Made on Staten Island,* 46; *Staten Island: A Resource Manual,* 78, 92–152; Shirley A. Zavin, *Staten Island: An Architectural History* (Staten Island, N.Y.: n.p., 1979), 2, 4–7; "Descriptive Sketch of Stapleton" (1893) and "Stapleton: A Look Back," files in the Stapleton Branch, NYPL; *Staten Island Register,* Nov. 13, 1975; *NYT,* May 4, 1997.

25. OH, 3; WS, 238; interviews with Harold Kiviat, Oct. 9, 1995, Jan. 28, 1996.

26. Interview with Harold Kiviat, Oct. 9, 1995; records of P.S. 14 archive; Henry G. Steinmeyer, "An Island Village Childhood," *Staten Island Historian* 3, no. 1 (1940), 4; Henry G. Steinmeyer, "How It Looked in 1885," *Staten Island Historian* 23, no. 3 (1962), 24; *Fifth Annual Report* (1903), 66–68, 346; *Annual Financial and Statistical Report of the Transactions of the Board of Education of New York, 1914* (New York: Board of Education of New York, 1914), 232–33; *The First Fifty Years: A Brief Review of Progress, 1898–1948, Fiftieth Annual Report of the Superintendent of Schools, Board of Education, the City of N.Y.* (New York: Board of Education of New York, 1948), 9, 20, 49–50; Maurice Denzil Hodgen, "Public Secondary Education in Staten Island: A Perspective," *Staten Island Historian* 21, no. 1 (1960): 11–12; Selma Berrol, *Immigrants at School, New York City, 1898–1914* (New York: Arno Press, 1978), 228–33.

27. OH, 20–22; interview with Harold Kiviat, Oct. 9, 1995; William H. Maxwell, *A Quarter Century of Public School Development* (New York: American Book Company, 1912), 58; Tyack, 180–81, 230–33; Deborah Dash Moore, *At Home in America* (New York: New York Univ. Press, 1981), 88–121. On the neighborhood's children of immigrants, see the U.S. Bureau of the Census, *Thirteenth Census.*

28. Interviews with Lucy Price, Toms River, N.J., Sept. 1, 1995, July 12, 1996; *SIA,* June 24, 1987; *Newark Star-Ledger,* May 19, 1991.

29. *NYT,* Dec. 17, 1905; Maxwell, 179, 410; *Sixth Annual Report of the City Superintendent of Schools, 1904* (New York: Board of Education of New York, 1904), 268–71; J. Thomas

Jable, "The Public Schools Athletic League of New York City: Organized Athletics for City Schoolchildren, 1903–1914," in *The American Sporting Experience: A Historical Anthology of Sport in America,* edited by Steven A. Riess (New York: Leisure Press, 1984), 219–38; Berrol, *Immigrants at School,* 241; Donald J. Mrozek, *Sport and American Mentality, 1880–1910* (Knoxville: Univ. of Tennessee Press, 1983), 61.

30. OH, 20, 24, 48; WS, 240; SIJHS; *NYT,* June 2, 9, 1907; *Sixth Annual Report of the City Superintendent of Schools, 1904,* 270; "On the Sport Trail with Hal J. Squier," *SIA,* n.d., TL; *Newark Star-Ledger,* May 19, 1991; Jable, "Public Schools Athletic League," 227–29. Kiviat's medal for winning the 1907 baseball title is in the Curtis High School display case with many of his other awards.

31. OH, 30, 87; interviews with Harold Kiviat, Oct. 9, 1995, Jan. 28, 1996; Alice Lawrence, "Staten Island's Early Automobiles," *Staten Island Historian* 13, no. 2 (1952), 11; D. Smith, *This Was Staten Island,* 127.

32. WS, 238–40, 246; OH, 3, 29; Carlson and Fogarty, *Tales of Gold,* 5–6; CF, 2; interviews with Harold Kiviat, Oct. 9, 1995, Jan. 28, 1996; interview with Esther Kiviat, Mar. 30, 1997; "Thomas J. Walsh," *SIA,* Oct. 10, 1955.

33. "The Athletes and Heroes," in *Bialystoker Memorial Book,* 29; Howe, *World of Our Fathers,* 182; "Sports," in *Encyclopedia Judaica,* 15:291.

34. OH, 53–57; CF, 2; interviews with Harold Kiviat, Oct. 9, 1995, Jan. 28, 1996; interview with Esther Kiviat, Mar. 30, 1997; *Staten Island: A Resource Manual,* 182–83; Samuel F. Grattan, "Famed Salvage Fleet Began in Stapleton 100 Years Ago," *SIA,* n.d., files of Stapleton Branch, NYPL; Harlow McMillen, "Staten Island Lager Beer Breweries, 1851–1962," *Staten Island Historian* 30, no. 3 (1969), 16, 20–21; *Staten Island Register,* Nov. 13, 1975; Sachs, *Made on Staten Island,* 46–47; floor plan of the Rubsam and Horrmann Atlantic Brewery in files of the Stapleton Branch, NYPL.

35. OH, 85; CF, 2; interview with Lucy Price, Sept. 1, 1995; *History of the Parish of Immaculate Conception, 1887–1962* (Staten Island, N.Y.: n.p., 1962), 23, 48 n. 24. In 1908–1909, Father McClure built the new Italian Renaissance–style brick building on Targee Street.

36. OH, 85; WS, 266; SIJHS; interview with Lucy Price, Toms River, N.J., July 13, 1996; letter to "The Exempt, Veteran and Volunteer Firemen's Association, E.F.D., Stapleton, S.I., Jan. 17, 1907," TL; obituary of Thomas Lennon, *NYT,* Apr. 5, 1967; *Staten Island: A Resource Manual,* 94–95, 151; "How It Looked in 1899," *Staten Island Historian* 18, no. 1 (1957), 7.

37. OH, 13, 17; interview with Esther Kiviat, Mar. 30, 1997; Michael Oriard, *Dreaming of Heroes* (Chicago: Nelson-Hall, 1982), 27–29, 46–49, 73–74; Oscar Handlin and Mary F. Handlin, *Facing Life: Youth and the Family in American History* (Boston: Little, Brown, 1971), 151, 201–2, 210.

38. OH, 20–22; WS, 239, 245; interviews with Harold Kiviat, Oct. 9, 1995, Jan. 28, 1996.

39. OH, 9; WS, 245–46; SIJHS; interview with Harold Kiviat, Oct. 9, 1995; Oscar Handlin, *Adventure in Freedom* (New York: McGraw-Hill, 1954), 118–19; Lloyd P. Gartner, ed., *Jewish Education in the United States: A Documentary History* (New York: Teacher's College Press, 1969), 10–12, 36–37, 123–24.

40. OH, 13, 15–16, 48–49; interviews with Harold Kiviat, Oct. 9, 1995, Jan. 28, 1996; interview with Dr. Patricia Halloran, Dec. 21, 1996, Stapleton, N.Y., during which Dr. John Halloran's daughter-in-law reminisced about him and showed the author the original 1905 blueprint of the family's Broad Street house. See also Charles W. Leng and William T. Davis, *Staten Island and Its People: A History, 1609–1929* (New York: Lewis Historical, 1930), 4:532; Henry G. Steinmeyer, "Sock and Buskin on Brook Street," *Staten Island Historian* 17, no. 4 (1956), 39; "Old Stapleton and the Flats," *Staten Island Historian* 16, no. 3 (1955), 21.

41. OH, 85–86; WS, 238; interview with Harold Kiviat, Oct. 9, 1995; interview with Esther Kiviat, Mar. 30, 1997; Frank Litsky, "Honors for Oldest Olympian," *NYT,* June 16, 1987; Weinberg, *World of Our Mothers,* 14–15, 26.

42. Interviews with Harold and Adele Kiviat, Oct. 9, 1995, East Windsor, N.J., and Jan. 28, 1996, Fort Lauderdale, Fla.; obituary notices of Zelda N. Kiviat, *NYT,* Mar. 6, 7, 1946; Litsky, "Honors for Oldest Olympian." On the role of the Polish Jewish woman, see Zable, *Jewels and Ashes,* 71, and Weinberg, *World of Our Mothers,* 3–20. In later life, Abel denied the racism of Stapleton in his youth.

43. OH, 30; WS, 244; interview with Harold Kiviat, Jan. 28, 1996; "On the Sport Trail with Hal J. Squier," n.d.; *Staten Island: A Resource Manual,* 169. The title of this concluding section is adapted from a classic novel about the conflict between an Orthodox Jewish immigrant father and his go-getting American son: Budd Schulberg, *What Makes Sammy Run?* (New York: Random House, 1941).

2. ALL–NEW YORK

1. Carol V. Wright, "St. George," in Jackson, 1034; *Staten Island: A Resource Manual,* 149–50, 212; CF, 3.

2. David Scobey, "Curtis, George William," in Jackson, 305–6.

3. Maurice Denzil Hodgen, "A High School in Perspective: The Characteristics of High School Life on Staten Island: 1881–1926," Ed.D. diss., Teachers College, Columbia Univ., 1959, 46, 104–5, 165–66. Abel Kiviat was one of twenty-three students from that era whom Hodgen interviewed. Hodgen concluded that the active support of the Chamber of Commerce was exceptional and that "there was little interest in Curtis High by the public-in-general." For an excellent treatment of C. B. J. Snyder, see Gary Hermalyn, "The Creation of Morris High School, 1896–1904: The First Public High School in the Bronx," Ed.D. diss., Teachers College, Columbia Univ., 1985, 103–16. See also Zavin, *Staten Island,* 7; Deborah S. Gardner, "Architecture," in Jackson, 47; Gary D. Hermalyn, "Morris High School," in Jackson, 773. For the context, see William J. Reese, *The Origins of the American High School* (New

Haven, Conn.: Yale Univ. Press, 1995), 175–80, 209, 257; Edward A. Krug, *The Shaping of the American High School, 1880–1920* (Madison: Univ. of Wisconsin Press, 1964), 169–89; David E. Tyack, ed., *Turning Points in American Educational History* (Waltham, Mass.: Xerox College, 1968), 386–96.

4. Hodgen, "A High School in Perspective," 159, 161; Maxwell, 91.

5. Hodgen, "A High School in Perspective," 123, 125–26, 172–77, 203.

6. Ibid., 196, for a report of an interview with Kiviat on his homework.

7. OH, 26; "Kiviat Abel," Permanent Scholarship Record, New York City Department of Education, Curtis High School archives; *The Year Book of the Curtis High School, Published by the Class of 1909*; Hodgen, "A High School in Perspective," 140–41.

8. Hodgen, "A High School in Perspective," 115–17.

9. "Kiviat Abel," Permanent Scholarship Record.

10. Hodgen, "A High School in Perspective," 166, 206–7. As an example of students' casual stereotyping of the Irish and Jews, see Mary O'Brien, "Not Stopping o'er the Modesty," in *A Class Book Published in New York by the Senior Class of Curtis High School 1908*, 40.

11. Hodgen, "A High School in Perspective," 155, 188–89; WS, 246–47 (italics added).

12. Seventy-eight percent of the nation's high schools fielded a team. Guy S. Lowman, "The Regulation and Control of Sports in Secondary Schools in the United States," *American Physical Education Review* 14 (1907), 245, as cited in S. W. Pope, *Patriotic Games: Sporting Traditions in the American Imagination, 1876–1926* (New York: Oxford Univ. Press, 1997), 128.

13. *The Curtis High School Monthly* (Dec. 1907), 173–74; Hodgen, "A High School in Perspective," 155. On the early decades of football, see Michael Oriard, *Reading Football* (Chapel Hill: Univ. of North Carolina Press, 1993), 56–133; John Sayle Watterson, *College Football* (Baltimore: Johns Hopkins Univ. Press, 2000), 102–7; John M. Carroll, *Red Grange and the Rise of Modern Football* (Urbana: Univ. of Illinois Press, 1999), 28–31.

14. WS, 240–41; interview with Harold Kiviat, Oct. 9, 1995; *NYT*, Jan. 26, 1908; James E. Sullivan, "Public Schools Athletic League Track," in *An Athletic Primer: Spalding's Athletic Library, 1910*, edited by James E. Sullivan (New York: American Sports, 1907), 73, 75.

15. CF, 3; OH, 20, 49; WS, 240–41; *Curtis High School Monthly* (Dec. 1907), 174–75.

16. WS, 243; *NYT*, Jan. 26, 1908; *Curtis High School Monthly* (Feb. 1908), 13–14; "Alumni Notes," *Curtis High School Monthly* (Mar. 1910), page not known; obituary of John Drebinger, *NYT*, Oct. 24, 1979; telephone conversation with John Warner Drebinger, Los Angeles, Aug. 9, 1998; "On the Sport Trail with Hal J. Squier," n.d.

17. *NYT*, Feb. 15, 16, 1908; *Curtis High School Monthly* (Mar. 1908), 40.

18. OH, 23–27; *Curtis High School Monthly* (Mar. 1908), 41; *NYT*, Mar. 22, 1908; Arthur D. Hittner, *Honus Wagner* (Jefferson, N.C.: McFarland, 1996), 3–9.

19. OH, 23–27; WS, 241; *Curtis High School Monthly* (May 1908), 95–97. For Elmer Ripley, see Robin Jonathan Deutsch, ed., *Basketball Hall of Fame Class of 1996 Yearbook*

(Springfield, Mass.: Basketball Hall of Fame, 1996); David S. Neft and Richard M. Cohen, *The Sports Encyclopedia: Pro Basketball*, 3rd ed. (New York: St. Martin's, 1990), 10–14.

20. OH, 23–27; WS, 241; Carlson and Fogarty, *Tales of Gold*, 6; SIJHS; *Curtis High School Monthly* (May 1908), 98 and track team photo; "On the Sport Trail with Hal J. Squier," n.d.; "On the Sport Trail with Hal J. Squier," *SIA*, July 25, 1952; Jay Price, "On Track to Immortality," *SIA*, June 9, 1992; Oriard, *Dreaming of Heroes*, 27–29. For Blanchard Preble, see "Alumni Notes," *Curtis High School Monthly* (Mar. 1910); *The Winged Foot* (Aug. 1911), 46; "Blanchard Mussey Preble," 1912 Harvard class album, HUD 312.04, Box 1666, Harvard Univ. Archives, Cambridge, Mass.

21. OH, 23–27, WS, 246–47; *Curtis High School Monthly* (May 1908), 98, (June 1908), 165, and track team photo; *NYT*, May 3, 24, 1908; John Drebinger ("Ten Flat"), "Staten Island's Great Miler Appears in Best of Condition," *SIA*, Feb. 9, 1923. Kiviat's medals for these races are on display at Curtis.

22. OH, 48–49; "Tommy Lennon, S.I.'s Crack Sprinter, Goes to Pennsy," *Richmond County Advance*, July 3, 1914; Sheppard, "Spiked Shoes," part 8, 91; "Elias Bernstein," in Leng and Davis, 4:429–30; George H. Douglas, *All Aboard! The Railroad in American Life* (New York: Paragon House, 1992), 275–78.

23. *NYT*, Aug. 30, 1908; Sheppard, "Spiked Shoes," part 7, 49–53; Alan H. Feiler, "The Durability of the Long Distance Runner," *Baltimore Jewish Times*, Dec. 29, 1989. For the London Olympiad, see Bill Mallon and Ian Buchanan, *The 1908 Olympic Games* (Jefferson, N.C.: McFarland, 2000).

24. "Kiviat Abel," Permanent Scholarship Record; WS, 244; Hodgen, "A High School in Perspective," 170–71.

25. The idea of the teenage years as a separate stage of human development was at this moment becoming understood by the public, in large part because of G. Stanley Hall's landmark study *Adolescence*, vols. 1 and 2 (New York: D. Appleton, 1904).

26. OH, 3, 17–18, 35–36; WS, 238–39, 242–43; interviews with Harold Kiviat, Oct. 9, 1995, Jan. 28, 1996; interviews with Esther Kiviat, Mar. 30, July 14, 1997; *SIA*, Aug. 14, 1964; *NYT*, June 16, 1987; Feiginoff, 26–27.

27. Interviews with Harold Kiviat, Oct. 9, 1995, Jan. 28, 1996; interview with Esther Kiviat, Mar. 30, 1996; obituaries of Zelda Kiviat, *NYT*, Mar. 6, 7, 1946; Litsky, "Honors for Oldest Olympian."

28. OH, 21–22; WS, 238, 248; interviews with Harold Kiviat, Oct. 9, 1995, Jan. 28, 1996; interview with Esther Kiviat, Mar. 30, 1997; interview with Lucy Price, July 13, 1996; untitled poem by Anne Kiviat (1969), SK; Howard Valentine, "Kiviat Needs a Long Rest, Says Robertson," *NYG*, July 10, 1913.

29. OH, 45, 50; WS, 241, 245–46; SIJHS; interviews with Harold Kiviat, Oct. 9, 1995, Jan. 28, 1996; Steven Heller, *The Swastika: Symbol beyond Redemption?* (New York: Allworth Press, 2000), 81–84, 90, 96. See Howe, *World of Our Fathers*, 256–63, for a valuable interpretation of the experience of second-generation adolescent Jews on the

Lower East Side that bears directly on Kiviat's experience in the remote outer borough of Staten Island.

30. *NYH*, Jan. 24, 1909; *High School Recorder* (Brooklyn Boys High) 19, no. 5 (1909), 27.

31. *NYT*, Dec. 6, 1908; *NYH*, Jan. 24, 1909; *Curtis High School Monthly* (Feb. 1909), 350; *High School Recorder* 19, no. 5 (1909), 27–28; *The Red and Black: A Year Book of the Brooklyn Boys High* 6 (June 1909), 107; "Oliver W. DeGruchy," *The Winged Foot* ([month not known] 1914), 22.

32. *Curtis High School Monthly* (Mar. 1909), 16.

33. "Kiviat Abel," Permanent Scholarship Record; Hodgen, "A High School in Perspective," 150–51, 161; Krug, *Shaping of the American High School*, 284–88.

34. OH, 26; WS, 241; CF, 3; *Curtis High School Monthly* (Mar. 1909), 16; *Year Book of the Curtis High School Published by the Class of 1909*.

35. *Curtis High School Monthly* (Apr. 1909), 17; "Track," in *Year Book of the Curtis High School 1909*.

36. OH, 29; *Curtis High School Monthly* (May 1909), 15–16; *Richmond County Advance*, May 1, 1909. Telephone conversation with John Warner Drebinger, Los Angeles, Aug. 7, 1998, during which John Drebinger's eighty-year-old son, himself a track star in the 1930s, reported the "Ten Flat" nickname.

37. *NYT*, May 2, 1909; *Curtis High School Monthly* (May 1909), 17.

38. OH, 37–38; *Curtis High School Monthly* (Mar. 1909), 16; "Baseball," in *Year Book of the Curtis High School 1909*; *NYH*, May 7, 16, 1909; *New York Evening Journal*, June 2, 1909; *New York Evening World*, June 12, 1909; *NYT*, June 20, 1909.

39. WS, 242; *New York Evening Journal*, May 29, June 2, 3, 1909; *NYH*, May 30, 1909; *NYT*, May 30, 1909; *Curtis High School Monthly* (Oct. 1909), 18–19; *High School Recorder* 19, no. 8 (May–June 1909), 31; obituary of Cedric Major, *NYT*, Apr. 29, 1961.

40. The PSAL track meet and the nearly concurrent selection to the *New York Evening World*'s "All–New York" baseball team were a constant in Kiviat's later interviews with the media and historians. He specifically linked them, telling interviewers that the all-city team was announced on the same day as the track meet, May 29. In fact, the *Evening World* published its selection on Saturday, June 12. The two events' psychological significance can be seen in OH, 28–29; WS, 242; and CF, 4.

41. OH, 27–28; WS, 242, 249; "Ed Hughes' Column," *Brooklyn Eagle*, Feb. 22, 1935. Sportswriter Howard Valentine quoted Kiviat's letter to David Keane in *NYG*, Apr. 1, 1912. Valentine, a medalist in the 1904 St. Louis Olympics, had an insider's knowledge of the New York track clubs, so it is probable that his version of how Kiviat joined the I-AAC was accurate.

3. THE PHENOM OF CELTIC PARK

1. For descriptions, photographs, and a map of Celtic Park and its environs, see SIJHS; OH, 47; Sheppard, "Spiked Shoes," part 4, 1–2; *New York Daily Tribune*, June 19, 1910;

Sullivan, "Public Schoools Athletic League Track," 73; *Belcher Hyde Map of Long Island City* (1903). For John Drebinger's brief career with the I-AAC, see *NYH, NYDT,* July 4, 1909. For descriptions of travel to Queens before the opening of the Fifty-ninth Street Bridge, see Vincent F. Seyfried and William Asadorian, *Old Queens, New York, in Early Photographs* (New York: Dover, 1991), 44, and Marion R. Casey, "From the East Side to the Seaside," in *The New York Irish,* edited by Ronald H. Bayor and Timothy J. Meagher (Baltimore: Johns Hopkins Univ. Press, 1996), 413. By the fall of 1909, Kiviat cut his travel time to Celtic Park by taking the trolley over the newly opened Queensboro Bridge. For the bridge's impact on Queens and the city, see *New York Evening Journal,* June 12, 1909; *NYH,* Sept. 18, 1909. For Laurel Hill, see "History of the Parish of St. Teresa of the Child Jesus, Woodside, New York," in *Solemn Dedication of the New Church, Oct. 26, 1942* (Woodside, N.Y.: n.p., 1942), 16–17, at the Archives Diocese of Brooklyn.

2. *NYH, NYDT,* July 11, 1909; Sheppard, "Spiked Shoes," part 3, 7, part 4, 4; "Travers Island: The Country Home of the N.Y.A.C.," *The Winged Foot* (June 1911): 7–10, 14; J. Willis and R. Wettan, "Social Stratification in New York City Athletic Clubs, 1865–1915," *Journal of Sport History* 3, no. 1 (1976): 45–63; Jesse Abramson, "Clubs in Their Greatest Glory," in the AAU National Track & Field Championships program, June 19 and 20, 1942; Steven A. Riess, *City Games: The Evolution of American Urban Society and the Rise of Sports* (Urbana: Univ. of Illinois Press, 1991), 57–58, 91; Melvin L. Adelman, "Sports," in Jackson, 1103–4; Jarvis, *From Vision to Victory,* 14; Kenneth Silverman, *Houdini!!! The Career of Ehrich Weiss* (New York: HarperCollins, 1996), 7–8.

3. For a suggestive parallel to the role of the public schools in an age of reform, see Lawrence A. Cremin, *The Transformation of the School: Progressivism in American Education, 1876–1957* (New York: Alfred A. Knopf, 1961), 85.

4. See *New York American,* Jan. 8, 1928, LR, for a physical description of Robertson. For successive generations of athletes' first encounters with Robertson, see Earl Eby, "There Was but One Robby . . . and Pennsylvania Will Not Forget Him," in *Franklin Field Illustrated—1953 Relay Program,* UP; Jean Shiley in Doris H. Pieroth, *Their Day in the Sun* (Seattle: Univ. of Washington Press, 1996), 10; conversations with author's uncle, Albert Green (Greenberg), a Penn middle-distance runner (1936). The athletes' impressions of Robertson were virtually identical.

5. *New York World,* Jan. 31, 1926, LR; *New York American,* Jan. 8, 1928, LR; *Philadelphia Bulletin,* July 30, 1936, UP; *Pennsylvania Bulletin,* Apr. 18, 1945, UP; *NYT,* July 8, 1947, UP; *Philadelphia Evening Bulletin,* Jan. 23, 1951, UP. For a contemporary's approach, see Keene Fitzpatrick, "How to Train for the Distance Run," in *The Book of Athletics,* edited by Paul Withington (Boston: Lothrop, Lee and Shepard, 1914), 177–88.

6. H. V. Valentine, "He'll Write on Olympic Games for the Globe," *NYG,* n.d. (1920), LR; *NYT,* July 8, 1947, UP; Hal Bateman, comp., *America's Best* (Indianapolis, Ind.: Press Information Department, The Athletics Congress, 1988), 75.

7. Charles W. Paddock, "Maker of Olympic Champions," *New York Herald Tribune,* June 14, 1931, LR; H. V. Valentine article, *NYG,* Aug. 3, 1909, LR; *New York World,* Jan. 31,

1926, LR; "Lawson Robertson," *New York American*, Jan. 8, 1928, LR; C. Peterman article, unidentified news clip, n.d. (ca. 1933), LR; *Spalding's Official Athletic Almanac 1909* (New York: American Sports, 1909).

8. *New York Evening World,* June 22, 1909.

9. Robertson's comments on training (italics added) are from the following sources: H. V. Valentine, *NYG,* Aug. 3, 1909, LR; Lawson Robertson, "Half-Mile Running" and "Distance Running," in *College Athletics,* edited by Lawson Robertson (New York: American Sports, 1923), 91 and 95–99; Lawson Robertson, *Modern Athletics* (New York: Harper, 1932), 152–58; Lawson Robertson, *How Champions Are Made* (N.p.: n.p., 1933), 34. That these ideas had a powerful impact on Kiviat is clear from OH, WS, and sundry news articles as late as the 1980s.

10. H. V. Valentine articles, *NYG,* May 26, Aug. 3, 1909, LR; Sprinter, "Why Did They Let Robbie Go?" unidentified news clip (1920), LR.

11. WS, 242, 249; journal of William Krapowicz, an I-AAC weight thrower, May 1909 to Apr. 19, 1910, in possession of his nephew, David Sokosh of New York.

12. *NYT,* Jan. 24, 1951, May 17, 18, 1954; L. P. Curtis, Jr., *Apes and Angels: The Irishman in Victorian Caricature,* rev. ed. (Washington, D.C.: Smithsonian Institution Press, 1997), 58–67, 105–8, and passim.

13. Sheppard, "Spiked Shoes," part 4, 5–18; *NYT,* Sept. 22, 1908; David Wallechinsky, *The Complete Book of the Olympics,* new ed. (New York: Penguin Books, 1988).

14. The untold story of the nineteenth-century precursor of the I-AAC has to be pieced together from contemporary newspapers. See, for example, *NYH,* June 24, 1879, May 17, 1882; *NYT,* Sept. 23, 26, 1880, June 26, 1881; Bill Mallon and Ian Buchanan, *The United States' National Championships in Track & Field Athletics, 1876–1985* (Indianapolis, Ind.: Press Information Department, The Athletics Congress/USA, 1985) 215; Glen McMicken, ed., *1997 USA Track & Field Media Guide* (Indianapolis, Ind.: USA Track & Field, 1997), 109–10. For Boston's Irish-American Athletic Club, see Stephen Hardy, *How Boston Played: Sport, Recreation, and Community, 1865–1915* (Boston: Northeastern University Press, 1982), 137–38. For the GAA, see Pat Davin's memoir, *Recollections of a Veteran Irish Athlete* (Dublin: Juverna Press, 1938), 20–34; W. F. Mandle, *The Gaelic Athletic Association and Irish National Politics, 1884–1924* (London: Christopher Helm, 1987), 71–72; Marcus De Burca, *The GAA: A History* (Dublin: Cumann Luthchleas Gael, 1980), 43–45.

15. Ed Van Every article, *New York Evening World,* Feb. 12, 1927; *NYT,* June 28, 1931, secs. 11 and 12, 10; obituary of P. J. Conway, *NYT,* Jan. 17, 1932. Background provided in Riess, *City Games,* 109, 199–201, 208–9, 216; and John T. Ridge, "Irish County Societies in New York, 1880–1914," in Bayor and Meagher, 290.

16. Peter Lovesey, *The Official Centenary History of the Amateur Athletic Association* (Enfield, U.K.: Guinness World Records, 1979), 48.

17. "Prinstein, Meyer," in *Quest for Gold: The Encyclopedia of American Olympians,* edited by Bill Mallon and Ian Buchanan (New York: Leisure Press, 1984), 336; Jay Cox, "The

Original Orange Olympic Champ," *Syracuse University Magazine* (summer 2000): 44–45; Joseph Siegman, *The International Jewish Sports Hall of Fame* (New York: SPI Books/Shapolsky, 1992), 174–75; McMicken, *Track & Field Media Guide,* 114, 116.

18. Ernest W. Hjertberg to Kristien Hellstrom, secretary, Swedish Olympic Committee, May 26, 1910, Stockholms Olympiaden 1912, O II a, 1, 2, 3, Riksarkivet, Stockholm, Sweden; S. S. Abrahams, "Introduction," in E. W. Hjertberg, *Athletics in Theory and Practice* (New York: G. P. Putnam's Sons, 1914), v–vii; E. W. Hjertberg, "A Veteran Looks Back," *The Amateur Athlete* (June 1942), 7; *NYT,* Apr. 8, 1947; Sheppard, "Spiked Shoes," part 3, 6. On the rise of the professional expert to serve the new bureaucratic society, see Robert Wiebe, *The Search for Order* (New York: Hill and Wang, 1967), 173–75; Mrozek, *Sport and American Mentality,* 73–81, 101–2, emphasizes the emergence of the professional coach.

19. Noel Carroll, *Sport in Ireland* (Dublin: Department of Foreign Affairs, 1979), 43; Mike Cronin, *Sport and Nationalism in Ireland* (Dublin: Four Courts Press, 1999), chap. 4. For Martin Sheridan, see *NYT,* Jan. 27, 1909, May 1, 1910, Mar. 28, 31, 1918; Sheppard, "Spiked Shoes," part 4, 12–13; "Ed Hughes' Column," *Brooklyn Eagle,* Feb. 22, 1935; Det. Mark D. Warren, "Memorabilia: Martin Sheridan Olympic Hero—Again, Again and Again!" *Spring 3100* (May–June 1994), 9; Bill Mallon, "Sheridan, Martin Joseph," in *American National Biography* (New York: Oxford Univ. Press, 1999), 19:804–5; "Martin Sheridan," in Mallon and Buchanan, *Quest for Gold,* 343–44; Roberto Quercetani, *A World History of Track & Field Athletics, 1864–1964* (London: Oxford Univ. Press, 1964), 280–81. There has been debate among writers about Sheridan and Rose's respective roles in the flag incident at London. The definitive analysis is in Mallon and Buchanan, *The 1908 Olympic Games,* 314–19, which concludes that flag bearer Rose did not dip the flag to King Edward. See also John A. Lucas, "Rose, Ralph Waldo," in *American National Biography,* 18:866–67; Dyreson, *Making the American Team,* 136, 234 n. 37; and, especially, Arthur Daley column, *NYT,* Feb. 26, 1936, on Sheridan's role in the controversy.

20. Sheppard, "Spiked Shoes," part 1, 4–18, part 2, 6–16, part 3, 6–15; *NYT,* Dec. 17, 1905.

21. Norman Baker, "Amateurism: Whose Hegemony? The Origins of the Amateur Ethos in Nineteenth-Century English Society," unpublished paper presented at North American Society for Sport History Conference, Columbus, Ohio, May 2003; Lovesey, *The Official Centenary History,* 29–30. For the transfer of the idea to America, see Pope, *Patriotic Games,* 18–34; John Cumming, *Runners and Walkers* (Chicago: Regnery Gateway, 1981), 129, 155–56; Robert Korsgaard, "A History of the Amateur Athletic Union of the United States," Ed.D diss., Teachers College, Columbia Univ., 1952, 242–73, 275; Ronald A. Smith, *Sports and Freedom* (New York: Oxford Univ. Press, 1988), 172–74.

22. Michelle Brattain, "Sullivan, James Edward," in *American National Biography,* 21:112–14; Arthur J. Daley, "Sullivan, James Edward," in *Dictionary of American Biography* (New York: C. Scribner's Sons, 1936), 9:191–92; Gustavus Tom Kirby, "AAU Reminiscences," *The Amateur Athlete* (Dec. 1938), 4, 24, 39; Peter Levine, *A. G. Spalding and the*

Rise of Baseball (New York: Oxford Univ. Press, 1985), 82–83, 86, 88, 95. See also *NYDT,* Nov. 16, 1909, for excerpts from Sullivan's address to the AAU annual meeting on the continuing problem of "misconduct" by amateur athletes.

23. Cumming, *Runners and Walkers,* 101–28, and Sears, 80–162, provide detailed accounts of the professional pedestrians. See Peter Lovesey, *The Kings of Distance: A Study of Five Great Runners* (London: Eyre and Spottiswoode, 1968), 64–65; and D. H. Potts, *Lon* (Mountain View, Calif.: Tafnews Press, 1993), 53–56, 135–63, for Lon Myers and Walter George. Potts quotes at length contemporaries' charges of professionalism against Myers in 1884, 88–95. See also Sheppard, "Spiked Shoes," part 4, 3, part 7, 51, and part 11, 98–99.

24. OH, 28; telephone conversation with Steven Wheeler, archivist, New York Stock Exchange, Dec. 11, 2006; Martin S. Fridson, *It Was a Very Good Year: Extraordinary Moments in Stock Market History* (New York: John Wiley, 1998), 1–28.

25. WS, 242, 244, 251–52; OH, 54; "Kiviat Is Training for the Mile Run," *Brooklyn Eagle,* July 22, 1909; *NYH,* Oct. 25, 1909, for a photograph of Kiviat in the crouch start before a race. For Robertson's comments on the "technique of the crouch start," see Robertson, *College Athletics,* 64–69. The technique was then only two decades old, with diverse claimants to its invention.

26. *NYH, NYDT, NYT,* July 4, 11, 1909.

27. *NYH, NYDT, NYT,* July 12, 1909.

28. *NYH,* July 18, 1909; Douglas, 312.

29. *NYT,* July 25, 1909; unidentified news clips, July 14, 24, 1909, HED; *Curtis High School Monthly* (Oct. 1909), 19. For a profile of John Moakley, "wizard of track," see Robert J. Kane, *Good Sports: A History of Cornell Athletics* (Ithaca, N.Y.: Cornell University, 1992), 9–11. For the career of Bill Bingham, who was later a prominent director of athletics at Harvard, see *Spalding's Official Athletic Almanac 1910* (New York: American Sports, 1910), 129; *Harvard Magazine* (Sept.–Oct. 1998), 37.

30. *NYG,* May 26, Aug. 3, 1909, LR; *NYH,* July 20, Aug. 2, 1909; Robertson, *Modern Athletics,* 47–48, 52–53; "Ed Hughes' Column," *Brooklyn Eagle,* Feb. 22, 1935.

31. *NYDT, NYH,* Aug. 2, 1909; *NYG,* May 26, Aug. 3, 1909, LR. On the Clan-na-Gael, see Lawrence J. McCaffrey, "Forging Forward and Looking Back," David Brundage, "'In Time of Peace, Prepare for War': Key Themes in the Social Thought of New York's Irish Nationalists, 1890–1916," and Chris McNickle, "When New York Was Irish and After," all in Bayor and Meagher, 223–26, 331–33, 349; *NYH,* July 19, 1909.

32. *NYDT,* Aug. 8, 1909; *The Eagle,* unidentified news clip, Aug. 7, 1909, New York Roadrunners Club Scrapbook; *New York Evening Journal,* Oct. 11, 1909; *Curtis High School Monthly* (Oct. 1909), 19; Russell Roberts and Rich Youmans, *Down the Jersey Shore* (New Brunswick, N.J.: Rutgers Univ. Press, 1994), 22–25, 34, 50, 105–7.

33. *NYDT,* Aug. 23, 1909.

34. *NYDT,* Sept. 26, 1909; "Athletic News and Notes," *New York Evening Journal,* Sept. 9, 23, Oct. 27, 1909. For a perceptive treatment of "the deeply embedded historic stereotype

of the inherently intelligent and crafty Jew" in an American context, see Joseph W. Bendersky, *The "Jewish Threat": Anti-Semitic Politics of the U.S. Army* (New York: Basic Books, 2000), 44–46.

35. *NYH*, Sept. 13, 1909; "Ed Hughes' Column," *Brooklyn Eagle*, Feb. 22, 1935.

36. OH, 54; Sheppard, "Spiked Shoes," part 4, 4–5; *NYDT*, Sept. 16, 20, 1909; *NYH*, Sept. 16, 1909; *Spalding's Official Athletic Almanac 1910*, 67, 95–97; Jarvis, *From Vision to Victory*, 19–21; Lucius Beebe and Charles Clegg, *The Trains We Rode* (New York: Promontory Press, 1990), 917.

37. *NYH*, Sept. 15, 19, 1909; *NYT, NYDT*, Sept. 19, 1909; *Curtis High School Monthly* (Oct., 1909), 19.

38. *NYT*, Sept. 26, 1909; *NYDT*, Sept. 26, Oct. 3, 1909; *NYH*, Oct. 3, 4, 1909. Stan Saplin reviews the early history of the U.S. indoor national championships in the chapter "Track & Field," in *Madison Square Garden*, edited by Zander Hollander (New York: Hawthorn Books, 1973), 129–33.

39. NB, 3; *NYT*, Oct. 5, 6, 1909; *NYH*, Oct. 5, 1909; *NYDT*, Oct. 6, 1909. Stanford White's Garden was the second one on the site. For an excellent brief history of the structure, see Joseph Durso, "The Four Gardens and How They Grew," in Hollander, 4–13, supplemented by Wally Donovan, *A History of Indoor Track & Field* (El Cajun, Calif.: Edward Jules, 1976), 9–10. See also Miriam Berman, *Madison Square: The Park and Its Celebrated Landmarks* (Salt Lake City: Gibbs Smith, 2001), 48. The hotel Kiviat referred to was undoubtedly the Madison Square, then the last hotel on the square.

40. *NYDT*, Oct. 3, 1909; *NYT*, Nov. 1, 1910; Earl Eby, "The Sports Parade," *Philadelphia Evening Bulletin*, Jan. 24, 1942, UP; Donovan, *Indoor Track & Field*, 41.

41. *NYDT, NYT, NYH*, Oct. 5, 6, 1909; McMicken, *Track & Field Media Guide*, 30–36; Sullivan, *An Athletic Primer*, 90–92.

42. For descriptions of the Celtic Park track, see CF, supplemental page; Mel Sheppard, "Third Decade—1908 to 1918," *The Amateur Athlete* (Dec. 1938), 41. For the four-mile relay race, see *NYH, NYT, NYDT*, Oct. 11, 1909. The I-AAC record lasted until 1913; see *Meadowbrook Club Year Book* (Philadelphia: n.p., 1919), 139.

43. No Wanamaker's personnel records survive from that era; telephone conversation with Laura Beardsley, Historical Society of Pennsylvania, June 17, 1998. For background on Wanamaker's, see Elaine Abelson, "Department Stores," and David B. Sicilia, "Wanamaker's," both in Jackson, 327–28, 1235; Wolfe, *New York*, 164–65; Leon Harris, *Merchant Princes* (New York: Viking, 1979), 379n.; Howe, *World of Our Fathers*, 166. David Nasaw, *Children of the City: At Work and at Play* (Garden City, N.Y.: Anchor, Doubleday, 1985), 1–5, has an excellent interpretation of the early-twentieth-century department stores and their impact on city dwellers.

44. WS, 242, 248, 252; OH, 33, 35–36. Jacob Messing's pharmacy was at 113 Broad Street, next door to the Kiviat home. See "Druggists," *The Standard Directory of Richmond Borough 1897–1898*, 338; *Richmond Borough Directory 1912*, Staten Island Museum, 38; interview with Dr. Patricia Halloran, Dec. 21, 1996.

45. OH, 43; interviews with Harold Kiviat, Oct. 9, 1995, Jan. 23, 1996.

46. WS, 243; Fred Schmertz, *The Wanamaker Millrose Story: History of the Wanamaker Millrose Athletic Association 1908–1967* (Yonkers, N.Y.: Millrose Athletic Association, 1967), 15, 17–19; Riess, *City Games,* 84–85; Stephen Hardy, "Adopted by All the Leading Clubs: Sporting Goods and the Shaping of Leisure," in *For Fun and Profit,* edited by Richard Butsch (Philadelphia: Temple University Press, 1990), 71–101.

47. WS, 244; OH, 37; "Kiviat Abel," Permanent Scholarship Record. On high school dropouts, see Maxwell, 84–95; Howe, *World of Our Fathers,* 277–78; Sherman Dorn, *Creating the Dropout: An Institutional and Social History of School Failure* (Westport, Conn.: Praeger, 1996), 28–34; Michael R. Olneck and Marvin Lazerson, "The Achievement of Immigrant Children: 1900–1930," *History of Education Quarterly* 14, no. 4 (1974): 453–82; Nancy Foner, *From Ellis Island to JFK* (New Haven, Conn.: Yale Univ. Press, 2000), 188–96, 279 n. 37.

48. OH, 31, 46; Sheppard, "Spiked Shoes," part 4, 9–11; Robert M. Fogelson, *America's Armories: Architecture, Society, and Public Order* (Cambridge, Mass.: Harvard Univ. Press, 1989), 7, 16, 36–37, 42–43, 79, 208–9, 213–15, 218; Pope, *Patriotic Games,* 121, 139–44.

49. OH, 31; *Harper's Weekly* (Apr. 28, 1894), 404; A. W. A. Pollock, "The 'National Guard': A Hint from the United States," *The Nineteenth Century* (Nov. 1909), 918; Pamela W. Hawkes, "Armories," in Jackson, 54; Fogelson, 83–117, 137–140. According to Fogelson, most late-nineteenth-century armories were built in wealthier and more remote neighborhoods to provide an attractive clublike setting for their regiments.

50. OH, 31; *NYT,* Mar. 22, 1908, Apr. 2, 1911. The building serves today as a shelter operated by the New York City Division of Homeless Services.

51. OH, 46; WS, 244; *NYT,* Nov. 21, 1897, Dec. 5, 1902; George Trevor, "Kiviat's Comeback," *Brooklyn Eagle,* Mar. 16, 1924; Fogelson, 92. For the development of the MAL, see Martin H. Glynn to Lindley M. Garrison, Sept. 24, 1913, RG 94, Office of the Adjutant General, Document File 188701–940, Box no. 1188, AGO Restricted, NA.

52. OH, 13–16; WS, 238–39; interviews with Harold Kiviat, Oct. 9, 1995, Jan. 28, 1996. A census enumerator placed the Kiviats at 156 Broad Street in April 1910. Abel Kiviat's final Curtis transcript still had his address as 101 Broad Street, so it is likely the family moved shortly before the winter season of 1909–10. On February 24, 2005, Richard Dickenson, the Staten Island/Richmond County Borough historian, faxed to the author copies of a 1930s photograph of 156 Broad Street and a property card. The house was demolished for an urban renewal project in 1962.

53. OH, 14; WS, 252.

54. *NYT,* Dec. 26, 1909.

4. "THE CHAMP" IN THE MELTING POT

1. For portraits of the quasi-amateur world of nineteenth-century track, see Cumming, *Runners and Walkers,* 129–76, and Sears, 80–162. See also comments in Riess, *City Games,* 58.

2. *NYDT, NYT, NYH,* Feb. 6, 1910.

3. *NYH,* Mar. 13, 1910; "Hunter Mile for B.A.A. Games," unidentified news clip, n.d., HED; obituary of H. H. Baxter, *NYT,* Dec. 29, 1945; John A. Lucas, "The First Great International Track Meet," *Sports Illustrated* (Oct. 23, 1972): M6, M8.

4. *NYT,* Feb. 27, 1910; obituary of George Bonhag, *NYT,* Nov. 1, 1960; *Pittsburg Press,* July 1, 2, 1911; Howard Valentine, "George Bonhag Shatters Theory on Length of 'Athletic Life,'" *NYG,* Jan. 6, 1912; *Spalding's Official Athletic Almanac 1913* (New York: American Sports, 1913), 242; Donovan, *Indoor Track & Field,* 30; Jacques Carmelli, Steven J. McPeek, and Giorgio Malisani, *The Evolution of Indoor Records in Track & Field Athletics World-Europe-Italy* (Ferrara, Italy: Tipografia Artigiana, 1986), 62–63; "Bonhag, George V.," in Mallon and Buchanan, *Quest for Gold,* 275–76.

5. *NYT, NYH, Brooklyn Eagle,* Mar. 13, 1910; *Spalding's Official Athletic Almanac 1913,* 243.

6. *New York Herald Tribune,* Mar. 11, 1934; F. A. M. Webster, *Athletics of To-Day: History, Development, and Training* (London: F. Warne, 1929), 81–82; George Smith, *All Out for the Mile: A History of the Mile Race: 1864–1955* (London: Forbes Robertson, 1955), 190; Quercetani, *World History of Track & Field,* 99–100. See OH, 54, for Kiviat's idea of racing a fast final quarter-mile.

7. Donovan, *Indoor Track & Field,* 41; "Kiviat Close to '12 Win," *SIA,* Aug. 14, 1964.

8. *NYG,* Nov. 11, 1912.

9. *NYT,* May 31, June 19, Aug. 28, 1910; *NYH,* May 31, June 6, 19, 26, July 18, Aug. 1, 8, 1910; Sheppard, "Spiked Shoes," part 8, 90, 91, 93.

10. For Billy Paull, see the brief obituary by Grace Harwood Paull, "Wilton Colt Paull, Class of 1910," UP; *NYH,* July 12, Aug. 22, 1910. For the Ancient Order of Hibernians race, see *NYT,* Aug. 28, 1910; *NYH,* Aug. 22, 29, 1910; unidentified news clip, n.d., HED.

11. *NYDT,* Sept. 6, 1910; *NYT,* Sept. 6, 1910; *Progression of World Best Performances and IAAF Approved World Records* (Monaco: International Athletic Foundation, 1987), 165.

12. *New York Athletic Club Journal* (Oct. 1910): 14–16; "Official Athletic Almanac for 1911," in *Spalding's Athletic Library* (New York: American Sports, 1911), 95, 108, 110; Edward Bushnell, "Was Great Meet," unidentified news clip, June 1911, JPJ; Sheppard, "Spiked Shoes," part 8, 96.

13. *NYT,* Sept. 25, 1910; unidentified news clip, Sept., 1910, HED.

14. Sheppard, "Spiked Shoes," part 4, 14, and part 8, 96; *New York Athletic Club Journal* (Nov. 1910), 20; *New Orleans Times-Democrat,* Oct. 15, 16, 1910; unidentified new clip, Sept. 1910, HED.

15. *NYH,* July 20, 1910; *New Orleans Times-Democrat,* Oct. 11, 17, 1910; *New York Athletic Club Journal* (Nov. 1910), 23; Edward F. Haas, *Political Leadership in a Southern City: New Orleans in the Progressive Era, 1896–1902* (Rushton, La.: McGinty, 1988), 137–55.

16. *New Orleans Times-Democrat,* Oct. 11, 13, 1910; *New York Athletic Club Journal* (Nov. 1910): 20–22; Charles Dudley Warner, "Sui Generis," in *The World from Jackson Square: A New Orleans Reader,* edited by Etolia S. Basso (New York: Farrar, Straus, 1948), 309; John

R. Kemp, preface in *Martin Behrman of New Orleans: Memoirs of a City Boss,* edited by John R. Kemp (Baton Rouge: Louisiana State Univ. Press, 1977), xxiii; "The Chaotic 1910 Session of the General Assembly," in Kemp, 239–43; Dale A. Somers, *The Rise of Sports in New Orleans, 1850–1900* (Baton Rouge: Louisiana State Univ. Press, 1977), 289.

17. *New Orleans Times-Democrat,* Oct. 13, 15, 16, 17, 1910; *NYT,* Oct. 16, 1910; *NYAC Journal* (Nov. 1910): 20–23; *Spalding's Official Athletic Library,* 85; Sheppard, "Spiked Shoes," part 8, 97.

18. *NYT,* Dec. 25, 1910; *NYDT,* Jan. 9, 1911; Jesse Abramson, "Prodigies Face Task 'Breaking Through,'" in *American Track & Field Championships* (program), Randall's Island Stadium, New York, June 17 and 18, 1944, 40–41.

19. WS, 248, where Abel claimed mistakenly that the violinist was Sam Kiviat; interview with Berenice Kaufman, Hallandale, Fla., Jan. 26, 1996; interview with Harold Kiviat, Jan. 28, 1996.

20. Interview with Harold Kiviat, Jan. 28, 1996; *SIA,* May 8, 1976; *Richmond Borough Directory, 1912;* "Kiviette," *Questionnaire* (spring 1942): 1–2, Fashion and Costume Sketch Collection, designer files, Brooklyn Museum Libraries and Archives, Brooklyn, N.Y.; George Boardman, *The Oxford Companion to American Theater,* 2d ed. (New York: Oxford Univ. Press, 1992), 407; Bobbi Owen, *Costume Design on Broadway: Designers and Their Credits, 1915–1985* (Westport, Conn.: Greenwood Press, 1987), 88.

21. WS, 248; OH, 35–36, 106–7.

22. George V. Brown to Oscar Hedlund, Jan. 24, 1911, HED; unidentified 1911 news clip, n.d., HED.

23. OH, 101–2; *NYAC Journal* (Mar. 1911), 16; unidentified news clip, Feb. 19, 1911, HED. For background about the early years of the BAA, see Hal Higdon, *Boston: A Celebration of Running; Celebrating the 100th Anniversary of the Boston Athletic Association Marathon* (Emmaus, Pa.: Rodale Press, 1995), 22–23; Tom Derderian, *Boston Marathon* (Champaign: Human Kinetics, 1994), xviii–xix. For Mechanics' Hall, see Walter Muir Whitehall, *Boston: A Topographical History* (Cambridge, Mass.: Belknap Press of Harvard Univ. Press, 1959), 178–79; Walter H. Kilham, *Boston after Bulfinch* (Cambridge, Mass.: Harvard Univ. Press, 1946), 85.

24. Interview with Louise Mercer, Little Compton, R.I., July 17, 1997. See the 1910 profile by Hugh C. McGrath, "Oscar Hedlund, Brookline's Pride on the Track," *Boston Traveler,* n.d., HED; unidentified 1911 news clip, n.d., HED; *Spalding's Official Athletic Almanac 1913,* 243.

25. Slightly divergent accounts of the Hunter race are given in *New York Athletic Club Journal* (Mar. 1911), 17; *NYT,* Feb. 12, 1911; and unidentified news clip, Feb. 19, 1911, HED.

26. OH, 78; *New York Athletic Club Journal* (Feb. 1911): 20–21, (Mar. 1911): 8–10; *NYT,* Feb. 11–12, 14, 1911; *NYDT,* Feb. 12, 18–19, 1911; unidentified news clips dated Feb. 18–19, 1911, HED. Because Columbia University was unable to continue sponsorship of its

annual meet, Hugh Baxter was only too happy to transfer the race to his own NYAC's indoor games.

27. *NYDT,* Feb. 23, 25, 27, Mar. 15, 1911; see also *NYT,* Feb. 25, Mar. 12, 15, 19, 1911.

28. *NYT,* Apr. 2, 7, 23, 1911; *NYG,* May 1, 1911; unidentified 1911 news clip, n.d., HED; Carmelli, McPeek, and Malisani, *Evolution of Indoor Records,* 58; Stan Saplin to Giorgio Malisani, June 6, 1991, SS, in which Saplin shared his extensive research on Kiviat's indoor career and confirmed Kiviat's new world record in the 880.

29. Sheppard, "Spiked Shoes," part 4, 1–3.

30. CF, 7; OH, 40, 45; Sheppard, "Spiked Shoes," part 8, 87, 91; *NYT,* May 17, 18, 1954; *The Amateur Athlete* (June 1946), 8; NB, 7.

31. *Irish-American,* July 2, 1910; Howard Valentine, "M'Donald Most Worthy Rival of Great Ralph Rose," *NYG,* Mar. 20, 1912; *NYT,* May 17, 18, 1954; John A. Lucas, "McDonald, Babe," in *American National Biography,* 15:10–11; William R. Taylor, ed., *Inventing Times Square: Commerce and Culture at the Crossroads of the World* (New York: Russell Sage Foundation, 1991).

32. Valentine, "M'Donald"; Hjertberg, *Athletics in Theory and Practice,* 229–30, 238; *The Amateur Athlete* (June 1946), 8; *NYT,* May 18, 1954.

33. For Ryan, see Gerald Lawson, *World Record Breakers in Track & Field Athletics* (Champaign, Ill.: Human Kinetics, 1997), 263–64; "Ryan, Patrick James," in Mallon and Buchanan, *Quest for Gold,* 339. For McGrath, see *NYT,* Jan. 29, Feb. 2, 1941; Adam R. Hornbuckle, "McGrath, Matthew J.," in *American National Biography,* 15:68; Det. Mark D. Warren, "Memorabilia: Matthew McGrath—The Olympic Legend Who Picked-Up Where Martin Sheridan Left Off," *Spring 3100* (July–Aug. 1994), 9; Quercetani, *World History of Track & Field,* 292–93. There is an excellent portrait of the "Whales," rich with anecdote, in Bob Considine and Fred G. Jarvis, *The First Hundred Years: A Portrait of the NYAC* (London: MacMillan, 1969), 99–104. Although these vivid tales of the weight throwers' masculine bravado were honestly observed and reported, at times the sources seem suspiciously predisposed to the old Paddy stereotypes discussed in Curtis's book *Apes and Angels,* especially 58–67.

34. On Riley, see OH, 40; *NYDT,* Jan. 9, 1911. On Rosenberger, see Howard Valentine, "Be It Known That 'Rosie' Is a Son of St. Patrick," *NYG,* Apr. 4, 1912; unidentified news clip, n.d., LR; *New York Evening World,* Feb. 12, 1927, LR.

35. Unidentified news clip, Sept. 25, 1911, LR; Edward R. Bushnell, "Lawson Robertson—An Olympic Landmark," *Pennsylvania Gazette,* Sept. 1947, UP; Lawson Robertson obituary, unidentified news clip, Jan. 23, 1951, UP; *NYT,* Jan. 24, 1951; Eby, "There Was but One Robby."

36. For the view that Robertson was a regressive influence on track & field, see, for example, Frank Zarnowski, *The Decathlon: A Colorful History of Track & Field's Most Challenging Event* (Champaign, Ill.: Human Kinetics, 1989), 166, supplemented by the

author's conversations with various track officials. Robertson's positive impact on his prewar charges was described in *NYDT*, July 10, Sept. 11, 1911; unidentified news clip, Sept. 25, 1911, LR.

37. Harold Abrahams, "Foreword" to Lovesey, *The Kings of Distance*, 10. See also Quercetani, *World History of Track & Field*, xviii; unidentified news clip, n.d. (1912), LR.

38. WS, 251–52; OH, 39.

39. Lawson, *World Record Breakers*, 263–64; "Ryan, Patrick James," 339; Art Morrow, "Maker of Champions," in *Official Program: Second Annual Track Meet*, Philadelphia Inquirer Charities, Inc., Convention Hall, Philadelphia, Jan. 25, 1946, 20–21, 30–32. Particularly useful for this section was Steven A. Riess, "Sports and Machine Politics in New York City, 1870–1920," in *Sport in America: From Wicked Amusement to National Obsession*, edited by David K. Wiggins, 163–84 (Champaign, Ill.: Human Kinetics, 1995).

40. WS, 250; OH, 33.

41. *Irish-American*, June 10, 1911; Judge Daniel F. Cohalan, "The Irishman in New York," *The Metropolis* 1, no. 6 (Mar. 15, 1921): 5, 7; Barrett, "Americanization," 1001–2; Chris McNickle, "Overview: When New York Was Irish, and After," in Bayor and Meagher, 337–41; M. Gordon, *Assimilation in American Life*, 84–131; Howe, *World of Our Fathers*, 374–77.

42. For an excellent brief history of the I-AAC and its leadership, see *New York Evening World*, Feb. 12, 1927. For obituaries of Daniel F. Cohalan, see *NYT*, Nov. 13, 1946; of James J. Frawley, *NYT*, Sept. 2, 1926; of John Cloughen, who was the father of Olympic sprinter Bobby Cloughen, *NYT*, Dec. 28, 1911; and of Victor J. Dowling, *NYT*, Mar. 24, 1934. See also the *Irish-American*, 1909–15, for the central place of sport in New York Irish life. See also "Greeting," in I-AAC program, Madison Square Garden, Feb. 8, 1908, American Irish Historical Society Papers, New York.

43. OH, 84; WS, 250; interview with Harold Kiviat, Oct. 9, 1995. See also the *Irish World and Industrial Liberator*, Mar. 25, 1911, and 1910–11, passim; *Irish-American*, July 8, 1911, Mar. 16, June 8, 1912; Lawrence J. McCaffrey, "Overview: Forging Forward and Looking Back," in Bayor and Meagher, 229; Leonard Dinnerstein, *Antisemitism in America* (New York: Oxford Univ. Press, 1994), 69–72; Marion R. Casey, "Film and History Review," *New York Irish History Roundtable Newsletter* (fall 1993), at http://www.irishnyhistory.com/new.htm. For suggestive treatments of *The Melting Pot* and the silent film *Abie's Irish Rose* (1928), see Charles Musser, "Ethnicity, Role-Playing, and American Film Comedy: From Chinese Laundry Scene to Whoopee (1894–1930)," in *Unspeakable Images*, edited by Lester D. Friedman, 53–60 (Urbana: Univ. of Illinois Press, 1991).

44. WS, 249–50; *Irish-American*, Apr. 23, 30, 1910, July 8, 1911; *NYH*, May 29, 1910; Vincent Seyfried to author, Dec. 8, 1995, with documentation about I-AAC's officers, membership, and clubhouses. In "Class, Culture, and Immigrant Group Identity in the United States: The Case of Irish-American Ethnicity," in *Immigration Reconsidered: History, Sociology, and Politics*, edited by Virginia Yans-McLaughlin, 96–129 (New York:

Oxford Univ. Press, 1990), Kerby A. Miller analyzes the role of early-twentieth-century Irish American associations in the development of its members' middle-class values.

45. OH, 100–102; interview with Harold Kiviat, Oct. 9, 1995.

46. Kiviat claimed modestly "I don't know" when historian William Simons in 1985 asked him if Jewish track fans "identified" with him. See WS, 258; OH, 34; Sam Friedland to Joseph Siegman, n.d. (ca. 1979), "U.S. Committee Sports for Israel, Inc." File, SK; obituary of Samuel N. Friedland, *NYT*, Apr. 11, 1985; interviews with Harold Kiviat, Oct. 9, 1995, Jan. 28, 1996; interview with Esther Kiviat, Mar. 30, 1997; obituary of Zelda Kiviat, *NYT*, Mar. 7, 1946. For the story of the Rabbi Jacob Joseph funeral and Jewish-Irish tensions generally, see Dinnerstein, *Antisemitism in America*, 69–72.

47. *NYT*, May 22, 29, 30, and 31, 1911; *NYG*, May 18, 30, 1911; *Boston Herald*, June 24, 1911, HED; Grace Harwood Paull, "Wilton Colt Paull," UP; Quercetani, *World History of Track & Field*, 260–61.

48. "Tremendous Success of Meet," *Pittsburg Press*, July 2, 1911; Hittner, *Honus Wagner*, 180; Lawrence S. Ritter, *Lost Ballparks: A Celebration of Baseball's Legendary Fields* (New York: Viking Studio Books, 1992), 63–65.

49. Sheppard, "Spiked Shoes," part 10, 43–44; *Pittsburgh Post*, June 30, 1911.

50. *Pittsburg Press*, July 1, 1911; *Pittsburgh Post*, July 2, 1911; *NYDT*, July 2, 1911; *The Winged Foot* (Aug. 1911): 42–43.

51. *Pittsburg Press*, July 2, 1911; John J. Hallahan, "No Doubt Now about Kiviat," *Boston Herald*, June 24 [*sic*], 1911, HED; unidentified news clip, July 2, 1911, HED; Howard Valentine, "America's Olympic Athletes," unidentified news clip, May 19, 1912, HED; *Spalding's Official Athletic Almanac Nineteen Hundred and Twelve* (New York: American Sports, 1912), 51.

52. *NYDT*, July 2, 1911; *Pittsburg Press*, July 2, 1911; *Pittsburgh Post*, July 2, 1911; *NYG*, July 3, 1911.

53. *NYDT*, July 1, 2, 1911; Hallahan; "Tremendous Success of Meet," *Pittsburg Press*, July 2, 1911; and "Meet Greatest Ever Is Opinion of All at A.A.U. Contests," *Pittsburg Press*, July 2, 1911. For a more sober perspective, see *The Winged Foot* (Aug. 1911): 43–44.

54. *Irish-American*, July 8, 1911.

55. *NYG*, July 3, 1911; *Boston Globe*, July 5, 1911; *Boston Evening Transcript*, July 5, 1911. Late in life, Kiviat liked to show a seven-jewel Waltham pocket watch he claimed he won for this race in Somerville, Massachusetts. He actually won it for an earlier victory over Hedlund in Revere, Massachusetts. See "For Distinguished Service," *NYT*, June 14, 1982. See also unidentified news clip, n.d. (ca. spring 1911), HED; in "Kiviat Needs a Long Rest," Valentine reviewed this aspect of Kiviat's I-AAC career from its beginning.

56. Howard Valentine, "Jones versus Hedlund versus Kiviat," *NYG*, Apr. 5, 1912, HED.

57. H. V. Valentine, "J. P. Jones in Fine Shape for Big Race on Saturday," *NYG*, July 26, 1911; and Howard Valentine, "Many Cracks Are in St. Agnes A.C. Games," *NYG*, July 28, 1911.

58. Official world records would be listed for the first time only after the 1912 Olympics, with the founding of the IAAF. H. V. Valentine, "J. P. Jones May Compete Here Soon," *NYG*, May 30, 1911; Howard Valentine, "Another John Paul Jones Who Is Expected to Subdue the British," *NYG*, Apr. 9, 1912; Samuel A. Munford, "John Paul Jones—All-Round College Man," *Outing* 62, no. 6 (1913): 715–20; John Paul Jones to Gordon Cobbledick, May 20, 1963, JPJ; George Raborn, "Jones, Nurmi Compare to Ryun, Clarke," *Glendale News-Press*, July 1967, JPJ; Nelson and Quercetani, *The Milers*, 20. For Coach Moakley, see Kane, *Good Sports*, 9–11, 204–8, 389; *The Cornellian* (1913), 455.

59. *The Cornellian* (1913), 152, 515; "John Paul Jones," in *Personal Sketches—District of Columbia* (publication information unknown, fragment in the Jones Family Archive, Tucson, Ariz.), 233–34, JPJ; obituary of Ruth Jones, *Washington Times-Herald*, Sept. 18, 1940, JPJ; interview with Mary-Lou Palmer, Tucson, Ariz., Aug. 2, 2007; Robert J. Kane, "The Esteemed John Paul Jones '13," *Cornell Alumni News* (Apr. 1970), 30–31.

60. *NYG*, July 26, 1911; *NYDT*, July 30, 1911; *NYT*, July 30, 1911. For Washington Park, see Michael Benson, *Ballparks of North America* (Jefferson, N.C.: McFarland, 1989), 60–62; Lawrence S. Ritter, *East Side, West Side: Tales of New York Sporting Life, 1910–1960* (New York: Total Sports, 1998), 53–54; Peter C. Bjarkman, *The Dodgers* (New York: Gallery Books, 1990), 16.

61. *NYT*, July 30, 1911; *NYH*, July 30, 1911; H. V. Valentine, "Jones Toyed with the Local Mile Runners," *NYG*, July 31, 1911; Trevor, "Kiviat's Comeback."

62. *NYDT*, July 30, 1911; Valentine, "Jones versus Hedlund versus Kiviat"; H. V. Valentine articles, July 31, Aug. 1, 1911, *NYG*; "The Eccentric Firemen's Great Games," *Irish-American*, Aug. 5, 1911.

63. "Abel Kiviat," Mecca Cigarettes Series of Champion Athletes, 1911; Derderian, 46–47. For the context, see the introduction to Bert Randolph Sugar, ed., *Classic Boxing Cards: 56 Full-Color Reproductions from the Mecca Cigarette Sets, 1909–1910* (New York: Dover, 1988). Mecca allegedly paid Kiviat twenty-five dollars; see Don Holst and Marcia Popp, *American Men of Olympic Track & Field: Interviews with Athletes and Coaches* (Jefferson, N.C.: McFarland, 2005), 81.

64. For Alvah T. Meyer, see U.S. Bureau of the Census, *Thirteenth Census of the United States: 1910—Population, Borough of Manhattan, New York, NY* (Washington, D.C.: National Archives and Records Administration, 1910); WS, 247, 249, 257; *Boston Evening Transcript*, July 1, 1911; *NYT*, Aug. 25, 1914; "Alvah Meyer Ranks with Best Sprinters," *Anaconda Standard*, July 25, 1915; "Wills for Probate, Adele Carey Meyer," *NYT*, Dec. 4, 1937; obituary of Alvah T. Meyer, *Arizona Daily Star*, Dec. 20, 1939; Bernard Postal, Jess Silver, and Roy Silver, *Encyclopedia of Jews in Sports* (New York: Bloch, 1964), 474. *Hasia Diner's: The Second Migration, 1820–1880* (Baltimore: Johns Hopkins Univ. Press, 1992) offers a new and challenging interpretation of this era.

65. *NYT*, Sept. 3, 5, 1911; *NYDT*, Sept. 5, 1911.

66. *NYT*, Sept. 17, 24, 1911; *NYDT*, Sept. 16, 17, 1911; *Spalding's Official Athletic Almanac Nineteen Hundred and Twelve*, 81; *Irish-American*, Sept. 30, 1911; unidentified news clip, Sept. 24, 1911, HED; "Hedlund to Join Unicorn," unidentified news clip, Sept. 1911, HED.

67. *NYT*, Oct. 2, 4, 29, 1911; Valentine, "Jones versus Hedlund versus Kiviat"; Barrett, "Americanization," 1012.

5. OLYMPIC TRIALS

1. Interview with Hal Bateman, Indianapolis, Ind., Feb. 11, 2000. Tom McNab, *The Complete Book of Track & Field* (New York: Exeter Books, 1980), 14–15; Istvan Gyulai, ed., *IAAF—80 Years for Athletics* (London: International Association of Athletics Federations, 1992); "1912—A Step Back in Athletics Time," in *IAAF 90th Jubilee* (Lausanne, Switzerland: International Association of Athletics Federations, 2002); V. J. Casey, "Olympic Games Standardized," *The Winged Foot* (Sept. 1913), 27; Paul Withington, "Track Athletics," in Withington, 153–54.

2. *NYT*, Dec. 27, 1911; Carmelli, McPeek, and Malisani, *Evolution of Indoor Records*, 58; Stan Saplin to Giorgio Malisani, June 6, 1991, SS.

3. *NYT*, Dec. 28, 1911; Stan Saplin to Giorgio Malisani, June 6, 1991, SS; Carmelli, McPeek, and Malisani, *Evolution of Indoor Records*, 56; McMicken, *Track & Field Media Guide*, 30–31.

4. *NYT*, Jan. 18, 25, Feb. 12, 1912; WS, 250; Robertson, "Distance Running," 101, 103; Sheppard, "Spiked Shoes," part 10, 44.

5. Unidentified news clips, Feb. 1912, HED; "Hunter Mile," unidentified news clip, n.d., HED; "Hedlund Trains Runners' Emotions," *Boston Herald*, Jan. 17, 1932, HED.

6. "Hunter Mile"; "Varsity," unidentified column, 1912, HED; *NYG*, Feb. 15, 17, 1912.

7. *Spalding's Official Athletic Almanac 1913*, 95; *NYG*, Feb. 13, 16, 1912; Valentine, "Jones versus Hedlund versus Kiviat"; *NYT*, Feb. 12, 13, 1912; unidentified news clip, Feb. 17, 1912, HED. Kiviat's time for the three-quarter mile on a flat floor track was an unofficial indoor record of 3:08.9.

8. *NYT*, Feb. 17, 18, 1912; *NYG*, Feb. 19, 20, 1912; "Kiviat Wins Baxter," unidentified news clip, Feb. 17, 1912, HED; "Kiviat Beats Hedlund in the Baxter Mile," *Boston Herald*, Feb. 17, 1912, HED; Howard Valentine, "Staten Island Boy Sure to Be Prominent in Middle Distance Events at Sweden," *NYG*, Apr. 1, 1912, HED; Howard Valentine, "America's Olympic Athletes," *NYG*, May 19, 1912, HED.

9. Howard Valentine, "Catholic Relay Big Feature of Fordham's Meet," *NYG*, Feb. 24, 1912.

10. *Troy Times*, Feb. 23, 1912, HED; *Boston Evening Transcript*, Feb. 23, 1912; *The Winged Foot* (May 1912): 32–33; Brad Lewis, "The Oldest Olympian," *The Olympian* (July–

Aug. 1989), 13. For the state armory, see Rutherford Hayner, *Troy and Rensselaer County: A History* (New York: Lewis Historical, 1925), 671–72.

11. *Troy Times,* Feb. 23, 1912, HED; "Sporting Topics of the Moment," unidentified news clip, Feb. 20, 1912 [*sic*], HED; "Hedlund Really Broke World's Record at Troy," unidentified news clip, Feb. 19, 1912 [*sic*], HED; *NYT,* Mar. 6, 1912.

12. *NYT,* Oct. 23, Nov. 12, 28, 1912. See chapter 9 for the disposition of this and other allegations by Roscoe Campbell.

13. *NYG,* Mar. 11, 1912; Valentine, "Staten Island Boy"; *NYT,* Mar. 14, 1912.

14. *NYT,* Apr. 8, 23, 1912; Valentine, "Staten Island Boy"; Sprinter, "New York's Athletes to Begin Training for Olympic Games," unidentified news clip, spring 1912, LR.

15. OH, 45–47; WS, 245.

16. Howard Valentine, "Kiviat Declares Athletes Start Work Too Early," *NYG,* Apr. 23, 1912.

17. *NYT,* May 3, 4, 1912; see Robertson, "Distance Running," 95–97, for Lawson Robertson's ideas about early season training for the mile. For Julia Richman and Judah Magnes, see Howe, *World of Our Fathers,* 134–35, 197, 206, 275–76, 278; Arthur Hertzberg, *The Jews in America: Four Centuries of an Uneasy Encounter: A History* (New York: Simon and Schuster, 1989), 222–23. For detailed data and analysis of the Jewish children and their families in the blocks immediately surrounding the Seventh Ward Athletic Field, see Howe, *World of Our Fathers,* 141–44, and Herbert G. Gutman, appendix B, in *The Black Family in Slavery and Freedom, 1750–1925* (New York: Pantheon Books, 1976).

18. *NYT,* May 14, 1912.

19. *NYT,* May 15, 1912.

20. Valentine, "Staten Island Boy"; *NYT,* May 18, 19, 1912; James E. Sullivan, "Organization of the American Committee," in Sullivan, *Olympic Games, Stockholm 1912,* 29–35.

21. BG, 1; NB, 6; WS, 257; CF, 6. The standard biography of Thorpe is Robert W. Wheeler, *Jim Thorpe: World's Greatest Athlete* (Norman: Univ. of Oklahoma Press, 1979), 82–98. For an insightful interpretation, see Nicholas Lemann, "Jim Thorpe: The Natural," in *Sports Century,* edited by Michael MacCambridge, 58–70 (New York: Hyperion, 1999).

22. *NYT,* May 19, 21, 1912; Zarnowski, 99.

23. *Irish-American,* May 25, 1912. That spring, the New York and Boston sports pages debated regularly the respective merits of the top milers. See, for example, Valentine, "Staten Island Boy." For the statement that Jones "discontinued all training, excepting [*sic*] to spend his vacation as a master in a boy's camp," see Samuel A. Munsford, "John Paul Jones—All-Round College Man," *Outing* 62, no. 6 (Sept. 1913), 716–17. Nelson and Quercetani, *The Milers,* 12, accepted this statement. However, a report to the *New York Times* from Ithaca dated May 19, 1912, stated categorically: "It is well understood here that the crack runner will go with the team if he is chosen."

24. Quercetani, *World History of Track & Field,* 95–97 (italics in the original); Nelson and Quercetani, *The Milers,* 14; "1500 Metres," IAAF, at http://www.iaaf.org/sport/trackfield/19.html, accessed Oct. 29, 1998.

25. *NYT,* May 27, 28, 1912; *Irish-American,* June 1, 1912; "Start and Winner of 1,500 Meter Race at Celtic Park," unidentified news clip, May 26, 1912, HED; "Kiviat Close to '12 Win," *SIA,* Aug. 14, 1964; *Official IAAF World Records,* 63; Lawson, *World Record Breakers,* 247.

26. *NYT,* May 29, 1912.

27. The AAU meet netted more than four thousand dollars for the Olympic Committee, a not insubstantial sum then. *NYT,* June 2, 3, 1912; *Irish-American,* June 8, 1912; *The Winged Foot* (July 1912): 37.

28. WS, 253; *NYT,* June 7, 8, 1912; Hal J. Squier, "On the Sport Trail," *SIA,* July 25, 1952; Robert Harron, "Which Race Is Hardest?" *Princeton Athletic News* 8 (June 15, 1935): 28–29, for the friendship between Coaches Tom Keane and Lawson Robertson.

29. OH, 78; Robertson, "Distance Running," 98.

30. Trevor, "Kiviat's Comeback." For Norman Taber, see interview with Mary Honey, Rhinebeck, N.Y., July 14, 1997; "Taber of Brown Lands Second in World's Record 1500 Metres," *Providence Journal,* June 8, 1912, in Athletics Scrapbook, NT; "Scholarship and Athletics Do Mix," n.d., in Athletics Scrapbook, NT; "Studies of Present American Champions," unidentified article, 1915, in Athletics Scrapbook, NT; "Forty-Four Years of Brown Sports," *Providence Evening Bulletin,* Apr. 25, 1934, in Athletics Scrapbook, NT; untitled article in Athletics Scrapbook, NT; *NYT,* June 2, 9, 1912; *Spalding's Official Athletic Almanac 1913,* 244; G. Smith, *All Out for the Mile,* 28.

31. OH, 78; *NYT,* June 9, 1912; *New York Evening World,* June 10, 1912; *Providence Journal,* June 8, 1912, in Athletics Scrapbook, NT; unidentified news clip, June 9, 1912, HED; Trevor, "Kiviat's Comeback"; Jay Price, "Abe Kiviat: At 96 Years of Age, He's Olympic History," *SIA,* July 12, 1988. *Official IAAF World Records,* 54, lists Kiviat's 1,500 record and, below it, the proverbial asterisk of sports record books: "Kiviat continued to complete 1 mile in 4:15 3/5, a time which was not accepted by the IAAF as a world mile record—as John Paul Jones had run 4:15 2/5 on May 27, 1911 in Cambridge, Mass. (this too was not accepted)."

32. "Taber of Brown Lands Second in World's Record 1500 Metres," *Providence Journal,* June 8, 1912, in Athletics Scrapbook, NT; *NYT,* June 9, 1912; Robert Edgren column, *New York Evening World,* June 10, 1912; *Spalding's Official Athletic Almanac 1913,* 178–79; Sheppard, "Spiked Shoes," part 6, 6, part 10, 44–45.

33. *NYT,* June 9–10, 1912.

34. Lettergram from James E. Sullivan to Oscar Hedlund, June 10, 1912, HED; *Boston Globe,* June 11, 1912, HED; *NYT,* June 10–12, 1912; Sullivan, "The Steamship *Finland* Trip," 37; Postal, Silver, and Silver, *Encyclopedia of Jews in Sports,* 474.

35. The photograph of the team parade at League Park was in *The Amateur Athlete* (Dec. 1938), 24. See also the comments of Ralph Craig, "The Olympic Games of 1912," in

Withington, 233–34. For Mayor Gaynor, see Robert F. Wesser, "Gaynor, William J(ay)," in Jackson, 455. Olympian McClure's son, Walter McClure, Jr., coached Steve Prefontaine to national high school distance records in the 1960s; Kenny Moore, *Bowerman and the Men of Oregon: The Story of Oregon's Legendary Coach and Nike's Cofounder* (Emmaus, Pa.: Rodale, 2006), 325.

36. *NYT,* June 1, 1912; Howard Valentine, "Fast Little Hopi Indian Is Being Groomed for Marathon," *NYG,* Apr. 13, 1912, was an appreciative brief portrait of Louis Tewanima, replete with the accepted stereotypical language of the day.

37. *NYT,* June 1, 12, 1912; *The Winged Foot* (July 1912): 16.

38. OH, 51; John R. Case Diary, June 12–13, 1912, John R. Case Papers (Record Series 26/20/65), Univ. of Illinois Archives, Urbana; *NYT,* June 13, 1912.

6. GOLDEN STOCKHOLM DAYS

1. *NYT,* June 14, 1912. For Col. Thompson and "the idea of a sporting republic," see Dyreson, *Making the American Team,* 176–79. See also "Col. R. M. Thompson for President," *New York Athletic Club Journal* (Jan. 1911): 11–12; John A. Lucas, "Setting the Foundation and Governance of the American Olympic Association: The Efforts of Robert Means Thompson, 1911–1919 and 1922–1926," *Journal of Sport History* 29, no. 3 (2002): 457–68. See Noel-Baker, "V Stockholm 1912," 74–84, for the chapter title.

2. NB, 2; Taber, Olympic diary, June 13, 20, 1912, NT; M. P. Halpin, "How the Team Trained on the *Finland,*" in Sullivan, *Olympic Games, Stockholm 1912,* 237; Craig, "Olympic Games of 1912," 233–34.

3. *NYT,* June 15, 1912; Sheppard, "Spiked Shoes," part 10, 45–46; *The Winged Foot* (July 1912): 12–15; Andy Edelstein, "Kiviat, 87, Once Record Runner, Strong for Boycotting Moscow," *Jewish Telegraph Agency (JTA),* Jan. 27, 1980; "The Gentleman Recalls His Glory Days," *Ocean County Reporter,* Mar. 29, 1980, TL.

4. OH, 51; WS, 247; *NYT,* Feb. 27, 1912; R. Wheeler, *Jim Thorpe,* 100; Grace Thorpe, "The Original Natural," *Newsweek* (Oct. 25, 1999): 49. For the *Finland,* see *Steamers, Sailing Vessels, and Owners,* vol. 1 of *Lloyd's Register of Shipping, 1916–17* (London: Lloyd's Register of Shipping, 1916–17); *Dictionary of American Naval Fighting Ships* (reprint, Washington, D.C.: U.S. Navy Department, 1977), 2:406.

5. Sheppard, "Spiked Shoes," part 10, 46; James E. Sullivan, "Organization of the American Committee" and "The Steamship *Finland* Trip," in Sullivan, *Olympic Games Stockholm 1912,* 33–35 and 36–37; Lucas, "Setting the Foundation," 463; Jarvis, *From Vision to Victory,* 78–88.

6. Sullivan, "The Steamship *Finland* Trip," 37–41; Sheppard, "Spiked Shoes," part 10, 46; Jarvis, *From Vision to Victory,* 94.

7. OH, 41; WS, 254; Sullivan, "The Steamship *Finland* Trip," 37, 43.

8. WS, 255; NB, 7; OH, 57; Taber, Olympic diary, June 14, 1912; *NYT,* June 15, 1912; Sullivan, "The Steamship *Finland* Trip," 39.

9. OH, 41, 43; CF, 9; WS, 247; interview with Harold Kiviat, Jan. 28, 1996; Taber, Olympic diary, June 14, 1912. Interviews with Jean Drew Lightfoot and Howard P. Drew, Jr., Aug. 26, 2000, Washington, D.C., gathered the background information on Howard Drew. See also "Drew Stands Chance to Equal Art Duffy's Mark," unidentified news clip, Mar. 18, 1913, HDS; Howard P. Drew, "U.S. Men Owe Much to Instruction of Irishman," *Los Angeles Express,* June 8, 1914, HDS; Howard P. Drew, "Clean Living Responsible for Victories over Other Nations, Drew Asserts," unidentified 1914 news clip, n.d., HDS; "Howard Drew Recalls Old Days as Sprint Star Here," Mar. 11, 1947, unidentified news clip, Connecticut Valley Historical Museum, Springfield, Mass.; "The Whitney Building," *Western New England* (Jan. 1913): page unknown; *The Pnalka,* Springfield (Mass.) High School, 1912, 128; *Spalding's Official Athletic Almanac 1913,* 243; *The Winged Foot* (July 1912): 15; Arthur R. Ashe, Jr., *A Hard Road to Glory: A History of the African-American Athlete 1619–1918* (New York: Warner Books, 1988), 65; "Drew, Howard Porter," *American National Biography,* 6:909; *NYT,* Feb. 22, 1957; Robert Pariente, *La fabuleuse histoire de l'athletisme* (Paris: ODIL, 1976), 93. For the context, see Hasia Diner, *In the Almost Promised Land: American Jews and Blacks, 1915–1935* (Westport, Conn.: Greenwood Press, 1977), 28–88, 237–38.

10. CF, 4; Taber, Olympic diary, June 15, 1912; Case Diary, June 15, 1912; Sullivan, "The Steamship *Finland* Trip," 51. For Coach Murphy, see Michael C. Murphy, *Athletic Training* (New York: Charles Scribner's Sons, 1914); "Murphy, Michael Charles," in *American National Biography,* 16:141–42; Roberta J. Park, "Athletes and Their Training in Britain and America, 1800–1914," in *Sport and Exercise Science: Essays in the History of Sports Medicine,* edited by Jack W. Berryman and Roberta J. Park (Urbana: Univ. of Illinois Press, 1992), 93–95.

11. CF, 4; Drew, "U.S. Men Owe Much to Instruction of Irishman"; Craig, "Olympic Games of 1912," 235; Sullivan, "The Steamship *Finland* Trip," 37–43; Halpin, "How the Team Trained," 237, 239; Murphy, *Athletic Training,* 13–20.

12. OH, 45, 50; Taber, Olympic diary, June 15, 1912; Case Diary, June 15, 1912; Craig, "Olympic Games of 1912," 236.

13. WS, 254; Norman Taber, "The Fifth Olympiad," unpublished manuscript of an article (summer 1912), in Athletics Scrapbook, NT; unidentified news clip, July 16, 1912, NT; Taber, Olympic diary, June 16, 17, 21, 22, 1912; Case Diary, June 19, 20, 1912; Craig, "Olympic Games of 1912," 235; Sullivan, "The Steamship *Finland* Trip," 43; "Physical Directors Meet," *NYT,* Dec. 31, 1912.

14. OH, 42–43; NB, 17; R. Wheeler, *Jim Thorpe,* 100–102; Carlo D'Este, *Patton: A Genius for War* (New York: HarperCollins, 1995), 132.

15. NB, 4; WS, 255; CF, 6; unidentified news clip, July 16, 1912, in Athletics Scrapbook, NT.

16. OH, 57; Taber, Olympic diary, June 16, 18, 19, 20, 22, 1912; Case Diary, June 18, 21, 1912; Sullivan, "The Steamship *Finland* Trip," 43; James E. Sullivan, "The Fifth Olympiad," in Sullivan, *Olympic Games, Stockholm 1912*, 67–69; Howard Valentine, "Final of 1,500 Metre Run: Will Be a Thrilling Race," *NYG*, July 10, 1912; Arthur Daley, "Sports of the Times," *NYT*, Aug. 25, 1945; Robert J. Kane, "The Esteemed John Paul Jones '13," *Cornell Alumni News* (Apr. 1970): 30–31; Bud Greenspan, "A Day of Glory and Sadness," *Parade Magazine* (Apr. 16, 1989): 8; Jeff Benjamin, "In Memoriam: Abel Kiviat (1892–1991)," *Staten Island Athletic Club* (n.d.); Jarvis, *From Vision to Victory*, 94.

17. OH, 41; Taber, Olympic diary, June 16, 17, 19, 21, 22, 1912; Case Diary, June 19, 1912; *NYT*, June 25, 1912; Sullivan, "The Steamship *Finland* Trip," 39; R. Wheeler, *Jim Thorpe*, 102; Allen Guttmann, *The Games Must Go On: Avery Brundage and the Olympic Movement* (New York: Columbia Univ. Press, 1984), 24–25; Owen Johnson, *Stover at Yale* (New York: Frederick A. Stokes, 1912).

18. OH, 41; Taber, "The Fifth Olympiad"; Arthur Daley, "A True Olympian," *The Amateur Athlete* (June 1946): 8; Sullivan, "The Steamship *Finland* Trip," 39, and "How the Team Trained," 239; Considine and Jarvis, *First Hundred Years*, 99–104.

19. The Olympic teams of the period from 1900 to 1908 had only five minority members, Louis Tewanima and Frank Mt. Pleasant of Carlisle; Myer Prinstein; and George Poague of Wisconsin and John B. Taylor of Penn, both African Americans. Taber, Olympic diary, June 19, 22, 1912; NB, 8–10; Sullivan, "The Steamship *Finland* Trip," 45; Jarvis, *From Vision to Victory*, 107; Jim Nendel, "New Hawaiian Monarchy: The Media Representations of Duke Kahanamoku, 1911–1912," *Journal of Sport History* 31, no. 1 (2004): 33–52, for the negative stereotypes the swimmer regularly faced. For Dyreson's contention, see *Making the American Team*, 123–24.

20. Taber, Olympic diary, June 17, 1912; Riess, *City Games*, 29–30, 156–58.

21. WS, 254; Sheppard, "Spiked Shoes," part 10, 47–48; Taber, Olympic diary, June 23–26, 1912; Case Diary, June 23–26, 1912.

22. WS, 254; Sheppard, "Spiked Shoes," part 10, 47–48; Taber, Olympic diary, June 24–26, 1912; Case Diary, June 24–26, 1912.

23. Taber, Olympic diary, June 26–29, 1912; Case Diary, June 26–29, 1912; *NYT*, June 28, July 1, 1912; R. Wheeler, *Jim Thorpe*, 102. For Louis Madeira, see *NYT*, June 2, 1912; *The Record of the Class of 1914*, Univ. of Pennsylvania, 47, 291; *Philadelphia Record*, Mar. 21, 1943, UP; "Louis C. Madeira, III," *Pennsylvania Gazette*, June 1934, UP; obituary of Percy C. Madeira, *NYT*, Feb. 23, 1942; E. Digby Baltzell, *Philadelphia Gentlemen: The Making of a National Upper Class* (Glencoe, Ill.: Free Press, 1958), 118–20, 210–14, 297–300, 302, 307, 324–26, 347. For Frank J. Coyle, see *Spalding's Official Athletic Almanac 1913*, 242. For commentary about how class and ethnic tensions affected "the social realities" of the 1912 Olympians, see Dyreson, *Making the American Team*, 112–14, 125–26, 177–78. Eric Lott offers a subtle interpretation of the origins of the blackface phenomenon and its evolving cultural history in *Love and Theft: Blackface Minstrelsy and the American Working Class* (New

York: Oxford Univ. Press, 1993), 3–12, 249 n. 26. See also Michael Rogin, *Blackface, White Noise: Jewish Immigrants in the Hollywood Melting Pot* (Berkeley and Los Angeles: Univ. of California Press, 1996), 73–120. Rogin must be read with care. See Hasia Diner, "Trading Faces," *common quest* (summer 1997): 40–44, for a penetrating review of Rogin's "extravagant claims" based on his failure to locate the use of blackface by Jewish immigrants in an accurate historical context.

24. *NYT*, July 1, 1912; NB, 1; CF, 4, 6; Taber, Olympic diary, June 30, 1912; Case Diary, June 30, July 2, 1912; Craig, "Olympic Games of 1912," 237, 245; James E. Sullivan, "Receptions in Sweden," in Sullivan, *Olympic Games, Stockholm 1912*, 99–101; Bergvall, *The Fifth Olympiad*, 11, 41; Jarvis, *From Vision to Victory*, 94–95. For Ernie Hjertberg, see "The Stockholm Olympics 1912 Archives," boxes F II: 1–3, in the Riksarkivet, Stockholm.

25. NB, 6–7, 12; OH, 42–43; WS, 255; Sheppard, "Spiked Shoes," part 10, 48–49; Taber, Olympic diary, June 30, July 1, 1912; *NYT*, July 1, 4, 1912; Bergvall, *The Fifth Olympiad*, 349.

26. NB, 1; Trevor, "Kiviat's Comeback"; Taber, Olympic diary, June 30, July 1, 1912; Case Diary, July 1, 1912; Sheppard, "Spiked Shoes," part 10, 48–49; "Has Great Praise," unidentified 1912 news clip, n.d., HDS; *NYT*, Mar. 31, July 2, 1912; Bergvall, *The Fifth Olympiad*, 178–83, 218–19, 349; Claes Caldenby, Joran Lindvall, and Wilfried Wang, *Sweden: Twentieth Century Architecture* (Munich: Prestel, 1998), 29, 255, 379; Claes Britton, "Stockholm Stone City," *Stockholm New*, no. 12 (2002): 174–85.

27. Taber, Olympic diary, July 2–5, 1912; *NYT*, July 3, 4, 6, 1912; "From the Training Quarters," unidentified news clip, July 5, 1912, HED.

28. NB, 3; WS, 255–56; Taber, Olympic diary, July 4–5, 1912; Sheppard, "Spiked Shoes," part 10, 49; Sullivan, "The Fifth Olympiad," 67–69; unidentified 1912 news clip, n.d., TL; *NYT*, June 23, July 4, 6, 1912; *Richmond County Advance*, July 6, 1912.

29. NB, 1; Frank Litsky, "Politics Have Surpassed Idealism at the Olympics," *NYT*, May 13, 1984.

30. Taber, Olympic diary, July 4, 1912; Case Diary, July 4, 1912; *NYT*, July 2, 3, 1912; "From the Training Quarters," unidentified news clip, July 5, 1912, HED; Sullivan, "Receptions in Sweden," 103; A. N. S. Strode-Jackson, "Swedish Classic," in *Olympic Odyssey*, edited by Stan Tomlin (Croyden, U.K.: Modern Athlete, 1956), 17.

31. For the incident on the *Finland*, see OH, 41, 43, 44; NB, 10; Andy Edelstein, "Kiviat, 87, Once Record Runner, Strong for Boycotting Moscow," *JTA*, Jan. 27, 1980; CF, 7; WS, 247. Although Mark Dyreson interprets this incident as an example of Olympians "animated" by "the sporting republic's ideals," it was in reality merely another instance of the good-hearted Whales protecting their little I-AAC teammate. See Dyreson, *Making the American Team*, 160. For the context, see *NYT*, Feb. 26, May 10, 1912; Dinnerstein, *Antisemitism in America*, 58–77.

32. *America at the Olympics*; NB, 2; John Jeansonne, "Running Through the Past 90 Years," *Newsday*, June 26, 1982; Taber, Olympic diary, July 6, 1912; Case Diary, July 6, 1912;

NYT, July 6, 7, 1912; *Daily Telegraph* (London), July 8, 1912; *London Times,* July 8, 1912; Bergvall, *The Fifth Olympiad,* 184, 241–49, 307–11, 997. Definitive in its description of the opening ceremony as well as of many other aspects of the Stockholm Games is Bill Mallon and Ture Widlund, *The 1912 Olympic Games: Results for All Competitors in All Events, with Commentary* (Jefferson, N.C.: McFarland, 2002), 21. The richest interpretation of the Olympic rituals, with their origins located firmly in nineteenth-century European cultural history, is in John J. MacAloon, *This Great Symbol: Pierre de Coubertin and the Origins of the Modern Olympic Games* (Chicago: Univ. of Chicago Press, 1981), 136–38, 213–14, 270–71. The Olympic flag and oath did not debut until the 1920 games in Antwerp; see Nadjeda Lekarska, "Olympic Ceremonial," in Lord Killanin and Rodda, 157–59.

33. MacAloon, *This Great Symbol,* 20–21, 107, 164–65, 170–71, 188–89; John A. Lucas, *Future of the Olympic Games* (Champaign, Ill.: Human Kinetics, 1992), 8; John A. Lucas, *The Modern Olympic Games* (Cranbury, N.J.: A. S. Barnes, 1980), 14–44, 63, 74, 77–78; Allen Guttmann, *The Olympics: A History of the Modern Games* (Urbana: Univ. of Illinois Press, 1992), 1–9; David C. Young, *The Modern Olympics: A Struggle for Revival* (Baltimore: Johns Hopkins Univ. Press, 1996), 68–74.

34. D. C. Young, *The Modern Olympics,* 68–82, 100, 107, 168–70, and passim. Although the multilingual Young's close and perceptive reading of a wealth of newly discovered documents enabled him to identify the sources of Coubertin's ideas more accurately than earlier accounts, his interpretation is frequently polemical. MacAloon, Lucas, and Guttmann offer more dispassionate and balanced views of Olympic origins. See MacAloon, *This Great Symbol,* 138–53; Lucas, *Modern Olympic Games,* 28–73; Guttmann, *The Olympics,* 10–31.

35. Mallon and Widlund, *The 1912 Olympic Games,* 1–16, for the history of Swedish sport and the dynamic role of Victor Balck in the organization of this Olympiad. See also Bergvall, *The Fifth Olympiad,* 10–23, 51; Guttmann, *The Olympics,* 32; Edward S. Goldstein, "Sigfrid Edstrom," in *Historical Dictionary of the Modern Olympic Movement,* edited by John E. Findling and Kimberly D. Pelle (Westport, Conn.: Greenwood Press, 1996), 362–66.

36. Bergvall, *The Fifth Olympiad,* 79, 109–10, 185–86, 192, 311, 504–5, 555–56, and plates 116–17, 205–7, 214–17; NB, 10–11, 21; *America at the Olympics*; OH, 68; James E. Sullivan, "Introduction," in Sullivan, *Olympic Games, Stockholm 1912,* 13; Sullivan, "The Fifth Olympiad," 63; "Impressive Ceremony at the Stadion," unidentified news clip, in Athletics Scrapbook, NT.

37. Bergvall, *The Fifth Olympiad,* 350–52; *London Daily Telegraph,* July 8, 1912; *NYT,* July 7, 1912; Quercetani, *World History of Track & Field,* 7; interview with Jean Drew Lightfoot, Aug. 26, 2000. For other indications of Drew's feelings about Murphy, see "Has Great Praise"; Drew, "U.S. Men Owe Much to Instruction of Irishman." The surprise of the heats was the new Olympic record of 10.6 set by eighteen-year-old Don Lippincott of Penn, a late addition to the team. In 1913, the new IAAF recognized Lippincott's time as the first official world record for 100 meters.

38. OH, 43; "Has Great Praise"; Bergvall, *The Fifth Olympiad,* 352–53; *London Daily Telegraph,* July 8, 1912. Pariente has a photograph of Drew winning his opening heat with his bandaged leg clearly visible.

39. Bergvall, *The Fifth Olympiad,* 412–14; *NYT,* July 8, 1912; R. Wheeler, *Jim Thorpe,* 104–7.

40. NB, 7–8; WS, 247, 256; "Has Great Praise"; conversation with Ture Widlund, Stockholm, Aug. 1, 2002; Bergvall, *The Fifth Olympiad,* 327–28, 353–54, plates 122, 123; *NYT,* July 8, 1912; *London Daily Telegraph,* July 8, 1912; Pariente, 93; Maxwell Stiles, "The Greatest Sprinters," *Track & Field News* reprint (1959): 5.

41. NB, 8; Bergvall, *The Fifth Olympiad,* 368–71; *NYT,* July 9, 1912; John Kieran, *The Story of the Olympic Games* (Philadelphia: Lippincott, 1936), 78, 80–81; Ron Clarke and Norman Harris, *The Lonely Breed* (London: Pelham, 1967), 149–50; Lovesey, *The Kings of Distance,* 164; K. P. Silberg, *The Athletic Finn* (Hancock, Mich.: Suomi, 1927), 94–99; Quercetani, *World History of Track & Field,* 133–34. For a report on Kolehmainen's training regimen, see Howard Valentine in *NYG,* Feb. 18, 1913.

42. Mallon and Widlund, *The 1912 Olympic Games,* 73–74; Bergvall, *The Fifth Olympiad,* 50, 363; Sheppard, "Spiked Shoes," part 10, 49–50; *NYT,* July 9, 1912; Howard Valentine, "Meredith's Feat the Feature in the Stadium," *NYG,* July 9, 1912; Howard Valentine, "Still Talking about the Yankees' Victories at Stockholm," *NYG,* July 26, 1912 (italics added). Although Kiviat was entered in the heats of the 800, he admitted grudgingly that America "had enough men who were faster than me," causing him to focus on the 1,500. See OH, 66–67.

43. Taber had scratched out the original "could touch" and had written instead "was up to the standard of" in his hand-written text; see Taber, "The Fifth Olympiad," 14.

44. NB, 3, 19; Bergvall, *The Fifth Olympiad,* 364. In reconstructing the 1,500 trial heats and the final, I have been influenced by both the approach and the information in B. Gilmore, "Four Laps to Glory," 10–12. See also Nelson and Quercetani, *The Milers,* 21.

45. Taber, Olympic diary, July 9, 1912. For biographical detail about Baker, see D. J. Whittaker, *Fighter for Peace: Philip Noel-Baker 1889–1982* (York, U.K.: William Sessions, 1989), 7, 10–15; David Howell, "Baker, Philip John Noel-, Baron Noel-Baker (1889–1982)," in *Oxford Dictionary of National Biography,* edited by H. C. G. Matthew and Brian Harrison, 3:397–99 (Oxford: Oxford Univ. Press, 2004); obituary of Noel-Baker in the *London Times,* Oct. 9, 1982; Nelson and Quercetani, *The Milers,* 31; H. A. Meyer, ed., *Athletics by the Achilles Club* (London: J. M. Dent, 1951), v. On Baker's 1,500 heat, see G. Smith, *All Out for the Mile,* 26; Bergvall, *The Fifth Olympiad,* 364.

46. Conversations with Elizabeth Boardman, archivist, and Richard H. Laver, librarian, Brasenose College, Oxford, Nov. 20, 1996. For impressions of Jackson, see WS, 256; *Providence Journal,* Apr. 17, 1914, in Athletics Scrapbook, NT. For Jackson at Oxford, see *The Brazen Nose* (1973): 269–71; Arthur Daley, "Sports of the Times," *NYT,* Aug. 10, 1945; obituary of Jackson, *London Times,* Nov. 17, 1972; John Bryant, *3:59.4: The Quest to Break the 4 Minute*

Mile (London: Arrow, 2004), 38–50; Ian Buchanan, *British Olympians* (London: Guinness Books, 1991), 94–95. Peter Lovesey recounts the story of Clement Jackson, his athletic circle, and his approach to training in *The Official Centenary History*. For Arnold Jackson's running style, see Sullivan, "The Fifth Olympiad," 67–71; *Philadelphia Public Ledger*, Jan. 31, 1914, as quoted in G. Smith, *All Out for the Mile*, 27–28.

47. Strode-Jackson, "Swedish Classic," 16–18; *NYT*, July 11, 1912; *London Daily Telegraph*, July 9, 1912; Bergvall, *The Fifth Olympiad*, 364; Webster, *Athletics of To-Day*, 83; G. Smith, *All Out for the Mile*, 27–28; *The Brazen Nose* (1973), for the Brasenose College legend of "the fabulous Jacker."

48. Taber, Olympic diary, July 9, 1912; Taber, "The Fifth Olympiad," 14; John Paul Jones to Gordon Cobbledick, May 20, 1963, JPJ; Bergvall, *The Fifth Olympiad*, 364–65; *Spalding's Official Athletic Almanac 1913*, 197; Valentine, "Final of 1,500 Metre Run"; B. Gilmore, "Four Laps to Glory," 10; Jarvis, *From Vision to Victory*, 98; Nelson and Quercetani, *The Milers*, 22.

49. NB, 2; Taber, Olympic diary, July 10, 1912; Sheppard, "Spiked Shoes," part 10, 50–51; *NYT*, July 11, 1912.

50. NB, 3, 7; Bergvall, *The Fifth Olympiad*, 346; *NYT*, July 11, 1912; C. D. Fowler-Dixon, *Athletic News Agency*, July 11, 1912.

51. BG, 5; Valentine, "Final of 1,500 Metre Run"; Valentine, "Still Talking about the Yankees' Victories"; Bergvall, *The Fifth Olympiad*, 367–68. For superb accounts of the 5,000, see Clarke and Harris, *Lonely Breed*, 148–52, and especially Lovesey, *The Kings of Distance*, 92, 164–65, where he uses the phrase "metronomic tempo" to describe the almost identically even pace for the first and second halves of the race.

52. BG, 5; Noel-Baker, "V Stockholm 1912," 76–77.

53. NB, 8, 22; Taber, "The Fifth Olympiad," 2–3, 14; Sullivan, "The Fifth Olympiad," 69–71; Bergvall, *The Fifth Olympiad*, 109–10, 187–89, 192, 345–46; B. Gilmore, "Four Laps to Glory," 10.

54. Taber, Olympic diary, July 10, 1912; Bergvall, *The Fifth Olympiad*, 111, 365, plate 129; Sullivan, "The Fifth Olympiad," 69; B. Gilmore, "Four Laps to Glory," 11; Nelson and Quercetani, *The Milers*, 23.

55. Taber, "The Fifth Olympiad," 14; Taber, Olympic diary, July 10, 1912; Bergvall, *The Fifth Olympiad*, 365; Valentine, "Still Talking about the Yankees' Victories"; Nelson and Quercetani, *The Milers*, 23; B. Gilmore, "Four Laps to Glory," 11.

56. NB, 2; Taber, Olympic diary, July 10, 1912; Taber, "The Fifth Olympiad," 14; B. Gilmore, "Four Laps to Glory," 11; Nelson and Quercetani, *The Milers*, 23; Webster, *Athletics of To-Day*, 83.

57. NB, 2; OH, 68; Taber, Olympic diary, July 10, 1912; Taber, "The Fifth Olympiad," 14, NT; Sheppard, "Spiked Shoes," part 10, 50–51; B. Gilmore, "Four Laps to Glory," 11; Nelson and Quercetani, *The Milers*, 23; Webster, *Athletics of To-Day*, 365; G. Smith, *All Out for the Mile*, 26.

58. For the last lap, see Lawson Robertson, "Briton and Two Yankees Finish Tenth of a Second Apart in Thrilling Race," *New York Evening World,* July 10, 1912; Bergvall, *The Fifth Olympiad,* 366; Nelson and Quercetani, *The Milers,* 23; B. Gilmore, "Four Laps to Glory," 11. For Kiviat's perspective, see NB, 3; WS, 256; Carlson and Fogarty, *Tales of Gold,* 8. For Taber's viewpoint, see Taber, Olympic diary, July 10, 1912; Taber, "The Fifth Olympiad," 14; *Providence Journal,* Aug. 1, 1912, in Athletics Scrapbook, NT, in which Taber stated that he beat Kiviat to the finish line. Several American athletes did support Taber, including the hurdler John Case, who noted in his diary for July 10: "Jackson of England 1, Taber really 2, and Kiviat 3 in 1500m." For James E. Sullivan's initial reaction, see Francis [Frank Albertanti], "Kiviat Comes Back as the Whirlwind King," *NYEM,* Mar. 7, 1913, HDS.

59. *New York Evening World,* July 10, 1912; *Providence Journal,* July 30, Aug. 1, 1912, in Athletics Scrapbook, NT; B. Gilmore, "Four Laps to Glory," 11; Mallon and Widlund, *The 1912 Olympic Games,* 16 (italics added). The series of official photographs of the 1,500 finish appear to be lost, according to Olympic historian Ture Widlund, who has searched unsuccessfully for them in Swedish archives. Conversation with Ture Widlund, Stockholm, Aug. 1, 2002.

60. The most accurate results are in Mallon and Widlund, *The 1912 Olympic Games,* 78. See also Barry J. Hugman and Peter Arnold, *The Olympic Games: Complete Track & Field Results, 1896–1988* (New York: Facts on File, 1988), 59–66; Bergvall, *The Fifth Olympiad,* 343, 365–66; *New York Evening World,* July 10, 1912. Memories of the event endured: in their history of the mile, Nelson and Quercetani, *The Milers,* 21, call this particular competition "the greatest race ever run." And in a 2001 retrospective titled "[The Twentieth] Century's 100 Greatest Competitions" ranking all track & field events, Jeff Hollobaugh puts this race "Number 80;" see http://www.michtrack.org/century.htm.

61. Lawson Robertson told the story of Kiviat's handshake in the *New York Evening World,* July 10, 1912. Although Howard Valentine credited the sporting gesture to John Paul Jones in his *NYG* report of July 11, 1912, Robertson's version is the more compelling, given Kiviat's own detailed accounts of the incident. See, for example, NB, 9; OH, 58. The *New York Times*'s magazine of July 28, 1912, had a photograph of Philip Baker carrying Jackson off the field.

62. Valentine, "Still Talking about the Yankees' Victories"; Howard Valentine, "Week-End Meets Keep Track Athletes Busy," *NYG,* Aug. 17, 1912.

63. For Kiviat's reaction to his defeat, see OH, 68; BG, 3; NB, 15; William Gordon, "Olympic Memories," *Newark Star-Ledger,* Feb. 16, 1988; CF ("Additional Interview"). James E. Sullivan's appreciative comments about Kiviat were in *NYT,* July 11, 1912.

64. Valentine, "Still Talking about the Yankees' Victories."

65. OH, 58, 68; BG, 3; Litsky, "Honors for Oldest Olympian"; Mary Honey to Arthur Kiviat, Aug. 28, 1991, SS. Quotes from both William James and Kiviat can be found in Thomas Gilovich, Victoria Husted Medvec, and Scott F. Madey, "When Less Is More: Counterfactual

Thinking and Satisfaction among Olympic Medalists," *Journal of Personality and Social Psychology* 69 (1995): 603–10.

66. *New York Evening World,* July 10, 1912. For a sensitive treatment of "the most profound disappointment" of Olympic silver medalists, see Sebastion Coe with Nicholas Mason, *The Olympians: A Century of Gold* (London: Pavilion, 1996), 100–108.

67. Interview with Harold Kiviat, Oct. 9, 1995; OH, 58, 68.

68. Taber, Olympic diary, July 11, 12, 1912; Taber, "The Fifth Olympiad," 29.

69. For the 3,000 heats, see Bergvall, *The Fifth Olympiad,* 345, 376–77; Taber, Olympic diary, July 12, 1912; Taber, "The Fifth Olympiad," 29; "Australia and Germany Score in Swimming," unidentified news clip, July 13, 1912, in Athletics Scrapbook, NT; Howard Valentine, "Young's Disqualification Was an Unjust One," *NYG,* July 13, 1912, in Athletics Scrapbook, NT; "Invincible Finlander," *London Daily Telegraph,* July 13, 1912; *NYT,* July 13, 1912; *The Winged Foot* (Aug. 1912): 19; *IAAF World Records,* 80–81.

70. Bergvall, *The Fifth Olympiad,* 50, 87, 360; Tell Berna to Morris Bishop, Feb. 17, 1963, JPJ; Taber, "The Fifth Olympiad," 29; *London Times,* July 17, 1912; *NYT,* July 14, 1912.

71. For the 3,000 final, see Bergvall, *The Fifth Olympiad,* 160–61, 377–78, plates 16, 138–40; Mallon and Widlund, *The 1912 Olympic Games,* 95, assert that Kiviat and Louis Scott did not finish the team race. However, Tell Berna had a very different memory: "*If any of the five did not finish, that nation was disqualified.* . . . I finished first, and *since all the Americans survived,* and our score was the lowest, we won the event." Tell Berna to Morris Bishop, Feb. 17, 1963, JPJ (italics added). See also *NYT,* July 14, 1912; Taber, Olympic diary, July 13, 1912; Taber, "The Fifth Olympiad," 29; *Dagens Nyheter,* Stadion edition, July 13, 1912, with Norman Taber's handwritten notes on the places of the runners, lap by lap, in Athletics Scrapbook, NT; Photographs Scrapbook, NT.

72. OH, 40; NB, 14. For Daniel J. Ferris, secretary of the AAU from 1907 to 1927 and secretary-treasurer from 1927 to 1957, see his obituary in *NYT,* May 3, 1977; Schmertz, *Wanamaker Millrose Story,* 57. For the IOC's perspective on Kiviat's complaint, see Monique Berlioux to Stanley Saplin, June 15, 1982, SS.

73. OH, 68; BG, 3–4; NB, 3–4; *NYT,* July 15, 1912.

74. Bergvall, *The Fifth Olympiad,* 789; NB, 12–13; BG, 5; Craig, "Olympic Games of 1912," 247–49; Noel-Baker, "V Stockholm 1912," 43–44.

75. Sullivan, "The Fifth Olympiad," 83–89; no author (but probably Sullivan), "Base Ball at Stockholm, 1912," and a photograph of the Olympic baseball team at Stockholm captioned "Olympic Games at Stockholm, Sweden, 1912," in Sullivan, ed., *The Olympic Games, Stockholm 1912,* 198–99 and 210; Bergvall, *The Fifth Olympiad,* 823–25, plates 302–4. Pete Cava, "Baseball in the Olympics," *The National Pastime: A Review of Baseball History,* issue edited by Peter C. Bjarkman, no. 12 (1992): 2–8, has important information on the Stockholm games.

76. BG, 1–4; NB, 16; Bergvall, *The Fifth Olympiad,* 414–20; R. Wheeler, *Jim Thorpe,* 107–10; Wallechinsky, *Complete Book of the Olympics,* 116–17; Quercetani, *World History of Track & Field,* 316–17; Tim Crothers and John Garrity, *Greatest Athletes of the 20th Century* (New York: Sports Illustrated Books, 1999), 89. Stephen Jay Gould makes a powerful case for Thorpe in "The Athlete of the Century," *American Heritage* (Oct. 1998): 14–17.

77. Bergvall, *The Fifth Olympiad,* 784–85, plates 288–95; BG, 3; OH, 58; NB, 3–4; WS, 255; Taber, Olympic diary, July 15, 1912; *NYT,* July 16, 1912. The ceremony of awarding medals at the conclusion of individual Olympic events began in 1932. See Paul Zimmerman, "X Los Angeles 1932," in Lord Killanin and Rodda, 54.

78. Bud Greenspan, *America at the Olympics,* CBS-TV, 1984, television documentary.

79. R. Wheeler, *Jim Thorpe,* 110; *NYT,* July 16, 1912; see also Bettmann/CORBIS photograph BEO80123 entitled "American Athletes Posing at Olympics," Stockholm, 1912.

80. NB, 1, 21; BG, 4; *Olympic Games, Stockholm 1912,* 33–38, a pamphlet in the Royal Library, Stockholm; WS, 255; CF, 6; *NYT,* Mar. 31, 1912. Kiviat left no record of having any contact with Stockholm's small Jewish community, centered in the downtown Great Synagogue.

81. BG, 4–5; Taber, Olympic diary, July 16, 1912; Case Diary, July 16, 1912; Sullivan, "The Fifth Olympiad," 85–87; unknown author, "Baseball at Stockholm 1912," and photographs, in Sullivan, *Olympic Games, Stockholm 1912,* 199, 210, 212; *NYT,* July 17, 1912; Jerry Patch, "Abe Kiviat Came Close to Victory in 1912," *SIA,* Aug. 14, 1964; R. Wheeler, *Jim Thorpe,* 284; Cava, "Baseball in the Olympics," 4.

82. Mallon and Widlund, *The 1912 Olympic Games,* 382–83, on the role of Leopold Englund in creating the concept of the IAAF. See also Leif Nilsson, "1912–1932 Origins and the Earlier Years," in Gyulai, *IAAF,* 16, 18, 20; Quercetani, *World History of Track & Field,* xvi–xvii; Lawson, *World Record Breakers,* 21; McNab, *Complete Book of Track & Field,* 14–15; Edward S. Goldstein, "Sigfrid Edstrom," in *Historical Dictionary of the Olympic Movement,* edited by John E. Findling and Kimberly D. Pelle (Westport, Conn.: Greenwood Press, 1996), 362–66. Eighty-nine years after its formation, the IAAF voted to drop the word *amateur* from its name, while retaining the acronym. The name is now the "International Association of Athletics Federations."

83. Taber, Olympic diary, July 17, 1912; Craig; Sheppard, "Spiked Shoes," part 10, 52–59; Case Diary, July 18–Aug. 16, 1912; *NYH* (Paris ed.), July 23, 1912; Guttmann, *The Games Must Go On,* 28–29.

84. CF, 6; Kedem, "Russian Jews in 5672," *The American Hebrew and Jewish Messenger,* Sept. 13, 1912, 517–18; Henry L. Feingold, *Zion in America* (New York: Hippocrene Books, 1974), 244–48.

85. *The American Hebrew and Jewish Messenger,* July 26, 1912, 346.

86. CF, 6; WS, 257; *NYH* (Paris ed.), July 23, 1912; *Richmond County Advance,* Aug. 2, 1912. Richard Holt, *Sport and Society in Modern France* (Hamden, Conn.: Archon Books, 1981), 5, 10–11, 69–70, 73–74, 78–80, 194–96, 202, sets the stage for the I-AAC visit. Some French officials assigned to athletics the role of "social educator," useful in promoting the values of nationalism and interaction between social classes.

87. BG, May 31, 1975, 5; *NYG,* Aug. 6, 1912; Litsky, "Politics Have Surpassed Idealism."

88. *NYH* (Paris ed.), July 22, 24, 1912; *Le Temps* (Paris), July 23, 25, 1912. See also Jarvis, *From Vision to Victory,* 102, for social details of the Rheims visit.

89. *NYH* (Paris ed.), July 26, 29, 1912; *Le Matin,* July 29, 1912; *Le Temps,* July 30, 1912; *Richmond County Advance,* Aug. 2, 1912; *NYT,* July 29, 1912.

90. *NYT,* Aug. 4, 1912; Jarvis, *From Vision to Victory,* 102.

91. *Richmond County Advance,* Aug. 2, 1912; WS, 257; OH, 90. David Fitzpatrick, "Ireland since 1870," in *The Oxford Illustrated History of Ireland,* edited by R. F. Foster (New York: Oxford Univ. Press, 1989), 230–31, provides a brief review of the political troubles of 1912.

92. WS, 257; "Matt M'Grath v. Records," *The Freeman's Journal* (Dublin), Aug. 1, 1912; "S.S. Celtic," *New York Passenger Lists,* vols. 4255–57, Aug. 9, 1912, FHC no. 1400595, Family History Library, Salt Lake City; *NYT,* Aug. 11, 1912.

93. NB, 19, 22; "Kiviat to Run," *Richmond County Advance,* Aug. 30, 1912; interviews with Harold Kiviat, Oct. 9, 1995, Jan. 28, 1996.

94. "Olympic Winners Royally Feted," *The Winged Foot* (Sept. 1912): 8; James E. Sullivan, "New York Reception," in Sullivan, *Olympic Games, Stockholm 1912,* 229–30; *NYT,* Aug. 25, 1912.

95. "Parade of Olympic Athletes—Aug. 1912," Bain Collection, Prints and Photography Division, L.C.; Sullivan, "New York Reception," 226–32; *The Winged Foot* (Sept. 1912): 8–9; *NYT,* Aug. 1, 9, 18, 23, 25, 1912; R. Wheeler, *Jim Thorpe,* 116; Wesser, "Gaynor, William J(ay)," 455; Brooks McNamara, "Parades," in Jackson, 878–80.

96. *NYT,* Aug. 25, 1912; Sullivan, "New York Reception," 232–34. For the context, see Akira Iriye, *The Globalizing of America, 1913–1945* (Cambridge, U.K.: Cambridge Univ. Press, 1993), 14–18.

97. Taber, "The Fifth Olympiad," 50–52. For a similar viewpoint, see Craig, "Olympic Games of 1912," 246–47.

98. Dyreson notes how the social experiences of some early Olympic athletes diverged from the AAU leaders' sporting and political ideals. See *Making the American Team,* 98–126, 176–79, 206–7.

99. Noel-Baker, "V Stockholm 1912," 41; James E. "Ted" Meredith, "1912—Stockholm, Sweden," in *41st Annual Invitation Indoor Games of the Millrose Athletic Association, Madison Square Garden* (program), Jan. 31, 1948, 46–48. The facts bear Meredith out: at present, seven 1912 Olympians and three team officials are enshrined in the USA Track & Field Hall of Fame, and still others are eminently deserving.

100. Arnold Strode-Jackson to John Paul Jones, June 2, 1955, Jones to Strode-Jackson, June 17, 1955, JPJ; Robert A. Urban, *"Byers Engineering Company,* Cleveland, Ohio," June 3, 1996, JPJ; interview with Mary-Lou Palmer, Aug. 2, 2007; Webster, *Athletics of To-Day,* 81–82; obituary of Jones, *Cleveland Plain Dealer,* Jan. 8, 1970.

101. For the reunion of the milers, see *Sports Illustrated* (May 7, 1956): 17. As a Penn freshman, the author was on Franklin Field that afternoon when announcer Pincus Sober introduced Strode-Jackson and Kiviat to the crowd of thirty-five thousand. See also the photographs "BNC Hockey XI 1913" and "BNC Athletes 1914," Brasenose College Archives, Oxford University; *The Brazen Nose* (1973): 269–71; obituary of Col. A. Strode-Jackson, *London Times,* Nov. 17, 1972; Philip Noel-Baker, "Col. Strode-Jackson: Athlete and Soldier," *London Times,* Nov. 28, 1972; *NYT,* Apr. 26, 1914; Arthur Daley, "Sports of the Times," *NYT,* Aug. 10, 1945; Bryant, *3:59.4,* 44–50; Buchanan, *British Olympians,* 94–95; G. Smith, *All Out for the Mile,* 28. Jackson wrote *Kentucky Heyday* (New York: Vantage Press, 1956), a sensitive fictional treatment of the life of Matthew Harris Jowett, an early American artist.

102. After the London press ran an endless debate about Great Britain's performance at Stockholm, Arnold Jackson responded in the *London Times* of Aug. 5, 1912, and Philip Baker in *The Outlook* of Oct. 19, 1912. The debate is summarized in Dyreson, *Making the American Team,* 163–65.

103. *London Times,* Oct. 9, 25, 1982; *NYT,* Oct. 9, 1982; Sebastian Coe, *The Olympians* (London: Pavilion, 1996), 21; Whittaker; Howell, 397–99. Baker's personal life was less ideal. His 1915 marriage to Irene Noel, ten years older than himself, was unhappy, and he had a secret, longstanding, and conflicted love affair with Parliament member Megan Lloyd George, daughter of the prime minister. See Mervyn Jones, *A Radical Life: The Biography of Megan Lloyd George, 1902–66* (London: Hutchinson, 1991).

104. Nelson and Quercetani, *The Milers,* 22, 27–29; Lawson, *World Record Breakers,* 70.

105. It took seventy years, but in 1983 Thorpe's children received duplicates of the medals from IOC president Juan Antonio Samaranch. BG, 1–2; WS, 257; OH, 64, 70, 103–4; Mallon and Widlund, *The 1912 Olympic Games,* 405–14; R. Wheeler, *Jim Thorpe,* 164, 193; Gould, "Athlete of the Century," 14–17.

106. Noel-Baker, "V Stockholm 1912," 40–44; Bergvall, *The Fifth Olympiad,* 789; Wallechinsky, *Complete Book of the Olympics,* 37; Clarke and Harris, *Lonely Breed,* 154; "England Losing Athletes," *NYT,* Dec. 1, 1914.

107. Noel-Baker, "V Stockholm 1912," 44; *Washington Post,* Sept. 3, 1912; *Chicago Daily Tribune,* Sept. 3, 1912; "Sporting Views and Reviews," *Montreal Star,* Sept. 25, 1912; "Smooth Stride Chief Asset of Kolehmainen," *NYT,* Mar. 5, 1916.

7. "THE MOST VERSATILE RUNNER IN THE WORLD"

1. "Kiviat to Run"; *NYT,* Sept. 1, 3, 1912; R. Wheeler, *Jim Thorpe,* 117–18. For the context of this international initiative in 1912–14, see Iriye, 17–18. Dyreson, *Making the*

American Team, 163–69, analyzes the European criticism of America's approach to training elite athletes and the Americans' response. For this chapter's title, see *NYT,* Feb. 28, 1915.

2. NB, 7; *NYG,* Mar. 7, 1913; interview with Lucy Price, July 13, 1996.

3. *Princeton Athletic News* 57, no. 4 (Nov. 11, 1989), 33, 38.

4. Charles J. Dieges, "Timing," in Sullivan, *An Athletic Primer,* 98–104.

5. Telephone interviews with Richard Packer, Barrington, R.I., Feb. 6, 2001, and Bob Millan, Southern Pines, N.C., Mar. 27, 2001. See also "Dieges's Birthday Party," *NYT,* Oct. 27, 1915; Dieges's obituary, *NYT,* Sept. 15, 1953; Donovan, *Indoor Track & Field,* 137; "Col. Charles J. Dieges," *The Amateur Athlete* (Oct. 1953): 12; "Tribute Made Tangible," *The Amateur Athlete* (Mar. 1955): 9.

6. James O. Drummon, "Singer Building," in Jackson, 1072; Sarah Bradford Landau, "Skyscrapers," in Jackson, 1073–74; Wolfe, *New York,* 8, 49.

7. OH, 73, 103; interview with Harold Kiviat, Oct. 9, 1995.

8. *Troy Times* (New York), Sept. 6, 9, 1912; *NYEM,* Oct. 15, 1915; *NYT,* Oct. 22, 1915. For the subsequent role of this race in Kiviat's banishment from AAU sport, see chapter 9. See also *The Winged Foot* (Feb. 1913): 12–13, about the payment of illegal appearance money.

9. *Pittsburgh Post,* Sept. 8, 15, 18, 1912; *Pittsburg Press,* Sept. 19, 1912; "Athletes Gather at Pittsburgh," unidentified news clip, n.d. (Sept. 1912), HDS.

10. *NYT,* Sept. 22, 1912 (italics added); "Kiviat Breaks Old Record for the One-Mile Run," *Pittsburg Press,* Sept. 22, 1912; "Irish Club Wins Senior Nationals," *The Winged Foot* (Oct. 1912): 29–30; *Boston Post,* Sept. 20, 1912; "Arthur Duffey's Column," *Boston Post,* Sept. 23, 1912; *Chicago Tribune,* Sept. 22, 1912.

11. *NYT,* Sept. 22, 1912; *The Winged Foot* (Oct. 1912): 29–30.

12. *NYG,* Sept. 23, 1912; *NYT,* Sept. 26, 27, 1912; *Montreal Daily Star,* Sept. 27, 28, 30, 1912.

13. *NYT,* Oct. 4, 1912; *NYG,* Oct. 4, 5, 9, 11, 1912.

14. *NYT,* Oct. 13, 1912; Howard Valentine article, *NYG,* Oct. 18, 1912. Alfred Shrubb of England had set the world record of 9:08.4 at Glasgow in 1904. Paul Withington of Harvard held the American outdoor mark. Tell Berna's 9:17.6 for Cornell in 1912 was not accepted as the American standard because of the condition of the Ithaca track.

15. Howard Valentine columns in *NYG,* Nov. 8, 9, 11, 1912.

16. Carmelli, McPeek, and Malisani, *Evolution of Indoor Records,* 62. For serious questions about the legitimacy of Bonhag's 1910 performance, see *NYT,* Mar. 18, 1913. For the Fourteenth Regiment Armory, see Hawkes, "Armories," 55.

17. Howard Valentine, "Hannes at Last Gets a Beating," *NYG,* Nov. 11, 1912.

18. Lawrence Robinson, "Welcome to a Visiting Fireman," AAU National Track & Field Championships program, June 19–20, 1943. Howard Valentine described Kolehmainen's training regimen in *NYG,* Feb. 18, 1913.

19. *NYT,* Nov. 20, 24, 28, Dec. 5, 1912; *NYG,* Nov. 26, Dec. 2, 1912. Kiviat won in 6:48.2. The unsystematic nature of the era's indoor record keeping precludes certainty, but the time appears to have been a new world standard.

20. For Robertson's remark, see *NYG,* Dec. 4, 1912. The Kiviat quote is in Patricia C. Turner, "Oldest Olympian," *Newark Star-Ledger,* May 19, 1991; however, her story, based on his ancient recollections, conflated his cross-country races in 1912 and 1913 into a single event.

21. *NYT,* Dec. 1, 1912; *Spalding's Official Athletic Almanac 1913,* 114; *NYG,* Dec. 4, 18, 1912.

22. *NYG,* Dec. 2, 1912.

23. *NYG,* Dec. 6, 1912; *NYT,* Dec. 15, 1912, Jan. 1, 1913. See WS, 256, and Tom Mahon, "Sports People," *Philadelphia Daily News,* Feb. 23, 1984, for examples of Kiviat's statements that he disregarded records and ran only to win.

24. *NYT,* Dec. 29, 1912, Jan. 19, 1913; Howard Valentine, "Notable Athletes of Year Now Waning," *NYG,* Dec. 5, 1912; Howard Valentine, "N.Y.A.C. Progressives Name Their Ticket," *NYG,* Dec. 31, 1912.

25. *NYT,* Jan. 16, 17, 18, 24, 26, 1913; *NYG,* Jan. 17, 27, 1913; Sheppard, "Spiked Shoes," part 11, 99.

26. *NYT,* Jan. 30, 1913.

27. *NYG,* Dec. 26, 1912, Feb. 12, 1913; *NYT,* Feb. 9, 1913.

28. *The Winged Foot* (Jan. 1913): 17 and (Feb. 1913): 12–13; *NYT,* Jan. 29, Feb. 10, 1913.

29. Howard Valentine articles, *NYG,* Feb. 11–12, 1913.

30. OH, 48; *NYT, NYG,* Feb. 13, 1913; *The Winged Foot* (Feb. 1913): 12 and (Mar. 1913): 16–18; Carl Warton, "Hedlund Trains Runners' Emotions," *Boston Herald,* Jan. 17, 1932, HED. Although in the Warton article Hedlund confused some of the details, he was referring to the 1913 NYAC meet. See also Carmelli, McPeek, and Malisani, *Evolution of Indoor Records,* 60. Hedlund's mile time bettered by a full second the old record he shared with Harold Trube, the former Cornell and NYAC runner.

31. OH, 48. Articles by Howard Valentine, *NYG,* Feb. 14, 15, 17, 1913; *NYT,* Feb. 16, 1913, Feb. 12, 1938; *The Winged Foot* (Apr. 1913): 42; *SIA,* Mar. 21, 1936, Feb. 17, 1951, Oct. 20, 1972; Carmelli, McPeek, and Malisani, *Evolution of Indoor Records,* 60. Miler Matty Geis later coached a generation of track stars at Princeton.

32. *The Winged Foot* (Feb. 1913): 44; *NYG,* Feb. 19, 25–26, Mar. 1, 3, 4, 6, 1913; *NYT,* Feb. 17, 23, Mar. 2, 1913; *Philadelphia Evening Bulletin,* Feb. 20, 1913; *Philadelphia Inquirer,* Feb. 20, 1913; *Washington Post,* Feb. 16, 20–24, 1913. In *How Champions Are Made* (1933), 37–38, Lawson Robertson described the same approach to training Ted Meredith at Penn in 1916 that he had used with Kiviat for the 1913 indoor nationals.

33. *NYT,* Mar. 6–7, 1913; *NYG,* Mar. 6–7, 1913; Francis [Frank Albertanti], "Kiviat Comes Back as the Whirlwind King," *NYEM,* Mar. 7, 1913, HDS; *The Winged Foot* (Apr. 1913): 13; V. J. Casey, "Homer Baker, Champion Half-Miler," *The Winged Foot*

(Aug. 1913): 21; Arthur Daley, "Homer Baker Makes a Call," *The Amateur Athlete* (Dec. 1944): 4.

34. Sheppard, "Spiked Shoes," part 11, 99–102; *NYT*, Mar. 7, 1913; Francis, "Kiviat Comes Back as the Whirlwind King", HDS; *NYG*, Mar. 6, 7, 10, 1913; *The Winged Foot* (Apr. 1913): 44.

35. Bob Paul, "The Men Who Have Made Indoor Track Thrilling," *The Amateur Athlete* (Mar. 1963), 29; Schmertz, *Wanamaker Millrose Story*, 17; official program, USA/Mobil Indoor Track & Field Championships, Feb. 26, 1988, 19–21, 91; Stan Saplin, "Abel Kiviat, 95 Today, America's Oldest Living Olympic Medalist," June 23, 1987, notes for a New York Road Runners Club press release, SS.

36. Francis, "Kiviat Comes Back as the Whirlwind King"; *NYT*, Mar. 7, 1913; *NYG*, Mar. 7, 1913; official program, USA/Mobil Indoor Track & Field Championships, Feb. 26, 1988, 19–21, 90.

37. *NYT*, Mar. 9, 1913; *NYG*, Mar. 10, 20, 1913. His 880 time of 1:58 was a new MAL championship record.

38. *NYT*, Mar. 16, 18, Apr. 20, 1913; Howard Valentine columns in *NYG*, Mar. 17–19, July 10, 1913; Nelson and Quercetani, *The Milers*, 25. Although Driscoll's stunning 3:07 broke Kiviat's unofficial indoor record by 1.6 seconds, experts viewed marks set on the Buffalo track with suspicion.

39. *NYG*, Mar. 20, 1913; *NYT*, Mar. 23, Apr. 20, 1913; "James E. Sullivan's All-American Track Team," *Boston Post*, Jan. 17, 1914, HDS.

40. *NYT*, Apr. 20, 29, May 12, 1913; *NYG*, Apr. 22, 1913; John Paul Jones, "Preface," in G. Smith, *All Out for the Mile*, x. Henry F. May's *The End of American Innocence: A Study of the First Years of Our Own Time, 1912–1917* (New York: Alfred A. Knopf, 1959), focuses on high culture but has implications for the world of athletics.

41. *NYG*, *NYT*, June 5, 1913.

42. *San Francisco Call*, Apr. 6, 1913; *San Francisco Examiner*, Aug. 15, 1917; *NYG*, Apr. 11, 1913; *NYT*, July 22, Oct. 29, Nov. 5, 1913.

43. *NYT*, Aug. 10, 22, 24, Dec. 6, 27, 1913. For Lon Myers in Australia, see Potts, 153–63. Dyreson notes the emerging role of sports in the theory and practice of international relations after Stockholm; see *Making the American Team*, 52, 175–76. John Keegan, *The First World War* (New York: Vintage, 1999), 10–18, surveys Western economic and cultural interdependence on the eve of battle.

44. *NYT*, May 8, Aug. 22, 27, Nov. 18, Dec. 1, 28, 1913; *NYG*, Aug. 27, Sept. 27, 1913. For Carl Diem and the German Olympic Commission in the United States, see David Clay Large, *Nazi Games: The Olympics of 1936* (New York: W. W. Norton, 2007), 33–35. Dr. Otto Herschmann, a Jewish athlete, died in the concentration camp of Izbica in 1942. See Siegman, *International Jewish Sports Hall of Fame*, 151; Mallon and Widlund, *The 1912 Olympic Games*, 439.

45. *NYT,* Aug. 22, 1913.

46. James C. Whorton, "'Athlete's Heart': The Medical Debate over Athleticism, 1870–1920," in Berryman and Park, 118, 126–30, 132 n. 42; Park, "Athletes and Their Training," 75, 76–78, 88–96; Hjertberg, "A Veteran Looks Back," 7.

47. Gail Bederman, *Manliness and Civilization* (Chicago: Univ. of Chicago Press, 1995), 16–20, 218–32. Although Bederman discusses African Americans and Native Americans at length, she mentions immigrants only in an extended footnote. See page 279, note 103.

48. *NYT,* Dec. 1, 1912; NB, 6; Riess, *City Games,* 15–16, 82.

49. See chapter 9 for a fuller treatment of excessive expense payments.

50. *NYG,* Apr. 23, May 10, June 3, 13, 16, 1913; *NYT,* June 15, 1913; *The Winged Foot* (July 1913): 18–20, 30.

51. *Providence Journal,* July 6, 1913, in Athletics Scrapbook, NT; *Chicago Tribune,* July 6, 1913; *NYT,* July 6, 1913; *NYG,* July 10, 1913. The Whales saved the Irish Club, scoring twenty-two points in the weight events to give the Winged Fist the team trophy.

52. Howard Valentine article, *NYG,* July 10, 1913.

53. *NYT,* July 27, Aug. 18, 30, 31, 1913; *NYG,* July 29, 31, Aug. 27, 1913.

54. *NYT,* Sept. 14, 21, 1913; *NYG,* Sept. 19, 1913; *The Winged Foot* (Oct. 1913): 24–25.

55. *NYG,* Oct. 15, 1913; interview with Harold Kiviat, Oct. 9, 1995. For the Frank and Beilis cases, see Dinnerstein, *Antisemitism in America,* 58–77, 181–85; Albert S. Lindemann, *The Jew Accused: Three Anti-Semitic Affairs (Dreyfus, Beilis, Frank) 1894–1915* (Cambridge, U.K.: Cambridge Univ. Press, 1991); *NYT,* Oct. 26, 1913.

56. *NYT,* Oct. 5, 16, 1913; *NYG,* Oct. 15, 1913; WS, 250; Sheppard, "Spiked Shoes," part 11, 103.

57. *NYG,* Oct. 15, Nov. 6, 11, 19, 1913; *NYT,* Oct. 27, 1913. On John Eke, a Swedish American who represented Sweden in the 1912 Olympic cross-county race, see Bergvall, *The Fifth Olympiad,* 290–91, 378–81.

58. *NYT,* Nov. 10, 16, 1913; *NYG,* Nov. 17, 1913.

59. "Harriers Healthy, Robertson Thinks," *NYT,* Feb. 19, 1916; Hjertberg, *Athletics in Theory and Practice,* 133–38.

60. *NYT,* Nov. 10, Dec. 5–7, 1913, Oct. 8, 25, 1914; *NYG,* Dec. 9, 1913.

61. *NYT,* Dec. 7, 1913; *NYG,* Dec. 9, 1913.

62. CF, supplementary page; J. E. Sullivan, *Spalding's Official Athletic Almanac 1914* (New York: American Sports, 1914), 127; *NYT,* Dec. 7, 1913; *Brooklyn Eagle,* Dec. 7, 1913; *NYG,* Dec. 9, 1913.

63. John Drebinger, "The Sporting Review of the Year," *Richmond County Advance,* Dec. 26, 1913; *NYG,* Dec. 8, 1913; *NYT,* Dec. 14, 1913, Jan. 4, 11, 17, 1914; "James E. Sullivan's All-American Track Team," *Boston Post,* Jan. 17, 1914, HDS; "All American Crack Team," *The Winged Foot* (Feb. 1914): 41; Saplin, "Abel Kiviat, 95 Today," SS.

8. AN "UP-AND-DOWN LIFE"

1. *NYT,* Sept. 30, Dec. 17, 23, 1913, Jan. 19, 27, Mar. 25, 30, 1914; Sheppard, "Spiked Shoes," part 11, 103–4. For I-AAC membership statistics, see *Eagle Almanac* (Brooklyn: Brooklyn Daily Eagle, 1914–28). The chapter title is from the Howard Valentine article, *NYG,* Mar. 17, 1914.

2. A glimpse of what to expect from the newly elected Registration Committee is given in the Howard Valentine article, *NYG,* Sept. 20, 1912, and in *NYT,* Oct. 22, 1912.

3. *NYT,* Oct. 16, 1913; *NYG,* Jan. 27, 1914.

4. On Kiviat's work with Dieges & Clust, see *NYG,* Jan. 26, 1914. On his relationship with Yetta Schimansky, see OH, 35–36, 106–7; *Richmond County Advance,* July 24, 1914; Owen, 88–89.

5. *NYT,* Jan. 20, 26, 1914; *NYG,* Jan. 26, 1914.

6. *NYT,* Jan. 11, 18, 22, 27, 1914; *NYG,* Jan. 26, 1914; *The Winged Foot* (Feb. 1914): 18–19.

7. *NYT,* Jan. 28, 1914.

8. *NYG,* Jan. 22, 24, 1914; *NYT,* Feb. 5, 1914.

9. *NYT,* Jan. 25, 1914; *NYG,* Jan. 26, 1914.

10. *NYT,* Jan. 25, 26, 27, 1914; *NYG,* Jan. 26, 27, 1914; *Brooklyn Eagle,* Jan. 27, 1914; A. Franco and J. C. Diaz, "Wars Stimulated the Development of Anaesthesia," *Current Anaesthesia and Critical Care* 11 (2000), 138.

11. *NYT,* Jan. 26, 28, 1914. The claim made by the later Millrose director and historian Fred Schmertz that in 1914 "[t]he 1000 Yard Handicap, with 59 starters, had Abel Kiviat on scratch" was incorrect; see Schmertz, *Wanamaker Millrose Story,* 59.

12. *NYT,* Jan. 31, Feb. 5, 1914; *NYG,* Feb. 5, 1914; obituary of John T. Dooling in *NYT,* Nov. 16, 1949.

13. *NYG,* Jan. 27, 1914; obituary of committee chairman Jacob W. Stumpf in *NYT,* June 30, 1954; obituary of committee member John J. Deignan in *NYT,* Aug. 31, 1946; Sheppard, "Spiked Shoes," part 8, 88–89. On James E. Sullivan and the definition of an amateur athlete, see *NYT,* Oct. 24, 26, 31, 1913, Jan. 19, 1914. See also Korsgaard, chap. 11.

14. OH, 101; *NYG,* Feb. 5, 1914; *NYT,* Feb. 8, 1914; *The Winged Foot* (Jan. 1914): 44; interview with Louise Mercer, July 17, 1997.

15. *NYT,* Feb. 12, 1914; *The Winged Foot* (Mar. 1914): 20–21; "The Gordon Boys," *The Winged Foot* (Sept. 1914): 18–19.

16. *NYG,* Mar. 2, 1914; *NYT,* Feb. 2, 10, 15, 24, Mar. 1, 2, 1914.

17. *NYT,* Mar. 2, 3, 1914; *NYG,* Mar. 2, 3, 4, 1914.

18. *NYT,* Mar. 15, 20, 1914; *NYG,* Mar. 17, 1914 (italics added); Dinnerstein, *Antisemitism in America,* 61–70.

19. *NYT,* Mar. 8, 15, 17, 1914; *NYG,* Mar. 17, 1914; Patricia Hills, "Armory Show," in Jackson, 55.

20. *NYT,* Mar. 25, Apr. 4, 15, May 6, 21, July 3, 1914; *NYG,* June 24, 1914; *NYEM,* May 9, 1914; George B. Underwood, "He Follows Hjertberg, Kranzlein, and Coplan to Europe," unidentified news clip, July 2, 1914, LR; "Tommy Lennon, S.I.'s Crack Sprinter, Goes to Pennsy," *Richmond County Advance,* July 3, 1914.

21. OH, 69–70; *NYT,* Apr. 4, 1914; "Certificate # 16790, State of N.Y. Certificate and Record of Marriage, the City of N.Y. Dept. of Health," June 24, 1914, Municipal Archives of New York City; interview with Berenice Kaufman, Jan. 26, 1996; telephone conversation with Roz Attinson, Staten Island, N.Y., Feb. 19, 1996.

22. *Richmond County Advance,* July 24, 1914. For Sacandaga Park, see Herbert M. Engel, *Shtetl in the Adirondacks: The Story of Gloversville and Its Jews* (Fleischmanns, N.Y.: Purple Mountain Press, 1991), 91–110, 179–80; Adele S. Thompson, "Sacandaga: Coney Island of the North," *Adirondack Life* (spring 1976): page numbers not available.

23. *Richmond County Advance,* July 24, 1914; Elizabeth Hawes, *New York, New York* (New York: Alfred A. Knopf, 1993), 211, for the Lloyd Morris quote; June Sochen, *The New Woman: Feminism in Greenwich Village, 1910–1920* (New York: Quadrangle Books, 1972), 5–6; Caroline F. Ware, *Greenwich Village, 1920–1930* (Boston: Octagon Books, 1935); Ross Wetzsteon, *Republic of Dreams: Greenwich Village, the American Bohemia, 1910–1960* (New York: Simon and Schuster, 2002).

24. Underwood, "He Follows Hjertberg,"; Howard Valentine article, *NYG,* n.d., LR; *NYT,* July 3, 8, 24, 30, 1914.

25. *NYT,* Aug. 9, 17, 23, Sept. 6, 1914; *Baltimore News,* Sept. 7, 1914; *NYG,* Sept. 14, 1914.

26. *NYT,* Apr. 1, Aug. 25, Sept. 6, 10, 13, 1914; *NYG,* Sept. 11, 14, 1914; *Baltimore Sun,* Sept. 6, 12, 1914; *Baltimore News,* Sept. 7–13, 1914; *Washington Post,* Sept. 13, 1914; *The Winged Foot* (Oct. 1914): 14. For the early career of Joie Ray, see *NYT,* Mar. 24, 1918; Nelson and Quercetani, *The Milers,* 29–30.

27. *NYT,* Sept. 17, 20, 22, Nov. 17, 1914; obituary of Frederick W. Rubien, *NYT,* July 6, 1951; "F. W. Rubien," *The Amateur Athlete* (Aug. 1951): 9; Sullivan, *Olympic Games, Stockholm 1912,* 30, for a photo of Rubien; Howard P. Drew, "Rubien Is Fitted for Position," unidentified news clip, n.d. (Sept. 1914), HDS; Gustavus T. Kirby to Avery Brundage, Nov. 2, 1933, Avery Brundage Papers, Univ. of Illinois Archives, Urbana; Shirley Povich, "Berlin, 1936: At the Olympics, Achievements of the Brave in a Year of Cowardice," *Washington Post,* July 6, 1996; Guttmann, *The Olympics,* 39, 65.

28. *NYT,* Sept. 23, 27, Oct. 2, 1914; *The Winged Foot* (Oct. 1914): 6–9, 16.

29. *NYT,* Oct. 4, 6, 1914; Arthur J. Daley article, *NYT,* Aug. 10, 1930; OH, 40. In the oral memoir, Kiviat made the unusual (for him) double mistakes of remembering Frank Riley as the captain he succeeded and Reisenweber's Restaurant off Columbus Circle as the site of his election.

30. *NYT,* Nov. 8, 18, 21, 22, 25, Dec. 20, 1914; *NYG,* Nov. 28, 30, 1914.

31. *NYG,* Nov. 28, 30, 1914; *NYT,* Nov. 29, 1914; *Philadelphia Daily News,* Feb. 23, 1984.

32. *NYT,* Dec. 16-17, 1914. There was a good description of an I-AAC track captain's duties in *Brooklyn Daily Eagle,* June 14, 1908, LR.

33. The *New York Times* figure of five hundred thousand spectators was probably a conservative estimate. *NYT,* Dec. 13, 20, 1914, Jan. 4, 10, Feb. 9, 1915; *NYG,* Dec. 21, 1914.

34. OH, 69-70; WS, 259; Sam Kiviat, Jan. 2, 1915, entry in calendar book, SK.

35. *NYT,* Jan. 1, 1915.

36. "Kiviette," *Questionnaire* (spring 1942), 1-3, Brooklyn Museum Libraries and Archives; Joanne L. Goodwin, "Women Workers in Applied Design: The History of the New York School of Applied Design for Women, 1892-1917," MA thesis, Sarah Lawrence College, 1983, 48, 50, 57, 110; WS, 258. See also Valerie Steele, "Women Fashioning American Fashion," in *Women Designers in the USA, 1900–2000: Diversity and Difference,* edited by Pat Kirkham, 185-91 (New Haven, Conn.: Yale Univ. Press, 2000).

37. Interview with Frances Kiviette, Englewood, N.J., Sept. 3, 1995; interview with Lucy Price, Sept. 1, 1995.

38. Kiviat's claim to historian William Simons that he and Yetta moved to St. Nicholas Avenue after they lived on Riverside Drive is contradicted by the sources. WS, 259; *New York City Directory, 1915–16,* NYHS; Sam Kiviat, Jan. 1917, entry in calendar book, SK.

39. OH, 87.

40. Interview with Berenice Kaufman, Jan. 26, 1996; interviews with Harold Kiviat, Oct. 9, 1995, Jan. 28, 1996; telephone conversation with Roz Attinson, Feb. 19, 1996.

41. *NYT,* Jan. 31, Feb. 6-7, 11-13, 18, 21, Mar. 20, 1915; George B. Underwood, unidentified news clip, Feb. 11, 1915, New York Roadrunners Club Scrapbook; *Chicago Sunday Tribune,* Feb. 28, 1915; Sheppard, "Spiked Shoes," part 11, 104-6. For summaries of the literature of psychosomatic illness emphasizing the gastrointestinal system, see David T. Graham, "Psychosomatic Medicine," in *Handbook of Psychophysiology,* edited by Norman S. Greenfield and Richard A. Sternbach, 839-924 (New York: Holt, Rinehart and Winston, 1972); H. G. Morgan, "General Medical Disorders," in *Mental Disorders and Somatic Illness,* vol. 2 of *Handbook of Psychiatry,* edited by M. H. Lader, 24-27 (Cambridge, U.K.: Cambridge Univ. Press, 1983).

42. *NYT,* Feb. 28, Mar. 5, 20, 1915; Frank Litsky article, *NYT,* June 14, 2003.

43. *NYT,* Mar. 14, 17, 20, 23, 1915.

44. *NYT,* Apr. 12, 17, May 13, 23, June 12, 13, 15, 16, 19, 20, 1915; *The Winged Foot* (July 1915): 16-17; *Anaconda Standard* (Montana), July 20, 1915.

45. *NYT,* June 24, 26, 1915; "Studies of Present American Champions"; *Providence Evening Bulletin,* Apr. 25, 1934, in Athletics Scrapbook, NT.; "Olympics," JBCF (unidentified abbreviation), July 14, 1996, in Athletics Scrapbook, NT; Nelson and Quercetani, *The Milers,* 26.

46. Nelson and Quercetani, *The Milers,* 22, 26; Webster, *Athletics of To-Day,* 82.

47. *NYT,* June 27, July 4, 6, 10, 11 (italics added), 1915; *Boston Evening Transcript,* July 17, 1915; "Records Go in Tryouts," unidentified news clip, June 27, 1915, in Athletics Scrapbook, NT; "Studies of Present American Champions."

48. *NYT,* July 17, 20, 1915; *Boston Evening Transcript,* July 17, 1915; "Studies of Present American Champions"; "Taber Breaks World's Mark," unidentified news clip, July 17, 1915, in Athletics Scrapbook, NT; Charles E. Parker, "Hold [*sic*] That Taber Can Beat Mark," unidentified news clip, n.d. (July 1915), in Athletics Scrapbook, NT; typed list titled "Wonderful Miles Run by Norman Taber," in Athletics Scrapbook, NT; W. R. "Bill" Schroeder, "The Story of the One-Mile Run," *The Amateur Athlete* (July 1957): 10; Nelson and Quercetani, *The Milers,* 26–27.

49. *NYT,* Dec. 22, 1914, July 9, 16, 20, 24, 25, 27, 1915; for the Underwood quote, see the *Anaconda Standard,* July 17, 1915; for the quote on the role of sport in Irish American culture, see Riess, *City Games,* 94. See also the photograph of Kiviat and his wife leaving New York for the Panama-Pacific Expo, July 15, 1915, U30556INP Bettmann/CORBIS.

50. *Anaconda Standard,* July 22, 25, 1915.

51. *Anaconda Standard,* July 16–26, 1915. For a detailed and insightful study of Butte's Irish community that bears directly on the I-AAC visit, see David Emmons, *The Butte Irish: Class and Ethnicity in an American Mining Town, 1875–1925* (Urbana: Univ. of Illinois Press, 1989), 13, 262–63, 305–7, 345–48, 400–401.

52. Ironically, Senator Myers later proposed federal legislation that became the Sedition Act of 1918, specifically targeting the foreign born and radicals. *Anaconda Standard,* July 26, 1915; Emmons, 315–16, 345–47; Geoffrey R. Stone, *Perilous Times: Free Speech in Wartime* (New York: W. W. Norton, 2004), 185–86.

53. *NYT,* July 20, 1915; *Anaconda Standard,* July 16, 26, 1915; *Oregonian* (Portland), Aug. 1, 2, 3, 1915; *San Francisco Chronicle,* Aug. 5, 1915.

54. *San Francisco Chronicle,* Aug. 5, 1915; *Chicago Tribune,* Aug. 2, 5, 1915; *Oregonian,* Aug. 6, 1915; *NYT,* Aug. 7, 1915; Gary Brechin, *Imperial San Francisco: Urban Power, Earthly Ruin* (Berkeley and Los Angeles: Univ. of California Press, 1999), 245–48, 270–72; Donna Ewald and Peter Clute, *San Francisco Invites the World: The Panama-Pacific International Exposition of 1915* (San Francisco: Chronicle Books, 1991), 5–9.

55. *NYT,* Mar. 31, July 27, 1915; *Washington Post,* May 2, 1915; *Oregonian,* Aug. 1, 1915; *Chicago Tribune,* Aug. 2, 1915; *San Francisco Chronicle,* Aug. 5, 1915.

56. *Chicago Tribune,* July 19, Aug. 3, 4, 5, 1915; *NYT,* Aug. 6, 25, 1915; "Studies of Present American Champions."

57. *San Francisco Chronicle,* Aug. 5, 8, 1915; *Chicago Tribune,* Aug. 8, 1915; *NYT,* Aug. 8, 10, 1915; "Studies of Present American Champions"; Nelson and Quercetani, *The Milers,* 29–30, 46–47. Track writers of the interwar years more familiar with Ray's brilliant achievements unfairly labeled Kiviat "the Joie Ray of his day." See, for example, Stanley Frank, "Irish-American A.C. Gave Workingman a Break," *New York Post,* Jan. 5, 1935, LR.

58. *San Francisco Chronicle,* Aug. 8, 1915; *Chicago Tribune,* Aug. 8, 1915; *NYT,* Aug. 9, 1915; Bert Keane, "Calling Em Right," unidentified news clip, n.d. (ca. 1935–36), HDS. After graduating from the University of Southern California and Drake University Law School, Drew became, in turn, the first African American appointed as assistant clerk of the Hartford City Court and as an acting judge. For Drew's posttrack career: interviews with Howard P. Drew (Jr.) and Jean Drew Lightfoot, Aug. 26, 2000; obituary, *Hartford Courant,* Feb. 21, 1957; Adam R. Hornbuckle, "Drew, Howard Porter," in *American National Biography,* 6:909.

59. *NYT,* Aug. 7, 1915; *Oregonian* (Portland), Aug. 10, 1915.

60. *NYT,* Aug. 10, 11, 22, 1915.

9. ORDEAL: *The AAU v. Kiviat*

1. *NYT,* Aug. 18, 19, 22, 26, 1915 ; *NYEM,* Sept. 24, 1915. For the link between Kiviat's problems with the AAU and those of the I-AAC, see the column by Howard Valentine in *NYG,* Oct. 25, 1915.

2. *NYT,* Sept. 7, 12, 19, 1915; *Boston Evening Transcript,* Sept. 9, 1915; *Brooklyn Eagle,* Oct. 12, 1915; *NYEM,* Oct. 15, 1915. Taber had already decided to retire and pursue his career in municipal finance. See obituary of Norman Taber, *NYT,* July 16, 1952.

3. *NYEM,* Sept. 23, 24, Sept. 28, Nov. 11, 1915; *Troy Times,* Sept. 15, 20, 1915, for details of the Schenectady meet. See *NYT,* Mar. 21, 1915, for the new AAU code. In a sense, the devastatingly swift conduct of the Thorpe episode prepared two of the principals, Weeks and Kirby, to conduct an extended series of trials of Kiviat. See Bill Crawford, *All American: The Rise and Fall of Jim Thorpe* (Hoboken, N.J.: John Wiley and Sons, 2005), 205–7.

4. *NYT,* Sept. 21, 1915; *NYEM,* Sept. 21, 1915. Obituary of Charles A. Elbert, *NYT,* Jan. 9, 1944; obituary of Charles F. Ericksen, *NYT,* Feb. 26, 1916; obituary of Stephen A. Byrne, *NYT,* July 24, 1950.

5. *Troy Times,* Sept. 30, Oct. 2, 29, 1915; *NYEM,* Oct. 6, 1915; *NYT,* Oct. 12, 1915; *NYG,* Oct. 13, 1915.

6. *NYT,* Oct. 7, 1915. Burke, a talented Bostonian, had paced Taber to his world mile record in July at Harvard Stadium.

7. *NYEM,* Oct. 12, 1915; *NYG,* Oct. 12, 13, 1915; *NYT,* Sept. 17, Oct. 12, 1915; *Troy Times,* Oct. 12, 1915. Obituary of Terence Foley, *NYT,* Feb. 27, 1925; obituary of Murray Hulbert, *NYT,* Apr. 27, 1950.

8. *NYEM,* Oct. 13, 14, 1915; *NYG,* Oct. 13, 1915.

9. For biographical information about Weeks and his father, Col. Henry Astor Weeks, M.D., see the entries in *The National Cyclopaedia of American Biography* (New York: J. T. White, 1921), 2:486–87; the front-page obituary, *NYT,* Feb. 4, 1922; the story of Weeks's funeral in *NYT,* Feb. 9, 1922; Considine and Jarvis, *First Hundred Years,* 27, 42, 44, 53, 65; and Jarvis, *From Vision to Victory,* 88. A sense of Weeks's beliefs can be pieced together

from *NYT,* Apr. 22, May 8, 17, Oct. 13, 1913, Apr. 28, 1914, Dec. 2, 1915. For an engaging portrait of Weeks's milieu, see Edwin G. Burrows and Mike Wallace, *Gotham: A History of New York City to 1898* (New York: Oxford Univ. Press, 1999), 452–55, 951–55, 1083–88, 1206–8.

10. *NYT,* Apr. 22, 1913, Nov. 7, 1914; photograph of Weeks in Sullivan, *Olympic Games, Stockholm 1912,* 18; Considine and Jarvis, *First Hundred Years,* 44.

11. *NYEM,* Oct. 15, 25, 1915; *NYT,* Oct. 16, 17, 1915.

12. *Troy Times,* Oct. 2, Nov. 6, Dec. 2, 22, 1915; *NYT,* Oct. 17, 1915; *NYEM,* Oct. 23, 1915; *NYG,* Dec. 24, 1915; Korsgaard, 265–73.

13. For the October 14 hearing, see *NYEM,* Oct. 15, 19, 1915; *NYG,* Oct. 15, 1915; *NYT,* Oct. 15, 1915; *Brooklyn Eagle,* Oct. 15, 1915; and *Troy Times,* Oct. 15, 1915. The *NYEM* of Oct. 25, 1915, reprinted substantial extracts from a statement by Pat Conway that included useful details about the hearings and an acid critique of Justice Weeks and his AAU associates.

14. *Troy Times,* Oct. 16, 1915.

15. *NYEM,* Oct. 16, 18, 1915; *NYT,* Oct. 18, 1915; *NYG,* Oct. 22, 1915; *Spalding's Official Athletic Almanac 1916* (New York: American Sports, 1916) ran a photograph of the finish of the mile.

16. *NYT,* Oct. 18, 1915; *NYG,* Oct. 18, 1915; *NYEM,* Oct. 20, 21, 1915; *Troy Times,* Oct. 21, 1915. See also Pat Conway's statement in *NYEM,* Oct. 25, 1915.

17. *NYEM,* Oct. 22, 1915; *NYT,* Oct. 22, 1915; *NYG,* Oct. 22, 1915; *New York American,* Oct. 22, 1915; *Troy Times,* Oct. 22, 1915. These accounts vary about the length of the executive session, but the *New York Times* report that it was two hours is most realistic. See the obituary of Roscoe C. Campbell, with photograph, in the *Troy Times Record,* Oct. 26, 1937.

18. *NYG,* Oct. 22, 1915; *NYEM,* Oct. 23, 1915; *NYT,* Oct. 23, 1915.

19. *NYG,* Oct. 25, 1915.

20. *NYG,* Oct. 25, Nov. 5, 1915; *NYEM,* Oct. 25, 26, 27, 30, Nov. 2, 9, 1915; *NYT,* Oct. 26, 30, 1915.

21. Povich, "Berlin, 1936"; Guttmann, *The Olympics,* 39, 65. For the contrast between Rubien and Sullivan, see *NYEM,* Oct. 25, 1915, and John Lucas, "The Hegemonic Rule of the American Amateur Athletic Union 1888–1914: James Edward Sullivan as Prime Mover," *International Journal of the History of Sport* 2, no. 3 (1994): 355–71.

22. *Brooklyn Eagle,* Nov. 10, 1915; *NYEM,* Nov. 10, 11, 1915; *NYG,* Nov. 10, 11, 1915; *NYT,* Nov. 10, 1915; *Troy Times,* Nov. 11, 1915.

23. Commissioner Eaton of Schenectady had already written to Rubien "withdrawing his resignation," and Rubien wanted to retain him in spite of the widespread criticism. *NYEM,* Nov. 11, 1915; *NYG,* Nov. 11, 1915; *Troy Times,* Oct. 29, Nov. 11, 1915; *NYT,* Nov. 12, 1915.

24. *NYEM,* Nov. 17, 26, 1915; *NYG,* Nov. 22, 1915.

25. For George J. Turner, see obituary in *NYT,* Jan. 10, 1936; *Troy Times,* Nov. 16, Dec. 1, 1915; *NYEM,* Nov. 16, 1915; *NYT,* Nov. 17, 1915. For Edward E. Babb, see obituary in *NYT,* Dec. 27, 1931; photograph of Babb in Sullivan, *Olympic Games Stockholm 1912,* 32.

26. For background on Kirby, see the obituary in *NYT,* Feb. 27, 1956; *The National Cyclopaedia of American Biography,* 45:20–21; Kirby, "A.A.U. Reminiscences." Offering additional insight is Kirby's delightful memoir *I Wonder Why?* (New York: Coward-McCann, 1954), 30–31. Allen Guttmann's comment is in *The Olympics,* 13, 30–31. John A. Lucas's article "Gustavus Tom Kirby: Doyen of American Amateur Athletics and His Inadmissibility into the International Olympic Committee," *Stadion* 21–22 (1995–96): 171–92, is an important study of character.

27. See Gus Kirby to Avery Brundage, Nov. 2, 1933, Box 28, and May 27, 1936, Box 29, Avery Brundage Papers; Kirby to Mrs. Arthur Hays Sulzberger, Apr. 7, May 1, 1936, Box 5, Folder 99, Kirby Papers, U.S. Olympic Committee Archives, Colorado Springs, Colo.; Leo Rosten, *The Joys of Yiddish* (New York: Pocketbooks, 1970), 181–82, for *kike*; Ted Husing, *Ten Years before the Mike* (New York: Farrar and Rhinehart, 1935), 54.

28. *NYT,* Nov. 28, 1915.

29. *NYT,* Nov. 28, 29, 1915; *NYEM,* Nov. 17, 29, 1915; *New York American,* Nov. 29, 1915; *Troy Times,* Nov. 29, 1915.

30. The sports columnist for the *Troy Times,* Bat Wright, protested the dismissal of Campbell and Livingston. Capt. Livingston circulated a letter he wrote to Rubien claiming he "had nothing whatever to do with the managing of" the February 1912 meet in the Troy armory. *Troy Times,* Dec. 14, 18, 1915; *NYT,* Dec. 18, 1915. See also Bat Wright, "Poor Method of Discipline," *Troy Times,* Dec. 20, 1915; Captain John Livingston, "In His Own Behalf," *Troy Times,* Dec. 21, 1915.

31. *Minutes of the Annual Meeting of the Amateur Athletic Union of the United States, at the Hotel Astor, New York City, Nov. 20th, 1916,* 121–23, LA84 Foundation Library, Los Angeles; *Brooklyn Eagle,* Jan. 15, Feb. 4, 1916.

32. *SIA,* Dec. 30, 1983.

33. OH, 72–74, 104–6.

34. Gordon Allport, *The Nature of Prejudice* (New York: Doubleday, Anchor, 1958), 238.

10. FROM DOUGHBOY TO "WONDER MAN"

1. OH, 72–74, 87; WS, 259; Sam Kiviat, Sept. 7, 1917, entry in calendar book, SK; "Would Lift Ban on Noted Athlete," *NYT,* Oct. 31, 1922; interviews with Harold Kiviat, Oct. 9, 1995, Jan. 28, 1996; P. Turner, "Oldest Olympian"; Andrew Alpern, *New York's Fabulous Luxury Apartments* (New York: Dover, 1975), 70; Hawes, *New York, New York,* 94, 109–10, 235–36, 243. On the demise of the I-AAC, see "Kolehmainen Quits I.-A.A.C.," *NYT,* Oct. 24, 1916; "Robertson to Assist at Penn This Spring," unidentified news clip, Apr. 22, 1916, UP; *Philadelphia Evening Bulletin,* Mar. 22, 1943, UP; *NYT,*

Jan. 8, 1917, Jan. 1, 1919; Eileen M. Kennedy to author, Jan. 12, 1996, regarding the erection of the Celtic Park Apartments on the site of the old stadium in 1931. On Sam Kiviat's track career at Curtis, see *NYT,* Dec. 19, 1916; "Athletic News and Notes," *New York Journal,* Jan. 2, 1917; *New York Journal,* Feb. 2, 1917; and, especially, unidentified news clip, n.d. (ca. 1917), SK.

2. *NYT,* Nov. 20, 1917; Owen, 17–18, 88.

3. *NYEM,* Dec. 17, 21, 1917, Jan. 5, 1918; *Brooklyn Eagle,* Dec. 16, 1917; "Lennon Quits Penn for Aviation Corps," *Philadelphia Evening Bulletin,* n.d. (1917), Thomas Lennon File, UP; "Military Record" of Lawson Robertson, UP; Sheppard, "Spiked Shoes," part 9, 91–92; David M. Kennedy, *Over Here: First World War and American Society* (New York: Oxford Univ. Press, 1980), 216–18.

4. "Kiviat, Abel R.," World War I card, Form No. 724-1½ AGO, Mar. 12, 1920, New York State Archives; *NYEM,* Dec. 17, 1917; *NYT,* Dec. 17, 1917; Holst and Popp, *American Men,* 78.

5. OH, 73–74; *59th Regiment, C.A.C. Supply Co., S/Rs, Correspondence Bks., Misc. Corresp., HDQRS,* Orders, Box No. 816, RG 391, Records of U.S. Army Regular Army Mobile Units, World War I, NA; *History of the 59th Artillery,* Coast Artillery Regiments (59th Regt. Through 60th Regt.), Coast Artillery Corps, 1–2, Folder 132-11.4, Box 332, RG 165, Records of the War Department General and Special Staffs, Records of the Historical Section Relating to the History of the War Department, 1900–41, NA; *NYEM,* Dec. 29, 1917, Jan. 16, 29, 1918; *Brooklyn Eagle,* Mar. 16, 1924; *New York City Guide* (New York: Random House, 1939), 469; Russell S. Gilmore, "Fort Hamilton," in Jackson, 429; David M. Ludlum, "Weather," in Jackson, 1249.

6. *Brooklyn Daily Eagle,* Jan. 20, 1918; *NYEM,* Dec. 29, 1917, Jan. 21, 23, 24, 1918; *NYT,* Jan. 24, 1918; Schmertz, *Wanamaker Millrose Story,* 59, 61.

7. *NYEM,* Jan. 31, 1918.

8. OH, 57; *History of the 59th Artillery,* 2; WS, 257; Sam Kiviat, Mar. 28, 1918, entry in calendar book, SK.

9. OH, 57; *59th Artillery Regiment—War Diary,* 2, Folder 132-33.5, RG 165, NA; Frank Freidel, *Over There: The Story of America's First Great Overseas Crusade,* rev. ed. (Philadelphia: Temple Univ. Press, 1990), 16–36; Edward M. Coffman, *The War to End All Wars: The American Military Experience in World War I* (Madison: Univ. of Wisconsin Press, 1986), 109–10.

10. OH, 79; *History of the 59th Artillery,* 2; *59th Artillery Regiment—War Diary,* 2; "The 59th Coastal Artillery in France," Casement Museum, Fortress Monroe, Va., at http://www.worldwar1.com/dbc/coast59.htm; American Battle Monuments Commission, *American Armies and Battlefields in Europe: A History, Guide, and Reference Book* (Washington, D.C.: U.S. Government Printing Office, 1938), 447.

11. OH, 79; *59th Artillery Regiment—War Diary,* 2–4; *History of the 59th Artillery,* 2–3; "The 59th Coastal Artillery in France."

12. Abel Kiviat to Sam Kiviat, Nov. 11, 1918, SK; Gordon, "Olympic Memories"; *NYT,* Jan. 26, 1919; Pope, *Patriotic Games,* 139–55; Wanda Ellen Wakefield, *Sports and the American Military, 1898–1945* (Albany: State Univ. of New York Press, 1997), 14–15, 22–23, 29, 145 n. 16; *Summary of World War Work of the American YMCA* (N.p.: privately distributed, 1920), 132–48.

13. *NYH* (Paris ed.), May 18, 28, 29, 30, 31, 1918; Trevor, "Kiviat's Comeback"; *SIA,* Oct. 14, 1926; Jack Eller photographs, "American Soldier Athletes Behind the Lines in France," in *Spalding's Official Athletic Almanac 1919* (New York: American Sports, 1919).

14. *NYT,* Oct. 24, 1916; *NYH* (Paris ed.), July 5, 1918; Eller photographs, *Spalding's Official Athletic Almanac 1919.*

15. *NYH* (Paris ed.), Aug. 15, 19, Sept. 13, 15, 16, 1918; *History of the 59th Artillery,* 3–6; "Record of Events," July and Aug. 1918, 59th Regiment, C.A.C. Supply Co., S/Rs, Box no. 816, RG 391, NA; "The 59th Coastal Artillery in France"; *NYT,* Jan. 25, 1919; Coffman, 262–64, 277; John S. D. Eisenhower, *Yanks: The Epic Story of the American Army in World War I* (New York: Free Press, 2001), 102–3, 127–28, 163–74, 180–84, 190–95.

16. Abel Kiviat to Sam Kiviat, Nov. 11, 1918, SK; "Record of Events," Sept. 1918, 59th Regiment, C.A.C. Supply Co., S/Rs; *NYH* (Paris ed.), Aug. 16, 1918; Charles S. Bernheimer, "Jewish Welfare Board," in *The Universal Jewish Encyclopedia,* edited by Isaac Landman (New York: n.p., 1942), 6:147–48.

17. "Record of Events," Sept. 1918; *History of the 59th Artillery,* 7; "The 59th Coastal Artillery in France"; Eisenhower, 198–209; Coffman, 299–300; Freidel, 147–48.

18. *History of the 59th Artillery,* 7, 9–10; American Battle Monuments Commission, 172–83, 216, has a photograph of an army supply truck driving through the devastation of Cheppy on October 6, 1918; Paul Braim, *The Test of Battle: The American Expeditionary Forces in the Meuse-Argonne Campaign* (Newark: Univ. of Delaware Press, 1987), 97; Eisenhower, 250–55; Coffman, 306–29; Robert H. Zieger, *America's Great War: World War I and the American Experience* (Lanham, Md.: Rowman and Littlefield, 2000), 100–107; Kennedy, 203.

19. OH, 79; WS, 258; "The 59th Coastal Artillery in France"; Zieger, 108.

20. Interview with Harold Kiviat, Oct. 9, 1995.

21. *History of the 59th Artillery,* 10–14; "Record of Events," Oct. 1–31, 1918, 59th Regiment, C.A.C. Supply Co., S/Rs; Abel Kiviat to Sam Kiviat, Nov. 11, 1918, SK; Ken Murray, "Kiviat, 97, Enjoys Golden Years, If Not 1912 Medal," *Baltimore Evening Sun,* n.d. (1990), SS.

22. Abel Kiviat to Sam Kiviat, Nov. 11, 1918, SK; "Record of Events," Nov. 1–21, 1918, 59th Regiment, C.A.C. Supply Col., S/Rs; *History of the 59th Artillery,* 11, 14; Braim, 133, 136–37.

23. *History of the 59th Artillery,* 15–17; "Record of Events," Jan. 1919, 59th Regiment, C.A.C. Supply Co., S/Rs; "Kiviat, Abel R.," World War I card; Abel Kiviat to Sam Kiviat,

Nov. 11, 1918, SK; Sam Kiviat, Jan. 24, 1919, entry in calendar book, SK; *NYT,* Jan. 24, 25, 26, 31, 1919; "The 59th Coastal Artillery in France"; Freidel, 228–29, 231–32.

24. OH, 102; NB, 7.

25. OH, 87; Sam Kiviat, Jan. 31, Feb. 1, 1919, entries in calendar book, SK; interview with Harold Kiviat, Jan. 28, 1996; *NYT,* Nov. 5, 1918.

26. Sam Kiviat, Apr. 25, 26, 1919, entries in calendar book, SK.

27. BG, 1–2; WS, 257; *NYT,* Apr. 27, May 22, 1919; R. Wheeler, *Jim Thorpe,* 164, 193; Kennedy, 218–30.

28. Interview with Harold Kiviat, Oct. 9, 1995; obituary of Herman Pomeranz, *NYT,* Oct. 29, 1956; Herman Pomeranz, "Goethe's Words," *NYT,* Oct. 9, 1914; *SIA,* May 19, 1930.

29. OH, 57, 87–88, 107. Abel Richard Kiviat and Isabel Solomon, marriage license, Registered M 10433, New York State Department of Health, Apr. 13, 1948, cited adultery as the grounds for Abel's divorce from Yetta in 1919. For divorce in New York State, see Hyacinthe Ringrose, ed., *Marriage and Divorce Laws of the World* (London: Musson-Draper, 1911), 181. For the Pomeranz marriage, see *SIA,* May 19, 24, 1930; interview with Harold Kiviat, Jan. 28, 1996; interview with Frances Kiviette, Sept. 3, 1995; interview with Dennis Goldner, Brooklyn, N.Y., Aug. 3, 2001. Kiviat's son enrolled in the fifth grade of Manhattan's elite Columbia Grammar School as "Arthur Louis Pomeranz" in 1923. He studied there until 1929. Telephone conversation with Helen Jarvis of the Columbia Grammar School staff, May 21, 2002.

30. For Staten Island at this time, see U.S. Bureau of the Census, *1920 Census of the U.S., for Staten Island* (Washington, D.C.: National Archives and Records Administration, 1920), K 130, Vol. 315, Sheet 8, ED 1557, Line 35; Vernon B. Hampton, *Staten Island's Claim to Fame* (Staten Island, N.Y.: Richmond Borough, 1925), 182; WS, 259; interviews with Harold Kiviat, Oct. 9, 1995, Jan. 28, 1996; telephone conversation with Staten Island office, New York City Department of Buildings, May 8, 2002.

31. *1920 Census of the U.S.,* K 130, Vol. 315, listed Kiviat as a "dry goods salesman"; Alan H. Feiler, "The Durability of the Long Distance Runner," *Baltimore Jewish Times,* Dec. 29, 1989, 48. Kiviat's father died less than a decade later (1930) from heart and liver diseases; see "Morris Kiviat," Standard Certificate of Death, no. 811, Bureau of Records, Department of Health of the City of New York, State of New York, Apr. 28, 1930, New York City Municipal Archives.

32. Telephone conversation with Phebe (Hirshon) Baugher, Port Washington, N.Y., Nov. 13, 2002; obituary of Hugh H. Hirshon, *NYT,* May 16, 1955; *New York City Directory, 1922–1923,* NYHS; Trevor, "Kiviat's Comeback"; Peter Levine, *Ellis Island to Ebbets Field: Sport and the American Jewish Experience* (New York: Oxford Univ. Press, 1992), 26–51; Steven A. Riess, "Sports and the American Jew: An Introduction," in *Sports and the American Jew,* edited by Steven A. Reiss (Syracuse, N.Y.: Syracuse Univ. Press, 1998), 22–23; Riess, *City Games,* 107–8.

33. *SIA*, Sept. 19, 1921, May 15, 31, 1922; "On the Sport Trail with Hal J. Squier," *SIA*, July 25, 1952; Charles V. Morris, "Athletes and Athletics—Staten Island's Claim to Fame," in *Tercentenary Booklet* (Staten Island, N.Y.: Tercentennial Commission, 1961), 42–46.

34. *SIA*, Oct. 27, Nov. 10, 1919, Oct. 10, 1921; "On the Sport Trail with Hal J. Squier," *SIA*, July 25, 1952; "Early Teams Played Against Opponents and Fans," *SIA*, Mar. 27, 1986; Morris, 44–45; Ken Strong, "From Staten Island to Manhattan, I Couldn't Get Out of New York," in *The Fireside Book of Pro Football*, edited by Richard Whittingham (New York: Simon and Schuster, 1989), 273–74. The Stapes played in the NFL from 1929 to 1931.

35. Trevor, "Kiviat's Comeback"; *NYT*, Oct. 31, 1922.

36. OH, 91–92; *NYT*, Oct. 31, Nov. 20, 21, 1922.

37. *NYT*, Nov. 1, 9, 20, 21, 1922; obituary of Murray Hulbert, *NYT*, Apr. 27, 1950; obituary of Jeremiah T. Mahoney, *NYT*, June 20, 1970; Dinnerstein, *Antisemitism in America*, 78–84. Throughout this period, the Registration Committee still adhered rigidly to its cardinal principle of prohibiting amateur athletes from accepting financial rewards for performances. See, for example, *NYT*, Jan. 29, 1923, Mar. 18, 1924; John A. Lucas, "In the Eye of the Storm: Paavo Nurmi and the American Athletic Amateur-Professional Struggle (1925 and 1929)," *Stadion* 17 (1992), 226–27.

38. John Drebinger ("Ten Flat"), "The Sporting Viewpoint," *SIA*, Nov. 23, 1922; Ed Hughes, "The Wonder Man of the Wilco Games," *NYTEM*, Feb. 16, 1924; "Kiviat's Comeback." On Jones and Taber as heroes of the postwar athletes, see *Ye Domesday Booke 1923* (Georgetown University yearbook).

39. For track's resurgence after World War I, see *NYT*, 1920–23, passim, especially Jan. 23, 1923, Sept. 20, 1927; McMicken, *Track & Field Media Guide*, 30–36, 106–18; Nelson and Quercetani, *The Milers*, 29–46; Lovesey, *The Kings of Distance*, 91–99; and especially Lucas, "In the Eye," 225–45. For the 1922–23 record holders, see Lawson, *World Record Breakers*; Wallechinsky, *Complete Book of the Olympics*.

40. Dyreson, *Making the American Team*, 199–203; Mark Dyreson, "Johnny Weismuller and the Old Global Capitalism: The Federal Blueprint for Selling American Culture in the 1920s and 1930s," in *Proceedings of the Twenty-ninth NASSH Conference, at London, Ontario, Canada, May 25–28, 2001* (N.p.: North American Society for Sport History, 2001).

41. John Drebinger ("Ten Flat"), "The Sporting Viewpoint," *SIA*, Dec. 21, 1922, Feb. 3, 1923; *Brooklyn Eagle*, Dec. 7, 1922; Eddie Mayo column, *Brooklyn Eagle*, Dec. 20, 1922; Homer Baker, letter to the editor, *Brooklyn Eagle*, Jan. 14, 1923; *NYT*, Jan. 21, Feb. 6, 12, 1923; Trevor, "Kiviat's Comeback"; Nelson and Quercetani, *The Milers*, 45.

42. John Drebinger ("Ten Flat") article, *SIA*, Feb. 9, 1923; *NYT*, Feb. 11, 13, 18, 22, 1923; Hughes, "The Wonder Man of the Wilco Games"; Trevor, "Kiviat's Comeback."

43. SIJHS; interview with Harold Kiviat, Oct. 9, 1995; telephone conversation with Pastor John Futchs, Wilmington, N.C., Jan. 18, 1996; *SIA*, Apr. 24, 25, May 26, 1923, Mar. 3, 1924; *The Kallista* (Wagner College), 1923, 86–88; *The Kallista*, 1924, n.p.; *The Kallista*, 1925, 66–67; "Ed Hughes' Column," *Brooklyn Eagle*, Feb. 22, 1935; "Pastor Frederic Sutter's

Recollections of Wagner College," *Staten Island Historian* 1, no. 3 (1984): 26–30; *Staten Island: A Resource Manual*, 206–7; Howard Weiner, "Wagner College," in Jackson, 1231–32; Dinnerstein, *Antisemitism in America*, 78–104. At Kiviat's urging, Wagner was instrumental in organizing Staten Island schools into a league for track meets, a concept soon broadened to baseball and basketball games.

44. *NYT*, Aug. 25–26, Sept. 2–4, 8–9, 1923; *Brooklyn Eagle*, Jan. 11, 1924; Trevor, "Kiviat's Comeback"; H. V. Valentine columns, *NYTEM*, Mar. 16, 24, 1924; OH, 74; NB, 18; WS, 258; CF, 8; Nelson and Quercetani, *The Milers*, 40–52. Kiviat claimed in OH (1984) that he was training "for the 3,000 meter flat race" and not for the team event. Although the American Olympic Committee did hold a 3,000-meter race in its final trials as a qualifier for the team event, there was no men's individual 3,000 on the Olympic program in Paris or in subsequent Olympiads.

45. *NYT*, Jan. 30, Feb. 6, 12, 14, 16, 17, 1924; *Brooklyn Eagle*, Feb. 12, 1924; "Ed Hughes' Column," *NYTEM*, Feb. 16, 1924.

46. Buker and Hahn finished fifth and sixth, respectively, to Nurmi in the Olympic 1,500 final in Paris. For the indoor nationals, see Howard Valentine column, *NYTEM*, Mar. 6, 1924; *Washington Post*, Mar. 5, 6, 1924; *NYT*, Mar. 5, 6, 1924; WS, 258.

47. H. V. Valentine column, *NYTEM*, Mar. 12, 1924; *NYT*, Mar. 8, 9, 11, 12, 1924; Trevor, "Kiviat's Comeback."

48. Hal J. Squier, "On the Sport Trail," *SIA*, Mar. 13, 1924; *NYT*, Apr. 5, 16, 30, May 20, 1924; "America Deficient in Long-Distance Runners," *Dearborn Independent*, Apr. 19, 1924, LR. For attacks in the *Independent* on Jewish participation in popular culture during the 1920s, including baseball, see Neil Baldwin, *Henry Ford and the Jews: The Mass Production of Hate* (New York: Public Affairs, 2001), 162, 200; Dinnerstein, *Antisemitism in America*, 80–83.

49. H. V. Valentine, "Kiviat to Try Steeplechase," *NYTEM*, Mar. 24, 1924; *NYTEM*, Apr. 10, 1924; *NYT*, May 29–31, 1924; Hal J. Squier columns and articles, *SIA*, May 9, 19, 26, 1924.

50. Hal J. Squier articles, *SIA*, June 9, 12, 1924.

51. Howard Valentine column in *NYTEM*, June 16, 1924; "The Final Olympic Try Outs," June 13 and 14, 1924, HUD 8420, Harvard University Archives, Cambridge, Mass.; OH, 74; WS, 258; NB, 18; Carlson and Fogarty, *Tales of Gold*, 9.

52. *Boston Globe*, June 15, 1924; *NYTEM*, June 14, 1924; *NYT*, June 15, 1924; *Columbus Dispatch*, June 15, 1924; OH, 74; CF, 8; NB, 18.

53. OH, 74; WS, 258; Carlson and Fogarty, *Tales of Gold*, 9; *Boston Globe*, June 15, 1924; *NYT*, June 14, 15, 1924; *NYTEM*, June 14, 1924; Hal J. Squier article, *SIA*, June 23, 1924. Marty Glickman wrote in his autobiography that Coach Robertson apologized to him after the 400-meter relay race in Berlin for making "a terrible mistake" and asked for forgiveness. Cromwell, whom Glickman believed was culpable in the affair along with Avery Brundage (he calls them "anti-Semites of the first order"), never spoke with Glickman. See Marty Glickman,

with Stan Isaacs, *The Fastest Kid on the Block: The Marty Glickman Story* (Syracuse, N.Y.: Syracuse Univ. Press, 1996), 26–29; Peter Gambaccini, "Marty Glickman: A Remembrance," *Runner's World Daily News,* Jan. 9, 2001. In *Triumph: The Untold Story of Jesse Owens and Hitler's Olympics* (Boston: Houghton Mifflin, 2007), 185, Jeremy Schaap couples Robertson with Cromwell as fellow racists. The overwhelming evidence from Robertson's career at the I-AAC and at Penn disproves this allegation. For example, he never again took a Penn team to Annapolis after the Naval Academy team barred his African American cross-country captain, Willis Cummings, from competing there in 1919. On Cummings, see James Smart, "He Sprinted Ahead of His Time," unidentified article, n.d., courtesy of Betty McKean. David Clay Large offers a thoughtful treatment of the relay controversy in *Nazi Games: The Olympics of 1936,* 240–43.

54. *NYT,* Jan. 7, 16, Feb. 7, 21, Mar. 9, 10, 21, Dec. 23, 1925, Feb. 14, 1926.

55. George B. Underwood, "New Garden on Eighth Avenue," *NYTEM,* June 18, 1924.

11. "A RUNNER WHOM RENOWN OUTRAN"

1. A. E. Housman, "To an Athlete Dying Young," in *A Shropshire Lad* (New York: Henry Holt, 1920), 26–28; Terence Allan Hoagland, *A. E. Housman Revisited* (New York: Twayne, 1995), 58–59. See WS, 236, for the view that Kiviat "lived in relative obscurity" from 1925 until 1982.

2. Sam Kiviat, July 19, Aug. 13, 1925, entries in calendar book, SK.

3. Sam Kiviat, July 19, Aug. 13, 1925, entries in calendar book, SK; "Personal History Statement of Abel Kiviat," Administrative Office of the U.S. Courts, Nov. 16, 1944, Reference Service Branch, National Personnel Records Center, NA; SIJHS; interviews with Harold Kiviat, Oct. 9, 1995, Jan. 28, 1996; Dinnerstein, *Antisemitism in America,* 89. Rhoades & Co. merged with Carl M. Loeb & Co. in 1937 to form Loeb, Rhoades. There are no surviving company records from the 1920s; however, see obituary of John L. Loeb, Sr., *NYT,* Dec. 9, 1996, and Charles R. Geisst, *The Last Partnerships: Inside the Great Wall Street Money Dynasties* (New York: McGraw-Hill, 2001), 73.

4. Sam Kiviat, July 19, 1925, entry in calendar book, SK; *SIA,* May 7, 15, Aug. 2, 10, Sept. 21, 1925, Apr. 17, May 20, 1926, July 5, 1927; Hal J. Squier, "On the Sport Trail," *SIA,* July 18, 1927; Hittner, *Honus Wagner,* 245. Unlike in the case of Jim Thorpe, the AAU under the presidency of Murray Hulbert apparently took no notice of Kiviat's concurrent baseball career and permitted him to run in its meets. See *NYT,* May 27, 1925, Feb. 14, 1926.

5. *The Kallista,* 1928, 72; SIJHS; *SIA,* Sept. 22, 1927, Mar. 28, Apr. 5, 1928.

6. "Personal History Statement of Abel Kiviat," NA; "Report of the Personnel Dept., New York Stock Exchange," Sept. 1, 1929, 22–32, New York Stock Exchange Archives; *NYT,* Feb. 20, 1930, Feb. 11, 1932; "Abel R. Kiviat," New York Stock Exchange Employment Badge, Dec. 31, 1932, TL; *Brooklyn Eagle,* Jan. 17, 1933.

7. *Supreme Court: Richmond County. Henry Joblin, Plaintiff, vs. Ruth Joblin, Defendant: State of N.Y.: County of Richmond, Nov. 21, 1931,* 1079/31, S.I. 853, New York City Municipal Archives; *SIA,* Nov. 17, 1931.

8. Interviews with Harold Kiviat, Oct. 9, 1995, Jan. 28, 1996; interview with Esther Kiviat, Mar. 30, 1997; interview with Lucy Price, July 13, 1996; SIJHS; Henry G. Steinmeyer, "South Beach: The Resort Era," *Staten Island Historian* 19 (1958): 17–22; *Staten Island: A Resource Manual,* 168.

9. Sam Kiviat, 1919, 1922, entries in calendar book, SK; "Camp Pontoosuc, Pittsfield, Mass., 1921-22-23" File, SK; telephone interview with Bruce Conrad-Reingold, Rochester, N.Y., Mar. 9, 2003; Bruce Conrad-Reingold to author, Mar. 16, 27, 2003; Sally Bedell Smith, *In All His Glory: The Life of William Paley, the Legendary Tycoon and His Brilliant Circle* (New York: Simon and Schuster, 1990), 41, 44. For Sam Kiviat, see also *The 1921 Record* (Univ. of Pennsylvania), 77, 295, UP; *The 1924 Record* (School of Dentistry, Univ. of Pennsylvania) 87, 210, UP; *Pennsylvania Gazette,* Mar. 26, 1926, Feb. 1, 1929, UP; "*Confidential.* Univ. of Penn. Background Statement for Solicitation of Dr. Samuel W. Kiviat," Apr. 4, 1966, UP.

10. Sam Kiviat, 1924, entry in calendar book, SK; "Profile of an Independent Resident Camp: 1980 Marks Ken-Mont and Ken-Wood's 57th Season," *New England Camping Magazine* (May 1980), SK; Sam Kiviat, "A Tribute to Joe Gawel," n.d., SK. See the insightful brief essays by Daniel Cohen and Jenna Weisman Joselit in *A Worthy Use of Summer: Jewish Summer Camping in America* (Philadelphia: National Museum of American Jewish History, 1993), 10–28.

11. Israel Kiviat administered the camps' kitchen and dining room after South Beach fell into disrepair. OH, 5; *The 1924 Record* (School of Dentistry, Univ. of Pennsylvania), 87, 210, UP; Lloyd Albin to Dr. and Mrs. Samuel Kiviat, Dec. 22, 1981, "70–71 Camp Correspondence" File, SK; interviews with Harold Kiviat, Oct. 9, 1995, Jan. 28, 1996; interview with Lucy Price, July 13, 1996; interview with Esther Kiviat, Mar. 30, 1997; telephone interview with Lloyd Albin, Kent, Conn., Apr. 5, 2003; Sam Kiviat to Anne Kiviat, Jan. 6, 1954, SK; "Some Well-Known K-M & K-W Clientele and Alumnus" File, n.d., SK. For Kiviat family conflicts at the camps, see Sam Kiviat to Iz and Harold Kiviat, June 13, 1945, SK; Sam Kiviat to Harold Kiviat, July 18, 1945, SK; Sam Kiviat to I. J. Kiviat, Feb. 16, 1951, July 11, 1952, SK. The success of the Kiviat camps is highlighted in the Bill Becker article, *NYT,* June 29, 1958.

12. OH, 88; Sam Kiviat's calendar book, 1927, contained Yetta Pomeranz's home telephone number, SK; Gerald Bordman, *The Oxford Companion to American Theatre,* 2d ed. (New York: Oxford Univ. Press, 1992), 407; Owen, 88–89.

13. *1931 Old Gold and Blue* (Peddie School), 55; "Peddie School Gives Diplomas to 78 Boys," *NYT,* June 2, 1931; telephone conversation with Dolly Crujeiras, Peddie School, Hightstown, N.J., May 17, 2002; *SIA,* May 13, 19, 24, June 20, 1930.

14. OH, 88–91; interview with Lucy Price, Sept. 1, 1995; photograph of Abel and Arthur Kiviat at Camp Kenmont, summer 1935, TL; interview with Esther Kiviat, Mar. 30, 1997; interview with Berenice Kaufman, Jan. 26, 1996; Neal Gabler, *Winchell: Gossip, Power, and*

the Culture of Celebrity (New York: Alfred A. Knopf, 1994), 187–89, locates the Stork Club at West Fifty-eighth Street until late 1931, which supports Kiviat's account of the time and place of the reunion. Arthur still listed his family name as "Pomeranz" for his graduation exercises at Peddie, but he enrolled at Penn in the fall as Arthur Lewis Kiviat. See "Arthur Lewis Kiviat," Wharton School freshman enrollment form, n.d., UP. For additional information about his undergraduate years at Penn, see "Arthur L. Kiviat," Alumni Records Office, June 2, 1936, UP; *The 1936 Record* (Univ. of Pennsylvania), 88, UP.

15. Interview with Dennis Goldner, Aug. 3, 2001; interview with Esther Kiviat, Mar. 30, 1997; interview with Harold Kiviat, Jan. 28, 1996.

16. OH, 91; "Arthur L. Kiviat," Alumni Records Office, June 2, 1936, UP; Alumni Records Office to Vice Dean Thos. A. Budd, Wharton School, Aug. 30, 1940, UP; "Wharton Record," Wharton School, n.d., UP; "Penn Alumni Census, 1987–1988," UP; interview with Berenice Kaufman, Jan. 26, 1996; interview with Dennis Goldner, Aug. 3, 2001; telephone conversation with Litzi Goldner, Roslyn Estates, N.Y., Apr. 30, 2005.

17. *SIA,* July 4, 1924, Sept. 6, 1926, July 18, 1927.

18. *SIA,* July 18, Aug. 4, Sept. 19–20, 1927; *Brooklyn Eagle,* June 22, 1927, Jan. 17, 1933; *NYT,* June 22, Sep. 18, 1927, Nov. 8, 1928; Bernie Beglane, "All-America [*sic*] Press Steward," in IC4A program, Mar. 8, 1969; Bill Welsh, "Abel Kiviat: The Longest 15 Minutes Ever," Curtis High School Alumni Association, Staten Island, N.Y.; Dinnerstein, *Antisemitism in America,* 78–79.

19. Hal J. Squier columns, *SIA,* Sept. 20, 1927, Apr. 18, May 24, 1928; George Currie column, *Brooklyn Eagle,* Feb. 18, 1935; "Ed Hughes' Column," *Brooklyn Eagle,* Feb. 22, 1935; James P. Dawson article, *NYT,* Nov. 18, 1944; Arthur Daley, "Sports of the Times," *NYT,* Apr. 12, 1950; Beglane, "All-America Press Steward"; telephone conversation with Eric Seiff, New York City, Feb. 25, 2003; OH, 83; CF, 5; WS, 261.

20. SIJHS; WS, 261; Robertson, *College Athletics,* 111; obituary of Thomas Lennon, *NYT,* Apr. 5, 1967; Beglane, "All-America Press Steward"; telephone conversation with David Johnson, Penn Relays staff, Nov. 1995.

21. "Program, Third Annual Invitation Track Meet," *Princeton Athletic News* 4, no. 6 (1936): 1–2; John Lucas, "The Princeton Invitation Meet—Aristocrat of International Track & Field 1934–1940," in *National College Physical Education Association for Men, Proceedings of the 74th Annual Meeting,* edited by C. E. Mueller (Portland, Ore.: National College Physical Education Association for Men, 1970), 197–202.

22. Husing, 149–50, 203–13, 228–30.

23. CF, 5; "Today on the Radio," *NYT,* June 13, 1936. In *Play-by-Play: Radio, Television, and Big-Time College Sport* (Baltimore: Johns Hopkins Univ. Press, 2001), 26–28, 238 n. 1, Ronald A. Smith unfortunately focuses his analysis almost exclusively on football and slights the significant early media history of track & field.

24. "Ed Hughes' Column," *Brooklyn Eagle,* Feb. 22, 1935; *NYT,* Jan. 24, Dec. 23, 1934, Feb. 28, 1935; Ira Berkow, ed., *Hank Greenberg* (New York: Times Books, 1989), 71; George

Eisen, "The Maccabiah Games: A History of the Jewish Olympics," Ph.D. diss., Univ. of Maryland, 1979, 224–25, 227–28. In his interview with William Simons, Kiviat was more modest about his role in the Maccabiah movement than the facts warranted; see WS, 260.

25. *NYT,* Oct. 9, Dec. 8–9, 1935; obituary of Jeremiah T. Mahoney, *NYT,* June 20, 1970; Povich, "Berlin, 1936"; Avery Brundage to Charles L. Ornstein, Oct. 8, 1934, Box 234, Avery Brundage Papers. The most accessible summary of the entire episode is in Large, 69–109.

26. J. P. Abramson articles, *New York Herald Tribune,* Feb. 29, Mar. 2, 1936; Pamela Cooper, *The American Marathon* (Syracuse, N.Y.: Syracuse Univ. Press, 1998), 81–82.

27. *NYT,* June 4, 25, July 26, Aug. 5, 9, 12, 29, 1936; Arthur Daley article, *NYT,* Jan. 31, 1938; obituary of Charles L. Ornstein, *NYT,* Sept. 9, 1966. The history of the meet is recounted by Edward L. Shapiro in "The World Labor Athletic Carnival of 1936: An American Anti-Nazi Protest," *American Jewish History* 74 (1985): 255–73; see page 266 for the role of the Jewish press. See also Large, 286–89; Riess, "Sports and the American Jew," 33–35.

28. *NYT,* Aug. 14–17, 1936.

29. SIJHS; *Brooklyn Eagle,* Jan. 17, 1933; *SIA,* Oct. 20, 1972; "Personal History Statement of Abel Kiviat," NA; "Abel Richard Kiviat," Application for Account Number, U.S. Social Security Act, Oct. 21, 1938, Social Security Administration. Beth S. Wenger, *New York Jews and the Great Depression: Uncertain Promise* (New Haven, Conn.: Yale Univ. Press, 1996), 16–17, 233, is outstanding on the context.

30. "Abel Richard Kiviat," Social Security Administration; OH, 102; obituary of Jeremiah T. Mahoney, *NYT,* June 20, 1972; Wenger, *New York Jews,* 130–33.

31. "Personal History Statement of Abel Kiviat," NA; obituary of Murray Hulbert, *NYT,* Apr. 27, 1950; Wenger, *New York Jews,* 46.

32. "Ed Hughes' Column," *Brooklyn Eagle,* Feb. 22, 1935; John Kieran, "Sports of the Times," *NYT,* Feb. 19, 1938, Mar. 4, June 24, July 20, 1939; "Letters to the Sports Editor," *NYT,* Mar. 11, 18, 1939; sports poll: *NYT,* Feb. 1, 13, 14, 17, 1944; Arthur Daley, "Sports of the Times," *NYT,* June 27, Aug. 10, 25, 1945, Apr. 12, 1950.

33. Kiviat served with the marshals from January 26, 1942, until November 15, 1944. "Personal History Statement," NA; interview with Harold Kiviat, Oct. 9, 1995; telephone conversation with Dave Turk, U.S. Marshals Service, Washington, D.C., Apr. 24, 2003; *New York City Guide,* 102; Wenger, *New York Jews,* 22.

34. "Abel R. Kiviat," swearing-in ceremony, Nov. 16, 1944, Kiviat File, NA; Assistant Director [of the Administrative Office of the U.S. Courts] to George J. H. Follmer, Nov. 18, 1944, and Assistant Director to William V. Connell, June 11, 1946, Kiviat File, NA; Joseph M. Fitzpatrick to Herbert A. Charlson, May 17, 1960, TL; SIJHS; OH, 107–9; WS, 261; interview with Joe Cloidt, New York, Aug. 30, 1995; interview with Kenneth Murphy, Columbus, Ohio, May 2, 2003.

35. Michael R. Belknap, "Cold War, Communism, and Free Speech," in *Historic U.S. Court Cases, 1690–1990: An Encyclopedia,* edited by John W. Johnson, 511–18 (New York:

Garland, 1992); *NYT,* May 29, 1952; *Corrected Opinion of Harold R. Medina, United States Circuit Judge in United States of America, Plaintiff, v. Henry S. Morgan, Harold Stanley, et al, doing business as Morgan Stanley & Co., et al, Defendants, Filed, Feb. 4, 1954* (New York: District Court, 1975); W. Graham Claytor, Jr., to William V. Connell, May 26, 1953, and Arthur H. Dean to William V. Connell, May 27, 1953, Kiviat File, NA.

36. Obituary of Zelda N. Kiviat, *NYT,* Mar. 6–7, 1946; interview with Lucy Price, May 18, 1996; interview with Esther Kiviat, Mar. 30, 1997; marriage license, Abel Richard Kiviat and Isabel Solomon, Registered M 10433, New York State Department of Health, Apr. 13, 1948; P. Turner, "Oldest Olympian"; Wenger, *New York Jews,* 72–73, on the Jews' "particular tendency to avoid marriage during the Depression."

37. For the Solomon family, see *1920 Census of the U.S.,* Beaver Falls, Pa.; *Beaver Valley Directory,* 1907, 1910–11, 1912–13, 1915–16, 1922, 1925–26, Beaver County Research Center for Local History, Beaver Falls, Penn.; Beaver County Research Center for Local History to author, Apr. 30, 2003. See also CF, 1; WS, 259; OH, 80.

38. Interview with Harold Kiviat, Jan. 28, 1996; interview with Esther Kiviat, Mar. 30, 1997; interview with Lucy Price, Sept. 1, 1995; *Newark Star-Ledger,* May 19, 1991; WS, 259–60.

39. Marriage license, Abel Richard Kiviat and Isabel Solomon, Apr. 13, 1948; WS, 259, 266; obituary of Thomas Lennon, *NYT,* Apr. 5, 1967; interviews with Lucy Price, Sept. 1, 1995, May 18, 1996; photograph of Abel R. Kiviat and Isabel Kiviat in the Lennons' Park Avenue apartment, Oct. 1948, TL. For anti-Semitism in the postwar era, see Dinnerstein, *Antisemitism in America,* 162–66.

40. OH, 37, 80; WS, 259; annual evaluations: Kiviat File, NA; interview with Lucy Price, Sept. 1, 1995; CF, 1.

41. Interview with Lucy Price, Sept. 1, 1995; interview with Dolly Kiviette, Englewood, N.J., Sept. 3, 1995; interview with Harold Kiviat, Jan. 28, 1996.

42. OH, 93–97, 102; WS, 259–60. For the history of the Civic Center Synagogue, see *NYT,* May 21, Dec. 3, 1956, May 1, 1964, May 26, 1968, Sept. 8, 1969, Jan. 24, 1972; *Civic Center Synagogue News,* Feb. 1984, notes Kiviat as a member. Hertzberg, 316–33, provides a rich cultural context for Kiviat's postwar religious experience.

43. OH, 83; WS, 261; Millrose Games program, Feb. 6, 1954; telephone conversation with Eric Seiff, Feb. 25, 2003.

44. Interview with Bud Greenspan, New York, July 25, 1995; telephone conversation with Eric Seiff, Feb. 25, 2003; telephone conversation with Robert Hersh, Roslyn Heights, N.Y., May 9, 2005.

45. Interview with Stanley Saplin, New York, Aug. 30, 1995; Millrose Games program, Feb. 6, 1943; "Saplin Appointed Director of AAU's New York Office," *Amateur Athlete* (1974); obituary of Stan Saplin, *NYT,* Mar. 5, 2002.

46. "Ed Hughes' Column," *Brooklyn Eagle,* Feb. 22, 1935; *NYT,* Apr. 7, 1950; Arthur Daley, "Sports of the Times," *NYT,* Apr. 12, 1950; interview with Bud Greenspan, July 25,

1995; Beglane, "All-America Press Steward"; CF, 4–5. Among the many track friendships Kiviat formed, one was with John Woodruff, the 1936 Olympic 800-meter champion and a longtime AAU official. On Woodruff and Kiviat, see Harold Kiviat to Anne Kiviat, July 23, 1981, SK.

47. WS, 253; John Paul Jones to Gordon Cobbledick, May 20, 1963, JPJ; Quercetani, *World History of Track & Field*, xvii–xxi.

48. Paul, "Men Who Have Made Indoor Track Thrilling," 10, 29.

49. OH, 104–6; WS, 253–54; AAU indoor nationals, program, Feb. 28, 1975; Steven A. Riess, "Madison Square Garden," in Jackson, 712–13. Joseph M. Turini, "'It Was Communism versus the Free World': The USA-USSR Dual Track Meet Series and the Development of Track & Field in the United States, 1958–1985," *Journal of Sport History* 28, no. 3 (2001): 427–71, provides an excellent brief history of the sport in the third quarter of the twentieth century.

50. OH, 108–9. On Kiviat's court career: Herbert A. Charlson to Will Shafroth, Mar. 15, 1962, Kiviat File, NA; "Kiviat, Once a World-Beater, Is Still Active in Track at 70," *NYT*, June 24, 1962; William T. Barnes to John Livingston, Nov. 4, 1969, and Livingston to Barnes, Nov. 7, 1969, Kiviat File, NA; obituary of Sylvester J. Ryan, *NYT*, Apr. 11, 1981; interview with Joe Cloidt, Aug. 30, 1995; interview with Esther Kiviat, Mar. 30, 1997.

51. Obituary of Arthur L. Kiviette, *NYT*, Jan. 6, 1992; interview with Lucy Price, Sept. 1, 1995; interview with Dolly Kiviette, Sept. 3, 1995; interview with Berenice Kaufman, Jan. 26, 1996; interview with Dennis Goldner, Aug. 3, 2001; telephone conversation with Litzi Goldner, June 19, 2003; Robert A. Caro, *The Power Broker: Robert A. Moses and the Fall of New York* (New York: Vintage, 1974), 1089.

52. WS, 266; obituary of Thomas Lennon, *NYT*, Apr. 5, 1967; interviews with Lucy Price, Sept. 1, 1995, July 13, 1996; interview with Dolly Kiviette, Sept. 3, 1995; interview with Harold Kiviat, Jan. 28, 1996. Drebinger also included in his retirement story the fact that he had run track with Kiviat at Curtis High School. See "John Drebinger Retires Today after 40 Years with the *Times*," *NYT*, Apr. 1, 1964.

53. OH, 107; Irving Spiegel, "Court Pays Honor to Retiring Clerk; Ryan Cites Valeche's 41 Years of Public Service," *NYT*, Dec. 18, 1965; John Livingston to William T. Barnes, Apr. 23, 1971, and "Notice of Separation, Abel R. Kiviat," June 7, 1971, Kiviat File, NA; *Newark Star-Ledger*, May 19, 1991. Kiviat left office with "240 hours of accumulated annual leave" and "1,092 hours of unused sick leave."

54. OH, 97–98; WS, 266; Anne M. Kivat, notarized letter, Apr. 2, 1984, Cappy Productions Papers; Litsky, "Honors for Oldest Olympian."

55. OH, 97–98; WS, 260, 265; Andy Edelstein article, *JTA*, Jan. 27, 1980; Litsky, "Honors for Oldest Olympian"; interview with Stan Saplin, New York, Aug. 31, 1995; interview with Lucy Price, Sept. 1, 1995; interview with Dennis Goldner, Aug. 3, 2001; telephone conversation with Bill Reingold, June 1, 2003; Kiviat family photographs, TL. For the context, see Howe, *World of Our Fathers*, 613–21; Eli Lederhendler, *New York Jews*

and the Decline of Urban Ethnicity, 1950–1970 (Syracuse, N.Y.: Syracuse Univ. Press, 2001), 148–54.

56. OH, 99; Jess Silver, "Two Great Names in Track History," *JTA*, n.d. (ca. 1971); *USOC Newsletter* (Oct. 1973): 7, TL; Alan B. Helffrich to Abel R. Kiviat, Jan. 10, 1974, TL.

57. Obituary of Isabel Kiviat, *Asbury Park Press,* Jan. 17, 1981; WS, 266; Frank Litsky article, *NYT,* June 16, 1987; Harold Kiviat to Anne Kiviat, July 23, 1981, Harold Kiviat file, SK; interview with Lucy Price, July 13, 1996; interview with Esther Kiviat, Mar. 30, 1997.

12. FOLK HERO

1. The notion that Kiviat "became a folk hero" after his rediscovery in the 1980s was suggested by Frank Litsky in his obituary of the great runner, "Abel Kiviat, Runner, Dies at 99; Held World 1,500-Meter Record," *NYT,* Aug. 26, 1991. The story of Stan Saplin's inspiration can be pieced together from "PSAL Inducts Kiviat, Ripley," *SIA,* Dec. 4, 1981; obituary of Elmer Ripley, *NYT,* Apr. 30, 1982; Elliott Denman column, *Asbury Park Press,* June 20, 1982; Stan Saplin, "Abel's Still Ready and Willing," *New York Running News* (Aug.–Sept. 1982): 7–10; Abel R. Kiviat to Stan Saplin, May 29, 1983, SS; obituary of Stanley Saplin, *NYT,* Mar. 5, 2002; Frank Litsky, "Marathon Mania," *NYT,* Oct. 29, 1982; "Abel Still Carries a Torch," *Modern Maturity* (June–July 1984): 11; Fred Lebow, with Richard Woodley, *Inside the World of Big-Time Marathoning* (New York: Rawson Associates, 1984); Elliott Denman, "93 and Still Running," *The Olympian* (May 1986): 22–23; Jim Reisler, "Abel Kiviat: An Athlete with a Dash of History," *Asbury Park Press,* n.d. (1990), TL. Cooper's *The American Marathon,* 139–56, provides a valuable analysis of the "marathon boom" of the 1970s and 1980s, highlighting the central role of Fred Lebow and his Road Runners Club. See also Ron Rubin's insightful biographical study *Anything for a T-Shirt: Fred Lebow and the New York City Marathon, the World's Greatest Footrace* (Syracuse, N.Y.: Syracuse Univ. Press, 2004), and Frank Litsky, "A Visionary and a Winner in the Race of Life," *NYT,* Oct. 10, 1999, for the sports promoter's methods and achievement. For the characteristics of "very old age," see Barbara M. Newman and Philip R. Newman, *Development Through Life: A Psychosocial Approach,* 5th ed. (Pacific Grove, Calif.: Brooks/Cole, 1991), 604–39.

2. Telephone interview of Dr. Richard Yeager, Toms River, N.J., Nov. 25, 1998.

3. Abel Kiviat to Stan Saplin, Feb. 8, Apr. 23, 30, May 12, June 4, 5, 1982, SS.

4. OH, 55–56; "Sports World Specials," *NYT,* June 14, 1982; Elliott Denman column, *Asbury Park Press,* June 20, 1982; Saplin, "Abel's Still Ready," 7–10; Jay Price, "Abe Kiviat: Still Going Strong at 90," *SIA,* June 24, 1982; Charles Carillo, "Jogging Away the Years," *New York Post,* June 24, 1982; Abel R. Kiviat to Stan Saplin, July 6, 1982, and Saplin to Kiviat, Aug. 2, 1982, SS.

5. Photograph U2131593 captioned "Olympians Wilma Rudolph and Abel Kiviat Holding Vitalis Cup," Dec. 29, 1983, Bettmann/CORBIS; Dory Devlin, "Olympic Medalist to Carry '84 Torch," unidentified news clip, Jan. 8, 1984, TL; George Vecsey, "Olympian's One

Regret," *NYT,* Jan. 13, 1984; Frank Litsky, "Politics Have Surpassed Idealism at the Olympics," *NYT,* May 13, 1984; "Abel Kiviat, Dead at 99, Was Oldest Marathon Runner," *JTA,* Aug. 30, 1991.

6. Interview with Sydney Thayer, July 25, 1995; Sydney Thayer to Rosanne Pool, Passport Services, Mar. 26, 1984, and notarized statement of Anne M. Kiviat, Apr. 2, 1984, Cappy Productions Papers.

7. Interview with Sydney Thayer, July 25, 1995; Lena Katarina Swanberg, "Back 72 Years after the Olympic Silver" (Swedish), *Stockholm Expressen,* Apr. 27, 1984; NB; *America at the Olympics.*

8. WS, 264; Sanne Young, "Area Runner Will Help Carry Olympic Torch," *Asbury Park Press,* n.d. (winter 1984), TL; Walter F. Naedele, "Olympian at Age 91: Why Keep in Shape?" *Philadelphia Inquirer,* Feb. 22, 1984; Frank Litsky, "Olympic Flame to Start Odyssey across U.S.," *NYT,* May 8, 1984; "Abel Still Carries a Torch," 11; Mickey Herskowitz, *One with the Flame: Carrying the Olympic Torch across America* (New York: New American Library, 1985), 15–39, is the fullest account of this episode.

9. WS, 264; Jay Price article, *SIA,* May 8, 1984; Frank Litsky articles, *NYT,* May 8, 9, 1984; "Saturday News Quiz," *NYT,* May 12, 1984; Nancy Jaffer, "Bearers of the Flame Begin Olympian Run Undaunted by Politics," unidentified news clip, May 9, 1984, TL; Herskowitz, 69.

10. WS, 264–65.

11. Howard Rosenberg, "Greenspan's High Moments of Truth," *Los Angeles Times,* July 4, 1984; John Corry, "TV Review: Americans in Olympics," *NYT,* July 4, 1984; *America at the Olympics.*

12. Nat Holman to Sam Kiviat, Nov. 20, 1979, and Sam Kiviat to Nat Holman, Dec. 10, 21, 1979, U.S. Committee Sports for Israel, Inc., File, SK; Sam Friedland to Joseph Siegman, n.d., U.S. Committee Sports for Israel, Inc., File, SK; Sam Kiviat to "Dear 'Kiviat'!!" Jan. 13, 1982, SK; Dr. Uriel Simri to Abel Kiviat, June 10, 1984, and Abel R. Kiviat to International Jewish Sport Hall of Fame, June 10, 1984, EK; "Seven Are Named to Sports 'Hall,'" *Buffalo Jewish Review,* n.d., EK; Siegman, *International Jewish Sports Hall of Fame,* 3–7, 172.

13. OH, 98–99, 102.

14. OH, 5–6; Sam Kiviat to David Kiviat, Dec. 26, 1945, David Kiviat File, SK; interview with Lucy Price, July 13, 1996; telephone conversation with Dorothy Kiviat, Williamsburg, Va., Dec. 31, 1996; interview with Esther Kiviat, Mar. 30, 1997.

15. Interviews with Lucy Price, Sept. 1, 1995, Mar. 1, 2001; interview with Dolly Kiviette, Sept. 3, 1995; Devlin.

16. WS, 265; interview with Esther Kiviat, Mar. 30, 1997.

17. Elliott Denman, "Abel Kiviat Finally Gets Some Fame," *Asbury Park Press,* July 9, 1985; Abel Kiviat photograph in *Asbury Park Press,* July 15, 1985; Denman, "93 and Still Running," 22–23.

18. Stan Saplin to Berny Wagner, Feb. 27, 1985, Saplin to Abel Kiviat, Feb. 27, 1985, Saplin to Arthur Kiviette, Feb. 27, 1985, and "Athlete Recommendation and Information Form," National Track & Field Hall of Fame, Indianapolis, Feb. 27, 1985, SS. For Carl B. "Berny" Wagner, see Holst and Popp, *American Men*, 161–71. The Hall of Fame moved from Indianapolis to the restored Armory Track Center in Manhattan in 2004. A decade after Kiviat's death, track journalist Marc Bloom selected Kiviat as number fifteen on his list of America's all-time greatest male distance runners. Frank Shorter tops the list, and Mel Sheppard, the first of Kiviat's contemporaries, is eleventh. Although acknowledging that his list is "subjective," Bloom has Kiviat outranking the likes of Johnny Hayes, George Bonhag, Joie Ray, and Norman Taber. He omits John Paul Jones completely, which would have astonished Kiviat. See Marc Bloom, *Run with the Champions: Training Programs and Secrets of America's 50 Greatest Runners* (Emmaus, Pa.: Rodale, 2001), viii–ix, 14, 59–62, 75–78, 139–40.

19. For the Hall of Fame induction, see Denman, "93 and Still Running," 22–23; interview with Pete Cava, Indianapolis, Ind., Mar. 14, 1996; interview with Hal Bateman, Jan. 28, 1997; telephone interview with Sanford (Sandy) Kalb, Howell, N.J., Aug. 13, 2003. Martin Gottfried, *George Burns and the Hundred-Year Dash* (Thorndike, Me.: G. K. Hall, 1996), 347, 351–52, is useful.

20. Anne M. Kiviat to *Pennsylvania Gazette,* July 5, 1986, UP; OH, 5–6; WS, 248, 260.

21. Interview with Lucy Price, Sept. 1, 1995; "Kiviat at 95 Still Ticks Just about Perfectly," *SIA,* June 24, 1987.

22. "Still on the Run," *NYT,* Mar. 13, 1986; photograph of Abel Kiviat and Mary Lou Retton, Mar. 1986, TL; Elliott Denman article, *Asbury Park Press,* Apr. 12, 1986; Frederick W. Byrd, "Fitness and Aging," *Newark Star-Ledger,* June 8, 1986.

23. Litsky, "Honors for Oldest Olympian"; "Still Running at 95," *NYT,* June 24, 1987; Jay Price article, *SIA,* June 24, 1987; Elliott Denman article, *Asbury Park Press,* June 24, 1987.

24. "Senior Olympics," *New Jersey Courier-Post,* Feb. 9, 1988, TL; Malcolm Moran, "A Telling Finish Indoors," *NYT,* Feb. 28, 1988; obituary of Glenn Cunningham, *NYT,* Mar. 11, 1988; photograph of benefit for multiple sclerosis, *Newark Star-Ledger,* Apr. 30, 1989; Reisler, "Abel Kiviat"; obituary of Abel R. Kiviat, *SIA,* Aug. 26, 1991.

25. Interview with Esther Kiviat, Mar. 30, 1997; Leo Braudy, *The Frenzy of Renown: Fame and Its History* (New York: Oxford Univ. Press, 1986), 572–76.

26. Interview with Lucy Price, Sept. 1, 1995; interview with Glenn Kasper, Wall, N.J., July 13, 1996; interview with Hal Bateman, Jan. 28, 1997.

27. Interview with Glenn Kasper, July 13, 1996; Glenn Kasper to Juan Antonio Samaranch, Mar. 8, 1988, and press release, New Jersey Governor's Council on Physical Fitness and Sports, Apr. 11, 1988, GK; "Physical Fitness and Sports: World's Oldest Olympian Receives Royal Gift," *DC Advisor* (New Jersey Department of Community Affairs) (spring 1989): 3, GK; Steve Chambers, "Olympic Winner Has Mettle for Royalty," *Asbury*

Park Press, Apr. 14, 1988; "Sweden's King Honors Oldest Olympian," *NYT,* Apr. 15, 1988; "The Region," H4, *Asbury Park Press,* Apr. 17, 1988; unidentified news photos, n.d., TL.

28. Interview with Glenn Kasper, July 13, 1996; "Oldest Olympian Will Meet Bush," *Newark Star-Ledger,* May 14, 1989; Larry McDonnell, "Oldest Olympian Meets with President Bush," *Asbury Park Press,* May 17, 1989; group photograph of Kiviat meeting with President Bush, May 16, 1989, TL.

29. Marilou Berry, "Olympic Experience Binds All Ages Together," *Courier* (city unknown), July 9, 1989, and Elaine Boies article, *SIA,* Sept. 1989, TL.

30. See, for example, program for "Senior Fitness Day at Essex Community College, Baltimore County, MD, May 2, 1990," GK; interview with Glenn Kasper, July 13, 1996.

31. Christine A. Rowett, "Senior Games Attract 800 Enthusiastic Athletes," *Asbury Park Press,* Sept. 16, 1990, TL; *1990 Fifth Annual Senior Games of NJ,* a booklet of event results (Trenton: New Jersey Governor's Council on Physical Fitness and Sports, 1990), and *Olympic Torch* (Newark: Communications and Creative Services Department, Blue Cross and Blue Shield of New Jersey, Nov. 1990), 3, 5, both in GK; interview with Glenn Kasper, July 13, 1996.

32. Reisler, "Abel Kiviat"; Jim Reisler, "At 98, an Ex-Olympian Has a New Spurt of Fame," *NYT* (New Jersey Weekly section), Aug. 26, 1990. See also Alan H. Feiler articles about Abel Kiviat, *Baltimore Jewish Times,* Dec. 29, 1989, Nov. 9, 1990, Aug. 21, 1992; Lisa Molinaro, "Oldest Olympic Medalist Talks to TR North Students," *Toms River Reporter,* Dec. 12, 1990; "World's Oldest Olympic Medalist Named to Council," unidentified news clip, Dec. 1990, TL. In 1987, Fred Lebow had urged Juan Antonio Samaranch to include Kiviat in the opening ceremonies for the 1992 Olympiad in Barcelona. Fred Lebow to Hon. Juan Antonio Samaranch, June 23, 1987, SS.

33. Interview with Lucy Price, Sept. 1, 1995; interview with Glenn Kasper, July 13, 1996; interview with Dennis Goldner, Aug. 3, 2001; P. Turner, "Oldest Olympian."

34. Abel R. Kiviat to Fred Lebow, Mar. 27, 1991, SS; interview with Lucy Price, Sept. 1, 1995; interview with Esther Kiviat, Mar. 30, 1997; Janet Nelson, "In Senior Olympics, Age Is Barely a Hurdle," *NYT,* June 22, 1991.

35. Interview with Lucy Price, Sept. 1, 1995; interview with Glenn Kasper, July 13, 1996; invitation to ninety-ninth birthday of Abel R. Kiviat, June 23, 1991, GK; Ira Berkow, "Oldest Olympian Still Making Time," *NYT,* June 24, 1991; Elliott Denman, "Olympian Kiviat Celebrates His 99th Birthday," *Asbury Park Press,* June 24, 1991; Fred Lebow, "My Friend, Abel," *Seton Hall Journal of Sport Law* 2 (1992), 339.

36. Interview with Lucy Price, Sept. 1, 1995; interview with Glenn Kasper, July 13, 1996; interview with Esther Kiviat, Mar. 30, 1997; interview with Dennis Goldner, Aug. 3, 2001.

37. Interview with Lucy Price, Washington, D.C., Mar. 1, 2001; Litsky, "Abel Kiviat, Runner, Dies at 99"; obituary of Abel R. Kiviat, *SIA,* Aug. 26, 1991.

38. Arthur Kiviette to Stan Saplin, n.d. (ca. Aug. 1991), SS; interview with Harold Kiviat, Oct. 9, 1995; telephone conversation with Lucy Price, Washington, D.C., Nov. 23, 2003; Karen E. Wall, "Olympic Running Star of 1912 Dies at Age 99," *Asbury Park Press,* Aug. 26, 1991; Litsky, "Abel Kiviat, Runner, Dies at 99"; obituary of Abel Kiviat, *SIA,* Aug. 26, 1991; obituary of Abel Kiviat, *JTA,* Aug. 30, 1991; Lebow, "My Friend, Abel," 339–40.

39. Quercetani, *World History of Track & Field,* 70, 94.

40. Interview with Lucy Price, Sept. 1, 1995; "Ed Hughes' Column," *Brooklyn Eagle,* Feb. 22, 1935; George Kochman, "Track at Curtis Dedicated to Kiviat," *SIA,* June 21, 1992; Staten Island Sports Hall of Fame Inaugural Installation Ceremony, program, College of Staten Island, Dec. 3, 1995; induction ceremony, First Annual Curtis High School Association of Alumni and Friends Hall of Fame, Apr. 22, 2001; "Harris' High Jump at Armory Best in Nation," *Daily Princetonian* (Princeton University), Feb. 6, 2002.

41. Sam Friedland to Joseph Siegman, n.d., U.S. Committee Sports for Israel, Inc., File, SK; WS, 260, 265; Litsky, "Honors for Oldest Olympian."

Selected Bibliography

ORAL HISTORIES

"Abel R. Kiviat." Unpublished text of an oral history, May 23, 1984, Lakehurst, N.J.
American Jewish Committee Oral History Collection, Dorot Jewish Division,
New York Public Library, Astor, Lenox and Tilden Foundation.

Beffa, Nancy, and Cappy Productions. Unpublished text of interview with Abel Kiviat, Apr. 27, 1984, Stockholm, Sweden.

Carlson, Lewis H., and John J. Fogarty. "Abel Richard Kiviat." In *Tales of Gold: An Oral History of the Summer Olympic Games Told by America's Gold Medal Winners*, 4–10. Chicago: Contemporary Books, 1987.

———. "Kiviat, Abel R." Unpublished text of interview, winter 1986, Lakehurst, N.J.

Greenspan, Bud, and Cappy Productions. "Abel Kiviat/Olympiad." Unpublished text of interview, May 31, 1975, Lakehurst, N.J.

Jewish Historical Society of Staten Island. "Interview with Abel Kiviat, July 3rd, 1984." Unpublished text, New York.

Simons, William. "Abel Kiviat Interview." *Journal of Sport History* 13, no. 3 (winter 1986): 235–66.

THE HISTORY OF TRACK AND FIELD IN AMERICA

Berryman, Jack W., and Roberta J. Park, eds. *Sport and Exercise Science: Essays in the History of Sports Medicine*. Urbana: Univ. of Illinois Press, 1992.

Bloom, Marc. *Run with the Champions: Training Programs and Secrets of America's Fifty Greatest Runners*. Emmaus, Pa.: Rodale, 2001.

Bryant, John. *3:59.4: The Quest to Break the 4 Minute Mile*. London: Arrow, 2004.

Carmelli, Jacques, Steven J. McPeek, and Giorio Malisani. *The Evolution of Indoor Records in Track and Field Athletics World-Europe-Italy*. Ferrara, Italy: Tipografia Artigiana, 1986.

Considine, Bob, and Fred G. Jarvis. *The First Hundred Years: A Portrait of the NYAC*. London: MacMillan, 1969.

Cooper, Pamela. *The American Marathon*. Syracuse, N.Y.: Syracuse Univ. Press, 1998.

Cumming, John. *Runners and Walkers*. Chicago: Regnery Gateway, 1981.

Derderian, Tom. *Boston Marathon*. Champaign, Ill.: Human Kinetics, 1994.

Donovan, Wally. *A History of Indoor Track & Field*. El Cajun, Calif.: Edward Jules, 1976.

Dyreson, Mark. *Making the American Team: Sport, Culture, and the Olympic Experience*. Urbana: Univ. of Illinois Press, 1998.

Glickman, Marty, with Stan Isaacs. *The Fastest Kid on the Block: The Marty Glickman Story*. Syracuse, N.Y.: Syracuse Univ. Press, 1996.

Guttmann, Allen. *The Games Must Go On: Avery Brundage and the Olympic Movement*. New York: Columbia Univ. Press, 1984.

Gyulai, Istvan, ed. *IAAF—80 Years for Athletics*. London: International Amateur Athletic Federation, 1992.

Higdon, Hal. *Boston: A Celebration of Running; Celebrating the 100th Anniversary of the Boston Athletic Association Marathon*. Emmaus, Pa.: Rodale Press, 1995.

Hjertberg, E. W. *Athletics in Theory and Practice*. New York: G. P. Putnam's Sons, 1914.

Hollander, Zander, ed. *Madison Square Garden*. New York: Hawthorn Books, 1973.

Husing, Ted. *Ten Years Before the Mike*. New York: Farrar and Rhinehart, 1935.

Jable, J. Thomas. "The Public Schools Athletic League of New York City: Organized Athletics for City Schoolchildren, 1903–1914." In *The American Sporting Experience: A Historical Anthology of Sport in America*, edited by Steven A. Riess, 219–38. New York: Leisure Press, 1984.

Jarvis, Fred G. *From Vision to Victory: America's Role in Establishing the Modern Olympic Games*. New York: United States Olympic Committee, 1996.

Killanen, Lord, and John Rodda, eds. *The Olympic Games*. New York: Collier Books, 1976.

Korsgaard, Robert. "A History of the Amateur Athletic Union of the United States." Ed.D. diss., Teachers College, Columbia Univ., 1952.

Large, David Clay. *Nazi Games: The Olympics of 1936*. New York: W. W. Norton, 2007.

Lawson, Gerald. *World Record Breakers in Track & Field Athletics*. Champaign, Ill.: Human Kinetics, 1997.

Levine, Peter. *Ellis Island to Ebbets Field: Sport and the American Jewish Experience*. New York: Oxford Univ. Press, 1992.

Lovesey, Peter. *The Kings of Distance: A Study of Five Great Runners*. London: Eyre and Spottiswoode, 1968.

Lucas, John A. "Gustavus Tom Kirby: Doyen of American Amateur Athletics and His Inadmissibility into the International Olympic Committee." *Stadion* 21–22 (1995–96): 171–92.

———. "The Hegemonic Rule of the American Amateur Athletic Union 1888–1914: James Edward Sullivan as Prime Mover." *International Journal of the History of Sport* 2, no. 3 (1994): 355–71.

———. "In the Eye of the Storm: Paavo Nurmi and the American Athletic Amateur-Professional Struggle (1925 and 1929)." *Stadion* 17 (1992): 225–45.

———. "The Princeton Invitation Meet—Aristocrat of International Track & Field 1934–1940." In *National College Physical Education Association for Men, Proceedings Of 74th Annual Meeting*, edited by C. E. Mueller, 197–202. Portland, Ore.: National College Physical Education Association for Men, 1970.

Mallon, Bill, and Ian Buchanan. *The 1908 Olympic Games*. Jefferson, N.C.: McFarland, 2000.

———, eds. *Quest for Gold: The Encyclopedia of American Olympians*. New York: Leisure Press, 1984.

———. *The United States' National Championships in Track and Field Athletics, 1876–1985*. Indianapolis, Ind.: Press Information Department, The Athletics Congress/USA, 1985.

Mallon, Bill, and Ture Widlund. *The 1912 Olympic Games: Results for All Competitors in All Events, with Commentary*. Jefferson, N.C.: McFarland, 2002.

McNab, Tom. *The Complete Book of Track & Field*. New York: Exeter Books, 1980.

Mrozek, Donald J. *Sport and American Mentality, 1880–1910*. Knoxville: Univ. of Tennessee Press, 1983.

Murphy, Michael C. *Athletic Training*. New York: Charles Scribner's Sons, 1914.

Nelson, Cordner, and Roberto Quercetani. *The Milers*. Los Altos, Calif.: Tafnews Press, 1985.

Pope, S. W. *Patriotic Games: Sporting Traditions in the American Imagination, 1876–1926*. New York: Oxford Univ. Press, 1997.

Potts, D. H. *Lon*. Mountain View, Calif.: Tafnews Press, 1993.

Quercetani, Roberto. *A World History of Track and Field Athletics, 1864–1964*. London: Oxford Univ. Press, 1964.

Riess, Steven A. *City Games: The Evolution of American Urban Society and the Rise of Sports.* Urbana: Univ. of Illinois Press, 1991.

Robertson, Lawson, ed. *College Athletics.* New York: American Sports, 1923.

Rubin, Ron. *Anything for a T-Shirt: Fred Lebow and the New York City Marathon, the World's Greatest Footrace.* Syracuse, N.Y.: Syracuse Univ. Press, 2004.

Schmertz, Fred. *The Wanamaker Millrose Story: History of the Wanamaker Millrose Athletic Association, 1908–1967.* Yonkers, N.Y.: Millrose Athletic Association, 1967.

Sears, Edward S. *Running Through the Ages.* Jefferson, N.C.: McFarland, 2001.

Sheppard, Melvin W. "Spiked Shoes and Cinder Paths: An Athlete's Story," parts 1–11. *Sport Story Magazine* 3, nos. 5–6 and others (unknown) (1924). Collected into one volume by the Sheppard family, and a copy given to the author.

Silberg, K. P. *The Athletic Finn.* Hancock, Miss.: Suomi, 1927.

Smith, George. *All Out for the Mile: A History of the Mile Race, 1864–1955.* London: Forbes Robertson, 1955.

Smith, Ronald A. *Sports and Freedom.* New York: Oxford Univ. Press, 1988.

Sullivan, James E., ed. *The Olympic Games, Stockholm 1912.* New York: American Sports, 1912.

Turrini, Joseph M. "'It Was Communism Versus the Free World': The USA-USSR Dual Track Meet Series and the Development of Track and Field in the United States, 1958–1985." *Journal of Sport History* 28, no. 3 (2001): 427–71.

Wallechinsky, David. *The Complete Book of the Olympics.* New ed. New York: Penguin Books, 1988.

Wheeler, Robert. *Jim Thorpe: World's Greatest Athlete.* Norman: Univ. of Oklahoma Press, 1979.

Withington, Paul, ed. *The Book of Athletics.* Boston: Lothrop, Lee and Shepard, 1914.

Zarnowski, Fred. *The Decathlon: A Colorful History of Track and Field's Most Challenging Event.* Champaign, Ill.: Human Kinetics, 1989.

Index

Italic page numbers denote illustrations.

OTHER TITLES IN SPORTS AND ENTERTAINMENT